EZRA POUND
and the
visual
arts

D1568287

Alvin Coburn, *Vortograph of Ezra Pound* (1917). International
Museum of Photography at George Eastman House, Rochester, New
York.

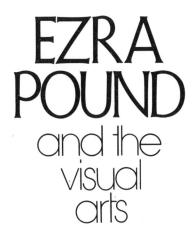

EZRA POUND
and the visual arts

Edited with an introduction by Harriet Zinnes

with usura
seeth no man Gonzaga his heirs and his concubines
no picture is made to endure nor to live with
but it is made to sell and sell quickly
Canto XLV

and: what art do you handle?
"The best" And the moderns? "Oh, nothing modern
we couldn't sell anything modern."
Canto LXXIV

A NEW DIRECTIONS BOOK

Manufactured in the United States of America
First published clothbound by New Directions in 1980
Published simultaneously in Canada by George J. McLeod, Ltd., Toronto

Library of Congress Cataloging in Publication Data

Pound, Ezra Loomis, 1885–1972.
    Ezra Pound and the visual arts.
    (A New Directions Book)
    Includes index.
    1. Arts—Addresses, essays, lectures.   I. Zinnes,
Harriet.   II. Title.
N7445.2.P675   1980   700   80-36720
ISBN 0-8112-0772-2

New Directions Books are published for James Laughlin by New Directions Publishing Corporation, 80 Eighth Avenue, New York 10011

Contents

List of Illustrations

Frontispiece:
   Alvin Coburn, *Vortograph of Ezra Pound*

Preface

Ezra Pound's work as an art critic is little known. Without the recent books[1] by Richard Cork and William C. Wees on vorticism, his efforts to promote the first English avant-garde art movement would have remained more or less in obscurity. This collection of Pound's art criticism should make more widely known another significant phase of his career.

Pound's involvement with the visual arts was yet another manifestation of his encyclopedic reach (often sneered at by the English cognoscenti of his early years in London). Since his music criticism has already been published (*Ezra Pound and Music*, 1977), surely it is time for his writings on art to receive the attention of those interested in his poetry as well as of those among the wider public interested in modernism as a whole.

Pound himself realized that a volume of the John Quinn letters with *The New Age* article that opened the correspondence between him and the art collector would be of value, as he writes in a letter of October 7, 1956, to Quinn's friend Mrs. Jeanne Robert Foster. But he probably did not consider that his other numerous writings on art, in which he engaged primarily, as he put it, "for the rent," were equally significant. The editor hopes that this collection will demonstrate that significance.

This volume is composed not only of articles in various periodicals by means of which Pound tried to eke out some kind of living, but also of those materials in books and letters that relate to the subject of the visual arts. All his comments on art are not included, however. A decision has been made not to include casual statements but only more or less extended comments or comments which, though repeated elsewhere, are in one particular place expressed with special perception or concision.

The selections, on the whole, are arranged chronologically within the separate sections, and no cross index of the chronology of the writings will be given. (Pound's writings on art, however, like his entire *oeuvre*, are so filled with his uncommon energy, his boundless enthusiasm, his precision of phrase of the very "first intensity," that for most readers chronology will be irrelevant.)

The first section contains the articles published in *The New Age*. Pound's work in the vorticist publication *Blast* comprises the next section, as well as his writings on vortography. The section that follows reprints articles in other magazines for which he wrote, arranged alphabetically according to magazine title, though maintaining a chronological sequence within each grouping. The John Quinn correspondence is then introduced, and immediately afterward materials are excerpted from Pound's published books relating to visual arts, the latter again arranged in alphabetical order according to book title. Relevant unpublished materials from the Yale Pound archives and from other library collections end the text. (It should be noted that all correspondence published here for the first time has been edited in conformity with the usage adopted in D. D. Paige's *Selected Letters of Ezra Pound 1907-1941*. For the most part, the original spelling and punctuation have been kept, except for an occasional silent editing of misprints and obvious errors.)

A glossary is also appended, but neither footnotes nor glossary contain identifications or explanations that are self-explanatory in the text or of little consequence to meaning.

The editor wishes to note her indebtedness to, among other standard Pound references, such books as the two volumes edited by Richard Cork entitled *Vorticism and Abstract Art in the First Machine Age* (I, London 1976; II, Berkeley and Los Angeles, 1976); William C. Wees's *Vorticism and the English Avant-Garde* (Toronto, 1972); B. L. Reid's *The Man from New York: John Quinn and His Friends* (New York, 1968); Walter Michel's *Wyndham Lewis: Paintings and Drawings*, introduced by Hugh Kenner (London, 1971). Catalogues that were also of assistance include *Vorticism and Its Allies*, published by the Arts Council of Great Britain and edited by Richard Cork, covering the exhibition at the Hayward Gallery, London, March 27-June 2, 1974; the Cork catalogue covering the Davis and Long Company's New York exhibition of *Vorticism and Abstract Art in the First Machine Age*, April 5-30, 1977; as well as that for the Sheffield University Library exhibition called *Ezra Pound: The London Years*, held April 23-May 13, 1976.

My indebtedness to Donald Gallup's *A Bibliography of Ezra Pound* (London, 1969) cannot be measured. I must also extend my gratitude to Professor Gallup for his special courtesy to me during my Yale visits as I searched for Pound's art writing in the archives of the Beinecke Library. Dr. Peter Dzwonkoski, Professor Gallup's assistant, must also be thanked for his continued willingness to ferret out within the archives materials that I requested. I should also like to thank the other members of the Beinecke staff for their kindnesses during my visits.

I am particularly indebted to Mrs. Mimi Penchansky of the Queens College Library and to her devoted staff at the Interlibrary Loan Department. I am especially grateful to the Dean of the Division of the Arts, Saul Novack, and to the Chairman of the Department of English, Professor Michael Timko, both of Queens College of the City University of New York, for granting me a six-month faculty award to complete my research as well as for financing some hours of work by graduate student Elizabeth Jaffe. I should also like to express my gratitude to my daughter Alice Zinnes, painter, for her constant encouragement and practical suggestions.

I also acknowledge with thanks the generosity of the following libraries, either for their particular courtesies or for their permission to examine and/or to publish their Pound materials: State University of New York at Buffalo, Lockwood Memorial Library, Poetry Collection; University of Chicago; Cornell University; Houghton Library, Harvard University; Northwestern University; University of Pennsylvania; and the New York Public Library, both the Manuscripts and Archives Division and the Berg Collection, and especially of that collection, Mrs. Lola L. Szadits, Curator.

In addition, I want particularly to thank the American Council of Learned Societies for their granting me financial support to continue my research.

I want also to thank Mary de Rachwiltz, Ezra Pound's daughter, for her warm and kind responses to my requests as well as for her personal and devoted encouragement.

I am also particularly indebted to Peter Glassgold of New Directions for his indefatigable editorial direction.

To James Laughlin I am indeed indebted most of all: first, for his acceptance of the proposal that I undertake the book; and second, for his unusual attention, his constant encouragement, his incisive suggestions throughout the rewarding correspondence that this exciting project drew forth.

I must also mention a visit in Venice with the late Ezra Pound and Miss Olga Rudge in April 1969 which, though long before the art criticism project was conceived, sealed my deep enthusiasm of the poet's work.

I should like to express my everlasting gratitude to my physicist-musician husband Irving, who has not lived to see the completion of this book but whose continuous encouragement made it possible. I dedicate this book to him in memory of a love that survived arguments against modernism by a lover of the baroque.

I am happy to have some little part in calling attention to contemporary readers a long overlooked contribution by Ezra Pound to the history of the visual arts.

HARRIET ZINNES

NOTES

[1]Timothy Materer, *Vortex: Pound, Eliot, and Lewis,* Ithaca and London, 1979, appeared during the final stages of the production of the present volume.

Introduction

By the fall of 1908, when Ezra Pound was settled in London, he had already developed a strong interest in the visual arts. He had arrived there with his first book of poems, *A Lume Spento* (which he translated as "With Tapers Quenched"), just published for him by A. Antonini in Venice. The title comes from Dante's *Purgatorio* III. 132, and as with Dante's phrase, Pound's alludes to premature death. The reference is to the death of the poet's "first friend" (at fifteen or sixteen), the painter William Brooke Smith,[1] whose loss led Pound to write as late as 1921 to William Carlos Williams: "How in Christ's name he came to be in Phila.—and to know what he did know at the age of 17–25—I don't know. At any rate, thirteen years are gone! I haven't replaced him and shan't and no longer hope to."

Pound's discussions on art, therefore, began at least with Smith in Philadelphia. Even as an undergraduate, however, long before he became an art critic for *The New Age* under the pseudonym of B. H. Dias,[1a] he had written what one may call loosely "art criticism," in the form of a theme on Uccello's battle picture in the Louvre, while in 1906, after seeing the Velásquez in the Prado, "with Whistler as gospel," he had "wondered what all the fuss was about." In July 1907, he had also written an essay on Rembrandt and Fra Angelico that was never printed. The poet had even shown early the kind of arrogance that later would prompt the sculptor Gaudier-Brzeska to say in 1913, when both he and Pound were examining Sir Jacob Epstein's *Rock-Drill* in the sculptor's studio: "Shut up, you understand nothing." Apparently, Epstein did not agree, for in his autobiography, *Let There Be Sculpture*,[2] he included Pound's "estimates" of his exhibitions that were published in *The Egoist* for March 16, 1914, directly after quoting Gaudier's derogatory remark.

Yet Pound rarely doubted his judgments on art. Even when, for example, he was literally under fire, along with his father and friends on February 8, 1907, when rescuing paintings from the burning Wanamaker "country place" called "Lindenhurst," about three quarters of a mile from the Pound home in Wyncote, Pennsylvania, the poet's quick eyes examined the paintings, whereupon he immediately concluded: the Rembrandts, Van Dykes, and Velásquezes he was carrying out were fakes![3]

In addition to having local contacts with the arts, Pound at an early age had been able to study at first hand the great Western masters. In 1898, he had traveled to Gibraltar, Tunis, and Venice with his great-aunt, and in 1901, to London with his father. In 1906, after obtaining his Master of Arts at the University of Pennsylvania, he went for further study in "Romanics" to Spain, Provence, and Italy. Though in 1907 he was back in the States as an instructor of Romance languages at Wabash College in Crawfordsville, Indiana, fortunately for the arts his academic career ended abruptly, even before he had completed one semester, because of "Bohemian" behavior. Soon he was off to London, "because I thought Yeats knew more about poetry than anybody else."

For a young poet who was soon to astonish Yeats and help promote a revolution in the literary and visual arts, his arrival in England in 1908 was propitious. Paris had already been in an artistic ferment. The year 1907 saw a memorial exhibition of Cézanne, who was now considered the Master of Aix, and in the same year Picasso painted (though never "finished") *Les Demoiselles d'Avignon*. Cubism had been born. Soon Pound was to foster first imagism and then the related movement, vorticism, as a consequence of his close involvement in London with the philosopher T. E. Hulme and with such artists as Wyndham Lewis and Gaudier-Brzeska. England would leave the nineteenth century behind her and enter the modern world, for late Edwardian London had lured not only Pound but the sculptor Jacob Epstein from New York and the young Gaudier from France. Though World War I would soon count Gaudier among the soldier dead as well as Hulme ("the best, among them/For an old bitch gone in the teeth,/For a botched civilization"), in the years preceding the outbreak of war the London art world was seething. The first machine age was claiming its aesthetic response. In the autumn of 1910, there had been Roger Fry's *Manet and the Post-Impressionists* exhibition, but the one that startled Londoners was the March 1912 *Exhibition of Works by the Italian Futurist Painters*. As Richard Cork pointed out in his catalogue of the vorticist show at the Hayward Gallery in 1974 in London, a show that demonstrated a renewed interest in the vorticists,[4] the 1912 futurist exhibition had been the mere initiator of such "scandalous" shows as were to follow:

> Fry's more advanced *Second Post-Impressionist Exhibition, British, French and Russian Artists* later the same year, Severini's one-man show in April 1913, a *Modern German Art* in the spring of 1914, another *Exhibition of the Works of Italian Futurist Painters and Sculptors* in April and finally, during the early summer of 1914, a large exhibition at the Whitechapel Art Gallery entitled *Twentieth Century Art, A Review of Modern Movements.*

At about the time of Fry's Manet exhibition, Pound was making statements about poetry and painting that already indicate how he held the two arts in conjunction—and these statements came almost four years before he wrote his first article completely organized around art, entitled "The New Sculpture," in *The Egoist* of February 16, 1914. (He had earlier discussed the American painter James Abbott McNeill Whistler in *The New Age* in September 1912 in an early installment of *Patria Mia*.) He noted on November 15, 1910, in his introduction to the Cavalcanti poems:

> As for verse itself: I believe in an ultimate and absolute rhythm as I believe in an absolute symbol or metaphor. The perception of the intellect is given in the word, that of the emotions in the cadence. It is only, then, in perfect rhythm joined to the perfect word that the two-fold vision can be recorded. I would liken Guido's cadence to nothing less powerful than line in Blake's drawing.
>
> In painting, the colour is always finite. It may match the colour of the infinite spheres, but it is in a way confined within the frame and its appearance is modified by the colours about it. The line is unbounded, it makes the passage of a force, it continues beyond the frame.

In the very next paragraph, anticipating some of the futurist, if not the vorticist principles, the unfledged art critic continues:

> Rodin's belief that energy is beauty holds thus far, namely, that all our ideas of beauty of line are in some way connected with our ideas of swiftness or easy power of motion, and we consider ugly those lines which connote unwieldy slowness in moving.

That Pound continues with cogent remarks about music makes it clear that as early as 1910 the poet was consumed with an interest in the fundamental principles of all of the arts. That interest was nurtured during the years that followed and produced the two movements already mentioned, imagism and vorticism. Richard Cork in his catalogue to the 1974 vorticist show at the Hayward Gallery, writing from the point of view of the art historian, describes the excitement of the early days of the movement through Pound's eyes. "No wonder Pound thought of a vortex," he notes. It was Pound who named the English art movement vorticism,[5] and it was he who was to promote it with a fervor equal to that of the Italian Filippo Marinetti in his promotion of futurism. Although Wyndham Lewis was to say in 1956 that "Vorticism was what I, personally, did and said at a certain period," without Pound, who with Lewis and Gaudier, was the theorist of the movement, and without such other artists as David Bomberg, Christopher Nevinson, William Roberts, and Edward Wadsworth, even the radical new energy of Lewis would not have made the movement anything more than local. But it did become more than local, and it had had an international provocation and origin.

The movement was officially launched in the summer of 1914 in the form of a monster, puce-covered magazine[6]—for sensational, promotional purposes—entitled *Blast*, in which Pound, Lewis,[7] and others issued their manifestoes in an attempt to lead England out of its stifling insularity, its middle-class virtues, and dead aesthetics. The effect of their blasts, unfortunately, was as nothing compared to the blasts of the guns of 1914. War not art became central. Harriet Monroe, editor of *Poetry* in Chicago, put the beginning and end succinctly:

> At the end of June, 1914, Wyndham Lewis and Ezra Pound had issued the first number of their cyclonic *Blast*, which was to blow away, in thick black capitals half an inch high, the Victorian Vampire; the Britannic Aesthete; Cream of the Snobbish Earth, Humor, and its First Cousin and Accomplice, Sport; and many other props of British civilization; including the Climate; also, crossing the Channel, Sentimental Gallic Gush, Sensationalism, and Fussiness. In fact, the list of Blasts and Curses covered eleven twelve-by-nine pages of a sizzling Manifesto. Never in historic time was any outcry of rebellion so promptly answered; for the huge magazine had scarcely appeared when all its blasts and curses were smothered, swallowed up, reduced to ignominy, by the counterblast of Mars.[8]

In July 1915, however, there was a second issue. *Blast No. 2* was a "War Number" (this time with an obviously symbolic monochrome cover). English art by now had clearly arrived into the modern age. Machine forms proliferated in its sculpture and painting, but many artists were at the front, and it was left for Pound to continue promoting his vorticist friends. *Blast* would have no other issue. Pound was an expert at publicity. He promoted vorticism with his usual energy in his "Affirmation" essays in *The New Age* and in other articles in such places as *The Egoist*. His memorial to Gaudier-Brzeska, however, was his most significant contribution to the cause. The book was made up largely of previously published articles by both Pound and Gaudier from *The Egoist, Fortnightly Review*, and *The New Age*, and from the vorticist magazine *Blast*. But the arrangement, its thrust, and its dedicatory zeal make it a document of the new art, both the visual and the literary. The impact of imagism on vorticism becomes clear in its pages, as does Pound's leadership in promulgating both movements. By the time of the Gaudier-Brzeska volume, however, Pound had transferred his promotional activity to vorticism. The vortex for Pound had superseded the image, and it was the vortex that stood for all forms of modernism.

He was right, for vorticism meant abstraction, and abstraction is modernism, the most honored form of art for the past seventy years. As Pound put it in a late interview with the poet Donald Hall,

> . . . vorticism from my angle was a renewal of the sense of construction. Color went dead and Manet and the impressionists revived it. Then what I would call the sense of form was blurred, and vorticism, as distinct from cubism, was an attempt to revive the sense of form. . . .[9]

Pound clearly saw that modernism, in brief, is an emphasis on pure form.

Only recently have various forms of realism competed with abstraction for exhibition space. Yet in April 1977, at a time when realism was slowly usurping some of abstraction's prestige, the Davis and Long Gallery presented New York with its very first vorticist show. In fact, with the '70s came a new interest in the art that Pound had so vigorously promoted. The monumental work of Richard Cork, for example, called *Vorticism and Abstract Art in the First Machine Age*, gives authority to the first significant English art movement dedicated to abstraction. The two exhibitions mentioned also indicate the renewal of interest in the movement, as does the book by William C. Wees, *Vorticism and the English Avant-Garde*, and the appearance of the vorticist artists *as* vorticists in such shows as the 1977 *British Drawings* at the Museum of Modern Art and the first American one-man show of the sculptor

Gaudier-Brzeska at the New York Gruenebaum Gallery in October 1977.

Art critic John Russell of *The New York Times* noted the change when he reviewed the above-mentioned Hayward Gallery exhibition on April 14, 1974. He wrote, in part,

> Over the last 15 years it has been generally agreed that David Bomberg's "In the Hold" and "The Mud-Bath" are the strongest and most original English paintings of their date (1913–15). As an expression of man's relationship with his machines, Epstein's "The Rock-Drill" seems to many people as prescient as it is sinister. Curiosity about Edward Wadsworth, about the early William Roberts, and about the early C. R. W. Nevinson has stirred continually. And although Wyndham Lewis could not always tell bluster from eloquence, there were those who believed him when, as an old man on the verge of blindness, he spoke of Vorticism as "more than just picture-making: One was manufacturing fresh eyes for people, and fresh souls to go with the eyes. That was the feeling."

Ezra Pound's enthusiasm obviously has been vindicated. This collection of the poet's writing on art should be useful, therefore, to lend an immediacy to the vorticist[9a] scene. Pound was there, as theorist, as friend of the participants, and even as art-participant, for although there is no real vorticist poetry, there is the imagist, and imagism not only influenced the art movement but is its parallel movement in the poetic art. It should be said, however, that at the time of his rebel enthusiasms Pound did not make simple connections between the art forms. He wrote in *The Egoist* of July 1914: "The force that leads a poet to leave out a moral reflection may lead a painter to leave out representation. The resultant poem may not suggest the resultant painting." Yet the poet had explained imagism as "poetry wherein the feelings of painting and sculpture are predominant."[10] Later Pound did make hard-driving connections, connections that are less aesthetic than mystical, when he wrote in *Guide to Kulchur*, "These disjunct paragraphs belong together, Gaudier, Great Bass, Leibniz, Erigena, are parts of one ideogram, they are not merely separate subjects."[11]

When Pound noted after the publication of *Blast No. 1*, however, that vorticism is "roughly speaking, expressionism, neo-cubism, and imagism gathered together in one camp and futurism in the other,"[12] he was writing not only as a critic of the plastic arts. He used the term "vorticist" as "a designation that would be equally applicable to a certain basis for all the arts." There had been a head-on collision between the futurists and the vorticists, some of whom had begun as futurists. To Pound, futurism was merely "an accelerated sort of impressionism," a movement he disdained. The vorticists as a whole, however, were less interested than the futurists in speed and movement, more static in their configurations. But a quick look at any of the paintings of Lewis, for example, even those with some figuration, reveals a cubist or, as Pound says, a "neo-cubist" influence.

Pound's linking of imagism to vorticism relates first of all to his feeling already mentioned that all arts have "some sort of common bond, some inter-recognition." (The age, like our own, was an age of intermedia arts. Consider Cocteau, Picabia, Picasso, etc.) But there was a specific bond that he saw in the rebel arts of the early decades of the century. Common to all was a hard, nonemotional, impersonal quality. In the case of the vorticist painters, that hardness was reflected in their mechanistic geometries. As Lewis stated quite bluntly, vorticism was "dogmatically anti-real. It was my ultimate aim to exclude from painting the everyday visual real altogether. The idea was to build up a visual language as abstract as music. . . . Another thing to remember is that I considered the world of machinery as real to us, or more so, as nature's forms, such as trees, leaves, and so forth, and that machine forms had an equal right to exist on our canvases."[13]

When Pound called for the elimination of rhetoric and emotional slither, and for an absolute rhythm under his imagist doctrine; when he asked for "non-representation" in painting, for a respect "not for the subject matter, but for the power of the artist—" he was asserting his dedication to formalism, or what is equivalent, to the hard abstraction of modernism, in both art and poetry. It is no wonder that Pound lacked sympathy for post-impressionism, as is mockingly indicated in the satiric thrust of "L'Art" of 1910:

> Green arsenic smeared on an egg-white cloth,
> Crushed strawberries! Come, let us feast our eyes.

On the other hand, the poet felt his early poem "The Return" is a poem that is "an objective reality and has a complicated significance, like Epstein's 'Sun God,' or Mr. Brzeska's 'Boy with Coney.'"[14]

That a poet, to whom early and late the visual arts were significant, wrote art criticism to enable him to round out his little income in his London years is not surprising. What is surprising is that until recently [15] critics have almost ignored the significance of this lifelong interest. Even the involvement with vorticism, though acknowledged, is slighted to the extent that Pound's own vortex statement is nowhere reprinted in its entirety as it appears in "Vortex," *Blast No. 1*. Part of the statement does appear in Pound's article on Brancusi (originally published in the *The Little Review* [Autumn 1921]), which is reprinted in the poet's study of Gaudier-Brzeska.

This collection of Pound's writings on art is therefore long past due. It documents his activities as a publicist for the new and revolutionary art of the first decades of the century. It shows how he performed a function in art very similar to the one he so notoriously performed in poetry. Through imagism he had revolutionized poetry and helped turned England away from the Victorian age and into the twentieth century. In art he was completely avant-garde. He argued early for abstraction and against the "representational." Pound was therefore in the forefront of both art and literary history. His statements on vorticism have historical interest. His championship of Gaudier-Brzeska and his equally enthusiastic championship of Brancusi after his move to Paris in 1921 demonstrate the poet's extraordinary ability to recognize genius even in the visual arts. His comments on other artists, such as Wyndham Lewis, Jacob Epstein, Edward Wadsworth, show a meticulously observant and educated eye. His frequently astute perceptions in sometimes unimportant reviews are often startling, such as, for example, his dislike of the "rhetorical" in Rodin or the condemnation of the kind of art scene "where pictures are made for museums,"[16] museums that "are the pest of our age";[17] or, his comment on Renoir: "However, it is very, very hard to write convincing forewords for collections of not quite the best work of artists who have deservedly large reputations. One might almost venture the formulation that these canvases of Renoir's show the effect of impressionism upon a fundamentally nineteenth century personality, who happened to be a good painter, with no psychology whatsoever."[18]

Pound's promotion during World War I of a College of Arts, though unsuccessful, shows the scope of his educational theories. The idea is still so radical that as far as I know no similar institution yet exists. Its lack of success had nothing to do with the anxieties of a war-burdened population.

Pound's exhortations to patrons, especially to the American John Quinn, to collect contemporary art, not the art of the dead, celebrated masters, indicate Pound's acute sense of the pernicious effect the art market can have on living artists. Despite his loyalties to tradition, Pound's tendency was not only to encourage the new but to sustain it—in the most literal sense, to "feed" it. These advanced notions on the economics of art led the poet to advocate economic aid to the artist while a work was being executed. Speculation in art, therefore, was anathema to him. He took it upon himself to proffer suggestions to collectors on how to avoid it.

Pound's art criticism is thus another source for an investigation into the poet's economic and political ideas. Such particular essays as "The Renaissance" and "Credit and the Fine Arts . . . A Practical Application" may be cited. His aesthetic élitism—always dangerous to the poet's shaky sympathies toward *political** democracy—is reflected in his art writing, such as the article already mentioned, "The New Sculpture," in *The Egoist* of February 16, 1914. Pound writes there, for example, "The artist has been at peace with his oppressors long enough. He had dabbled in democracy and he is now done with that folly."

But Pound's sympathy with an *economic* democracy is quite another matter, even if the means by which he thought he could achieve it in later life was notoriously undemocratic. Not only did he understand, however, that a starving artist could not produce work that would "speak the supreme sense of human values," but he realized the importance of leisure as "work unbartered." He writes in *The British Union Quarterly* of January/April 1937: "Leisure is necessary to any form of civilization higher than that of ants, apes, Kipling and his cousin Stan Baldwin."

Pound's interest in architecture bustles with his hatred of mere "acquisition" and extends to a very contemporary notion of city planning. He writes in an article in *The New Age* of September 19, 1918: "I *do not* know that anyone has attempted to formulate an aesthetic of good city building," and of course then promptly lists some general principles to follow. His articles on art, therefore, go beyond aesthetics to economic planning and development.

In the art criticism one also sees developing the poet's tendency to use an eccentric idiom that in the later *Cantos* turns to a hysterical language of hate. In a rather unpleasant, what I may call "dialect-of-diatribe," he can condemn offhandedly a painter he finds aesthetically offensive. To see this dialect applied in a non-political context may shed some light on his emerging state of mind. From calling a painter's work, for example, a rather tame "inexcusable rubbish" in an article in *The New Age* of August 1918, he becomes more irritatingly "playful" in a piece in *The*

*Pound made the following comment in an unpublished letter to John Quinn of September 3, 1916: "Naturally I am for individualism, civilization, a sort of Confucianism, at least enough of the mean that no one has any right to interfere with anyone else, and that a desire to coerce anyone else is barbarism." (The John Quinn Memorial Collection, New York Public Library)

Little Review of January/March 1921. Under the signature of Abel Sanders, he writes:

> My Khrist Kant somethin' be done about this man George G. Barnard. It aint Mikel Angerlo, an' it aint even Rodin. It's just mashed popatoz, and the following end of the last century's allegory. Before he spoils all that good marble can't somebody tell him about Egypt and Assyria, or pay his ticket so he can go look at some sculpshure made by someon' who had some idea of stone as distinct from oatmeal mush an molarsses. Hasn't even the sense of stone one finds in Barroque.

Pound's art criticism, however, is, as I have suggested, not just occasionally significant in itself but it is also of special interest as the continuation by an American writer of a tradition, particularly French, in which a man of letters devotes himself to art as well as to literary criticism. (Consider the art writing of the eighteenth- and nineteenth-century Diderot, Stendhal, Zola, Huysmans, the Goncourts, Baudelaire; later of Apollinaire; and the more recent works of Sartre, the poet Francis Ponge, and of Valéry; and in America of Frank O'Hara and John Ashbery.) For the student of literature, however, this collection will provide still another tool for the understanding of the *Cantos*. Pound's review of Adrian Stokes's book *Stones of Rimini*, appearing in *The Criterion* of April 1934, for example, seals the rather strong connection the book has with canto 17, among others, and is interesting in the light of what Donald Davie in his *Ezra Pound: Poet as Sculptor* (1965) has shown to have been Pound's influence on Stokes.

It is only recently that an interest in the history of art criticism itself has come into being. An important poet's contribution to that history is of some significance.

Pound's encouragement of the photographer Alvin Langdon Coburn in his cubist experiments with the vortoscope and his consequent art of vortography (a special technique named by the poet) shows finally the extent of Pound's radical involvement in the visual arts, as does his early interest in photographs of machines. His comments on the machine, for the first time made readily available, are superb examples of the continuing and deepening impact of vorticist principles.

It is unnecessary in this introduction to mention how throughout the *Cantos* (long after he gave up reviewing art "for the rent"), even in the midst of what had become more urgent matters, Pound demonstrates his continuing devotion to the visual arts—from the reference to the "eyes of Picasso" in canto 2 to canto 114, where poetry and painting are linked again ("And the literature of his time [Sandro's, Firenze] was in painting,"), through to the end when in *Canto CXVII et seq.* he urges "a church or an altar to Zagreus," the source, the god for Pound of all the arts, and recalls "Brancusi's bird/in the hollow of pine trunks."[19]

Pound also reveals in some of his criticism what may be disconcerting to feminists and women artists. Although he regularly covered the work of women in the course of his reviewing, and although there were three women associated with the vorticist movement, including his wife Dorothy Shakespear, he could still say: "Not wildly anti-feminist we are yet to be convinced that any woman ever invented anything in the arts. Mary Cassatt was doubtless a credit to Manet, etc., but we await proofs of invention."[20] Worse yet, he wrote to John Quinn in an unpublished letter of February 9, 1917: "I distrust the 'female artist' as much as even you can." Yet this statement occurred in a letter asking Quinn to help an unknown woman sculptor, Gwen Baxter. Pound's bark was always uglier than his bite.

Pound's zeal for the arts was unremitting. After his book on Gaudier-Brzeska (1916), for example, he began to plan two others: one on Wyndham Lewis, in the same style as the Gaudier but with a shorter text; the other, a monograph on Greek sculpture before Phidias. About five years later, his enthusiasm for Brancusi led him to want to write a book on the Rumanian-born French sculptor.

Everything Pound did for the arts followed his own rock-drill insistence in his correspondence and articles that, as he wrote to Harriet Monroe on June 20, 1915, "The arts have got to be kept up." This was Pound policy—aesthetic, economic, and political.

Finally, because Pound is a seminal influence on the poetry of our time, whatever he has written has some interest, whether in itself or in enlarging one's understanding of his more important *oeuvre*. Whatever he has to say, furthermore, is never dull, and it is always written with the kind of force and energy (if not *hubris*) characteristic only of a man of Ezra Pound's tremendous creative, exuberant intelligence.

NOTES

[1]In her memoir of Ezra Pound, *End to Torment* (New York, 1979, pp. 13–14), H. D. describes a meeting with Smith. She writes:

There is the first book, sent from Venice, *A Lume Spento* [1908]. It is dedicated to William Brooke Smith. Ezra had brought him to see me. He was an art student, tall, graceful, dark, with a "butterfly bow" tie, such as is seen in the early Yeats portraits. Ezra read me a letter he wrote; this is under the lamp at our sitting-room table. The letter was poetic, effusive, written, it appeared, with a careful spacing of lines and unextravagant margin. I only glimpsed the writing, Ezra did not hand the letter to me. The boy was consumptive. His sister had just died.

He waved to us from the car once.

[1a]Pound made the following statement in an unpublished letter of February 19, 1918, to John Quinn:

I am writing regularly for him [Orage] as B. H. Dias and Wm. Atheling. The former on art, where E. P. would be hopelessly suspect of Vorticist Propaganda, and the elderly Atheling on music because no one writer should publicly appear to know about everything. These wind shields are to be kept secret. Dias only puts over as much as the N.A. reader is supposed to be able to stand. (John Quinn Collection)

[2]Jacob Epstein, *Let There Be Sculpture*, London, 1940, p. 70.

[3]Noel Stock, *The Life of Ezra Pound*, New York, 1970, pp. 33–34. Often enough, however, Pound's confidence was justified. There is the blunt statement to John Quinn, with whom Pound had been in regular correspondence from January 1915, to help find art for a growing collection and simultaneously to encourage Quinn to become the patron of his friends. Pound suggested when Quinn was considering buying Epstein's *Birds*, "for God's sake get the two that are stuck together, not the pair in which one is standing up on its legs." (*The Selected Letters of Ezra Pound: 1907–1941*, ed. D. D. Paige, London, 1951, p. 95; New York, 1971, p. 52.) When Quinn hastily wrote to Epstein following Pound's suggestion the sculptor was none too pleased though he reassured his patron that he was to receive the called-for *Second Marble Doves*, adding that he "wondered by what right Pound was commenting on his work with such vehemence: Pound might mind his own business." (Epstein to Quinn, 28 April, 1915, paraphrased by B. L. Reid, *The Man from New York: John Quinn and His Friends*, Oxford, 1968, p. 203.)

[4]The critic Paul Overy made the following comments on the show: "These woodcuts [Edward Wadsworth's], which filled a large screen at the Hayward Gallery, together with Lewis's drawings and Epstein's *Rock-Drill*, are the most convincing examples of the vitality and originality of Vorticism and of its independence from Cubism and Futurism. And were any of the large lost oil paintings by Wadsworth and Lewis to turn up, these could only confirm this." ("Puce Monster," *The New Review*, June 1974, pp. 41–42.)

[5]Timothy Materer, in a brief article called "Pound's Vortex," notes that although "in 1914 the 'Vortex' seemed a catchy new term for an avant-garde development in the arts . . . the term was nevertheless grounded in Pound's study of ancient Greek philosophy." (*Paideuma*, Fall 1977, p. 176.) Actually, Materer's statement describes the fierce contradictions in Pound's nature: art revolutionary and arch traditionalist. Or perhaps it merely confirms that radical movements must come out of a tradition. Pound was steeped in a tradition and reluctant to

throw it off despite his avant-gardism: "All the outcry about Matisse and 'pure colour,'" he noted, "has not produced any colour better than that of Perugino." (*The New Age*, November 22, 1917, p. 74.) But looking back for Pound was only going forward. His characteristic statement in this connection was made in an unpublished letter to John Quinn of September 3, 1916: "You know I don't use this archaeology as a tomb, but as fodder for the living animal." (The John Quinn Memorial Collection)

[6] A characteristic contemporary response was the comment on the magazine in the *Morning Post*: "The first Futurist quarterly is a vast folio in pink paper covers, full of irrepressible imbecility which is not easily distinguished from the words and works of Marinetti's disciples." (Overy, p. 38.)

[7] Lewis later called *Blast* "that comic earthquake." (Wyndham Lewis, *Blasting and Bombardiering*, London, 1937, p. 54.) But Pound's early description, more serious, is more accurate. He calls it in a letter to Joyce of April 1914, a "Futurist, Cubist, Imagiste Quarterly." (*Pound/Joyce*, ed. Forrest Read, New York, 1967, p. 26.)

[8] *A Poet's Life*, New York, 1938, p. 355.

[9] "Interview with Ezra Pound," *Writers at Work*, Second Series, New York, 1963, p. 47.

[9a] Pound noted in a letter to Harriet Monroe that an article on "Imagisme" would be published under the title "Vorticism."(Harriet Monroe Collection, 1914, the University of Chicago Library.)

[10] "A List of Books," *The Little Review*, March 1918, p. 57.

[11] *Guide to Kulchur*, New York and London, 1952, p. 75.

[12] "Vorticism," *Fortnightly Review*, September 1, 1914, pp. 461–71; *Gaudier-Brzeska: A Memoir*, New York, 1970, p. 90.

[13] Walter Michel, *Wyndham Lewis: Paintings and Drawings*, London, 1971, pp. 443–44.

[14] *Fortnightly Review*, September 1, 1914, p. 464.

[15] See, for example, Jo Brantley Berryman, "'Medallion': Pound's Poem," *Paideuma*, Winter 1975, pp. 391–98.

[16] *Literary Essays*, New York and London, 1954, pp. 444–45.

[17] "The Curse," *Apple (of Beauty and Discord)*, January 1920, p. 22.

[18] *The New Age*, March 4, 1920, p. 292.

[19] Brancusi momentarily turned Pound into a sculptor! When the poet had lived in Paris—70 *bis* rue Notre Dame des Champs, a street on which Whistler had lived as a young man—he had odds and ends of Brancusi-like sculpture strewn on the floor. He had made them himself by hammering pieces of stone that were originally as near egg-shaped as possible. (Charles Norman, *Ezra Pound*, New York, 1960, p. 248.) I might add here that he had also tried painting. I have found no comment on those productions, but as a young man he did have some tubes of paint and brushes which he requested his mother to send him in London. He wrote from the Stone Cottage in Sussex sometime around the date of May 13, 1914:

> I wonder if you have ever seen some paint tubes and brushes that I acquired ages since. The paint will be dried past utility I suppose, but I'd be very glad if you would copy the name on the tubes, *the names of the colours*, as they were a carefully selected scale which I have forgotten. If they are

illegible you might get Whiteside to give you the list of his seven colour series, s. v. p.

Also I suppose the brushes are so light that they could be sent for tuppence.

Of course Pound may have wanted the materials for his wife, Dorothy Shakespear, whom he had married in April 1914. A much more likely possibility.

[20]*The New Age*, August 1, 1918, p. 223.

1
Selections from The New Age

WHISTLER[1]

I have taken deep delight in the novels of Mr. Henry James, I have gathered from the loan exhibit of Whistler's paintings now at the Tate (September, 1912), more courage for living than I have gathered from the Canal Bill or from any other manifest American energy whatsoever.

And thereanent I have written some bad poetry and burst into several incoherent conversations, endeavouring to explain what that exhibit means to the American artist.

Here in brief is the work of a man, born American, with all our forces of confusion within him, who has contrived to keep order in his work, who has attained the highest mastery, and this not by a natural facility, but by constant labour and searching.

For the benefit of the reader who has not seen this exhibition I may as well say that it contains not the expected array of "Nocturnes," but work in many styles, pastels of Greek motif, one pre-Raphaelite picture, and work after the Spanish, the northern and the Japanese models, and some earlier things under I know not what school.

The man's life struggle was set before one. He had tried all means, he had spared himself nothing, he had struggled in one direction until he had either achieved or found it inadequate for his expression. After he had achieved a thing, he never repeated. There were many struggles for the ultimate nocturnes.

I say all this badly. But here was a man come from us. Within him were drawbacks and hindrances at which no European can more than guess.

[1]*The New Age*, September 12, 1912, p. 466. Reprinted in *Selected Prose: 1909–1965*, ed. William Cookson, New York, 1957, pp. 116–17; *Patria Mia*, Chicago, 1950, pp. 50–51; *Patria Mia and the Treatise on Harmony*, London, 1962, pp. 34–35.

1

And Velásquez could not have painted little Miss Alexander's shoes, nor the scarf upon the chair. And Dürer could not have outdone the two faces, "Grenat et Or" and "Brown and Gold—de Race." The first is called also "Le Petit Cardinal."

These two pictures have in them a whole Shakespearean drama, though Whistler's comprehension and reticence would never have permitted any but the more austere discussion of their technique; of their painting as painting. And this technique is the only field of the art critic. It is the only phase of a work of art about which there can be any discussion. The rest you see, or you do not see. It is the painter's own private knowledge which he shares with you, if you understand it.

What Whistler has proved once and for all, is that being born an American does not eternally damn a man or prevent him from the ultimate and highest achievement in the arts.

And no man before him had proved this. And he proved it over many a hindrance and over many baffled attempts. He is, with Abraham Lincoln, the beginning of our Great Tradition.

AMERICA: CHANCES AND REMEDIES.[2]
Proposition III—The College of the Arts

In America you can be subsidised to study the development of ablauts in Middle High German; to make comments on the works of Quinet; to read Assyrian tablets; even to paint pictures, to sculp, and in one western college a man has been given a fellowship in musical composition. (I believe this happened at Oberlin and I pay the trustees my respects.)

No institution that I know of subsidises literary creation or experiment. There are certain prizes awarded. One man is being paid to translate the *Divina Commedia* into terza rima with feminine endings. The German Emperor encourages the ex-Germans in, I think, California. Mr. Fells is patron to a poet who advertised for a patron and whose name is not known to me.

Mr. Morgan, in finance, advocates "backing the man," and says he has lent a million dollars more than once to men whom he knew had nothing. In the arts he encourages the dead. I am very glad he sees fit to collect, for the presence of masterwork in the country will, in time, beget some sort of discrimination.

Retiring professors are pensioned by Mr. Carnegie, and all this is very nice and humane, but the careful expenditure of a bare two million

[2]*The New Age,* May 29, 1913, pp. 115–16.

2

dollars would bear a deal more fruit in sheer artistic creation, and would eventually pay the country many times over in actual possessions obtained; but let us have done with practicalities. I speak of something better.

The whole question of art patronage is too wide to go into, suffice it that the Ptolemies when they wished to lift the centre of the world's culture bodily into Alexandria, could find no better device. Cosimo de Medici, who may be regarded as a sound man and one little given to toying with chimeras, was of like mind in Florence.

I do not propose to talk social theory. I treat an immediate issue. I think there is any amount of willingness to patronise the arts now present in America, and that the point of fact need hardly be argued.

The question of the most advisable method remains. The American Academy at Rome is a most commendable model. Ten men are kept there, for a term of three years each—painters, sculptors, architects.

But why of necessity Rome? Why only ten men? Why only three sorts of art?

The mingling of young men engaged in *all* the different sorts of art has always proved most fruitful. One comes to a capital, in fact, in order that one may find the most dynamic minds of each variety.

My proposal is of the simplest. I want not ten men but a hundred. I want not Rome, but New York or Chicago.

I want these hundred men chosen with regard to their intentions and their capacities, not by an academic foot rule. I want them to be men who have done enough to show that their work is neither a passing whim nor a commercial predilection. I want painters, sculptors, musical composers, architects, scholars in the art of verse, and in the art of prose for that matter, and those who show some signs of being dramatists, and I should admit the occasional artists in the slightly divergent arts, say etchers or workers in bronze or in stained glass.

I should leave the charter so open that no dynamic man need be excluded. I should not have a freak committee, but as no institution has ever yet proved too revolutionary I should base the qualifications for admittance largely upon originality. I should insist, on the contrary that, save in rarest cases, the candidate should have reasonable knowledge of the prevailing fashions in the technique of his art. There is no effective revolution in art except that which comes from men who cast off bonds which they show themselves able to bear.

I would rather have the whole hundred of these artists chosen by one efficient artist than by any staid committee that was not composed of efficient artists. There is no hope for such an institution as this, unless the selecting committee be guided by an almost blind hatred of mediocrity, unless they have it branded and engraved upon their consciousness that

3

one fragment of perfect work outweighs forty salons of exhibitions without such a perfect fragment.

Longinus said it long ago in his book to young writers, "When you have composed such and such a thing, think how it would be received by Sophocles or Demosthenes." Until the American artist can work with some thought in his mind of how such and such a work would appeal to, let us say, Rodin, Anatole France, Henry James, or whatever master you will, dead or living, who is known to be reasonably severe, and to have a decent hatred of botches, until just such time is there no use in taking the American writer or artist seriously or of providing him with any plum cakes whatsoever.

But to return to our college. Presumably after the American neophyte in the arts has been beaten with a rope-end until he knows those things which any decent sailor man should know blind, drunk, or a-sleepin':

I should turn a hundred of him into a super-college, to wit, a college with no professors. I should give him enough yearly income (ranging from £100 to £200) so that he needn't worry about his actual food and lodging. I should take him on during the impossible years of an artist's life, to wit, along between twenty and thirty. I should keep him for from one to three years, according to his earnestness and his performance. (I would not have the three year limit absolute, though I think special provision outside the college could be made for unusual cases.) I would require nothing of him except that he painted the thing as he saw it, at his own rate and time, and that he showed up at a general sort of club rooms reasonably often, to quarrel, to dispute, to fraternise with, to backbite and to accelerate his fellows.

I would have at least ten per cent. of the fellows, foreigners summoned from abroad.

I would not have over twenty per cent. notably of any one religion.

I would have a reasonable fund to provide for bringing great artists from the corners of the earth to loaf about the club room and abuse the bad work of the fellows of the college, or to commend it on such rare occasions as any of it seemed worthy of commendation.

New York is an exceedingly beautiful city; any more than one intelligent man might find a worse way of spending a vacation.

The art of the world has come out of the capitals of the world, because it is only in the capitals of the world, at certain favoured periods, that the best minds among the older men and the ready minds of the younger enthusiasts have mingled and have taken fire one from another.

America is saved when she manages to make a capital, the segregation of officials at Washington has not done this. The game was better played at Alexandria and at Florence.

I write of this little school perhaps lightly, but I do not feel the need of it lightly, nor is my intention of seeing it real a passing fancy of the hour.

4

AFFIRMATIONS[3]
Vorticism

The New Age permits one to express beliefs which are in direct opposition to those held by the editing staff. In this, *The New Age* sets a most commendable example to certain other periodicals which not only demand that all writers in their columns shall turn themselves into a weak and puling copy of the editorial board, but even try to damage one's income if one ventures to express contrary beliefs in the columns of other papers.

There is perhaps no more authentic sign of the senility of a certain generation of publicists (now, thank heaven, gradually fading from the world) than their abject terror in the face of motive ideas. An age may be said to be decadent, or a generation may be said to be in a state of prone senility, when its creative minds are dead and when its survivors maintain a mental dignity—to wit, the dignity or stationariness of a corpse in its cerements. Excess or even absinthe is not the sure sign of decadence. If a man is capable of creative, or even of mobile, thought he will not go in terror of other men so endowed. He will not call for an inquisition or even a persecution of other men who happen to think something which he has not yet thought, or of which he may not yet have happened to hear.

The public divides itself into sections according to temper and alertness; it may think with living London, or with moribund London, or with Chicago, or Boston, or even with New Zealand; and behind all these there are possibly people who think on a level with Dublin, antiquarians, of course, and students of the previous age. For example, Sir Hugh Lane tried to give Dublin a collection of pictures, Degas, Corot and Manet, and they called him a charlatan and cried out for real pictures "like the lovely paintings which we see reproduced in our city art shops." I have even seen a paper from Belfast which brands J. M. Synge as a "decadent." Is such a country fit for Home Rule? I ask as the merest outsider having not the slightest interest in the question. I have met here in London two men still believing in Watts, and I suppose anything is possible—any form of atavism that you may be willing to name.

I suppose any new development or even any change in any art has to be pushed down the public throat with a ramrod. The public has always squealed. A public which has gushed over the sentimentalities of Rodin adorns Epstein's work with black butterflies, à cause de pudeur. The wickedest and most dashing publisher of "the nineties," of the "vicious, disreputable nineties," demands that our antiseptic works be submitted to ladylike censorship. And the papers in Trieste rejoice that futurism is a

[3]*The New Age*, January, 14, 1915, pp. 277-78.

5

thing of the past, that a new god is come to deliver them. Such is the state of the world at the beginning of A.D. 1915.

The political world is confronted with a great war, a species of insanity. The art world is confronted with a species of quiet and sober sanity called Vorticism, which I am for the third or fourth time called upon to define, quietly, lucidly, with precision.

Vorticism is the use of, or the belief in the use of, THE PRIMARY PIGMENT, straight through all of the arts.

If you are a cubist, or an expressionist, or an imagist, you may believe in one thing for painting and a very different thing for poetry. You may talk about volumes, or about colour that "moves in," or about a certain form of verse, without having a correlated aesthetic which carries you through all of the arts. Vorticism means that one is interested in the creative faculty as opposed to the mimetic. We believe that it is harder to make than to copy. We believe in maximum efficiency, and we go to a work of art not for tallow candles or cheese, but for something which we cannot get anywhere else. We go to a particular art for something which we cannot get in any other art. If we want form and colour we go to a painting, or we make a painting. If we want form without colour and in two dimensions, we want drawing or etching. If we want form in three dimensions, we want sculpture. If we want an image or a procession of images, we want poetry. If we want pure sound, we want music.

These different desires are not one and the same. They are divers desires and they demand divers sorts of satisfaction. The more intense the individual life, the more vivid are the divers desires of that life. The more alive and vital the mind, the less will it be content with dilutations; with diluted forms of satisfaction.

I might put it differently. I might say, "I like a man who goes the whole hog." If he wants one sort of, say, "philosophy," he goes to Spinoza. If he wants another sort of "philosophy," he goes to Swedenborg. But nothing under heaven will induce him to have recourse to the messy sort of author who tries to mix up these two incompatible sorts of thought, and who produces only a muddle. Art deals with certitude. There is no "certitude" about a thing which is pretending to be something else.

A painting is an arrangement of colour patches on a canvas, or on some other substance. It is a good or bad painting according as these colour-patches are well or ill arranged. After that it can be whatever it likes. It can represent the Blessed Virgin, or Jack Johnson, or it need not represent at all, it can be. These things are a matter of taste. A man may follow his whim in these matters without the least harm to his art sense, so long as he remembers that it is merely his whim and that it is not a matter of "art criticism" or of "aesthetics." When a man prefers a Blessed Virgin by Watts to a portrait of a nasty pawnbroker by Rembrandt, one ceases to consider him as a person seriously interested in painting. There is nothing very new about that. When a man begins to be more interested in the "arrangement" than in the dead matter arranged, then he begins "to have an eye for" the difference between the good, the bad and the mediocre in Chinese painting. His remarks on Byzantine, and Japanese, and on ultra-modern painting begin to be interesting and intelligible. You do not demand of a mountain or a tree that it shall be like something; you do not demand that "natural beauty" be limited to mean only a few freaks of nature, cliffs looking like faces, etc. The worst symbolist of my acquaintance—that is to say, the most fervent admirer of Watts' pictures—has said to me more than once, quoting Nietzsche most inadvertently, "The artist is part of nature, therefore he never imitates nature." That text serves very well for my side of the case. Is a man capable of admiring a picture on the same terms as he admires a mountain? The picture will never become the mountain. It will never have the mountain's perpetual variety. The photograph will reproduce the mountain's contour with greater exactitude. Let us say that a few people choose to admire the picture on more or less the same terms as those on which they admire the mountain. Then what do I mean by "forms well organised"? ·

An organisation of forms expresses a confluence of forces. These forces may be the "love of God," the "life-force," emotions, passions, what you will. For example: if you clap a strong magnet beneath a plateful of iron filings, the energies of the magnet will proceed to organise form. It is only by applying a particular and suitable force that you can bring order and vitality and thence beauty into a plate of iron filings, which are otherwise as "ugly" as anything under heaven. The design in the magnetised iron filings expresses a confluence of energy. It is not "meaningless" or "inexpressive."

There are, of course, various sorts or various subdivisions of energy. They are all capable of expressing themselves in "an organisation of form." I saw, some months since, the "automatic" paintings of Miss Florence Seth. They were quite charming. They were the best automatic paintings I have seen. "Automatic painting" means paintings done by people who begin to paint without preconception, who believe, or at least assert, that the painting is done without volition on their part, that their hands are guided by "spirits," or by some mysterious agency over which they have little or no control. "Will and consciousness are our vortex." The friend who sent me to see Miss Seth's painting did me a favour, but he was very much in the wrong if he thought my interest was aroused because Miss Seth's painting was vorticist.

Miss Seth's painting was quite beautiful. It was indeed much finer than her earlier mimetic work. It had richness of colour, it had the surety of articulation which one finds in leaves and in viscera. There was in it also an unconscious use of certain well-known symbols, often very beautifully disguised with elaborate detail. Often a symbol appeared only in a fragment, wholly unrecognisable in some pictures, but capable of making itself understood by comparison with other fragments of itself appearing in other pictures. Miss Seth had begun with painting obviously Christian symbols, doves, etc. She had gone on to paint less obvious symbols, of which she had no explanation. She had no theories about the work, save that it was in some way mediumistic. In her work, as in other "automatic" paintings which I have seen, the structure was similar to the structure of leaves and viscera. It was, that is to say, exclusively *organic*. It is not surprising that the human mind in a state of lassitude or passivity should take on again the faculties of the unconscious or sub-human energies or minds of nature; that the momentarily dominant atom of personality should, that is to say, retake the pattern-making faculty which lies in the flower-seed or in the grain or in the animal cell.

This is not vorticism. They say that an infant six weeks old is both aquatic and arboreal, that it can both swim and hang from a small branch by its fist, and that by the age of six months it has lost these faculties. I do not know whether or no this is true. It is a scientist's report, I have never tried it on a six-weeks-old infant. If it is so, we will say that instinct "revives" or that "memory throws back," or something of that sort. The same phrase would apply to the pattern-making instinct revived in somnolents or in mediumistic persons.

Note especially that their paintings have only organic structures, that their forms are the forms already familiar to us in sub-human nature. Their work is interesting as a psychological problem, not as creation. I give it, however, along with my paragraph on iron filings, as an example of energy expressing itself in pattern.

We do not enjoy an arrangement of "forms and colours" because it is a thing isolated in nature. Nothing is isolated in nature. This organisation of form and colour is "expression"; just as a musical arrangement of notes by Mozart is expression. The vorticist is expressing his complex consciousness. He is not like the iron filings, expressing electrical magnetism; not like the automatist, expressing a state of cell-memory, a vegetable or visceral energy. Not, however, that one despises vegetable energy or wishes to adorn the rose or the cyclamen, which are vegetable energies expressed in form. One, as a human being, cannot pretend fully to express oneself unless one express instinct and intellect together. The softness and the ultimate failure of interest in automatic painting are caused by a complete lack of conscious intellect. Where does this bring us? It brings us to this: Vorticism is a legitimate expression of life.

My personal conviction is as follows: Time was when I began to be interested in "the beauties of nature." According to impressionism I began to see the colour of shadows, etc. It was very interesting. I noted refinements in colour. It was very interesting. Time was when I began to make something of light and shade. I began to see that if you were representing a man's face you would represent the side on which light shone by very different paint from that whereby you would express the side which rested in shadow. All these things were, and are, interesting. One is more alive for having these swift-passing, departmentalised interests in the flow of life about one. It is by swift apperceptions of this sort that one differentiates oneself from the brute world. To be civilised is to have swift apperception of the complicated life of today; it is to have a subtle and instantaneous perception of it, such as savages and wild animals have of the necessities and dangers of the forest. It is to be no less alive or vital than the savage. It is a different kind of aliveness.

And vorticism, especially that part of vorticism having to do with form—to wit, vorticist painting and sculpture—has brought me a new series of apperceptions. It has not brought them solely to me. I have my new and swift perceptions of forms, of possible form-motifs; I have a double or treble or tenfold set of stimulae in going from my home to Piccadilly. What was a dull row of houses is become a magazine of forms. There are new ways of seeing them. There are ways of seeing the shape of the sky as it juts down between the houses. The tangle of telegraph wires is conceivable not merely as a repetition of lines; one sees the shapes defined by the different branches of wire. The lumber yards, the sidings of railways cease to be dreary.

The musical conception of form, that is to say the understanding that you can use form as a musician uses sound, that you can select motives of form from the forms before you, that you can recombine and recolour them and "organise" them into new form—this conception, this state of mental activity, brings with it a great joy and refreshment. I do not wish to convert anyone. I simply say that a certain sort of pleasure is available to anyone who wants it. It is one of the simple pleasures of those who have no money to spend on joy-rides and on suppers at the Ritz.

This "musical conception of form" is more than post-impressionism. Manet took impressions of colour. They say Cézanne began taking "impressions of form." That is not the same thing as conceiving the forms about one as a source of "form-motifs," which motifs one can use later at one's pleasure in more highly developed compositions.

It is possible that this search for form-motif will lead us to some synthesis of western life comparable to the synthesis of oriental life which we find in Chinese and Japanese painting. This lies with the future. Perhaps there is some adumbration of it in Mr. Wadsworth's "Harbour of Flushing."

At any rate I have put down some of my reasons for believing in the vorticist painters and sculptors. I have at least in part explained why I believe in Mr. Wyndham Lewis; why I think him a more significant artist than Kandinsky (admitting that I have not yet seen enough of Kandinsky's work to use a verb stronger than "think"); why I think that Mr. Lewis' work will contain certain elements not to be found in Picasso, whom I regard as a great artist, but who has not yet expressed all that we mean by vorticism.

Note that I am not trying to destroy anyone's enjoyment of the Quattrocento, nor of the Victory of Samothrace, nor of any work of art which is approximately the best of its kind. I state that there is a new gamut of artistic enjoyments and satisfactions; that vorticist painting is not meaningless; and that anyone who cares to may enjoy it.

AFFIRMATIONS[4]
Jacob Epstein

In the following January and February I had further opportunity for recording some of my thoughts on sculpture. I wrote rather bad temperedly in *The New Age* and was duly abused for it. There was one article on Epstein and another on Brzeska in a series of articles on the art of our decade. Mention of Brzeska is so mixed into the Epstein article that I print the two of them almost entire.

I wrote that the "nation," or, rather, the art critics and editorial writers of the orthodox press, had been prostrating themselves before M. Rodin and offering their paeans of praise. M. Rodin had made a very generous gift to England. To be sure, some of his sculpture seems made rather to please bankers with pink satin minds than to stir the lover of fine art; but even so, it was not for any loyal Englishman to mention the fact at this moment. And, moreover, M. Rodin has been the most striking figure in his generation of sculptors, and it is not proper to pluck at the beards of old men, especially when they are doing fine things.

The beard which one wishes to pluck is the collective beard of the English curators who did not realize Rodin in his best period, and who have left this island without examples of his best work. It is, of course, too late to mend the matter with Rodin; we must, as the *Times* says, look into the future. It would be at least sensible to take some count of the present. Whatever may be the ultimate opinion concerning their respective genius, there can be no doubt whatsoever that the work now being done by Jacob Epstein is better than anything which is likely to be accomplished by Rodin at the age of one hundred and three.

Yet I learn from fairly reliable sources that that sink of abomination, the Tate Gallery, has not bought any work of Epstein's (and its funds are, I believe, supposed to be used in acquiring representative modern art), but it has rushed further into the sloughs of stupidity by refusing, in an

[4]*The New Age*, January 21, 1915, pp. 311–12; *Gaudier-Brzeska*, New York, 1970, pp. 95–102.

indirect manner perhaps, yet refusing, one of the best of Epstein's works when it was offered as a gift. This is, to put it mildly, robbing the public.*

It may be answered that the public don't care. And the counter reply is that: the public don't know. Moreover, there is no surety that the public of fifty years hence will be plunged in a stupidity exactly identical with the present public stupidity. And besides all this, it is ridiculous even for the defenders of stupidity to pretend that there is not already a considerable part of the public who are "ready for Epstein."

The sculptors of England, with the exception of Epstein, are, or were until the beginning of the war, we suppose, engaged wholly in making gas-fittings and ornaments for electric light globes, etc. At least, we have little to prove the contrary. Of course, there's a living in it. And if people still want what Dublin calls "those beautiful productions displayed in the windows of our city art shops," one can only commend the soundness of certain commercial instincts. God forbid that we should interfere with any man's honest attempt to earn his sustenance. At the same time, there is a slender but, nevertheless, determined cult of the "creative element." A few, we say regretfully "a few," of us believe in the mobility of thought. We believe that human dignity consists very largely in humanity's ability to invent. One is, to put it mildly, weary with sculpture which consists of large, identical, allegorical ladies in night-gowns holding up symbols of Empire or Commerce or Righteousness, and bearing each one a different name, like "Manchester" or "Pittsburgh," or "Justitia." One can no longer feel that they are a full expression of what Kandinsky calls the "inner need." They are perhaps "classic ornament," and if one did not disapprove of having decorative columns made by the gross, one might irreverently suggest that such statues be made by the gross, with detachable labels. Unfortunately, one does not believe in having even columns made by the gross; one has the tradition that columns should be hand-cut and signed. It is only so that one can have really fine buildings. One's loftiest wish is that the mimetic sculptors should be set to making columns, and that the making of fine columns should be held in greater honour than the making of silly academy sculpture. The limits of the convention of columns and capitals might perhaps so press upon the mimetic sculptors as to result in something approaching intensity.

Of course, you will never awaken a general or popular art sense so long as you rely solely on the pretty, that is, the "caressable." We all of us like the caressable, but we most of us in the long run prefer the woman to the statue. That is the romance of Galatea. We prefer—if it is a contest in caressabilities—we prefer the figure in silk on the stairs to the "Victory" aloft on her pedestal-prow. We know that the "Victory" will be there

---

*I do not accuse Mr. Aitkin, I accuse the parties responsible, whatever may be their exquisite anonymity.

whenever we want her, and that the young lady in silk will pass on to the Salon Carré, and thence on toward the unknown and unfindable. That is the trouble with the caressable in art. The caressable is always a substitute.

Ideal of the caressable vary. In Persia, the Persia of its romances, the crown of beauty, male or female, goes to him or her whose buttocks have the largest dimensions. And we all remember the Hindoo who justified his desire for fatness with the phrase "same money, more wife."

Ideals change, even the ideals of the caressable are known to have altered. Note, for example, the change in the ballet and in "indecent" illustrations. Twenty years ago, the ideal was one with large hips and bosom. To-day the ideal is more "svelte." The heavier types appear only in very "low" papers. In fact, the modern ideal approaches more nearly to the "Greek type," which is, as Pater says, disappointing "to all save the highest culture." The development of Greek sculpture is simple; it moves steadily towards the caressable. One may even say that people very often set up Greek art as an ideal because they are incapable of understanding any other.

The weakness of the caressable work of art, of the work of art which depends upon the caressability of the subject, is, incidentally, that its stimulativeness diminishes as it becomes more familar. The work which depends upon an arrangement of forms becomes more interesting with familiarity in proportion as its forms are well organized. That is to say, the ideal vorticist is not the man of delicate incapabilities, who, being unable to get anything from life, finds himself reduced to taking a substitute in art.

Our respect is not for the subject-matter, but for the creative power of the artist; for that which he is capable of adding to his subject from himself; or, in fact, his capability to dispense with external subjects altogether, to create from himself or from elements. We hold that life has its own satisfactions, and that after a man has lived life up to the hilt, he should still have sufficient energy to go on to the satisfactions of art, which are different from the satisfactions of life. I will not say loftily: they are beyond it. The satisfactions of art differ from the satisfactions of life as the satisfactions of seeing differ from the satisfactions of hearing. There is no need to dispense with either. The artist who has no "ideas about art," like the man who has no ideas about life, is a dull dog.

The result of the attempt to mix the satisfactions of art and life is, naturally, muddle. There is downright *bad* art where the satisfactions offered or suggested are solely the satisfactions of life; for example the drawings in salacious "comics" or the domesticities of *Pear's Annual*— that Mecca of British Academicians. There is art, often very fine art, of mixed appeal: for example, in Rodin's "La Vieille Heaulmière," the "beauty" of the work depends in no appreciable degree on the subject, which is "hideous." The "beauty" is from Rodin. It is in the composition, as I remember it; in silhouettes. The "interest" is, largely, a life interest or a sentimental interest. It is a pathos for lost youth, etc., intensified by a title reminiscent of Villon. Without the title from Villon the bronze loses much of its force.

If you measure art by its emotional effect scarcely anyone will deny that Villon's poem is more efficient than the statue. It calls up an image no less vivid. And it is easier to carry about in one's pocket, or in one's memory, for that matter. The words are, in fact, nearly unforgettable, while it is very hard to conserve more than a blur or general impression of the bronze figure. Of course there is no denying that certain figures, more or less caressable, may have an artistic appeal based on "pure form"; on their composition and symmetry and balance, etc. Those who appreciate them on these grounds are nearer art than those who do not.

So far as I am concerned, Jacob Epstein was the first person who came talking about "form, not the *form of anything*." It may have been Mr. T. E. Hulme, quoting Epstein. I don't know that it matters much who said it first; he may have been a theorist with no more than a sort of scientific gift for discovery. He may have been a great sculptor capable of acting out his belief. However that may be, the acceptable doctrine of my generation is that:

"Sculptural feeling is the appreciation of masses in relation.

"Sculptural ability is the defining of these masses by planes."—(Gaudier-Brzeska, in *Blast*)

It is in accordance with this belief that one honours Epstein, apart entirely from one's sympathy or unsympathy with any particular work.

"Cynthia prima fuit?" what does it matter? Epstein is a "slow worker," perhaps. His mind works with the deliberation of the chisel driving through stone, perhaps. The work is conceived from the beginning, slow stroke by slow stroke, like some prehistoric, age-long upheaval in natural things, driven by natural forces . . . full of certitude and implacable and unswerving . . . perhaps. And perhaps these are only phrases and approximations and rhetoric. They are the sort of phrases that arise in the literary mind in the presence of Epstein's sculpture. At any rate we do not say "Here is a man who ought to have been writing a comedy of manners." We feel convinced that it is a man fit for his job.

Let me be quite definite about what I mean by the work of Jacob Epstein—the work as I know it consists of:
"The Strand Statues" (which are very early).
The Wilde Memorial (which is overornate, and which one, on the whole, rather dislikes).
A scrawny bronze head, more or less early renaissance, quite fine, and which Mr. Epstein will reprove me for praising. He always reproves you for liking the "work before last."

Head of a boy, in bright copper, or some such substance. That is to say, the top and back are burnished.

Head of an infant (quite representational).

"The Sun-God."

Two sets of pigeons. The heavier and closer is the better.

The two "Flenites," the finest work of the lot.

A bird preening itself (graceful).

The rock-drill.*

And in this dozen works there are three or four separate donations. One wonders how many great artists have been as temperate; how many have waited for such a degree of certitude before they ventured to encumber the earth with "yet another work of art." Surely there are two types of mind which the mediocre world hates most. There is this mind of the slow gestation, whose absoluteness terrifies "the man in the street." Roughly speaking, it is the neglected type of Buonarroti. There is the type "Leonardo," that follows the lightning for model, that strikes now here, now there with bewildering rapidity, and with a certitude of its own. The first type is escapable, or at least, temporarily evadable. You cannot contradict the man's affirmations, but you can at least leave him alone in his corner. You can kill time and avoid looking things in the face. This type is, let us say, the less alarming. The second type is, I suppose, the most hated; that is to say, the most feared. You never know where the man will turn up. You never know what he will do next, and, for that matter, when he won't do something or other better than you can, or pierce your belovédest delusion. The first type is crowned in due course, the second type, never till death. After Leonardo is dead professors can codify his results. They can produce a static dogma and return in peace to their slumbers.

I beg you may pardon digressions, but is it or is it not ludicrous that "The Sun-God" (and two other pieces which I have not seen) should be pawned, the whole lot, for some £60? And that six of the other works are still on the sculptor's hands? And this is not due to the war. It was so before this war was heard of.

One looks out upon American collectors buying autograph mss. of William Morris, faked Rembrandts and faked Vandykes. One looks out on a plutocracy and upon the remains of an aristocracy who ought to know by this time that keeping up the arts means keeping up living artists; that no age can be a great age which does not find its own genius. One sees buildings of a consummate silliness; buildings which are beautiful before they are finished, enchanting when they consist only of foundations and of a few great scaffoldings and cranes towering into the day or into the half-darkness. When they are finished they are a mass of curlycues and "futile adornments." Because?

*This is, of course, not a full catalogue of Epstein's work, merely the few pieces on which I based my criticism.

Because neither America nor England cares enough to elevate great men to control; because there is no office for the propagation of form; because there is no power to set Epstein, for example, where he should be, to wit, in some place where his work would be so prominent that people, and even British architects, would be forced to think about form. Of course, some of them do think about form; and then, after they have constructed a fine shape, go *gaga* with ornaments.

I do not mean by this that I would make Epstein an inspector of buildings, or that I would set him to supervise architects' plans. The two arts are different, though they both deal with three dimensional form. I mean simply that a contemplation of Epstein's work would instil a sense of form in the beholder. That is, perhaps, the highest thing one can say of a sculptor.

All this is very secondary and literary and sociological. There could be no such harangue among artists. One sees the work; one knows; or, even, one feels.

Trying to find some praise that shall be exact and technical, some few of us, not sculptors, but admirers, would turn to Brzeska's "Vortex," which will be undoubtedly the first textbook of sculpture in many academies before our generation has passed from this earth. Accepting his terminology we would say: Epstein has worked with the sphere, and with the cylinder. He has had "form-understanding"; he has not fallen into the abyss, into the decadence of all sculpture which is "the admiration of self."

Why should we try to pin labels on "what he has expressed"? Is there any profit in saying that his form-organisations express facts which were perhaps more violently true for the South Sea islander of three thousand years ago than for us, who are moderns? That sort of talk is mostly nonsense. It is the artist's job to express what is "true for himself." In such measure as he does this he is a good artist, and, in such measure as he himself exists, a great one.

As for "expressing the age," surely there are five thousand sculptors all busy expressing the inanities, the prettinesses, the sillinesses—the Gosses and Tademas, the Mayfairs and Hampsteads of the age. Of course the age is "not so bad as all that." But the man who tries to express his age, instead of expressing himself, is doomed to destruction.

But this, also, is a side track. I should not spend my lines in answering carpings. I should pile my objectives upon Epstein, or, better still, I should ask my opponents to argue, not with me, but to imagine themselves trying to argue with one of the Flenites, or with the energies of his "Sun-God." They'd "teach you to" talk about "expressing your age," and being the communal trumpet.

The test of a man is not the phrases of his critics; the test lies in the work, in its "certitude." What answer is to be made to the "Flenites"? With what sophistry will you be able to escape their assertion?

AFFIRMATIONS[5]
Gaudier-Brzeska

It may suit some of my friends to go about with their young noses pointing skyward, decrying the age and comparing us unfavourably to the dead men of Hellas or of Hesperian Italy. And the elders of my acquaintance may wander in the half-lights complaining that—

Queens have died young and fair.

But I, for one, have no intention of decreasing my enjoyment of this vale of tears by underestimating my own generation. The uncertainty regarding the number of lives allowed one is too great. Neither am I so jealous of other men's reputations that I must wait until they are dead before I will praise them.

Having written this, I turn to *Il Cortegiano*, "that great book of courtesies" which I have never yet been able to read from cover to cover. I find the Italian contemporaries of your King Henry VII already wrangling over feminism and supermen, over democracies and optimates and groups and herds: abstract topics which lead in the end to Polonius. They speak of the "white man's burden" and of the rational explanation of myths, and they talk about "the light of Christian truth" (in that phrase precisely).

The discourse is perhaps more readable when Cardinal Bibiena questions whether or no a perfect gentleman should carry a joke to the point of stealing a countryman's capons. The prose is musical and drowsy, so that if you read the Italian side of the page you feel no need of Paul Fort. (I am turning aside from the very reverent bilingual version of 1727.) The periods are perhaps more musical than the strophes of the modern prose poems. One reads on aloud until one's voice is tired, and finds one has taken in nothing. Or perhaps you awake at a paragraph which says:—

"Alexander the Great . . . built Alexandria in Egypt . . . Bucephalia, etc. And he had Thoughts also of reducing Mount Athos into the Shape of a Man. To raise on his left Hand a most ample City, and in his right to dig a large Bason, in which he designed to make a Conflux of all the Rivers, which flow'd from the Mountain, and from thence tumble them into the Sea; a Project truly noble, and worthy of the Great Alexander."

Perhaps, even, you persevere to the final discourse of Bembo on the nature of love and beauty, with its slightly stagey reminiscence of the Socratic trance. It is here that he calls beauty the sign manifest and insignia of the past victories of the soul. But for all their eloquence, for all the cradling cadences of the Italian speech, I find nothing to prove that

[5]*The New Age*, February 4, 1915, pp. 409–11; *Gaudier-Brzeska*, pp. 102–10.

the conversation at Urbino was any better than that which I have heard in dingy studios or in restaurants about Soho. I feel that Urbino was charming, that the scene is worthy of Veronese; and especially I feel that no modern ambassador or court functionary could write half so fine a book as *Il Cortegiano*. This proves nothing more nor less than that good talk and wide interest have abandoned court circles and taken up their abode in the studios, *in quadriviis et angiportis.*

Et in quadriviis et angiportis we have new topics, new ardours. We have lost the idolatry for the Greek which was one of the main forces of the Renaissance. We have kept, I believe, a respect for what was strong in the Greek, for what was sane in the Roman. We have other standards, we have gone on with the intentions of Pico, to China and Egypt.

The man among my friends who is loudest in his sighs for Urbino, and for lost beauty in general, has the habit of abusing modern art for its "want of culture." As a matter of fact, it is chiefly the impressionists he is intent on abusing, but like most folk of his generation, he "lumps the whole lot together." He says: They had no traditions and no education, and therefore they created an art that needed no introductory knowledge. This means that he separates the "impressionist" painters from the impressionist writers, but let that pass. Let us say that Manet and Monet and Renoir had no education; that the tradition of Crivelli's symbols meant less to them than the rendering of light and shadow. I shall not stop admiring their paintings. I shall not, for any argument whatsoever, cease to admire the work of minds creative and inventive in whatsoever form it may come or may have come. Nor, on the other hand, will I ever be brought to consider futurism as anything but gross cowardice. It may be that Italy was so sick that no other medicine could avail, but for any man, not a modern Italian, to shirk comparison with the best work of the past is gross cowardice. The Italian may shirk if he likes, but he will remain a parochial celebrity even so.

Urbino was charming for the contemporaries of Count Baldassar Castiglione. Most of Urbino's topics, not all, thank heaven, have been relegated to the *New Statesman*. The Lord Michael Montaigne no longer keeps a conceited, wise notebook in private. "We" keep our journals in public print, and when we go wrong or make a sideslip, we know it, we "hear of it," we receive intimations. I don't know that it matters. I am not even sure that we have lost the dignity of letters thereby, though we have lost the quiet security.

To return to the symboliste friend, I am not going to bother arguing the case for deceased impressionists; his phrase was that all "modern art" was the art of the ignorant; of the people who despised tradition not because they knew enough to know how far tradition might or might not be despicable, but who despised it without knowing what it was. I shall let other modern movements shift for themselves. But to bring such a charge against a movement having for one of its integral members Gaudier-Brzeska, is arrant nonsense.

Here is a man as well furnished with catalogued facts as a German professor, of the old type, before the war-school; a man who knows the cities of Europe, and who knows not merely the sculpture out of Reinach's Apollo but who can talk and think in the terms of world-sculpture and who is for ever letting out odd packets of knowledge about primitive African tribes or about Babylonia and Assyria, substantiated by quotations from the bulkiest authors, and who, moreover, carries this pack without pedantry and unbeknown to all save a few intimates.

Take, if you like, four typical vorticists: there is Brzeska, and another man digging about in recondite early woodcuts or in studies of Chinese painting, and another man mad about Korin, and another man whom even *The Spectator* has referred to as "learned." If these men set out to "produce horrors," obviously it is not from ignorance or from lack of respect for tradition. No. The sum of their so-called revolt is that they refuse to recognize parochial borders to the artistic tradition. That they think it not enough to be the best painter in Chelsea, S.W., or to excel all the past artists of Fulham. "Speak of perfection, my songs, and you will find yourselves exceedingly disliked." Vorticism refuses to discard any part of the tradition merely because it is a difficult bogey; because it is difficult perhaps to be as good a designer as Dürer, and is consequently more convenient to pretend that "the element of design is not so important."

There is another shibboleth of the artistic-slop crowd. It is the old cry about intellect being inartistic, or about art being "above," saving the word, "above" intellect. Art comes from intellect stirred by will, impulse, emotion, but art is emphatically not any of these others deprived of intellect, and out drunk on its 'lone, saying it is the "that which is beyond the intelligence."

There are, as often has been said, two sorts of artists: the artist who moves through his art, to whom it is truly a "medium" or a means of expression; and, secondly, there is the mediumistic artist, the one who can only exist in his art, who is passive to impulse, who approaches more or less nearly to the "sensitive," or to the somnambulistic "medium." The faculty of this second type is most useful as a part of the complete artist's equipment. And I do not hesitate to call Brzeska "complete artist." In him there is sculptural ability. That goes without saying. And there is "equipment" in the sense of wide knowledge of his art and of things outside it, and there is intellect. There is the correlating faculty, an ability to "arrange in order" not only the planes and volumes which are peculiarly *of* his art, but an ability for historical synthesis, an ability for bringing order into things apparently remote from the technique of his art.

In my paper on Epstein I referred to Brzeska's "Vortex" in *Blast*. It is not merely a remarkable document from a man whom people remember a twelve-month before as speaking English with difficulty, it is a remarkable arrangement of thought. I confess that I read it two or three times with nothing but a gaiety and exhilaration arising from the author's vigour of speech.

"They elevated the sphere in a splendid squatness and created the Horizontal.

"From Sargon to Amir-nasir-pal men built man-headed bulls in horizontal flight-walk. Men flayed their captives alive and erected howling lions: The Elongated Horizontal Sphere Buttressed on Four Columns, and their kingdoms disappeared."

I read that passage many times for the sake of its oratorical properties without bothering much for the meaning. Then a friend who detests vorticism but who "has to admire Gaudier-Brzeska," said rather reluctantly: "He has put the whole history of sculpture in three pages." It is quite true. He has summarised the whole history of sculpture. I said he had the knowledge of a German professor, but this faculty for synthesis is most untedescan.

The Paleolithic vortex, man intent upon animals. The Hamite vortex, Egypt, man in fear of the gods. The derivative Greek. The Semitic vortex, lust of war. Roman and later decadence, Western sculpture, each impulse with corresponding effects on form. In like manner he analyses the Chinese and Mexican and Oceanic forms. The sphere, the vertical, the horizontal, the cylinder and the pointed cone; and then the modern movement.

Naturally this means nothing to anyone who has not thought about sculpture; to anyone who has not tried to think why the official sculpture is so deadly uninteresting.

"Sculptural energy is the mountain."

"Sculptural feeling is the appreciation of masses in relation."

"Sculptural ability is the defining of these masses by planes."

I repeat what I said before; this Vortex Gaudier-Brzeska, which is the last three pages of *Blast* (the first number), will become the textbook in all academies of sculpture before our generation has passed from the earth. If *Blast* itself were no more than an eccentrically printed volume issued by a half a dozen aimless young men, then you could afford to neglect it. *Blast* has not been neglected. *Blast* has been greatly reviled; that is natural. Michael Agnolo fled from Pisa to escape the daggers of the artists who feared his competition. *Blast* has behind it some of the best brains in England, a set of artists who know quite well what they want. It is therefore significant. The large type and the flaring cover are merely bright plumage. They are the gay petals which lure.

19

*We have again arrived at an age when men can consider a statue as a statue. The hard stone is not the live coney. Its beauty cannot be the same beauty.**

Art is a matter of capitals. I dare say there are still people, even in London, who have not arisen to the charm of the Egyptian and Assyrian galleries of the British Museum. If our detractors are going to talk about art in terms of "Pears Soap's Annual," and of the Royal Academy, one dismisses the matter. If they are men of goodwill, considering art in the terms of the world's masterwork, then we say simply: What is the charm in Assurbanipal's hunting? What is the charm in Isis with the young Horus between her knees and the green stone wings drawn tight about them? What is the aesthetic-dynamic basis for our enjoyment of these various periods? What are the means at the artist's disposal? What quality have the bronzes of Shang?

And when they have answered these questions there is no longer any quarrel between us. There are questions of taste and of preference, but no dispute about art. So that we find the "men of traditions" in agreement or in sympathy. We find the men of no traditions, or of provincial traditions, against us. We find the unthinking against us. We find the men whose minds have petrified at forty, or at fifty, or at twenty, most resolutely against us.

This petrifaction of the mind is one of the most curious phenomena that I have found in England. I am far from believing it to be peculiarly or exclusively English, but I have lived mostly in England since I began to take note of it. Before that I remember an American lawyer, a man of thirty, who had had typhoid and a long nervous illness. He was complaining that his mind "no longer took in things." It had lost its ability to open and grasp. He was fighting against this debility. In his case it was a matter of strength. With the second type it is, perhaps, a matter of will. This second type I have noticed mostly in England, but I think it would be the same from Portugal to Siberia. This type of mind shuts, at eighteen, or at five and twenty, or at thirty or forty. The age of the closure varies but the effect is the same. You find a man one week young, interested, active, following your thought with his thought, parrying and countering, so that the thought you have between you is more alive than the thought you may have apart. And the next week (it is almost as sudden as that) he is senile. He is anchored to a dozen set phrases. He will deny a new thought about art. He will deny the potentialities of a new scientific discovery, without weighing either. You look sadly back over the gulf, as Ut Napishtim looked back at the shades of the dead, the live man is no longer with you. And then, like as not, some further process sets in. It is the sadisme of the intellect, it is blight of Tertullian. The man becomes

*This passage was not italicized in the first printing of this article.

not only a detester but a persecutor of living and unfolding ideas. He not only refuses them, but he wishes to prevent you from having them. He has gone from Elysium into the *basso inferno*. The speed of light, the absolute power of the planes in Egyptian sculpture have no charm left for such men. And the living move on without them.

So much for opponents. As for Brzeska's work itself: what more can I say of it? That I like it; that I believe in it; that I have lived with it, that its "definition of masses" seems to me expressive of emotional and intellectual forces; that I have bought such fragments as my limited means afford; that a man with Brzeska's skill could easily have a house in Park Lane and a seat in the Academy if he chose to make the pretty-pretties which the pink-satined bourgeosie desire. (The sequence is easy: you make for the market, you become rich; being rich, you are irresistible, honours are showered upon you.)

And it happens, this sculptor, instead of making pretty-pretties, chooses to make works of art. There are always two parties in "civilization." There is the party which believes that the stability of property is the end and the all. There are those who believe that the aim of civilization is to keep alive the creative, the intellectually-inventive-creative spirit and ability in man—and that a reasonable stability of property may be perhaps one of the many means to this end, or that it may not be detrimental, or even that it doesn't much matter. Because of this indifference to the stability of life and property on the part of one segment, this entire party is branded anarchic, or incendiary. "New art" is thought dangerous, and the dangerous is branded as "ugly." Those who fear the new art also hate it.

I had, for a long time, a "most hideous" Brzeska statue where the morning light came on it as it woke me, and because of this shifting light plane after plane, outline after expressive outline was given me day after day, emphasised, taken apart from the rest. This was a statue which I had chosen when I had but glanced at it and not fully taken it in. I cannot impose further tests. The beauty was first there in the mass. It was secondly there in the detail, which I now know thoroughly, and not merely as one knows a thing seen in the hurry of some exhibition. A man having this ability to make beauty which endures months of study and which does not decrease as you learn it more intimately, is what we call a great artist.

You, gracious reader, may be a charming woman who only like pretty men, a statue of a primitive man holding a rabbit may not be a matter of interest to you, but that is no reason for abusing the artist. Or, on the other hand, ferocious and intolerant reader, you may be a vigorous male, who likes nothing save pretty women, and who despises feminine opinions about the arts. In either case you are quite right in saying that you dislike the new sculpture, you are being no more than honest. But there is

21

no cause for calling it unenjoyable or even ugly, if you do you are but stupid, you hate the labour of beginning to understand a new form. As for me, I have no objection to "art as an Aphrodisiac," but there are other possible motifs.

And the "new form." What is it? It is what we have said. It is an arrangement of masses in relation. It is not an empty copy of empty Roman allegories that are themselves copies of copies. It is not a mimicry of external life. It is energy cut into stone, making the stone expressive in its fit and particular manner. It has regard to the stone. It is not something suitable for plaster or bronze transferred to stone by machines and underlings. It regards the nature of the medium, of both the tools and the matter. These are its conventions and limits.

And if the Germans succeed in damaging Gaudier-Brzeska they will have done more harm to art than they have by the destruction of Rheims Cathedral, for a building once made and recorded can, with some care, be remade, but the uncreated forms of a man of genius cannot be set forth by another.

It may not be out of place to quote still another article, "Analysis of the Decade,"[6] not merely because Brzeska is mentioned in it, but because I think any consideration of vorticist art is incomplete if it does not make some mention of a sense of awakening and of our belief in the present.

"Will and consciousness are our Vortex," and an integral part of that consciousness is the unwavering feeling that we live in a time as active and as significant as the Cinquecento. We feel this ingress and we are full of the will for its expression.

SYNCHROMATISM[7]

Sir,—Mr. Wright[8] is a capital fellow, and no doubt wishes to do well by the Synchromatists. I apologise for being so behindhand with this letter, but I wish to challenge his statement re Vorticism and Futurism.

I venture to suggest that Mr. Wright's knowledge of "Vorticist" work is confined to the once decorations of the "Cabaret." Not having seen any Synchromatist work (which exists, I believe, in New York), I do not venture to say who were its parents.

[6]See p. 23.
[7]*The New Age*, February 4, 1915, pp. 389-90.
[8]Stanton Macdonald-Wright (b. 1890), American painter who with his fellow American expatriate Morgan Russell (1886-1953) founded the first American *avant-garde* art movement, "Synchromism." The first synchromist exhibition was held in June 1913, in Paris the following October, and in New York in March 1914. The Whitney Museum of American Art reintroduced the art of the movement in its exhibition "Synchromism and American Color Abstraction: 1910-1925," which was held from January 24 to March 26, 1978.

I do ask in the name of common sense what work of Gaudier-Brzeska's, for instance, can by any flight of fancy be traced to Futurism; or what work of my own in verse; or where there is any trace of Futurism in Lewis' "Timon of Athens." As for the principles of Vorticism and Futurism they are in direct or almost direct opposition.

I think Mr. Wright's enthusiasm for the Synchromatists has led him into some exaggeration in a matter irrelevant to his main theme.

America has, I believe, one excellent Futurist and professed "Futurist," Stella, and one poet who practices the Futurist method, Vachel Lindsay.

Thought is not helped by a confusion such as Mr. Wright himself terms "the public's habit of generalising on topics of which it is ignorant." Mr. Wright's charge is too vague. Let him, if he likes, work out some elaborate thesis to prove that organised opposition is a species of descent. Let him adduce details based on careful study and an examination of intention. But let him desist from flinging mud merely in order to be able to put his Synchromatists at the top of an imaginary pyramid.

Judging from print and not from pictures, which are for the present inaccessible, Synchromatism would seem to be a praiseworthy department of Expressionism, making legitimate experiments in colour, but that is no reason why their advocates should call names and speak unsubstantiable abuse of others who are, at least for the present, inclined to regard Synchromatism with friendly eye. The question of what Mr. Wright means by "rationalising the palate" is not one that we would care to discuss until we have seen the painted results.

Are the Synchromatists working with colour as the Vorticist works with colour and form? In which case where is Mr. Wright's charge against Vorticism? Also, is his Minerva sprung from the forehead of Kandinsky?

EZRA POUND.

AFFIRMATIONS[9]
Analysis of This Decade

The Renaissance is a convenient stalking-horse for all young men with ideas. You can prove anything you like by the Renaissance; yet, for all that, there seems to be something in the study of the quattrocento which communicates vigour to the student of it, especially to such scholars as have considered the whole age, the composite life of the age, in contradistinction to those who have sentimentalised over its aesthetics. Burckhardt writes in German with the verve of the best French heavy prose. Villari's Italian is thoroughly Germanised; he writes always with an eye on modern national development for Italy, he has presumably an atrocious

[9]*The New Age*, February 11, 1915, pp. 409-411; *Gaudier-Brzeska*, pp. 111-117.

taste in pictures, he is out of sympathy with many of the Renaissance enthusiasms, and yet manages to be interesting and most shrewd in his critical estimates, even of things he dislikes (e.g., though he speaks with reverence of Raphael, he sees quite clearly the inferiority of Renaissance painting to the painting which went before, and attributes it to the right lack of energy).

Whatever one's party, the Renaissance is perhaps the only period in history that can be of much use to one—for the adducing of pious examples, and for showing "horrible results." It may be an hallucination, but one seems able to find modern civilisation in its simple elements in the Renaissance. The motive ideas were not then confused and mingled into so many fine shades and combinations one with the other.

Never was the life of arts so obviously and conspicuously intermingled with the life of power. Rightly or wrongly, it is looked back to as a sort of golden age for the arts and for the literati, and I suppose no student, however imperfect his equipment, can ever quite rest until he has made his own analysis, or written out his own book or essay. I shall not do that here; I shall only draw up a brief table of forces: first, those which seem to me to have been the effective propaganda of the Renaissance; secondly, those which seem to me the acting ideas of this decade—not that they are exclusively of this decade, but it seems that they have, in this decade, come in a curious way into focus, and have become at least in some degree operative. I shall identify the motive ideas in each case with the men who may, roughly, be considered as their incarnations or exponents.

The Renaissance, as you have all read forty times, was "caused" by the invention of printing and the consequently increased rapidity in the multiplication of books, by the fall of Constantinople (which happened after the Renaissance was somewhat well under way, granting that it—the Renaissance—had not been more or less under way since the fall of Rome). However, let us say that various causes worked together and caused, or assisted or accelerated, a complex result. The fall of Constantinople made necessary new trade routes, drove Columbus into the West Indies, sent Crisolora to Florence with a knowledge of Greek, and Filelfo to Milan with a bad temper. And these things synchronised with "the revival of classicism," and just preceded the shaping up of mediaeval Europe into more or less the modern "great States."

This "revival of classicism," a very vague phrase, is analysable, at the start, into a few very different men, with each one a very definite propaganda.

You had, for instance, Ficino, seized in his youth by Cosimo dei Medici and set to work translating a Greek that was in spirit anything but "classic." That is to say, you had ultimately a "Platonic" academy messing up Christian and Pagan mysticism, allegory, occultism, demonology, Trismegistus, Psellus, Porphyry, into a most eloquent and exciting and

24

exhilarating hotch potch, which "did for" the mediaeval fear of the *dies irae* and for human abasement generally. Ficino himself writes of Hermes Trismegistus in a New Testament Latin, and arranges his chronology by co-dating Hermes' great-grandfather with Moses.

Somewhat later Pico writes his *De Dignitate* in endless periods, among which is one so eloquent that it is being continually quoted.

Pico della Mirandola based his own propaganda on what we should call a very simple and obvious proposition. He claimed that science and knowledge generally were not, or, at least, should not, or need not be, grounded solely and exclusively on the knowledge of the Greeks and Romans. This created horrible scandal. People had indeed heard of Arabs and Hebrews, but this scoundrelly Pico insisted that there were still other languages and unexplored traditions. It was very inconvenient to hear that one was not omniscient. It still is. It was equally bad when Erasmus wanted scholars to begin using accent-marks over Greek letters. I sympathise with the scholars who objected to being bothered with "Tittle-tattles."

The finest force of the age, I think, came early—came from Lorenzo Valla. He had a great passion for exactness, and he valued the Roman vortex. By philology, by the "harmless" study of language, he dissipated the donation of Constantine. The revival of Roman Law, while not his private act, was made possible or accelerated by him. His dictum that eloquence and dialectic were one—i.e., that good sense is the backbone of eloquence—is still worth considering. I suppose anyone will now admit it in theory. Also, he taught the world once more how to write Latin, which was perhaps valuable. Seeing that they were drawing much of their thought from Latin sources, a lively familiarity with that tongue could not but clarify their impressions.

At this time, also, observation came back into vogue, stimulated, some say, by a reading of classics. The thing that mattered was a revival of the sense of realism: the substitution of Homer for Virgil; the attitude of Odysseus for that of the snivelling Aeneas, who was probably not so bad as Virgil makes out.

As Valla had come to exactness, it was possible for Machiavelli to write with clarity. I do not wish to become entoiled in the political phases save in so far as they are inextricably bound in with literature. Tyranny, democracy, etc., these things were, in the quattrocento and cinquecento, debatable ideas, transient facts. None of them could be taken for granted. In Machiavelli's prose we have a realism born perhaps from Valla's exactness and the realism of Homer, both coming to Machiavelli indirectly.

And in the midst of these awakenings Italy went to rot, destroyed by rhetoric, destroyed by the periodic sentence and by the flowing paragraph, as the Roman Empire had been destroyed before her. For when words cease to cling close to things, kingdoms fall, empires wane and diminish. Rome went because it was no longer the fashion to hit the nail on the head. They desired orators. And, curiously enough, in the mid-Renaissance, rhetoric and floridity were drawn out of the very Greek and Latin revival that had freed the world from mediaevalism and Aquinas.

Quintilian "did for" the direct sentence. And the Greek language was made an excuse for more adjectives. I know no place where this can be more readily seen than in the Hymns to the Gods appended to Divus' translation of the Odyssey into Latin. The attempt to reproduce Greek by Latin produced a new dialect that was never spoken and had never before been read. The rhetoric got into painting. The habit of having no definite conviction save that it was glorious to reflect life in a given determined costume or decoration "did for" the painters.

Our thought jumps from the Renaissance to the present because it is only recently that men have begun to combat the Renaissance. I do not mean that they merely react against it; that was done in the hideous and deadening counter-reformation; but we have begun deliberately to try to free ourselves from the Renaissance shackles, as the Renaissance freed itself from the Middle Ages.

We may regard all the intervening movements as revivals of the Renaissance or as continuations of special phases: for instance, the various forms of "classicism" getting "colder and colder," or more and more florid. Rousseau was almost born out of his due time, and Napoleon is but an exaggerated condottiere to the very detail of the Roman robe in which he surmounts the column Vendôme. It would be quite possible to sustain the thesis that we are still a continuation of certain Renaissance phases, that we still follow one or two dicta of Pico or Valla. But we have in so many ways made definite a divergence (not a volte-face, because we are scarcely returning to pious Catholicism or to limited mediaevalism). It is easier, it is clearer, to call this age a new focus. By focus I do not in the least mean that the forces focussed are in themselves new inventions. I mean that they begin to act. I mean, also, that the results are decidedly different from the results of Renaissance theory and aesthetics. It is not long since Springer wrote: "Durch Raffael ist das Madonnenideal Fleisch geworden." We remove ourselves from the state of mind of Herr Springer.

A certain number of fairly simple and now obvious ideas moved the Renaissance; their ramifications and interactions are still a force with the people. A certain number of simple and obvious ideas, running together and interacting, are making a new, and to many a most obnoxious, art. I need scarcely say that there were many people to whom the art of the quattrocento and the paganism of the Renaissance seemed equally damnable, unimportant, obnoxious. It was "Rome or Geneva." I shall give these simple ideas of this decade as directly as I have given the ideas which seem to me to be the motifs of the Renaissance. I shall give the names of men who embody them. I shall make some few explanations and no apology whatsoever.

Ford Hueffer, a sense of the *mot juste*. The belief that poetry should be at least as well written as prose, and that "good prose is just your conversation."

This is out of Flaubert and Turgenev and Stendhal, and what you will. It is not invention, but focus. I know quite well that Wordsworth talked about "common words," and that Leigh Hunt wrote to Byron advising him against clichés. But it did not deter Byron from clichés. The common word is not the same thing as *mot juste*, not by a long way. And it is possible to write in a stilted and bookish dialect without using clichés. When I say the idea "becomes operative" here I presumably mean that Mr. Hueffer is the first man who has made enemies by insisting on these ideas in England. That matter can be discussed, and it will aid to the clarity of the discussion if we discuss it quite apart from your opinion or my opinion of Mr. Hueffer's work "as a whole" or in detail.

Myself, an active sense not merely of comparative literature, but of the need for a uniform criticism of excellence based on world-poetry, and not of the fashion of any one particular decade of English verse, or even on English verse as a whole. The qualitative analysis in literature (practised but never formulated by Gaston Paris, Reinach in his *Manual of Classical Philology*, etc.). The Image.

Wyndham Lewis, a great faculty of design, synthesis of modern art movements, the sense of emotion in abstract design. A sense of the import of design not bounded by Continental achievement. A sense of dynamics.

Barzun's question: Pourquoi doubler l'image?

Gaudier-Brzeska. In him the "new" sculptural principle becomes articulate. "The feeling of masses in relation." (Practised by Epstein and countless "primitives" outside the Hellenic quasi-Renaissance tradition.) General thorough knowledge of world-sculpture. Sense of a standard not limited by 1870 or 1905.

Edward Wadsworth, sense of the need of "radicals in design," an attempt toward radicals in design. A feeling for ports and machines (most certainly not peculiar to himself, but I think a very natural and personal tendency, unstimulated in his case by Continental propaganda).

I consider this one of the age-tendencies, springing up naturally in many places and coming into the arts quite naturally and spontaneously in England, in America, and in Italy. We all know the small boy's delight in machines. It is a natural delight in a beauty that had not been pointed out by professional aesthetes. I remember young men with no care for aesthetics who certainly would not know what the devil this article was about, I remember them examining machinery catalogues, to my intense

27

bewilderment, commenting on machines that certainly they would never own and that could never by any flight of fancy be of the least use to them. This enjoyment of machinery is just as natural and just as significant a phase of this age as was the Renaissance "enjoyment of nature for its own sake," and not merely as an illustration of dogmatic ideas. The modern sense of the value of the "creative, constructive individual" (vide Allan Upward's constant propaganda, etc., etc.) is just as definite a doctrine as the Renaissance attitude De Dignitate, Humanism. As for external stimulus, new discoveries, new lands, new languages gradually opened to us; we have great advantage over the cinque- or quattrocento.

Ernest Fenollosa's finds in China and Japan, his intimate personal knowledge, are no less potent than Crisolora's manuscripts. China is no less stimulating than Greece, even if Fenollosa had not had insight. And this force of external stimuli is certainly not limited by "what we do"; these new masses of unexplored arts and facts are pouring into the vortex of London. They cannot help but bring about changes as great as the Renaissance changes, even if we set ourselves blindly against it. As it is, there is life in the fusion. The complete man must have more interest in things which are in seed and dynamic than in things which are dead, dying, static.

The interest and perhaps a good deal of the force of the group I mention lie in the fact that they have perfectly definite intentions; that they are, if you like, "arrogant" enough to dare to intend "to wake the dead" (quite as definitely as Cyriac of Ancona), that they dare to put forward specifications for a new art, quite as distinct as that of the Renaissance, and that they do not believe it impossible to achieve these results.

Many parallels will rise in the mind of the reader; I have only attempted certain obscure ones. The external forces of the Renaissance have been so often presented that one need not expatiate upon them. Certain inner causes are much less familiar, for which reason it has seemed worth while to underline the "simple directions" of Pico and Crisolora and Valla, and the good and evil of Greek. The Renaissance sought a realism and attained it. It rose in a search for precision and declined through rhetoric and rhetorical thinking, through a habit of defining things always "in the terms of something else."

Whatever force there may be in our own decade and vortex is likewise in a search for a certain precision; in a refusal to define things in the terms of something else; in the "primary pigment." The Renaissance sought for a lost reality, a lost freedom. We seek for a lost reality and a lost intensity. We believe that the Renaissance was in part the result of a programme. We believe in the value of a programme in contradistinction to, but not in contradiction of, the individual impulse. Without such vagrant impulse

28

there is no art, and the impulse is not subject to programme. The use and the limitation of force need not bring about mental confusion. An engine is not a confusion merely because it uses the force of steam and the physical principles of the lever and piston.

PROVINCIALISM THE ENEMY III[10]

. . . The "State" and the "universities" which are its bacilli work in a uniform way. In scholarship it leads to the connoisseur of sculpture who tells you, re the early Greek work, that your values are "merely aesthetic values," and, therefore, of no importance; he being intent only on archaeological values. (This is not fanciful but an actual incident.) It leads, in the general, to an uncritical acceptance of any schematised plan laid down by higher commands of one sort or another. These things have their relative "use" or convenience, or efficiency, but their ultimate human use is nil, or it is pernicious.

PROVINCIALISM THE ENEMY IV[11]

. . . It is a waste of time to arrange one's study of a literary period anywhere save in the British Museum. (No one who has not tried to start the examination of a period elsewhere can fully appreciate this.) I am taking a perhaps trifling illustration, but I wish to avoid ambiguity. It is a waste of time for a painter not to have both the Louvre and the National Gallery (and the Prado, for that matter) "under his thumb." Artists are not the only men to whom a metropolis is of value. They are not an isolated exception. I but take my illustration from the things most familiar to me. To put it another way: Civilisation is made by men of unusual intelligence. It is their product. And what man of unusual intelligence in our day, or in any day, has been content to live away from, or out of touch with, the biggest metropolis he could get to?

A lumping of Paris and London into one, or anything which approximates such a lumping, doubles all the faculties and facilities. Anything which stands in the way of this combination is a reaction and evil. And any man who does not do his part toward bringing the two cities together has set his hand against the best of humanity.

[10]*The New Age*, July 26, 1917, pp. 288-89; *Selected Prose*, London, p. 168; New York, p. 198.

[11]*The New Age*, August 2, 1917, p. 309; *Selected Prose*, London, pp. 172-73; New York, pp. 202-3.

ART NOTES[12]
At Heal's

The preponderant weakness, or, rather, the manifest sign of weakness, in the more rampant modern art movements is the rapidity with which they melt into stereotypes. The London Group has given, perhaps, twelve exhibitions, the schools to which its artists belong are none of them ancient, and yet anyone whose memory serves him, and who has been constant in attendance at picture shows, will agree that he has seen this exhibition before. He will feel that he has seen it at the Alpine Gallery and later repeatedly at the Goupil, and that it now appears deprived of several of its more startling and once prominent members.

The remaining members may have illuminated or deluminated each other, but the composite effect is unchanged. Let us in charity allow for the augmented cleanliness of the "atmosphere," due, perhaps, to the new spic-and-span gallery with the fortunate obscurity of its alcove. With this allowance and due pleasure therefore deducted, we find the familiar patchiness, blurriness, stickiness; or, in detail, we discover that No. 52 is a sticky blurr; No. 53 a blurr (greasy); 54, a blurr (muddy); 55, blurr pure and simple; 56, blurr (sticky); 57 is a sectionised blurr, a rather soggy, sectionised blurr leaning to the left and to Picasso; 58, a still muddier blurr; 59, a blurr with a glare on it; 60, patches; 62, a poster effort for Chu Chin Chow, inexcusable, but tempered by the kindly chiaroscuro of the alcove. And in this manner we might continue.

The old tendency to apply a convention of foliage which Gauguin found convenient for conveying cacti or other tropical foliage, is here, with less felicity, turned upon more northern orchards. Mr. Atkinson, as is his custom, obliges with the wonted homage to William Roberts; he has the inventiveness of the inlay workers of Naples and Capri, though the cunning workmanship of their knife-blades is perhaps more durable than the fruits of his brush. Miss Sands displays love of beautiful colour. No. 65 portrays dirty weather. No. 33 is romantic. Mr. Bevan has discovered that leaves either are, or, of a right, ought to be, little pasteboard "planes in relation," or whatever the new-fangled call them. His trees are Christmas trees, entirely covered with box-lids. The spirit is that of the early Impressionists, the pictures not unpleasing (if one likes one's trees with this dressing). S. de Karlowska seems either to have led, or followed, or accompanied him into the paradise of this verdure. No. 43 is a blurr; No. 51 is a blurr, called "The Washout." No 1 is a tin and oil composition; No. 6 approximates the texture of the pre-Victorian antimacassar,

[12]*The New Age*, November 22, 1917, pp. 74-75. This is the first of Pound's critical articles for *The New Age* signed with the pseudonym "B. H. Dias." They continue at intervals until April 8, 1920.

and represents, we presume, the London Group's longing to return toward the primitive. No. 2 is pale Bevan; No. 14 a bad imitation of Pryde, by an artist who exhibits three pictures imitative of as many different modes, which are, none of them, worth commending.

Messrs. Heal's cordial invitation to Visit the Furnished Flat offers temptations, and the layman may be justified in accepting it before he inspects Mr. Kauffer's melted ice-cream (42), or his painted ice-cream (47). The texture of these may be compared to that of the ceiling at the native "American Fountain," near Oxford Circus. There is some pretty blue paint to be found on canvas 17. 16 is simply bad.

Despite all this the show, on the whole, is not completely displeasing. The effect of cleanliness may not be wholly due to the newness of Messrs. Heal's Gallery. Some, at least, of the painters have made almost imperceptible, perhaps even imaginary, advances in technique. If there is no single picture as well painted as Chas. Shannon's portrait of Mr. Ricketts, shown in last Spring's "Academy," there is here and there in the general mass of the London Group a sign of improvement; of greater care in the use of the brush. 73 is a drawing of promise. Mr. Nash is amusing. His 75 is "modern," in the sense that it shows artificial flowers under a dome of glass, a steamboat of the 1875 pattern, and a young man (outside the window) wearing a bowler. 49 is one of several companion pieces to the public poster, "Is this worth fighting for?" 105 has been hung on its side by some hanger zealous for non-representation, and for a greater new-fangledness than is encouraged by the slightly timorous, hesitant revolutionism, which is the keynote of the Group. For the group is ceasing to be the art-student group, little by little. As the Chelsea Arts Club, with its air of fly-fishing, of "just back from the Derby," is gradually absorbed by the Academy, so the London Group drifts on insensibly toward the Arts Club, a little more sober than its once jaunty predecessors. Mr. Bevan, indeed, is almost ripe for Academy work. Impressionism is being received, and Mr. Bevan is at heart an Impressionist. He has trimmed up the edges of his leaves, but one must allow certain latitude.

Mr. McIntyre is amusing. The roguish lady in the mud-puddle (88) is much less entertaining. Mr. Kauffer's 78 is clean paint, at any rate. 31, a nude lady stepping over a dog, is, to my mind, without merit; 71 almost clean. One is inclined to wonder why this group, an essentially imitative body of men, have not chosen other models for their emulation. They manifest an unnatural desire for personality, or origination, yet they have none of them the inventiveness even to pitch upon a type of picture a little out of the common; they are all caught in the mode of the moment, or, rather, in the set of modes advocated during the last few years by French and German art critics. We have had books on Gauguin. El Greco's astigmatism has been exploited to the limit. The one characteristic common to all mild revolutionaries, and to nearly all revolutionaries is that they so seldom pitch upon a difficult mode. De Hooch, for example, or Mieris, for example, has never been made the point of departure for any artistic insurrection, yet their works are quite as different from the painting of contemporary academicians as is the work of El Greco. All the outcry about Matisse and "pure colour," has not produced any colour better than that of Perugino, who, in his turn, has produced no artistic-Sloboda.

LEICESTER GALLERY.

Mr. Epstein has left his quondam colleagues, and exhibits alone at the Leicester Gallery, seven pieces of sculpture: three portrait busts, left over from the larger Leicester Gallery exhibition; a wretched and rolling-pin travesty of his original and impressive mating pigeons; the ubiquitous bronze head of an ailing infant, which has been part of every Epstein exhibit for the last six or eight years; a portrait of Miss Keane, which does not much improve on her posters; and, lastly, a bronze idealisation of Mrs. Epstein worthy of any national museum; a masterpiece of no school and no period, not as portraiture, for the beauty is dependent in great measure on the narrowing and pointing of the face from cheek-bones downward, but a beautiful bronze demanding no dogma for its acceptance.

Mr. Epstein has left his abstractions, his Assyrian oddities, his South Sea grotesqueries; he has suggested the nomadic Arab type in this visage, or, perhaps, the Romany type in accord with his celebrated confrère of Chelsea. But this head is not simply an advertisement that Mr. Epstein can do pretty portraits; in fact, the accusation is made null by the accompanying head of the professionally pretty Miss Keane, which is, in his bronze, lacking in interest. The head of Mrs. Epstein has the beauty of antiquity, without, however, being Hellenic, without suggesting, as did one of the masks at Epstein's earlier show, that he was seeking Hellenic models. It will be a great comfort to Mr. Epstein's numerous admirers that he has shown himself capable of this mastery, unaccompanied by any peculiarity, or by any pronounced archaism, or exoticism, or by that misguided and excessive modernity which has never had any true place in his character.

ART NOTES[12a]
The Loan Exhibition at the Grafton

The Loan Exhibit at the Grafton Gallery centres about, we might almost say consists of, two magnificent Degas: one is a dancer; the other in the harder style of this master has for its subject two washerwomen; and both

[12a]*The New Age,* December 20, 1917, pp. 152-53. Signed "B. H. Dias."

canvases are of his best, both of them above praise. The effect of durable paint, the hardness of detail in the finish of one of the washerwomen's faces in its relation to the broadly done background, are so fine, so beyond any hasty critical sentence, that I am at loss whether I ought not to defer notice of the exhibit until I can muster a suitable homage. But, after all, this is only a chronicle. No art-lover will miss this show, bad as is the great bulk of it. The clean hard surface of the one Degas, and the roseate blurr of the other are worth the trouble of going to Bond Street, they are worth coming up from the provinces to look at; and no one need dwell on the rest of the paintings.

About thirty of these latter, nevertheless, repay inspection. Beneath the Degas hangs a small Whistler, as perfect in its rightness, in its quite unostentatious perfection, as are the former in their positive and assertive qualities. It is of four figures, one holding a parasol, done apparently at the time when Whistler was making his Hellenic studies, and having in its grace and its pallor nearly all of Condor's qualities, but having, as Condor never has, a very delectable firmness and surety. The tiny white Whistler to the left is not to be passed unmentioned, despite scant "acreage," for it is about the size of a cabinet photograph.

The Degas fan is not his best, though it was probably impossible for him to paint without making something of interest. The poise of dancers' feet, the effect of the stage seen through the wings, one figure particularly happy in its pattern value, where it is cut into by the scenery, lift the fan out of the commonplace.

Next in interest are "Max's" caricatures of Mr. Rosetti, his friends and his pictures (these latter rather better than the originals). There is shown a good Brabazon, and a rather good Sickert. Mr. Sargent's water-colours present technical interest, as does also one water-colour by Mr. Steer (the one on which he has written a word which looks like "Bilter" or "Bilten").

Mr. McEvoy is too much with us. From the first dribble of his "promise" to his last unfortunate efforts, he covers, or obscures, a great deal of wall-space. It is all remarkable that the admirers of this painter did not hit upon Kirchner, who would have satisfied all their aesthetic desires.

Mr. Strang's "No. 3" is deplorable. Mr. Philpot shows a Spanish subject, a sort of compromise between Boldini and Castelucho. He shows also a symbol of, we presume, a Labour movement, abortive. Harrington Mann has, perhaps, the distinction of having created the worst of the paintings present, but this distinction is hotly and multitudinously contested. Mr. Sims, for example, shows a Cupid sitting in the branches of a tree; it would not have seemed out of place in Pears' Annual for 1887. Watts' effort for the poster of "The Incoming Tide," has the finish of some Victorian textile. It might have served as a lambrequin, and one would not be surprised if one found it covering a Surbiton sofa, or draped upon a Clapham piano.

Monticelli always contrives to be interesting with his mastery of his own particular, rather unintelligent little business. The pictures here shown are not his finest, but they are worth a moment's attention.

The lenders of the few fine pictures have been most generous in risking them at this time, while the lenders of others may have their motives suspected. Still, the Gothas have avoided the Tate Gallery so far, and one can leave something to them.

SERBO-CROATIANS

The Serbo-Croatian artists at the Grafton Gallery are divided into three parts: Rosandic, Racki, and Mestrovic. On entering the first room, which is devoted to Rosandic, the spectator thinks he is looking at the new work of Mestrovic; that Mestrovic has been wise in confining himself for the most part to wood-carving; that he has been more careful than usual about his compositions, and their formality, but that he has lost in some degree the excellent wood-carver's "trade" work or technique, which showed in his earlier wood-cutting.

Rosandic's work is of uneven merit. "Mother's Treasure" is excellently formal. "Woman's Sorrow" is technically excellent. "The Grandmother" betrays his paucity of formal invention, for the same rectangular composition is used to better advantage in "Mother's Treasure." "The Vestal Virgin" is rubbish, with a few meritorious cuts; No. 13 is the old Mestrovic story; we saw it some time ago at S. Kensington. "A Girl" has merit. "Ecco Homo" is merely skinny. "Salome" is silly post-Beardsley. "The Little Shepherd" is extremely interesting. On the whole, Rosandic's work is hopeful, and I should be more inclined to trust him than his better-known confrère.

The painter Racki is uninteresting, a mixture of Dulac and Slavicised Millet, with some undigested Puvis and Goya thrown into the *olla,* from which emerge also various Mestrovician visages.

It is Mestrovic whom the visitors come for. When his illumination first burst upon the chiaroscuro of fad-ridden London, while thankful, as usual, for any relief from Sims, Frampton and Co., of Piccadilly, we noted certain defects in Mr. Mestrovic's talent. He had practically no feeling for stone. This is a very sad thing for a sculptor. He had very little feeling for form; his emphasis was got by purely literary means, and those of the crudest. The shape of his "Serbian Hero" mattered very little, the "terribility," or whatever it was intended for, was supposedly given by presenting the hero in the act of biting through an imaginary plate of sheet-iron. Other works were embellished with weakly barbaric symbology. The energy of Mr. Epstein's flenite figures was not to be found at the South Kensington exhibition. On the other hand, Mestrovic had an irrefutable wood-carver's technique, the fruit, we were told, of more than one generation. The wooden figures and the plasters taken from, or intended for wood, were executed with no mean talent.

The charming archaic-restoration of his imitation Greek vases gave us the key to the matter. We had in them the real Mestrovic, the Mestrovic as he would have been if left to himself; but no, he had been inoculated with an idea of being Victor Hugo, or someone of that sort. He had contracted the milkman's itch to be the eighty-third Michaelangelo, instead of simply the gentle Mr. Mestrovic, delighted with the refinements of Vienna. Turning his back upon the tea-cup of modernity he set out to be the Croatian Colossus. He constructed an idea of Serbian nationality, with the result that is known to us . . . and he would have made such exquisite snuff-boxes had he lived in the time of Louis XIV!

When a man's mind is so fundamentally uninteresting and uninventive as the mind displayed by Mr. Mestrovic in his sculpture, he would do well, as in the case of Monticelli, to stick to the matter of his craft, for we can get excellent art from men who have but one idea every ten years, on condition, be it stipulated, that they do not try to act as a megaphone for current notions. This megaphoning is the function of politicians who do it, perhaps, better than artists.

However, Mestrovic still inclines to "telling a story" instead of asserting a verity. (Note how utterly absent the narrative element is from Epstein's flenites, or from Egyptian sculpture, however memorial it may be, however many inscriptions there are to tell you all about Rameses or Amen Hotep.) Mestrovic's present exposition contains no surprises. What one thought at South Kensington, one is constrained to think again at the Grafton.

The influence of the archaic or Gnossian wave-pattern (as in the pre-classic bas-relief of "Venus Rising from the Waves"), is still active in Mestrovic's work (and in that of Rosandic). There is no objection to this pattern in itself. Mestrovic has seen John; he has encountered, possibly in Mayfair, a female twisting a shawl round her person, so as not too greatly to obscure certain salients. And he has, alas, taken less care in the actual cutting of his wood.

His pièce-de-résistance is a crucifix, not carved better than many of the nine-and-ninety million objects of this sort that sprang from the ages of faith. The crucifix at best is a displeasing and eminently (and, I dare say, intentionally) unaesthetic object. As a fetich it lacks notably the energy, the horrific energy, of African and Mexican fetiches; it had the Greek aesthetic to contend with; the ideas concerning Adonis were constantly getting mixed up with the idea of sacrifice. The two ideas neutralised; they were very nearly incompatible.

Mestrovic's crucifix met me first in a reproduction in *Colour*. This reproduction made me slightly ill. I had a definite qualm in the stomach. Any sheep in a butcher's-shop might have so yawed at the mouth. I mention this as a protest against bad reproduction, or rather reproduction obviously taken from some point of view from which the original statue will not be seen.

This unpleasantness is absent from the head as one sees it from the floor of a gallery, looking up at the figure. (Must we still go on quoting Aristotle?)

Mr. Nevinson, who resembles the pre-Raphaelites in that his work gains by being seen in reproduction, is represented also in *Colour* by a picture of wind. In this picture he has, as the editors of that periodical quite rightly claim, added something to his subject. I doubt if Mestrovic has added anything to his crucifix, unless it be a few extra inches of fingers and pedal phalanges. The question remains, Is this "Christ" any more effective than the usual Christ of the everyday crucifix? Do we get a new religious emotion from being asked to believe that He had prehensile toe-nails? And is this symbol of an age of faith, this symbol of a religion having now mainly a suburban interest, this symbol of individual sacrifice, particularly impressive at a time when every newspaper is throwing upon our daily imagination the vision of fields covered with dead, of hecatombs, and of calamities? Has it even the merit of being a psychological record? The chromos of Christ and the boy-scout, Christ and the dying soldier, are narrative, and do record the state and quality of contemporary people's thought. Does Mestrovic's crucifix do this? Or is it really more historic, does it represent the last gasp of Christianity, the last attempt by extraneous means, by distortion and exaggeration, to put some last life into a fading and irrevocable belief? If so, it is perhaps good as a record.

LETTERS TO THE EDITOR[13]
Contemporary Mentality. Art.

Sir,—There is no use arguing with these people. There is no use trying to make them understand the difference between the rhetoric of Victor Hugo rather messily transposed into stone or plaster, and sculpture which is an art of form, whose language is form and whose effects when they are lastingly impressive are by form produced. Mr. Ezra Pound attempted some such explanation in your paper years ago; it only produced a riot. But, then, he expressed himself very badly and in the jargon of his horrible vortex.

Still, he is better than the people who think that the obvious reproduction of sexual organs is the one means of producing "powerful" art. "Powerful" is a word these people are exceedingly fond of. They apply it

[13]*The New Age*, January 10, 1918, p. 219.

to messy fiction like that of Mr. Thomas Burke. They need and perceive nothing else.

Your correspondent drags in Mestrovic's temple. Surely this concerns architecture rather than sculpture. Architecture has laws and a technique of its own. A building has and must have what a statue has not, or need not of necessity have—namely, a hollow inside. I believe that once the talented Lutyens, carried away by excess of fancy, created a beautiful house-plan—with no stairways. Did your "powerful" Mestrovic enthusiast by any chance consider the lighting of Mestrovic's temple? Religion has, I admit, nearly always stood for the propagation of darkness. But a temple with *no* means of lighting is surely excessive. Perhaps it is intended to light it with pure genius, or from some secret Serbo-Croatian power station, the clue to which is denied us.

B. H. DIAS

ART[14]
The New English Art Club

In Rule 10 of the New English Art Club we read: "There are no restrictions as regards frames, except that paintings in oil must be framed in gold." Whether this quaint bit of folklore is an heritage from Cimabue or Madame Blavatsky or only from the aureate period of the late Sir Frederick Leighton, the present critic is unable to state. Indeed, as I only read the "Rules" after leaving the building, I am unable to say if the tenth rule is strictly observed in the present exhibition. The question whether or no all oils are gold-framed is, however, without reasonable doubt, vital to the health of the N.E.A.C., especially in the absence of Mr. Augustus John and Mr. William Orpen. Not that this absence is by any means as grave a matter to the club's health as the *Daily Mail* would have us believe. In reference to these two "most distinguished members" we say, however, that whatever British official art has been, the Canadian Government has recently set the rest of the Empire a fine example and that the committee in charge of the Canadian war records is to be congratulated on the courage and discrimination with which it has chosen for its work the best artists in the contemporary schools, without favour, and in defiance of various makers of municipal monuments, moulagers of mice and other official furniture.

There are there "for all tastes," from water-colours à la Turner (not bad), an oil à la Turner (appalling, by Mr. William Shackleton, really appalling!) to pseudo-Japanese backgrounds and Mr. Nevinson; from bad imitations of six or seven early Italian masters—imitation confined usually

[14]*The New Age,* January 17, 1918, pp. 235-36. Signed "B. H. Dias."

to one part of the picture, seldom covering in its discipleship the whole of any one canvas—to pointillism, spotty impressionism, de Smet, Mr. McEvoy (naturally), Mr. William Rothenstein, a "Pygmalion" poster (that is to say, a "Lithographed Fan," by Miss Margarite Janes, done in the style of those charming advertisements of "Pygmalion" that so used to adorn the "Metro" in La Ville Lumière).

Mr. Rothenstein's clear house with the storm cloud behind it is well painted. Mr. Nevinson's portrait of himself is a very good piece of work (with due debt to Picasso). ("Wind," as we suspected, gained by being reproduced in *Colour*.) A great deal of Mr. Nevinson's actual painting is not commendable. But in the "Outskirts of Montmartre" he has justified at least some of his enthusiasts. He has, naturally, chosen a different style for this picture. It is his habit to choose a "different style" on what seems an average of once a fortnight. In this case he has chosen a good firm, clear representational method, and executed with no mean skill. If by some act of God he could once make up his mind what good art really is— I do not mean in the sense that there is only one good art, but that for every fine artist there are certain things which must be to him in particular, "the best"—if Mr. Nevinson could really decide what the words "the best" mean to him, and thereafter please himself exclusively and leave off trying to suit everyone all at once, he would greatly strengthen our belief in his future. Cleverness and journalistic ability no one can be so rabid as to deny him.

Mr. F. S. Unwin, in "Man with a Scythe," seeks to temper the "old master" method with Segonzac. Miss Wynn George has seen the Ajunta[14a] cave frescoes or at least some Indian painting. She has got into her "Etching" a great deal of "beauty" as the term was understood in 1897; she has done this without weakness, without obliterating the Indian influence, or, I think, a little Dutch influence; but in the process she has found the beginning of a personal style. There is no reason why one should not use beauty à la 1897 if one so desire. Mr. D. W. Hawksley in the "Patient Griselda" has shown a pleasing contempt for history, reality and geography. Griselda's attendants may just as well have been Japanese as Italian.

Mr. C. Marco Pearce has found a style of his own; in black and white there is something wrong with every drawing, or it would seem with every drawing. One does not analyse, but one receives the distressing impression that the work has something wrong, something out of composition. But "La Foire dans la Place" comes off. Given colour, (late impressionist or pointiliste) this artist is most pleasing, and his crowd-grouping is excellent in this instance.

Mr. Thomas T. Baxter presents what appears to be a figure of Christ

---

[14a]Misspelling of "Ajantā."

teaching a dickey-bird to chew worms. This work is labelled "St. Francis" (D'Asise). I cannot concede his background, but the face is remarkable; it is painted with very great skill, and the frenetic modernist who rushes by the picture merely because of the demoded subject-matter will miss one of the best pieces of detail in the exhibition.

There are (naturally) points where the critic's patience gives out. The week's wash (entitled "A Shiny Night") by Miss Olive Gardner is one of them; so also are "The Bath" by Mr. R. Schwabe; "Bain on the River" by Mr. William Shackleton; "Interior of a Church" by Miss Coke; "The Rose Garden" by Mr. William Shackleton; "An Aeroplane Passes" by Mr. Derwent Lees; "The Burden of the Sea" by an artist already mentioned; "Gavin" by Mr. F. Dodd. "The Happy March" illustrates again the consummate inanity of trying to combine an Italian primitive (with a false naïveté substituted for the real), Puvis (minus his spacing), Rossetti (minus his molasses and his really well-painted jewelry).

The man who comes best out of the show is very probably Mr. Walter Taylor. His "Fragment of a Palace" has great charm and simplicity. His "Pavilion, Brighton" is done in the excellent clean colours of a Navajo blanket. Both these pictures are "ready to hang in one's room."

If we are still to retain Aristotle, and still to believe that the excellence of a work of art depends largely on what one intends to do with it, i.e., whether if made to stand on the pinnacle of a church-spire it is so made as to look well in that exalted position; if made to hang in a room, then so made as to look well in a room—we must take some count of the suitability of modern pictures for conceivable modern interiors.

Mr. Taylor's two pictures are made without any appearance of struggle, without any sign of eccentricity. There are other pictures in the show, and quite enough of them to make one feel that the show's average is rather high, in which the painters have shown the results of long and honest work—results such as to cheer anyone who has not a determined pessimism concerning English painters.

The general proclamation of the collection, as a whole, is that: There is no set current criterion; there is no type, and there are no ten types of picture that represent the present decade. Painting has achieved a condition of absolute individualism. Apart from knowing the work of at least a hundred painters, there are no common symptoms by which the future connoisseur will know the work of this generation. Anti-academism is having its innings, whether for better or worse I do not know. But it is having its innings, and if one will spend enough time at the N.E.A.C., one can find evidence of a good deal of thought and a good deal of skill among the exhibitors.

"Endymion," by Mr. H. Morley, is another of the points were patience fails. The head of Diana is cleanly drawn, but the rest of the work is a caramel, and a damned indigestible caramel. Mr. Meninsky is after John.

Mr. Dodd gets a likeness. Miss Lubov Letnikoff strains after the romantic, after the oo-oo of Celtic balladry. Mr. N. M. Summers shows merit. Mr. R. Schwabe presents a portrait, a perfectly good John, done with rather more care than the original painter has made habitual during later years. Miss Ethel Walker, in "The Sacrifice," uses her smeary colours and swirly lines to good effect.

To "The Chelsea Figure" one says a violent "No" at close range, but finds, from the other side of the gallery, that Mr. F. Harmer has put quite good work into it. "Le Chiffe d'Amour" has the amateur prettiness of a magazine cover. Mr. Steer's "Betty" shows well from a distance, but on approaching one finds that it is not really Velasquez. Mr. J. M. Jefferys shows "Dans un Studio Ami" all blubby-blubby, but not without merit. "West Bay" is our old friend: "Is this worth fighting for?"; but it is rather neater .in execution. Mr. Archibald Wells' "Portrait in Time," shows humour and a desire to make painting resemble a textile, and his light shows well from a distance. The pseudo-Goya of "Christopher St. John" cannot be called "achieved." Mr. McEvoy's sitter was lucky; this is one of the times he has painted quite a good portrait. "Stacking Turf" is one of Mr. Schwabe's better tries. Mr. Louis Sargent presents a "Portrait"; the young lady's face is mostly hidden by a veil. We have long sympathised with the painters of portraits. Mr. R. M. Hughes shows skill à la 1870; but there is no earthly reason why a man should not paint à la 1870 if he wants to, and if he is rather good at it. Mr. M. F. Wollard holds one up with his "Man and Child." Are we to endure this wooden-faced individual with the syrupy-carrot-hued hair? On the whole, we had better endure it; the colour is perhaps out of Matisse and les Indépendants, but the face is well carved, and most of the colour is clean. The pose and mass of the infant's body are excellent. The water-colours in the S.W. room are mostly just water-colours, some good, some bad, mainly indifferent.

ART—AND PASTELS[15]

Without being litigious we may say at once that most of the exhibits at the present exposure of the Pastel Society already show signs of decay, or at least of mortality and corruption, and that the sooner the process completes itself the better for all concerned.

This has, however, no bearing on the main question, that of durability. In so far as the current carelessness regarding durability is a parallel to the incursion of journalism upon literature; in so far as it is a desire to catch the day's audience with as little trouble as possible, and to care nothing for tomorrow, it is simple jerry-building, and most condemnable. In so far

[15]*The New Age*, February 14, 1918, p. 310. Signed "B. H. Dias."

as it is a revolt against dealers and connoisseurs; in so far as it bends the thought of the viewer toward what the artist has in him, what he knows or feels of colour and of design, it is excellent. The dealer cares nothing for the artist's temperament or his skill in invention; he wants a sound investment and beyond that an investment that will give lightning profits. In the main the minor virtues are safer for him, and in so far as he is able to dominate, or to influence the condition of art, he will always overemphasise detail, finish, and the qualities which he can comprehend.

Among the deceased members of the Pastel Society are Brabazon, Whistler, Carriere, and E. A. Abbey. (Let me see, is Abbey dead?)

The truth about pastel (notwithstanding advertisement at the beginning of the catalogue to the contrary) is that part of the pastel rubbed into a given sheet of paper will stay there for a good while. Particles sticking up from the paper in lumps and heavy lines will break off if the paper is creased, dropped on the floor too often, brushed violently by the housemaid, or used to wrap up parcels. All so-called fixatives are relative, and all of them affect the original colour in some degree. The better the artist the more annoyed he is with his fixatives. As an offset, pastel reproduces very well. Whistler got a great deal of Tanagra charm into his little figures in pastel, and most of this charm survives in the reproductions of these same pastels.

The Pastel Society hangs its exposures in groups; each group the work of one artist. Thus it concentrates the attention of the spectator upon the name and relative existence of the artist. We follow humbly. Eves, drawings a long way after Sargent. I had just decided that the portrait of the inevitable peeress must be intended for someone else, when that catalogue assured me that it was indeed Lady ——. (The name will spring instantly to the mind of every habitual reader.) Chappel, Blaycock, Jones, Holroyd, Pike, Willink, rubbish! I mean, present. Musprat, "The Blue Stockings," a desperate leap after Degas, minus the colour sense. Baldry, unspeakable, save for "The Pool," which suggests that he may once have seen a painting by Gustav Moreau. He has, however, learnt nothing of that artist's intensity, nor of the heat whereby Moreau welded an assortment of rather undesirable qualities into an art. By art I mean a means of expression or representation. Almost any qualities can be built into this, if the artist have sufficient emotion, and an abnormal degree of persistence. Fred Yates, trace of mood. Mary Yates, faint perception in one picture, and some finish in another. Linnel, no. Sheringham, a relief in the general waste, Dulac on Condor, but accomplished, clear, clean colour, competent. His design for a decorative panel is probably better as a design than it would ever be as a panel, unless the panel were very small, very small indeed. Williams, good student work. Bedford, worst possible dregs of pre-Raphaelitism, not even the value of S. Soloman. Humphrey, death. Lawrenson, not good student work, shows a craving for soul. Cohen, yearns to do Dürer drawings. Dowie, death. Hope, death. White, pavement artist. Smith, death. Hervey, has at least tried to have a style. "The Skirts of the Sea" is exquisitely original; has repeated the motif in some of the other studies. Foottet, has discovered dark blue, not the first man to do so, poetic in the worst sense of the word. Still one pauses to consider whether one could hang "Ludlow" or "The Roman Tower" in any room of one's own. One wouldn't. Dutton, in No. 163, succeeds in suggesting Turner. In 164, 165, 16- does not succeed in suggesting Turner. Hope (Mrs. Adrian, before mentioned), death. She has several groups of exposures and there is nothing else to be said of any of them. Rossiter, possibility of reprieve. Cohen, touch of merit in "Ruth." Williams, touch of colour in "The Shambles." Bax-Ironside: in "The Old Town, Cannes," the town is rather better done than its setting. Constable (Miss Sarah), no trace of J. Constable. Burn-Murdoch, trace of Wm. Hunt. Bedford, her "Mrs. Clemens Usher" appears to be successful portraiture. Her "Dorothy Bedford" appears to be an excellent portrait. She had better stick to adults. Her paintings of children are of the familiar Christmas Annual type. Fisher, also after Sargent, with charm (in not quite the best sense of the word). Landscape is not his talent; he should confine himself to people, preferably pretty ones who wish to look pretty in their pictures. Sheard, bilge. Marshall, tinted photos. Richmond, "In Dreamland," reminiscence of Condor; in the other exposures, reach after Innes and Van Gogh, a very faint reach. Fischer, hopeless, tinted photo. Crosley, careful drawing, but nothing added to pencil; that is to say, he has wasted his medium. Hitchens, colour in one exposure, but no control of it, no sense of values. Lyster, a yearn for ugliness. Fisher, a yearn for tinted photography. By "tinted photography" in this note I mean just the emotional values, and just the aesthetic intensity, of the tinted photos shown in the window of any tinting photographer. I do not refer disparagingly to an accurate transcript of natural objects. Wirgman, refined dilettante, should be able to secure work as an illustrator if he so wishes. Lyster (same, D. Lyster again). Slavic feeling in "Bushka," naturally. Look at the title. Smith, death, definitely. Hammond, honest, willing, Victorian, not of the best Victorian. Richter, has heard of decorative art. Wardle: "A Jaguar," obviously has never seen the animal, not even in a Zoo. There is at least some animal quality in the small unfinished feline set in the background of "Leopard." Littlejohns, "The Wave," symbolical, naturally a female nude; "The Fugitive," dramatic; also figures in symbolical positions showing reverence; also 18th century powdered hair. Luard, "Soyez bons pour les animaux," Millet, Rosa Bonheur, S.P.C.A. 228 "Harrowing," we cannot contest this title. Airy (Miss Anna, R.E., R.O.I.) "The Fair." The best thing in the show. True sense of colour, a full sense of the medium. Pastel is, after all, the means Whistler used in the Tanagra-like sketches. Still the public can hardly be asked a shilling to look at one good pastel.

Miss Airy's other group is composed of drawings à la Orpen and John. Small, Beata Beatrix gone very bad and Christmas Annual. Carter, death. Partridge, why? Fisher, death. Crosley, possibly for the Royal Geographical Society. Humphrey: "Betty," with an expression of most consummate inanity. Baumer, not without talent; merely trying to be pretty, but he has achieved a certain grace in so doing.

Any words of praise I have used in this present note must be taken in a suitably relative sense.

ART NOTES[16]
The National Portrait Society

The present exhibition of the National Portrait Society offers about as much nutriment to aesthetic rumination as the contents of the average family photograph album in the most average middle-class family. There is a certain commercial standard and standardising of product. "An Exhibition of Portraits of Their Majesties the King and Queen of the Belgians," by R. N. Speaight, of Speaight, Ltd., photographers and portrait painters, may serve the captious for ballast. Indeed, the pile of society portraits to be found at any of our best photographers will stimulate one to many comparative cogitations. If the pigment of Speaight, Ltd., is less well administered than that of the National Portrait Society, Messrs. Speaight, in any case, have their cameras to fall back on.

Portraiture has an aesthetic of its own slightly distinct from that of painting. By calling a thing a portrait you imply that it has a relation to something not itself; to an individual, not simply to mankind at large or to nature, or colour, or form, or to "laws" of painting, of filling and dividing the space of the canvas.

It is perhaps pedagogic to state that a "portrait" must be a good picture first, and that thereafter it may add the grace of being a portrait, a good portrait, or a likeness. This statement is not unexceptionable. Certain avowals on the part of the painter almost inhibit his painting of portraits. If he is deliberately more interested in light, in patches of colour, in accidental grimaces, in, yes, even in the texture of orange-coloured velvet, though this latter interest may in the present stage of portraiture serve his pocket in no mean degree it may hinder him in the making of portraits.

A portraitist is not limited to the photographic method. I would not limit him to any method. He may depict the form of his sitter's head and face. That is portraiture of one sort. On the other hand, the depiction of blobs of sunlight, of all sorts of accidentals and circumstances of the sitter, is not, in the best sense, portraiture, though it may be as fine painting as you like.

[16]*The New Age*, February 28, 1918, pp. 356–57. Signed "B. H. Dias."

The portraitist may also centre his attention on the character of his sitter (as he sees or imagines it), he may depict the clothing, surroundings, possessions of the sitter in order to illustrate the sitter. Moroni shows his tailor holding the shears. There are cruder methods of symbolism. But how far it is necessary to present the pearls and the plumage of society ladies in order that we may not mistake them for models, I will leave out of this diatribe.

The portrait painter's liberty runs just as far as is compatible with leaving the centre of interest *always* in the personality, the character, the individual who is the sitter. When this centre shifts the canvas becomes a fancy picture or whatever else you like, but it ceases to deserve attention as portraiture. Man used as an excuse for a study in sunlight, or even woman used as a clothes-horse, cannot rise to the apex of portrait-painting.

In the present show the Negro supporting the pink abortion is not, and is not labelled a portrait; neither is De Smet's picture of the back of a lady's neck. This neck and the two small boys are labelled "Mon Foyer." Other cases are not so clear. We may perhaps discard Creamer's "Decorative Portrait" in the worst phase of so-called modernism; and debate Swanzy's arrangement of brush-strokes in quadrilaterals. Katherine Mayer paints "Louise's" kimono so that the painting is quite as pretty as the dress goods, but she has neglected Louise's pretty face. The same painter shows Mrs. A. G. Eddy screwed into an attitude, there to squirm for posterity as Sisyphus or Ixion. Mr. Chas. Sims, R.A., appears to "have got a likeness" of Mrs. Brett, and he has put a nice tone into part of his very plain background. Let us return to the star performers, as shown in the "large" gallery or first room as you enter.

Mr. Ambrose McEvoy exhibits one of the best portraits of The Lady Diana Manners contained in this exhibition. True, his only competitor is Mr. Eves, and the tear concurrent with the expression of Mr. Eves' drawing has been incontinently taken away. In Mr. Eves' painting the lady's hand is neither drawn nor *stylisée*. Mr. McEvoy's portrait is "decorative"; the sitter or stander is in the posture of "This way up, ladies"; she appears as if leading to higher things. The canvas also appears as if it might have been cut out of some larger compostion, some fantasy after Reynolds or Gainsborough. There is tradition for this sort of thing. Sir Edwin Landseer was never able "to tell beforehand." He used to paint on the large and cut out as much as would "compose." One questions Mr. McEvoy's knowledge of anatomy, as one might question Landseer's sense of composition. As for McEvoy's pigment and colour-quality, we can only refer the reader again to the stucco ceiling of the soda-bar so convenient to the Oxford Circus "Central London."

Mr. Glyn Philpot, A.R.A., exhibits an infelicitous imitation of Picasso's "Mann am Tisch." (The public is unacquainted with the earlier work of Picasso.) Sir J. Lavery, A.R.A., in his "Mrs. P. Ford" displays all the

44

possible faults of muddiness, from the feet in a Boldini smear through the pink mud, the brown mud, the blue mud disposed on the rest of the canvas. McEvoy's "Young Man" is done in blobs of light, but the young man is recognisable. Mr. Strang makes an honest endeavour to transmit the face of his Picador's wife; the virtue is in the drawing not in the painting. Wm. Nicholson's rather bad picture is so hung as to look worse during daylight, the feet and spats are thrust into the lime-light and the face left in darkness. This is the fault of the hanging, for the picture should be more carefully condemned after the electric lights are turned on. Cadell in "Black Lace Veil" certainly shows how not to do it. Spencer Watson, at first wink, seems to have managed to do dress goods quite up to Tate Gallery standard; then one perceives that one cannot quite say whether the skirt *really* is satin. Swynnerton makes the young man's tennis shoes quite as interesting, as painting, as his face. Cadell, again, in "The Fawn Dress" seems scarcely the artist who could have painted the other picture attributed to him in the catalogue. Here he shows a typical French lightness and grace, and has placed his pretty figure most admirably on his canvas, which is a fit ornament for the most exquisite boudoir in Mayfair. The ruck of the exhibits do not merit individual condemnation. There is some poor archaism. One man has seen a book illustrated with prints of Gauguin and perhaps Matisse and Kandinsky, and has introduced a little of their stylisation judiciously, and with caution, into his background, "seeing how much the public will take." Philpot's "The Lady Mary Thynne" is reminiscent of "A Little Child Shall Lead Them."

The interest in the exhibition, such as it is, may well centre in Alvaro Guevara. I must confess to a preference for his dancers and acrobats. In this show his "Dorothy Warren" is a fancy picture, and the lady's hair is not that colour. His Mrs. Wallace is needlessly reminiscent of John. It "comes up better" at thirty yards distance—that is, from the very end of the other gallery; but paintings are not normally viewed from thirty yards' distance, and unless this portrait is particularly intended to decorate some unusually large room this focus is an error.

There is only one thing in the show that is "safe" for an art student to look at. It is labelled "Alf. Stevens," but the artist is given his full praenomen in the catalogue. The texture of the blue velvet in his picture is rendered with technique worthy of the name. It matches, despite its being wholly different, the technique of early Dutch masters; so also the surface of the paint on the screen and of the table-cover. The face is the weakest spot in the picture; the artist has turned it as far as possible from one, obviously wishing to make as pleasing a picture as possible of his sitter.

Axiom: The portrait painter not only attempts to make a good painting, but he attempts to bring that painting into a definite relation with an extraneous object called the "Sitter."

Obiter dictum: Between the revelation, or portrayal, or interpretation of "The Sitter," and the concealment of a society lady in her frills, frou-frous, and furbelows there is a gulf as yet unmeasured.

ART NOTES[17]
Processes

The Thirty-sixth Annual Exhibition of the Royal Society of Painter-Etchers and Engravers does not add greatly to our stock of knowledge. The work of the late Sir Charles Holroyd, especially his "Bishop's Tomb," shows distinction. The eye will be caught by his "Yew Tree." There is clarity in Béjot's "Honfleur." Turrell by his "St. Gregory, Valladolid" maintains the argument that etching is an excellent medium for recording Gothic architecture.

The scope of etching is still, I think, open to dispute. I cannot go the full length of the ultramodernist who has called it "a series of fakes from one end to the other," or even of the more moderate disapprover who calls it "a bad thing, on the whole." After all, Goya did choose this medium for "Mala Noche," and Méryon has left us a not too despicable heritage.

One cannot condemn a medium merely because some members of the R.S.P.-E. choose to make things that look like bad photogravures. Neither in the face of Goya and Whistler can one consider etching as fit merely for book-plates and book-illustrations. True, etching has suffered from con-noisseurship; and there has been very little real aesthetic discussion fo-cussed upon it. No one has asked any very searching questions about it. Elderly gentlemen with incomes have filled pages with discussions about "number of impressions" and details of printing. Should the printer "wipe" with a cloth or the palm of his hand? Biting, re-biting, burnish-ing, give the connoisseur ample scope for his researches, but do not fundamentally concern the art critic, whose business is with the result. Before we can begin to appraise even the smallest exhibit we must have made up our minds, or at least laid them open to certain lines of inquiry: whether, for instance, Rembrandt's portrait etchings do not fall short just in so far as they suggest that their subjects should have been painted, not etched?

I take it that an etcher is at liberty to produce any effect he is able to; that there are no illegitimate effects. Secondly, I take it that an artist may choose an apparently narrow medium for one or two reasons, or with one or two distinct results. He may by restricting his ambition achieve a sort of distinction in part of an art, that he would never achieve in the whole. For example, Méryon, who is perhaps unexcelled as an etcher, would have

[17]*The New Age*, April 4, 1918, pp. 456–57. Signed "B. H. Dias."

done worse had he chosen to be a third-rate painter. By narrowing his scope an artist may gain intensity.

On the other hand, this medium which tends in the hands of ordinary men to be extremely ordinary, to be, in brief, book-plates and book-illustrations has, at the hands of extraordinary men, shown itself capable of most violent revolutions, and been bent to the expression of most wayward and individual spirits; after which revolutions and renewals it has relapsed into set categories, following the wake of the innovators (or making obvious blends of their methods): Bauer, cobwebby; Van der Velde, rather uncommendable and reminiscent of engraving; Méryon, clear white, straight lines, clear delineation; Braquemond, Jaquemart, detail; Hollar, magnificent respect for his medium; Goya, perhaps indifferent to the medium, but capable of forcing his verve and vitality into any medium that he touched, and so on. Against these are the blurry and moody etchers, or Ribot with his broken lines, and black blotches.

One's only conclusion is, perhaps, that if the R.S.P.-E. had among their present members any great artist, or any man of marked individuality, this genius or talent would come out in the work.

About all one can gather from the present show is that etching may convey certain moods of nature, and, as I have said, that it is a good way of recording certain effects of Gothic architecture. There is nothing in the show which one has not seen before. A good deal of it does fall into the category of book-illustration. Griggs shows a moderately original composition (Botolph's Bridge), but it is not wholly convincing. Hartley has a touch of cubism, in uninteresting technique. Wright in his stage scene of Venice has light and shade, Dawson some charm in "In a Gondola." (One goes on "falling for" Venice, no doctrinaire attacks on romanticism will, in our time, eliminate this trait from our characters.) Marriot has clarity. Lee's "Ancient Street" is pleasant, Percival Gaskell shows clarity and neatness in his "Bridge-gate, Verona." Lancaster, Wright, Walcot catch the eye if one stays long enough and sets oneself to rather meticulous examination of the exhibits.

The Imperial Photographs Exhibition (Grafton Gallery) is most interesting, beginning with the magnificent and highly flattering portrait of "The Hun" in the entrance hall, which vies as art with most of the Royal Academy exhibits, and, apart from trying to reconcile us with our enemies or to fill us with untimely admiration of the subject, does definitely show how far a machine, in the hands of an expert, may be made to rival the brush in the hands of a second-rate painter; how far, in brief, the academic methods are sheer, translatable mechanism.

The photograph of tanks is interesting in composition, and "Reprisals," taken from the air, should satisfy even Mr. Wyndham Lewis and his wild crew in their demands for arrangement.

The reds, browns and yellows seem, on the whole, well rendered throughout the exhibition; the skies are usually too soft, or in some way out of scale. One is interested to see the purple in the camels' shadows, but it seems too red a purple. The greens are, on the whole, bad, save in one dark green Arab coat, where the brown element predominates. The *matte* surface of the big photos is felicitous, save, usually, in their skies.

It is difficult in this case to diagnose the faults without knowing the mechanism, but in the main, one is bothered; there is something wrong, probably in the relative registering of red and green; a scientist is required to determine whether this can be eliminated by any series of ray-screens, or whether all colours as we see them have not some intermixture of sub-red and ultra-violet which the present colour-photographers do not take count of; just as the colours in nature have intermixtures from different parts of the registered spectrum.

Timothy Cole's wood-cuts (Greatorex Galleries, Grafton Street) are an amazing display of technique. Why a man should spend a lifetime copying paintings by a process which should perhaps be called wood-engraving, rather than wood-cutting, I do not know. It is as if he had early become entoiled in an argument, and never stopped demonstrating the capacities of his medium for interpreting pigment colour in terms of black dot and line. At this game he is proficient, wonderfully and marvellously proficient, whether he take Hogarth or Constable for a subject. Artists in other sorts of black and white could learn a great deal from Cole, if they chose to study his variety and invention in conveying so many colour qualities with a means apparently so little varied. Blacks, whites, greys are here in every temper and for every colour equivalent.

A further inspection of etchers loose on the town might lead one to conclude that these gentlemen are for the most part rather conservative; that few of them have very much "made up their minds," or even considered as many problems of their art as I have found it necessary to consider before writing the opening paragraphs of this article. Their branch of the service is, perhaps, more than another, beset by the amateur, the connoisseur, and the dilettante. Mempes' work at the Greatorex shows the effect of his temporary proximity to a Master. Hall is old-fashioned. Leslie Mansfield shows considerable promise, "The Clearing" shows him attending to Méryon, perhaps best of all models for the young etcher. His "Old St. Michael's" is clean work. He gets blacks in good contrast in "Low Tide." In another place he shows Japanese influence. He has not yet evolved a uniform or personal style, and his work is still very uneven, but he has a chance of doing excellent things.

At the Dowdswell Galleries, Albany Howarth shows two quite beautiful drawings, among much work that is uneven, and among etchings still vaguer in their import. In "Ponte Vecchio" and in "Houghton's Tower" he has attained great charm, by the most conventional means, and his effects of light and water are most satisfying. In "Bamborough" the etcher's task is fully planned in the pencil drawing.

ART NOTES[18]
Water

The sheets displayed at the One Hundred and Ninth Exhibition of the Royal Institute of Painters in Water Colours are mostly of the school of "We-desire-to-succeed-to-the-market-of . . ." The blank dots may be filled in at pleasure according to the whim of the artist. The late Alma Tadema is not unpopular among them, and many of the masters of the Tate Gallery might here find their mildest disciples. Here also are sweet bits of rainbows, ponds and seas liquid with soup, many grassy and leafy smears, and even our old friend "the symbolic"; art nouveau in Mrs. Averil Burleigh; Condor *minus* in R. Vicaji; the nadir, the absolute bottom, in A. T. Nowell's "St. Mark's"; simplesse in Wm. Rainey; the nude submerged by M. I. Kees; and silk coats in abundance, the silk coat, silk-stocking period when somebody is always taking off a three-cornered hat and making a flourished bow with said hat swept out at arm's length; and, we need hardly say, landscape in all degrees of uncertainty; also a few wild animals with the Humane Society smile; plus at least one attempt to be comic.

D. W. Hawksley contributes a Japanese derivation, in smooth paint (that is something). The bottom half of E. Green's "Bowl of Spring Flowers" is entertaining. P. A. Hay, "The Minstrel" (Gosh!). C. E. Swan, "Indian Leopard" (Really!). R. Gemmell-Hutchinson, pseudo-oil. W. Tyndale, "Grocer's Shop," clear, at any rate, though tones of his colour are not unquestionable. N. Wier-Lewis, still life, visible. Mrs. J. B. Mathews "Carmen" (presumably Madame Delysia), carefully done, save the face and the appalling flesh tones. E. M. Harms, 81, horror. H. Copping, 96, ditto. Hal Hurst, "Youth" (Oh?), Ryland (Late Alma-Tadema, hopes to succeed to the market of . . .).

A. Van Anrooy, "Albi on the Tarn," paper effect, and well handled. Josh. Smith, "Rosebud of Womanhood," terrible strain to find something, anything, to do with a model. Chuji Kurihara has, at any rate, done what he pleased; his picture, "The Calmness," is in key with itself, and not a heterogeneous collection of second-hand furniture. John Hassall, theatrical, but with technical interest. W. Apperley, daring, not so much in subject as in execution, pseudo Rossetti-Botticelli. D. W. Hawksley, "Summer," cleanly executed figures in the foreground. J. W. Schofield, moody, house in distance, inferior to Wm. Rothenstein's at London Group. F. Matania, "Cubiculum," female with hideous face, mighty thigh, mosaic floor carefully executed.

George Graham, "Great Gable," clean, rain-swept landscape, quite beautifully done. J. R. Reid a few clean strokes. H. Banks, "Digging Cockles," possible to take a little pleasure in foreground figures. C. R.

[18]*The New Age*, April 11, 1918, p. 472. Signed "B. H. Dias."

Burnett shows enterprise (Millet's market?). A. J. W. Burgess, frosted porcelain finish, like numerous other exhibitors. A. H. Collings, variation on Messrs. Pears and Co.'s "Bubbles," with the actual soap-globes omitted. Hal Hurst, "The First Rays," so far inferior to Kirchner, or the pictures of midinettes and their hosiery which we pass in the art-shops of the Strand. F. Taylor, "Water Gate," largest sheet on show, brown tree in bold strokes, "impossible" greensward seen through arch, bright, clean colour, Paris nine years ago, gate broadly done, rest of sheet not so certain, shows well at a distance. C. Barnard, "Mermaid, Rye," clean in parts. D. Adamson, solferino, blue-pink-an'-purple horses. C. W. Simpson, white shovelled on with a manner. Gotch, chintz, still more Tategalleryish. G. Rogers, clean, not much waste. Thus pass the accomplishments of our mother's generation. There is also sculpture. G. Bayes shows aspiration toward breadth, and has quaint enamel insertions.

There are also miniatures. Josh. Smith's "Phryne" the worst. No Areopagus would have fallen. M. E. Wilson, clean work in "Gladys." F. Cooper, appalling in "Lady D. Manners," excellent in "Miss J. Buckmaster." G. Hughes, appalling nude, bad as Smith's. M. R. Peacock, excellent in "S. Hardy." (Where one miniature by an artist is mentioned, it is to be understood that the rest, by same hand, are without merit.) A. Underwood, quaint. S. Shillaker, fake enamel (as intended).

Mr. Nevinson (Leicester Gallery) has appealed unto Caesar. He is, in the process, a little hard on the family profession, and he seems to have misunderstood a few brief lines from these columns. We did not mean that he showed too great a variety, we noted an indecision of method; the underlying formula has always been sufficiently monotonous; it has always been to mix Picasso, or Lewis, or Severini, or some ultramodern with the old stand-by illustrators of the *Illustrated London News*. We did not imply that Mr. Nevinson isn't *the* man for his present job. We have no intention of siding with the *Saturday Review* in its imbecile attack on Mr. Nevinson's work. Mr. Nevinson *is* the man for his present job, which is illustrating the war, and he is one of the nippiest and alertest of illustrators. But he now appeals unto Caesar, the modern democracy, and, in substance, asks the critics either to praise him or to let him alone. We are quite ready to emulate Felix and let the appeal go through. It does not surprise us that Mr. Nevinson should prefer to be judged by the public than by the expert. (The *Saturday Review,* is, of course, the public with a vengeance, and its intelligence far below Mr. Nevinson's.) Being among the careful observers whom this artist disparages, we would caution the public to remember one thing alone: a good picture is a picture which does not wear out one's interest too quickly. To attract the eye is no trouble. I can by the simplest of expedients; by the mere throwing of a basin-full of paint at a sheer white stretch of canvas, produce something that will instantly catch the eye of every visitor to a gallery. I have seen a whole room "dominated" by the high, by the very high, light on the hind-side of an ill-painted cow. Rembrandt's formula of a light patch in the midst of surrounding obscurity is only too simple. Needless to say, it is not the only device of its sort. Mr. Nevinson wishes the public to judge him. We have no wish to thwart this democratic desire, but if the public wishes to be the true audience of philosophers it will try the artist by this one test; it will try to look at a Nevinson picture as long as it can look at a Degas, or a Cézanne, or a Picasso, or a Rousseau. Surely, Mr. Nevinson will not mind the public's employing these little tests, for all his scorn of the critic, with all his distaste for expert attention. He will not mind the public interest rising to such a pitch that it compares him with his fellow artists and his forebears. Or is this also forbidden? Do we await more manifestos, to the effect that the public is to judge his art by the method of snap-shot? The instant exposure of the retina to a picture is to be the test of the future?

We are indebted to M. J. Pupin for his "South Slav Monuments," profusely illustrated with photographs of Serbian churches, and containing valuable historic notes. The book indicates the spread of a culture from Byzantium, the Empire of the East approximating that of the West, so that San Zeno, of Verona, would not appear strange in the eyes of a Serbian; whereas the mosaic style of St. Mark's would, in so far as it preserves the Byzantine tradition, be even more native to him. We see round romanesques arches, and stone or brick in layers of different colours. Decani is fortunate in its church, and Lesnovo, and there is interesting ornament at Ravanica, and at Ljubostinja.

ART NOTES[19]
At the Alpine Club Gallery

The Friday Club gives us an excellent show. There is a prevalent impression of clean paint. I think nearly two-thirds of the exhibits may be worth individual attention, and such a percentage must be admitted as unusually high. One cannot claim for them origination, but the members are alert, the influences are creditable for the most part, and (let me repeat it with emphasis), they have, in the main, learned to paint with clean paint, and in this virtue can give points to most rival organisations. If we are to attribute the work to its very possible and plausible sources, it must be done seriatim:—

Dorothy Brett, "Umbrellas," Renoir-Rousseau blended in bright tin tonalities; Adam Slade, "Dyfferyn," Innes, rather poor Innes; Milne, "Burial," what bastard of Matisse!; Woestyne, "Etude," soft but clean

[19]*The New Age*, April 25, 1918, pp. 503–4. Signed "B. H. Dias."

Renoir with Maeterlinckian pallor; Kauffer, "Tugboat," Nevinson at his worst, a work which shows to better advantage when reproduced in *Colour*; Gilman, "Landscape," a relapse on himself; McNaught, pleasant; C. Doyle, "Two Rudders," clean, good sensible, hard edges, paint well put on, no hesitations, smears or smudges, uniform quality and care over all the surface; H. Daeye, "Baby," we presume Mary Cassatt, plus cream ices; Maresco Pearce, "Rain," in pointillisme gone sadly to seed; Miss Mathers, "Cornfield," clean water-colour, better than the horticultural exhibit in Bond Street.

M. Ellis, lithograph, amusing, and rather good. Mary McCrossen, "Snow Peaks," simple treatment, and deserves better place than in the crook of the stairs; M. Jones, pleasant lithograph; Wagemans, "Nu," Sickert pallidified; Kauffer, "Woodcut," here the disciple of Nevinson bobs up again as a disciple of Wadsworth; P. Nash, "Illustration to 'Tiriel'" (Blake), really this sort of thing might be left to the late W. Blake himself, among whose distinguished remains there are already a sufficient number of botches; R. Schwabe, "L. Carruthers," meritorious Slade; J. Nash, in "Purlieus of a City," is found retaining himself. P. Nash tries to take a farewell in "Lake Maiden." Gertler tries for an exit in "Figure Studies" (60), and might be allowed to disappear on this title; in "66" he does very poor Gaudier-Brzeska; in 72 we find the raised arm spherical triangle motif as from Gaudier-Brzeska.

M. Jeffereys, "Tamise," good of its school, tone quality of excellent slabs of biscuit glacé. A. Slade, "Downs" (75), Fry, rather sub-Fry; E. Walker, "Card Table," curious reminiscence of the "Eighties." J. Nash, "Viaduct," tries to convince us that the Nash family deteriorate. (It is remarkable that men on war-work have time to do anything, and one should not count a temporary slump too seriously.) H. Squire, sub-Innes, in "Undermillbeck"; Walker, "Bouquet," in mud; M. McDowell, "Conversation with Nature," clean, bright colour, in other respects, sub-John; Nevinson, "February," excellent bit of work of simple pre-Whistlerian period. In "Estuary" he is clean, in "Boat Race" he is at his very bad worst. Allinson, in "Quai de la Poissonière," shows exceeding bad Nevinson; Mrs. N. M. Summers' "Group" is the last gasp of Johnism, a superultimate diliquidation. Bevan appears just where we so amiably left him at the last "London Group"; Allinson, "Bedford Music Hall," without significance; Mrs. Summers' "Child with Straight Cut Fringe," a quite meritorious portrait, more Mrs. Summers than John; Hobart-Hampton, "Wall Decoration," orientalism with the reason for existence removed; Strang, "Armentiers," etching in soft blacks, not unpleasing; E. White, "Orchard and Hills," as was Nash; K. Baynes, "Landscape," cleanly done; Gertler, "Fruit Stall," a relapse; E. White, "Stone-Breaker," Puvis pietism of countenance; T. T. Baxter, " Study of Fox Terrier." Mr.

Baxter has been looking at Sotatsu's "Puppy with Convolvulus," and has profited to some extent, more in this study than in No. 119, but he has still something to learn from Sotats'.

To continue: K. Baynes, "Landscape" (4), high-shine tin-plate; E. McNaught, "Watching the Fishermen," John figures strayed into an Innes background; "The Meeting," last difluxion of John. J. Nash has lost some of his individuality, but manages atmosphere in both the Black Park pictures. H. Daye has not smudged in "Girl." Gertler, "Still Life," mild endeavour to "cube" à la Derain or Laurencin. M. James, "Lithograph Fan," pleasant Boutet de Monville; Gwendolen Schwabe, "Rotten Row," tailor and cutter. R. Kristian, "Drawing" (71), the weakest pseudo-Picasso I can remember. Maresco Pierce, "Summer, 1913," still pale pointillisme. . . .

A quoi pensent les jeunes gens? This show fairly answers the question, though some of the exhibitors are no longer in the first gay flush of leaping adolescence. My brief analysis of influences need not be taken for too severe a disparagement. All artists begin by imitating something or other, or by "being influenced." The significant thing about this group is that it is influenced by distinctly contemporary forces. If it is not a band of masters, it is, at any rate, a group concerned with art in the making, with the live matter, not with an atrophy of the taste, sense, and the senses.

It is nearly, perhaps wholly, free of the El Greco craze; it is not utterly set and anchored. It is, on the other hand, absolutely un-futurist, in the sense that there is (in this exhibit, at least) no trace either of Balla or of Severini, or of any distinctly futurist theories. If the French and English influences are not exactly in balance, they are very nearly in balance. The Slade school, Innes and John, do not dominate; they are, on the contrary, rather submerged in a flow of Parisian moderation. The "stunts" of Les Indépendants are toned down, there are none of the surprises which one had six or seven years ago in the long sheds by the left bank of the Seine. Matisse's definite revelations of colour value have been more or less applied, digested, and distributed. The kind of miscoloration that we still see in art vendors' windows of the more conservative sort does not flourish here. Impossible values as practised by the post-Landseer, post-pre-Raphaelites, and even post-Manet periods have at last been done away, or almost done away, with. Photographism on the one hand, and the almost equally meticulous literalism in the treatment of minutiae of light, have given way to the more modern emphasis, on the synthetic.

There are, doubtless, many people still alive (I heard specimens conversing at the "Gardens of England and Italy" show), who would find some of the Friday Club products "startling." But any one who has followed current work; any one who has even glanced at a few numbers of *Les Soirées de Paris,* will see that this group of painters is simply in the current of the time, moving with the current, pleasantly, and with that placidity which is the normal mark of the painting nature. They must not be attacked as fumistes, or as a dangerous revolution.

ART NOTES[20]
Water, Still More of It

The Royal Society of Painters in Water Colour must not be confused with the Royal Institute of that ilk. The Institute is giving its one hundred and ninth exhibition, but the "Society," founded in the year MDCCCIV of the Christian era, aged, therefore, one century and fourteen years, is now booked for its one hundredth and seventieth public performance.

One's impression on entering its more exiguous salon is that the painted parts of the pictures hold more paint, and that the white portions of said pictures are less painted than those of the Institute. One feels the impact at once of more pigment, and more uncontaminated paper surface. The general tone is more cheery; one flies to the conclusion that there must be several good pictures on show, and infers a half-dozen worthy exhibitors.

Here, indeed, is this Moffat Lindner with something that looks (from across the room) like a Turner. On close approach it appears a considerable improvement on the blurry method of that master; the job is done with fewer strokes of the brush. It is, indeed, a very clever analysis of the necessities behind the Turner sort of impression. This is not saying that Mr. Lindner's place in Teutonic histories of art-development will be more marked than that of Ruskin's favourite painter.

Approaching the most attractive pictures in the present show, one finds, however, that a reasonable or unreasonable number of them have been achieved by the same set of brushes. Lindner is at his best in "St. Mark's Basin." "San Giorgio Maggiore" does not come up to No. 4. "Venice from the Public Gardens" is a much weaker Turner. "Dutch Boats" does not gain by comparison with the "Mark's Basin." There is economy in his "Rhone Lagoon."

S. J. L. Birch shows a fine distinctness, ease, simplicity of treatment in "Spring." His "Near Caldy" also draws notice. Breadth is intended in his "Cornwall," but rather fails to arrive.

D. M. Smith shows merit in "Showery Weather"; R. W. Allen, clear hard sunlight in "Damascus Gate." T. M. Rooke is careful in "Barfreston"; C. A. Shepperson contributes the same slender feminine figures that *Punch* has made world-familiar; H. A. Pain is imaginative in "Storm Cloud"; he is better in "Sussex Village." H. Watson had an idea for his

[20]*The New Age*, May 9, 1918, p. 29. Signed "B. H. Dias."

water in "The Pool"; W. T. Wood shows intention in "Last Church, Dunwich."

W. Russell Flint is successful in the central figure and in the figure reclining in "West Highland Picnic." The back hill does not hang into the picture. One is surprised, however, to find that the picture is by Flint. One is accustomed to Flint as reproduced in *Colour,* and in the windows of art-shops, in the manner of another art-shop-window artist, whose name irritatingly escapes me, but is also world-familiar, more so than Shepperson. We all know that shepherdess in the act of being caressed. Roth . . . Ram . . . no, not Rothenstein. Griefenhagen, that is the name we are hunting for. On finding this "Highland Picnic," one is inclined to think Flint suffers by reproduction in *Colour;* but this feeling fades as one moves on to his other exhibits. He is at his worst in "Yellow-cap." "Summer ripples" would be improved rather than damaged by translation into the pages of our contemporary; in his "Phryne and the Slave" the same old model with the heavy teuto-classical limbs is shown as applied decoration, and should be acceptable as a magazine cover.

Mr. Alfred Parsons, R.A. (President), exhibits various studies of our indigenous flora; they are less interesting than those shown in the Elgood "Gardens of England and Italy" exhibit at the Fine Arts Gallery, Bond Street.

As for the rest of the show, W. Mathew Hale leads with "Sunset at Ronda" in the manner of the late Wm. Hunt or Alfred Hunt, or whichever was contemporary with Ruskin. F. Cayley Robinson (not to be confused with the spritely Heath Robinson) gives us a number of thrills. We have the death of Abel showing the advanced state of architecture doubtless familiar in that period of the world's progress; we have "Noah," a synthetic of scriptoro-aesthetic book or bilk illustration stretching vaguely from the era of William Blake to the era of Rackham and Frampton. "The Death of Rachel" displays still more of this funny old symbolism, bowed heads, heroic mantles lopped over them, same old story . . .

We could with equal ease avoid commending Miss Eleanor Fortescue-Brickdale for her "Guardian Angel" playing cat's-cradle with an aeroplane. G. Lawrence Bulleid's "Madonna" confers no lustre on the exhibit, and I find that three other scattered works of this painter have each of them struck me as execrable. The clever hanging committee evidently hoped to hide these small things by distributing them in various parts of the room (unavailingly!).

H. E. Crocket in "Midsummer Eve (in a Cornish Village)" tells a very old story, not up to "Carnation, Lily, Lily, Rose"; Cuthbert Rigby recalls some Hunt or other, William or Alfred, it doesn't much matter. W. Eyre Walker goes through no novel sponge-sopping in "Whitewater" and "A Dell in the Cotswold." Then, in my catalogue, as I write this, I come again upon Mr. Bulleid, "At the Well"; it is marked "Rotten Alma Tadema," but, perhaps, I should soften that phrase. It was, after all, put down in the heat of a first impression. Let us say, rather, "inferior Alma Tadema." J. C. Dollman gives us "the same old Tate" in "The Conversion of St. Hubert." R. W. Allen, "Antibes," Monet not attained. A. Hopkins, "The Interview Ended" (Victorian era still dragging on; most unfortunate). R. A. Bell, "Dance of Reapers before Juno, Ceres and Iris," weak Byam-Shawism.

D. Murray Smith shows "Mill on Dunes," pleasant, but tending to porcelain. Miss Katherine Turner, "June Bunch," in the tradition of, I suppose, 1860; A. Reginald Smith, "The Bridge," tradition of possibly 1887. Henry A. Payne, "Who is this who cometh from Edom with dyed garments from Bosra? I have trodden the winepress alone"—Hunt, this time Holman of that family, mixed rather with the text-cards of the Bible Society.

E. J. Sullivan, "Golden Days," possibly very poor Conder. Robert Little, "Hemingford Grey—Twilight," fog certainly. H. A. Payne, "The Sunset," refer to Tate, picture called, I think, "Vale of Rest."

Various other no longer fecund conventions are employed by other exhibitors. There is, as indicated, some clean application of colour, Lindner in particular helping to make the show seem rather better than that of the "Institute," though it very possibly isn't. Most of the unmentioned items sink in a general fogginess; into two or three familiar kinds of uninteresting Victoriana. Our mothers used to paint on china, our grandmothers used to make sketches along the lines here apparent. The things are not old enough *yet* to possess a romantic or antiquarian interest. The exhibitors at the Friday Club may show traceable derivations, but they have not settled down into a set derivativeness from an utterly finished tradition. It is possible, it is, indeed, absolutely certain, that one will find their next show different.

ART NOTES[21]
"Gaudier-Brzeska"

With the Academy and the International mopping up most of the public attention, the chief art-event of the week is nevertheless the Gaudier exhibit at the Leicester Gallery. It is the only one having any bearing on the history of the art of our time. The death of this artist at Neuville St. Vaast was one of the great losses of the war, and we need not quibble over Mr. Pound's statement (in the catalogue preface) that it was the greatest individual loss which the arts have sustained in war.

[21]*The New Age*, May 23, 1918, pp. 58–59. Signed "B. H. Dias."

The exhibit deserves the careful study of everybody interested in contemporary art, a far more careful study than the public or most of the critics will give to it. There are phases of the artist's work unnoted by, and until now perhaps unknown even to, Gaudier's most assiduous student and biographer, notably: "The Dancer" (11) bronze, early, in a French or even Parisian style, not in the least revolutionary, but interesting as showing Gaudier's very early interest in the crook'd-arm angle. Note that this form stays with the sculptor and is again in use after any number of revolutions of style, in the "Red Stone Dancer" (to which special attention is drawn in the catalogue preface). The unity of Gaudier's career, through all the bewildering external changes, shows here, as in the growth of the form of animal head and neck from plate XXX of the "Memoir," to plate XXIV. One can scarcely help being minutely technical in trying to make people understand the work of a master of his craft who is "so strange" to the public.

"Workman fallen from a scaffolding," early work, very fine, had not, I think, been shown before, and is unmentioned in the "Memoir." The "Fawn," lent by Mr. Dray, needs no treatise; it is so obviously better than anything by Rodin, and yet needs no new theory to explain it. It is one of the finest things in the show.

"The Russian Ballet" shows another unnoted phase, Gaudier blending the style of French eighteenth-century sphinxes with the negroid, but still "beautiful," as the unthinking employ that term. Thirty-three, a gorilla, is another Rodinesque triumph that is not Rodin by any means. The painted Madonna reminds one of the Gothic post-mortem figures of Toulouse. All of which points are marginalia.

The show is simply one for every art-lover to turn into for study, whether for the skill of the calligraphic drawings of stags, etc., or of the thick-line, more "abstract" drawings on the south wall.

The amazing thing is the finish of each of the varied modes chosen by the young artist; the brevity of the time in which he attained a convincing finality in work done on formulae so apparently different. We must consider the amount of close thought, over and above the impulse, genius, and so on, required to begin and to will. He had thought of, thought up, so much to do; and he attained so marvellous a proficiency before his twenty-third year. Even his youth is not the main point. The work would be remarkable if he died at fifty.

Sculpture should be seen from all angles. In the present show there are difficulties, but the thoughtful visitor will at least try to see the "Stone Dancer," the "Boy with a Coney," and the "Embracers," from various sides. Top light is suitable for pictures, scarcely for sculpture, and, in the present case, there are many planes that do not reveal themselves to the eye at first glance. The art student can with profit spend a full day in careful examination of the workings and innovations here shown. The cut brass deserves notice; the modelling of both the torsos (8 and 18) deserves attention, though "8" may be better seen in the "South Kensington" than in the cast here exhibited. We commend the synthesis in the smooth line drawings of the man on horse; the wrestlers; the men skipping; and the simplicity of 37: The "Bird Swallowing Fish" is one of the finest "form-combinations." The "Imp" is among the more interesting personal expressions, and is excellently contrived. The "Birds Erect" is before its time; it is still a waste of breath to call attention to this sort of work. The triangulation in 89 is interesting, and one should compare it with the quite different triangulation of 39.

The man's whole form-system is full of interest; full of evidence of his remarkable intuition; application; perseverance. The stone charm is excellently done, so also is the brass paper-weight, a remarkable composition. The "Serval" is interesting, less important; so also there are moments of fun in the coloured drawings. One is amazed, and the longer one looks and thinks, the greater the measure of surprise at the scope and variety of the man's work, the constant mental change and inventiveness, coupled with the unsurpassed faculty for bringing these things to a conclusion, a conclusion in a complete and finished method or style, in each case to be left with such promptitude for new artistic adventure. We have here the first comprehensive exhibit of a very remarkable artist, an indubitable genius, an artist having a definite niche in art history.

Mr. Nash's exhibit of war drawings in the next room is such that Mr. Nevinson may soon have to look to his laurels as the favourite portrayer of war; especially we note the tangle of wires over shell holes. The whole set of drawings is of interest.

George Belcher's "Life and Character" show in the entrance room, presents him as a much more skilful workman than anyone would ever guess from the reproductions of his work in the *Tatler*. He excels in his gradations of black and grey, and has in him, surprisingly, as much of the black and white artist as of the popular joker.

Murray Smith's show, which has just left the Leicester, deserved notice, which now comes too late. In the Corot and Barbizon traditions, he has a good deal of charm, with clear clean colours, airy space, and perhaps memories of Turner; but there is no need to confine himself to the water-colour by which he is better known. We hope to see more of his oil. Of sure touch, and clear pallor of colour, "Mellow Sunlight" is not unlike an early "hard" Corot. Plenty of room for a quiet efficient painter in this mode.

With these four shows in such a small time one almost wonders if, in the proprietors of the Leicester Gallery, we have come upon that incredible phenomenon, a firm of art dealers really interested in the development of painting and sculpture.

THE ROYAL ACADEMY[22]

The Royal Academy, Oh God, the Royal Academy! The Royal Academy is, before God, nothing to joke about. It is with groanings that the critic pulls up his cravat, hitches his braces, smoothes down his overcoat, plunges past the funny foreshortened plaster horse and its archaically costumed caballero, and lugubriously addresses himself to the entrance stairs. The Royal Academy (150th exposition) contains 1,622 items.

With colour out of all register, with ashes of Alma Tadema, with refuse of Tate, Luxembourg, Art Shop Windows, etc., brummagem. I decline to take the 1,600 items seriatim. If any of the exhibitors expect their work to be looked at seriously and carefully, they will doubtless exhibit it elsewhere. We pull up a few stray examples.

Strang ("Spanish Lady") improving. Strang ("The Singer") punk Zuloaga. Ewell (5), we note that the lettering on the façade is distinct. Sims ("A Sussex Landscape") has mood, not despicable; Sims ("Piping Boy"), the *really* idiotic. Clausen ("The Sleeper"), style of Le Doux in Salon des Indépendants for 1912, its hard-cream tonality and composure bearable, and even a relief among the rest of the pictures. Chas. Shannon, portrait of himself, not so successful as his portrait of Chas. Ricketts shown last year; at any rate, free from the almost omnipresent vulgarity of his co-exhibitors. Sir J. Lavery (portrait of Mr. Asquith), worse than any picture need be. Salisbury (panel for Royal Exchange), as might be expected. Hawksley (182), cheap Jap, plus symbolism. Shannon (James Jebusha, R.A.), "Girls Bathing," bad to the point of being comic, all the prurit of Watts, smartened up to oleograph register, false colour, steam-heated "nature." Anna Airy (210), comedy, *as intended,* good magazine illustration. "Jagger" (241), spirited Raemakers, coloured (Bolshevik, or "blood," red). M. L. Williams, "The Triumph," real French (old) Salon "shocker," Pierrot with the stigmata, school of—let us say, Zwintscher, skirt and lady's underfrillies show technique, flesh tints, especially in the face, less successful.

R. G. Eves (250), as in many other portraits in the show, the skirt is better painted than the face. Riviere (309) bad Boldini, like a few gross of other portraits here present. H. Hurst (393), punk salon cum Luxembourg. J. R. Reid (401), like so many others, etc., sea the colour it "ain't." Adrian Stokes (400) colours on this canvas are at least in relation to each other; *no common feat* in this company; not to be underestimated among so many exhibits in the tone of the "firelight" pictures so common in the Strand. "Lighting the cigarette," etc.

[22]*The New Age,* June 6, 1918, p. 91. Signed "B. H. Dias."

H. Morley (370) pseudo-Hellenic, cum Teuto-Hellenic, cum symbolic meaning. "Le Quesne" (372), incredible. B. Partridge (410), painted with a mop. H. Draper (406), little fairy soap ad. I. Codrington (407), B. Jones, the late, ashes of. 421 cf. Manet. 440 Tate. 444 cf. tinted photo.

G. Spenser Watson (portrait of H. Pinker) has at any rate made a portrait, painted the face, even if he got a little tired before quite finishing the rest of the canvas. Example for confrères who have apparently left the faces to be filled in at the end.

627, as "Before Aesculapius," but worse painted. 613, comedy (unintended). 610 F. Dicksee, not shining in his disciples. 285, school of the lady on the volant champagne cork. Sydney Lee (293), larky idea for stage scenery, might collaborate with Mr. Allinson.

We sink, we perambulate, among flowers à la 1829; among pre-Raphaelitisms with the definite detail and definite outlines removed; more Boldinis, more blasted Tademas; Partridge past belief again looms upon the exhausted vision; Cayley Robinson has pre-raphed with a Bengali innovation; Russel Flint, even Flint with his post-Boutet de Monville magazine covers comes as cooling and relief. One regrets having intended to write (or being about to write) that the London Group show was uninviting. (It was. It was painted in suet, but continue. The Academy is a dark forest, a psychological era, a morass, and so on. God help us.) More Boldini. Spenser Watson turns up again, spirited if bad painting. I have not noted the number. More history, allegory, paregory, paregoric, etc.

Most of the sculpture is comic. We note 1416; some rumour of something called form has reached this artist (F. Wiles). 1598, careful copy. 1583, suave. 1556, pseudo-Epstein, oh very-very-very-pseudo. 1558, trace of shape. 1507, usual Tate-Luxembourg bric-a-brac. 1489, pseudo cinque cento. 1481, pseudo-Rodin, very pseudo. 1498, beer-mug pottery, but good as such.

1497, Epstein's "Rom," very pseudo, very diluted, and one returns to the pigment section. 316, evidently as "modern" as is allowed "in," wide garish bad pointillism or late state of impressionist jab-jab. 317, ditto. 596, funny animals. Forgot to mention that there are a lot of pages out of the bestiary, fierce tigers, not burning very illuminedly, etc. 581, false colour beyond belief. 635, Tadema with the glaze off. H. Harvey (465), artist had an idea, and carried it out. My first moment of pleasure.

More smeary impressionism, tinted photos, official portraits of "robes." Hall Neal, interior. Impossible leopards by Wardle; pretty-pretty, by J. Duncan; then the 243, by Walter Bayes, "Pygmalion poster" school with the modishness of the Parisian firm removed; matte colour, flatness, very mild recognition of the present. "Oh, I dew think that's queer" (sic: queheh) whiff-whiffs the young lady behind me.

I suppose spectators of that sort have to have pictures to look at. There are, presumably, plenty of entrance shillings to represent that state of inanity. Bayes' picture is the first spot of interest in the show. It ought to be hung somewhere else.

Lastly, M. Green, in "The Step Dancer" (54), shows great charm, a picture well painted, pleasant, the colour in scale, and well put on, true lights, proper degree of dulness and lightness in register, a picture, in short, fit to hang with two dozen others in the drawing-room of some person of taste, who doesn't begin to think he or she "has a collection." Just a quiet piece of good work, lost in this mass of rubbish. There may be two or three others, but there is an end to one's patience.

The Rothenstein show of war pictures, is, or was, chiefly remarkable for the psychology displayed by the *Times* writer on painting, in dealing with it. The London Group give a poor show; a few clean drawings by Ginner, being the star feature. Karlowska's stuffed cat is less suety than most of the exhibits. Hamnett gaining admirers. Bevan had roughed up his trees a little. Only by contrast with the Academy does one unenjoyed hour at Heal's take on some glow in remembrance.

Quel métier! Quel métier!

ART NOTES[23]
Still the Academy

Slowly recovering from the depression, and hoping the patient reader is likewise, I am faced again with the "question" of the Academy. This matter is not a joke. I do not mean that the British Academy is not a subject for witticisms in all the known tongues of Europe. I mean that it should be considered, for a few moments, as seriously as the press of this country was some months ago considered in *The New Age*.

In my last article I could but stagger, could but utter vague grunts of discomfort, emerging as I was, fresh from the impact of all these horrible canvases. It would be hypocrisy to consider the Academy as anything save a great market, a stock exchange, a definitely trade concern, accepted in full cynicism by all its honest or even half-honest members. For an activist journal the question is merely: *can* this yearly debauch and appejoration of the national taste be in any way made less injurious? One doesn't want to suppress the "trade" utterly. It is perfectly suitable that there should be a yearly market of trade articles; one wonders, simply, whether this yearly rag-fair can be made less harmful to painting.

The net result of this year's show is, as I pointed out in my last article: one picture "good" in the sense that a brocaded sofa or some other article of Mayfair drawing-room furniture might be described by this adjective; a respectable portrait, done with a developed style by a serious painter

[23]*The New Age*, June 20, 1918, pp. 125–26. Signed "B. H. Dias."

(Chas. Shannon); a couple of other canvases (one a portrait, one a land-scape), both of which might equally well have appeared in any local provincial exhibit in Birmingham, Verona, Marseilles, Bilbao, or Cincinnati; and one painting by Bayes, which might conceivably be made the subject for a discussion of art among more or less intelligent people, more or less familiar with the painting of the last forty years. It was before this canvas that the young lady from (?) Bedfordshire, visiting her aunty in (?) the Belgravia end of S. Kensington, remarked: "Oeh, I deu think that's queuh!"

To cut the knot: The Royal Academy is *not* there to stimulate a critical state of mind in the spectator. It is *not there* to interest people who are acquainted with contemporary art or past masterwork, or who can compare one picture with another, to the disadvantage of the lamentable. The Royal Academy is there to "get off" as much painting (trade article) on to the public as the befoozled public will take. As in any country-fair full of gimcracks, glass beads, tin ware, etc., the articles are shown helter-skelter all in a jumble, so that the critical sense may be dazzled, or lulled, or confused. The bad Boldinis, the bad Tademas, the decalcimania or "transfer" flowers, the tinted photos are hurtled in side by side. A garish ninth-rate bit of impressionism may look fairly clean when placed next to a J. Jebusha Shannon. A perfectly ordinary bit of 1880 may gain by juxtaposition with a bit of grease-tin finish left over from a still earlier rummage. As a means of pensioning aged and inefficient painters, keeping 'em off the rates, all those devices may be excellent. . . . But the national taste?

What am *I* going to do about it? Vous me flattez. It is not to be supposed that one journalist can educate a whole nation at a blow. I can but point out that the one thing which would purge (purge, not kill) the Academy would be the awakening of a critical habit in the public. The one thing which must most terrify any true Academician is the thought that the general spectator MIGHT begin to compare one canvas with another; that the man on the floor, having spent one shilling to get in and one more for a list of pictures, MIGHT, not suddenly but gradually, begin to think about painting, about the verity of colour, about form, about composition, about the scale of colour-values, lighting, etc., about the various possible qualities and defects of a canvas.

I think it is only Mr. Bernard Shaw, among dramatists of our day, who has sighed for an audience of philosophers. I do not expect a public of art-critics and experts to rise up in an instant. I simply point out two little devices which would promote a comparing faculty and habit in the Academy public—and without dispossessing the Academician all at once, or preventing nice old inefficient octogenarians from "hanging on to their markets," or having their stuff shown in public.

1. It would be perfectly possible (and quite fair to the artists) to hang all the bad Boldinis together; to hang all tinted photographs in a line; to hang all the bad Tademas on one wall and all the "Tate" on another. In this manner the poor public would be faintly impelled to wonder *which* of the bad Boldinis was least offensive, and thence it would drift into a habit of comparisons. It might even think of comparing the annual society portraits with portraits at the National Gallery, or (if travelled) with those in the Louvre or the Prado. We can easily imagine the wail that would go up from the exhibitors IF their work should be hung like by like, instead of being subjected to the shell-game of "contrasts."

2. The alternative method would be to hang the work by periods. Thus Mr. Fustan Jaggson, who was a promising Slade student in 1801 and who was elected to the Academy in 1843 as a "safe man," might be hung next to Mr. Jappleton-Hexsom, who was a promising Slade pupil in 1805 and was admitted to the Academy (as a still safer proposition) in the year of grace MDCCCXLV. One could then tell, more or less easily, which of the old crocks was fairly active and intelligent in his day, and which of them merely tumbled into a fashion even after his better contemporaries were learning to abandon it.

The nonagenarian public could also get its little garden scenes, its pictures with touching subjects, etc., without being subjected to Bayes, or Clausen, or the terrible and unbounded moderns (as this term is Academically animadverted). The "queuh" pictures could also have part of a room to themselves; and the shockers could be segregated, and everybody *ought* to be pleased. Even the bilious critic could concentrate on the part of the show most likely to deserve his attention.

If the Academy were not composed of 98 per cent. of cowards we should see one of these devices adopted by the summer of 1919.

ART NOTES[24]
The International

This year's International is a mixture of brightness and frivolity. After immersion in the Academy one is filled with a spirit of tolerance; inclined to admire almost anything. Brightness greeted one. Sir John Lavery, A.R.A., presented what we may roughly call Boldini-Abbey, but carefully done (for him), with glittering colour well harmonised. F. Harmer (37) careful post-Manet. John S. Sargent (42) careless pseudo-Lawrence. DeSmet (27) dilution of Matisse, not quite despicable. D. Y. Cameron (10) landscape, clean rain-washed and pleasant. If H. Morley (12) had ever

[24]*The New Age,* July 4, 1918, p. 155. Signed "B. H. Dias."

looked at Picasso's early drawings of acrobats he would not foist such a botch upon us. Contemptible ignorance of all Picasso's phases save the last seems to reign in this island. A. Ludovici (15), might remember Degas, but doesn't. Remembrance would have prevented "15." McEvoy (23) likeness to his chief sitter, and more care than usual; 4 bad even for McEvoy. Strang (34) yearning for the Augustus of yesteryear. Newbury (62) bright and nippy, crescent moon clearly visible. A. Newton (67) technical stunt of bringing water-colour up to oil brightness. Guevara (74 and 75) nearer Matisse than DeSmet, but in very obvious derivation, lacking Matisse rhythm. Guevara has done better; grasp of anatomy as shown in some of the figures; too facile a lift. E. Albanesi (80) a likeness in large strokes. H. Daeye (96) sopped on with a blanket.

It is one of those shows where the pictures look better by the wall-full than when noted one by one. (My companion, *not* having been to the Academy, tells me that it is a distressing exhibit . . . which only goes to show how looking at a sea of bad pictures *will* put one's eye out.) The longer one stays, the less there is to rejoice one. Max's cartoons of the Rossettis are not so spirited as last year; if we go through the Methuen volume of his things printed in 1907 we shall find a few drawings interesting in actual forms employed; no such formal interest in the present lot. Orpen (3) below himself. L. Knight (20) trick of catching the eye by bright streak on darkish canvas. Chas. Ricketts . . . I will come back to Mr. Ricketts in a moment. H. Bishop (84) thoughtful, bland, careful, meritorious. L. Sargent (88) colourful. F. H. Newbury (102) relic of Burne-Jones and Rossetti.

Bits of sculpture should have gone direct to suburban cemetery or to electric-light ornament dealers. Wolmark (decorative panel) decorative rather than a panel, good division of space, grasp of unhackneyed pose. Bentley (114) gay study in human billets of wood. C. D'Erlanger (120) quiet, careful, paint excellently put on. E. Sargent (121) sanded and textile finish. J. Noble (134) Angelus remembered, tree-trunk gone a bright-dark pink, quite commendable as things go. E. Proctor (140) Rousseau diluted *a lot.* Vinall (151) ought to be in Academy, not much worse than anything I saw there. H. Blaker (153) width, inventiveness in his clouds. L. Richmond (175) the delicate and fragile in quite pretty colours. A. Burleigh might bury the Teuto-Hellenic. Meugens, Rackham looking backwards towards Idylls of a King. Flint (188) softened Tadema. E. Walker (220) Watts *very* deliquescent. Sheringham "Poetasters of Ispahan" passing from Conder to Dulac. Kurihara, post-Brangwyn. B. Young "Refugees" in colour suggesting rich decor, gay lights of 10,000 candles, crystal and drawing-rooms; had better look at Bayes' Academy picture.

Ricketts presents the only point of interest in the show. His "Don Juan" at first glance seems to be remembering the departed glories of

Tiepolo; but if we can lift ourselves out of the whole socket of current ideas and take this picture with an absolutely untouched mental plate, we find, first, Mr. Ricketts is obviously, absolutely contemptuous of *all* contemporary clamours; secondly, there is any amount of technique in the picture; thirdly, if the desirable aim of a twentieth-century artist is to produce "something like an old master," Mr. Ricketts has done it. If it is an academic ideal, it is, as here carried out, an ideal that would kill, annihilate, the present extant Academy. Grant against this that it has the air of being an objet d'art, of being a thing of virtu, of being something exceedingly valuable in itself; you cannot imagine it hung in a barn as you can imagine a Matisse; you cannot imagine it suitably hung on a simple plain-tinted wall as you can a Whistler; or among the slightly stuffy upper middle-class furniture where a Manet or a Degas could hang. It has nothing to do with modern life, in so far as you can only imagine it hung in a Renaissance palace, or in a modern multi-millionaire imitation of one.

It is, after all, the artist's business to express his desire; to paint what *he* wants, not something that he is bullied into, or that someone has told him. He can be with his age or against it; but he must express what *he* himself wants. Mr. Ricketts, in utter defiance of every current opinion and of all the "forces" or inertias about him, has taken a traditional subject, saturated with associations (Spanish play, French play, opera with a libretto in Italian, poems by Baudelaire, etc). The method of painting is also soaked in tradition, a polyglot tradition. I said "remembering Tiepolo"; but note how different this "remembering" is from that of the people who disconnectedly fake a "Piero della Francesca" or some primitive; or from the Academic remembrance based on traditions not the best of their kind.

The minute you try to ascribe Ricketts's picture to any one master you realise that without a whole library of technical history in your head or at your elbow, you are lost. The critic accustomed to judge and compare pictures by his eye alone, cannot make an historic analysis of this canvas. He can only say the high lights are built up, the paint is rather glazed, etc. His next question is: "Does such building, such a glazing," etc., belong to such and such an old master? Mr. Ricketts's work is a work of scholarship. He has not cribbed an old master, or the style of any old master; he has picked here and there, and worked out with infinite care a perfectly unified style—the lift of the curtain, the hard, creamy-white streaks, all these show comparison, analysis of a hundred old pictures, a care greater than Tiepolo's; the work of a connoisseur.

In 24 he has leapt a few centuries and produced something between a Boecklin and a Craig stage scene. But "Don Juan" infinitely like an old master could only have been done to-day; and is quite unlike any old master in particular. It is a bibelot, an objet d'art, a *specialité*, whatever you like; out of the "movement" and the "movements," but it is undoubtedly the result of great care, skill, experience, and it calls into court every assumption now gobbled by every art-public, and every art-student-bohemia. Of its kind you can't beat it; you can't explain it away; you may detest it, dislike it, ridicule it as an affectation, as millionaire's furniture; but this will not annihilate it. It is not an appeal for money, or sympathy, or admiration from people differently constituted; it is not a fake, a shift, a bluff; it is an assertion—of nearly every painting ideal now out of office, and as such it is intensely interesting. I am not expressing one jot of sympathy. But a man cannot do any sort of thing so well, so completely, with so great technical skill, without the result being "there"; without its existing in a way which the shoals of rubbishy things at the Academy, and the hoards of careless imitations of modes of the moment simply cannot achieve.

ART NOTES[25]
Nash, Nicholson, Orpen

It has been suggested to me that the Nash exhibit deserves more attention than I have given it. I had, previously, received some such idea from myself. I have investigated it further. My first impression of the show was that it was a Nevinson show and that Nevinson had taken a decided turn for the better; was using more care in execution. No. 4 was an interesting composition of circle and wave. No. 8 suggested reminiscence of a Wadsworth wood-cut. No. 12, good use of perpendiculars; 17, rather Nevinson; 26, good diagonals; 28, Nevinson; 29, not Innes; 34, typical effect of broken trees, interesting; 43, wave lines; 47, zig-zags and trees; 49, variation of waves and circles; 51, simple colour scheme, commendable; 52 or 53, colonnade; and 53 or 52, inverted V's. Net result: Nash is not endowed with any great formal inventiveness; he has made a show with variations on a few motifs; but, on the other hand, he has illustrated the war most creditably. The pictures look like war; they are not merely sketches, in peace time, of destroyed places, and they are not in peace mood. People returned from the front say that that is what the front is like.

The show was not a landmark in art history, but it was probably the best show of war art—that is, of pictures painted to Government order—that we have had.

[25]*The New Age*, July 18, 1918, p. 189. Signed "B. H. Dias."

NICHOLSON

William Nicholson has really pulled himself together again. His show demonstrates a good deal of thought in arrangement; it contains several distinct and different pictures; it is not simply a series of variants on an identical composition, or on five or six habitual themes. It is curiously uneven, but it has style. That is Nicholson's gift. He has had a conception of style all along, even when doing his worst work. By "style" I do not mean a uniform personal manner. I mean that in practically every canvas something has been done to the subject, some idiom of translation has been created, or moulded, or developed. Important or not, the artist has evolved a *way of saying*, or rather a way of painting, what he had to paint about his subject.

2, "Retour de La Joconde"; old impressionism, can't see its merit. There are curious blurrs in some of the pictures ("Henley's Hat," "Air Raid Night"); possibly they would come right in some lightings. There is a good deal of real Academy red in No. 7.

"Silver" is quiet, unassuming, skilfully and evenly painted. "Lustre Mug" is perhaps a shade too chaste for a world given over to evil. I, personally, happen to loathe the way the paint is put on "Ursula," but this is a matter of taste, not a matter of dogma. One does not, or should not, disapprove of things merely because they happen to be antipathetic to oneself. "Poet's Cottage" is a blob. No. 4 appears to me simply bad. The white blurr in 5 may need special lighting, but I doubt if one should paint in such a manner that the canvas must have an electric light just under the frame. The "Air Raid Night" does visibly improve if one gets into the opposite corner (northwest) of the room. No. 11 is superficially, if not fundamentally, Academy.

But there is the gift of style, and Mr. Nicholson, in contradistinction to practically all his contemporaries, has not "lain down." Here is a man past middle age who is still putting energy into his work; a man with a very considerable reputation who still *tries*, who still tries to make *each* canvas the best possible job he can make it. Mr. Nicholson is, therefore, very nearly in a class by himself.

SIR WILLIAM ORPEN

The Orpen show need not detain one—Slade, Slade Sketch Club, Society tinted-photos. Are the generals in tents or in Mayfair? In short, Sir William's message is that the war is very like peace-life in Belgravia— bright cheery tints, lemonish egg-yolk yellow. Any tone of war, any feeling of war, wholly absent—the usual pre-war Orpen drawings rather more hastily done. Ease, comfort, complexion soap, a little stage decoration. A pale cast of prettiness.

Tooth's Gallery, Bond Street

Exhibit of old masters: Two excellent Canalettos, showing synthesis within bounds of strict representation; clear, broad, though apparently close brushwork; convention of water, stylisation in sun on houseboats. Dark water, finer perhaps in the less charming "Salute," good grouping of three figures in lower left-hand corner. Jansen's[25a] "Portrait of a Lady," of interest. Intelligent breadth in the Raeburn. The F. Cotes (1726–76) remarkable for its Goyaesque quality. Distinct pleasure to be got from this small exhibit.

Lamorna Birch (Fine Art Society) might study Murray Smith to advantage. Sutton Palmer, old-fashioned bright water-colour. Clear, careful, dating possibly to Meissonier; just a faint touch of originality in clouds; 35 and 28 successful.

J. D. Fergusson has simplicity, a cellular construction visible in No. 10. (The Connell Gallery.) "Still Life" good. Bronze "Head of Painter," fine, simple representation, no nonsense, grasp of form. In the terra-cotta coloured substance he attempts a Botticellese prettiness uglified and convoluted. There is some distinction of character between one portrait and another; there is also hang-over from Futurist shows, from Matissian bulbous females disported in lush mangel-wurzels. The extent of Mr. Fergusson's misfortunes can, however, only be gleaned from his catalogue. One blames no artist wholly for his introducers, but such sentences as the following exclude sympathy:—

"Art is everything or nothing, and the art whose effort is not wholly devoted to being everything is of no account. Just as there is a false and a true art, so there is a false . . ." etc.

"Our universe of hopes and fears is but one changing facet of the great clear-shining jewel which the artist alone sees face to face, and we in his mirror."

An artist desiring public courtesy should not have his catalogue adorned with these festoons of twaddle. Space in *The New Age* is too valuable to quote further from this "Blue Review" entail. The country has had enough of it.

[25a]Probably Cornelius Johnson (Jonson), also called Jansen's, Janssen van Ceulen.

ART NOTES[26]
The Tenth London Salon of the Allied Artists Association

Miss Nina Hamnett has sent three of her best pictures to the Grafton Gallery: "Still Life" in simple cubicity, "Portrait" and "Roofs." Fifty-two of her works are also exhibited at the newly opened Eldar "Gallery" upstairs, around the corner; around, in fact, several corners at 40, Great Marlborough Street. Like Fergusson, she suffers from her introducer. That she should have been a careful disciple of Gaudier-Brzeska is well enough, and that she should have picked up something or other (vague and indefinite) from Modigliani is well enough, but to drag in Kristian and "the acumen and learning of R. Fry"; and to tell us that *"Like Hogarth,* she picks her sitters," doth but arouse the latent irony in our natures. Mr. Sickert shouldn't do it.

"Like Michael Angelo" he painted the Pope . . . etc. At the Eldar, Numbers 2, 4, 5, 8, 10, 12, 15, 24, 28*a*, 32, 40, show the influence of Gaudier-Brzeska in varying degree, but always with this difference, that whereas Gaudier used to "knock off" a hundred or so of these line drawings at a sitting, they being often a sort of range-finding on his part, and in most cases the preparation for sculpture, or at least for an abstract drawing in firm thick line, synthesising the whole series of studies, they are here done as if an end in themselves and with quite apparent laboriousness. What had been the sweep of the hand with the original genius is here a careful process, embodying usually some definite superficiality of some particular Gaudier drawing or series. In 31 one of Gaudier's modes of stylisation is modified, in 8 something is added, in 12 the inflow is less apparent.

The work is creditable, but before getting too excited over the drawings one should get one's eye in by reviewing the work of Gaudier or of Pascin. Not wildly anti-feminist we are yet to be convinced that any woman ever invented anything in the arts. Mary Cassatt was doubtless a credit to Manet, etc., but we await proofs of invention.

Eighteen is felicitous; 21 done broadly, 16, école de John, well painted, considerable skill. "Portrait of the Artist" about the best thing in the show, 46 no merit, 47 expresses some character.

GRAFTON GALLERY (NO PEARLS, BY REQUEST)

Cheer, gaiety, odds and ends from the Royal Watercolour outbreaks. Academy, etc., Swiss scenes à la 1824, china painting, pastel-photoism, etc. Keith Bayes "White Cottage," school of Ginner. David Sassoon,

[26]*The New Age,* August 1, 1918, pp. 223–34. Signed "B. H. Dias."

"Green and White" decorative, good drawing, pure colour; not so successful in his other two pictures. M. Arbuthnot, should return to Korin. Henriques, technique in parts of one canvas.

D. Fox-Pitt, Bevanism. R. McIntyre follows the moderns. Richard C. Carline, care and originality unobtrusively in "Hampstead." J. Kramer presents a "Portrait of M. Kerensky, ex-Premier of Russia," instantaneous, and evidently labouring under a bad attack of bright jaundice. Robert Bevan, care and cleanliness. H. Clements Hassell presents "Still Life": a hat not made by the milliner whose name appears on the box.

Arthur Stewart does oil in imitation of pastel; "Head" is better than "From Flanders." Grace J. Joel offers the worst sort of backwash of Watts via James Jebusha Shannon via the magazine cover school. Mary McCrossan does Venice in "Dutch" colour, simple, clear, bright, definite, not without merit. I trust Edward Ertz will not repeat his present performances, which I suspect of having been offered first to the Academy and rejected incontinent. Ben Dix, as of the Independents of yesteryear. Alfred Wolmark's "Groups of Nudes" (£150) is of rhythmic interest. Therese Lessore declines. Mervyn Lawrence pointillises decadently.

William Rodway-Barnes' "Mural Decorations" are not exactly a joke. It seems possible that he may have intended to do for the Rathskeller cum chromo-lithograph genre something more or less akin to what Rousseau did for the Sea-chest popular tradition. Given a darkened cellar, and having heard of cubism, and being rather too broadly-minded, a critic might "fall" for these works.

But Mary Donaldson should be discouraged in her attempts to sentimentalise cubism. Mary Stewart Robinson should be asked to retire. Jack B. Yeats is as usual, prices well up, verve, a personal style, the faces of interest, the landscape unobjectionable.

E. Garner is correct in the sun on the gabled house in No. 160, which is better than her other two pictures. Mrs. Luck's fortune is not apparent save in her name. S. de Karlowska has a recognisable style of her own, near to Bevan's; merit; colours from pure to purish. Emeline Deane: inexcusable rubbish. F. Tysoe-Smith, ditto.

Fanny Abbot applies some very poor Rousseauisation to the portrait school of 1830 and to a bad brace of primitives; employing the greasiest possible colour. Doubtless deliberate in her striving for results such as are here produced.

M. I. Beckley: spotlight on Fra Angelico. (??) H. Dallas, some hope in No. 251, belied by 250 and 252, W. Boreel pre-raphs. G. de-Braux demonstrates the inconvenience of *not* having a jury. J. Verney should be removed. Margaret Smith: careful delineation of features, with less skill than at first sight appears. D. F. Hirst, some impression of sunlight in No. 270:

G. L. Whelpton: Landseer and damn poor Landseer. V. Randolph: guff. A. K. Diver, rubbish. A. P. King: Gnashing, if the "G" be permitted us. P. Forbes-Robertson enjoying herself and harms no one. Walter Taylor; simplicity, not quite at his best in this show. L. W. M. Taylor, a yearn towards Beardsley. V. Lorein, careful discipleship of Picasso, meritorious, possible influence of Segonzac (or even of Gaudier-Brzeska??). Chas. Ginner, not at his best, pretty much the same as before, more little black lines between his bricks. J. W. Stephens, suet from Preraphaelite boule de suif. J. Noble knows what he wants, get it in part with the palate-knife.

Sculpture "and applied art," mostly pots, one by Wolmark (No. 10) not bad. K. Maltwood "Group" not particularly commendable.

System of hanging each exhibitor's work, three pictures one above the other with decent interval between the trios is very satisfactory. It gives each painter a comfortable space to himself, to appeal or repel; to establish what personality the gods have allowed him.

ART NOTES[27]
"Fresh wholesome sentiment"

"Ya no mi diga mucho a mi." We may even spell it *"muncho"* as the late Sir Alfred must often have heard it pronounced in Algeciras, where he observed that the colour was brilliant but did not "quite get" the vitreous quality of southern atmosphere. The remaining works in oil, water-colour, etc., of the late Sir Alfred East, R.A., P.R.B.A., at the Fine Art Society, Bond Street, consist in part of almost the worst possible oil-daubs. In the better oil he appears to have heard some rumour of Corot (as in 44, "A Pastoral") or of Alfred Stevens (in "Top of Wolds," 11), but he could have studied both masters to advantage. An old man named Hopkinson Smith who used to be seen painting in Venice could have given Sir Alfred valuable hints upon water-colour. East is sometimes broader, sometimes less broad than himself, sometimes fuzzier. In "Enchanted Castle" he turned out something like a Dulac, with a certain economy of pigment. "Taormina" is stage painting; in "Edge of Wood" (9) he appears as if edging toward Brangwyn, etc.

His death a few years ago was a severe loss to his friends, but art did not greatly suffer. After reading Mr. A. L. Baldry's preface about "true sentiment of nature," "fresh wholesome sentiment," etc., one does not greatly mind how much Mr. Baldry is bereaved.

[27]*The New Age*, August 15, 1918, pp. 255–56. Signed "B. H. Dias."

Largely mentioned as "Post-Impressionism," the New English Art Club again presents itself. Post-Impressionism would seem to consist largely of Post-Puvis-de-Chavannism, and somewhat of "old-master" compositions re-done in different colour schemes; simplesse, matt or gouache-like tone instead of oily glaze, etc., or even 18th-century pseudo-classic engravings adapted in oil-colour. There are a good many pictures which one would not mind on the walls of one's friends' drawing-rooms; but there is also a tendency to art that is "all in the shop-window": the picture that "looks modern," the picture that is arty; the picture that grows less interesting as you examine it.

The programme for New English painting run up by the Chantrey Bequest taste, complied with by the P.R.B., hallowed by tradition, is in favour of the picture that is *at least as interesting* when reproduced on an art-brown-ink postcard as when seen on the canvas. The Liverpool Gallery is stuffed with the most popular horrors. It is also a democratic tendency, this wish to reach as many casual glances as possible, this lust for the reader of *Vogue*, and of *Colour*. The artist cares less for the few people who will *see* the original work than for the ten thousand who will glance at the reproduction. Raverat's "Sirens" catch the eye, for the necessary instant, when reproduced. It is a prize example of the sort of thing I mean: Puvis, Manet's Olympia, the old formula for the "pleasing" shown in the derivative middle figure, the forward figure baggy and podgy, a bit more "modern" in the undesirable sense, an after-thought of Botticelli in the middle figure to make up. It is distinctly the sort of picture from which interest fades rapidly; the type of painting with "everything in the window," nothing in reserve. Raverat's "Judas, etc.," looks like a desperate stab at the old masters, via Kramer.

There is something to be said for old Hellenism, and Renaissance Hellenism revived. A man whose name I forget used to do it in Les Indépendants seven or eight years ago considerably better than the present exhibitors.

The North-West Room contains two John drawings and the usual better class magazine or book illustrations; R. Nahebidian very mild; F. S. Unwin (44), Sickert-Gaudier; T. Proctor (49) Shannoning (Chas.) toward illustration; F. Dodd, "Fo'castle" natural cubo-vorto composition; E. White (61) Nashing. Central Gallery: M. Jefferies "Teintes d'Orient" tricky but skilful, successful portrait. Sidney Lee's "Yorkshire Hill-side," care and extremely unobtrusive invention, dull colour giving impression of sunlight correctly. Leon de Smet's work, recognisable by its uncommendableness (68). Morley's "The Bather," example of type of thing borrowed from eighteenth-century "classic" engravings. A. N. Lewis,

"Three South African Women," Gauguinesque bluff. L. Pissarro (73, etc.), a greatly over-rated artist. E. Walker (74), not commendable.

C. M. Pearce, "Piccadilly Circus" and "Motor 'Bus"—Mr. Pearce's systematised product in a stylisation that is becoming rather wearisome. A. Roche, "Cottage Interior," sloppy, with derivation, ultimately, from the Dutch. W. Shackleton "Old Age," fake Rembrandt.

L. Pickhard (82), "The Mantel Piece," good colour, and good drawing under a superficial confusion, contrasts without violence, as in difference of tone between the room and the room seen in the mirror, Pickhard is to be picked out of the "general run." O. Gardner (88) worst type of fake Puvis. W. Rothenstein (90), "Three Children Singing" in the manner of the Tate Gallery Corale, with their surfaces roughed up for the occasion.

M. Jeffries' "Potiche et Fleurs de Papier" is commendable; note this commendation. In contrast to Raverat, Jeffries' picture has in it more skill than shows at first glance. Also in E. Walker's "Decoration Lileth" we find a conventionalisation of smear carried to point of interest; there is a unity of feeling in the brightish confused colour; it is all in the key of the whole; there is better drawing than at first sight appears, in the figure, in the animals, in the flowers.

L. Lancaster (96) very bad Puvis. M. McCrossan "Pink Chestnut," spotty pointillism, poor colour sense, poor relation of colour. M. E. Atkins, bright blue, bright white, bright green, simple tricolour that for some reason does not weary one, possibly because of contrast with usual English weather. W. Shackleton (106), daring resurrection of a colour-scheme long laid away in the Luxembourg, a sort of Conderism in yellow and orange. He shows also a filthy post-Wattsism (195), 217 is in the red and brown-orange. However, there is not much hope for him. The "Nu au Salon" is represented by Tonks and F. Harmar. Bevan is recognisable by his style of very mild cubing or octagoning of trees, matte colour, commendable. E. Darwin (186), in quest of naiveté. E. White (205), Nashing. M. Jeffries, in love with "beauty, charm, enchantment." Walter Taylor at his average; one always finds oneself stopping before Taylor's unshouting work.

Various Boutet de Monville followers. Vegetarian pseudo-naive in E. Hughes (234). Russian fadism meeting Japanese fadism in R. M. Hutching's "St. Francis preaching to birds."

ART NOTES[28]
Buildings—I

Outside a few technical journals, architecture has no modern critics. There are antiquarians who bring out two-volume studies of Palladio;

[28]*The New Age*, August 29, 1918, pp. 287–88. Signed "B. H. Dias."

there are professors of the Beaux Arts who have presumably taught Parisian builders to make their exteriors as much like interiors as possible. There are practical architects, Government architects, and arty architects; but the society which flocks to the Royal Academy, Institute, International, Futurist, Water-Colour, and Etchers' shows does not discuss the aesthetics of building. They restore old places in the country, or with infinite labour they preserve the grey-blue-green painted panelling of old London boudoirs, withdrawing-rooms, and powder-closets. "Rooms" are transported and reconstructed; old ceilings look down new walls.

London has been called the most modest city in the world, because of her concealment of treasure. She is said to have the worst architecture of any city of magnitude. This is, however, a gross and exaggerated attack. The worst houses in the world are on Campden Hill; they are brick of an undistinguished red, with whitish stone ornaments and borders and stripes and gew-gaws and scroll-saw effects favoured in the late middle of the last century.

But these deformations are neither typical of nor peculiar to London. You will find the same type of thing in any French jerry-built suburb. London is much too large and her building much too various to be criticised, or praised, or attacked all together. Reform is impossible; at least, mechanical and legislated reform is out of the question; but a discussion is not impossible, and an intolerance of certain faults might be developed.

Apart from beautiful curiosities like the old houses in Holborn, which are impractical for contemporary use, London has riches and models. There is the old eighteenth-century brick, and there are the beautiful Regency houses, both preferable to the work of 1850 and after, the work of the Prince Consort period and the modern aping of America. (Americans, by the way, tell me that London gets only second and third rate American designs; but I will come to that later.)

The horror of London is its grey-yellow brick. It is the horror of Islington; it is the horror of the districts south of the Thames through which one passes on train coming from Dover. In the more pretentious houses there is added to this the horror of machine-cut stone trimmings. I do not know whether these borders, copings, cornices, and so on are stone or a composition moulded into horrible forms and indented with "ornaments." The borders are common both to yellow and bad-red brick houses.

They are also found dividing the brickwork in the imitations of the Hampton Court period. My general impression is that there is no good work done in this mixture of brick and whitish stone, although I know I have seen houses in Mayfair done more carefully than elsewhere. The style is dangerous and almost never successful. The earlier (presumably the

1875 to 1895) middle-grade house adds the horror of bad machine designs in stained glass, ascending toward Walter Craneism.

Some of the best Georgian brick is in Sloane Street, and here at least one finds, in some cases, one hallmark of the good façade, the graduation of windows. As the beauty of a Greek temple depends on the irregularity of the spacing of its pillars, so the simple composition of the oblong house front, punctuated by the four, six, or more smaller oblongs, depends almost wholly upon the careful proportion of the smaller oblongs. When one thinks of house after house, often called palazzi, in Italy, made beautiful by ever so little ornament, but by ever so fine a proportion of windows, one is inclined to curse modern builders. Grant a ground floor of rough stone, the doorway need not be, but is often, arched, the single window covered with a heavy hand-wrought iron grill, the two or three great windows of the *piano nobile,* perhaps a balcony or several balconies, the narrower lower windows above it, and the still smaller windows at the top if the house has a fourth floor, one has the beginning of a beautiful city, and a model practical for the town living-house of today. Grant even the early Georgian restraint, the difference between the fine old and the cheap hideous modern, in this *genre* where there is a complete absence of ornament, is *solely* in the proportion of the ascending rows of windows, and, perhaps, a few pounds more expenditure for the doorway. But the graduation of windows is not a matter of building cost, it is a matter of architectural taste and knowledge and care.

Like all the properties of good art it is of an utter simplicity. It is the veriest beginning of things. I walk down Dean Street finding a house with half of its ground floor devoted to groceries and the other to dingy furniture; there is a beautiful grill over the door; there is a glimpse of a spacious and beautiful stairway. All through Dean Street and the streets adjoining are beautiful doorways and well-cut frames for the doors. I do not believe that these houses were more expensive than the bad houses built us today, but granting that short-lease tenants will not pay for carved door-posts, the question of windows remains.

Is anything but the indifference of owners and stupidity of architects responsible for this fundamental perversity?

A basement-house has certain difficulties to overcome which the Italian palazzo has not; to keep the basement from being hideous one has to use either priceless city space *or* be very careful. Let us not run mad with theory or go building garden suburbs too rashly. But there are sound principles of architecture, and architecture can be an art, though it must be a very accommodating art. Its technique *is* the art of fitting a building to a use, and the evils of architecture are all, or nearly all, due to non-utilitarian excrescence. The worst architecture is architecture that tries to be "artistic." It should aim at being architectural. The aesthetic of the

75

architectural is the least explored aesthetic of our time. There are fine examples of it in London, and in buildings constructed within the last ten or twenty years, but their qualities are very often concealed from us by a wash of bad "ornament" stultifying the whole. Yet the architect is, or can be, quite as much, or more, of an artist than the adolescent who pays a guinea for the privilege of exhibiting a few sketches; he may have as much right to individual recognition, outside his purely business relations. He might even send private-view cards to "representatives of the Press."

ART NOTES[29]
Building: Ornamentation!

It is impossible to look with any attention at the individual buildings in Oxford Street and New Oxford Street from Marble Arch to Chancery Lane, without at the same time experiencing an almost uninterrupted series of rather acute disgusts.

John Ruskin was the only man who ever worried over the horrors of 19th-century British architecture and John Ruskin was driven insane. Ruskin's fussy little copies of the Stones of Venice and Ruskin's final insanity should be perfectly understandable to anyone who spends even half an hour in observing the ornamentation of Oxford Street. No one does observe this ornamentation. The sensitive foreigner might well believe that the denizens of this district had been afflicted with some marasmic obsession; but they really have had no obsession, they have not looked at the buildings, and they have perhaps been wise in their obese self-protection.

Neither law, reason, nor the requirements of 20th-century business advertising oblige men to ornament buildings. The ornamentation is a mendacity, for ornament implies care, it implies affection for the surfaces treated with ornament. Here there has been no affection, nothing but an evasiveness, a desire to get through a mean job with the least possible expenditure of thought, taste, time, money, or the better habits of craftsmanship.

In the streets running west from Southampton Row you will find, by contrast, the fanlights, beautiful fanlights, ugly fanlights, and in some cases plain half circles of glass where the fine old frames have worn out. Under many of the frames, good, bad and cheaply renewed, you will find a single line of carved wood in a simplified wall-of-Troy pattern; and in this is a fine tradition of carpentry.

Westward from Marble Arch by the Park a patient observer will find cast-iron balcony railings full of mendacity, and, alternating with them, a

[29]*The New Age*, September 12, 1918, p. 320. Signed "B. H. Dias."

few fine balconies in perfectly plain slender bars. This is not a matter of cost. The clean line of the well-proportioned plain iron costs no more than the lies.

Complications and convolutions in these machine-made "ornaments" are lies, because the ornamented surface is an implication that it has cost more trouble than the plain. The lie deceives no one, and it has never attained the dignity of a convention.

As the first printed books were made to look like written manuscript, the first iron castings may have deceived a few people, and the cheap-jack may have had the hypocritical pleasure of passing off a cheap house for a good one, but that naïveté is past.

One sighs for the stone window-frames of Verona. Simplex munditiis, how fine the simple notching and grooving of the stone, how fine the simple grooving of the patterned wood in the old London doorways! I am not sighing for the impossibilities of fine carving, I do not expect people in our time to have a gross of Pietro Lombardos sent down from Sheffield and Birmingham to fill London with beautiful doorways and balconies.

But there are any number of fine patterns which do not require individual artists to repeat them, and which might even be made by machine without being hideous. The cement imitations of Pietro Lombardo's mermaids set into brick façades are unspeakable abomination.

One walks into Russell Square and wishes that before erecting prominent structures people would decide whether they want a Chinese pagoda or a French Renaissance château. One finds in Oxford Street isolated, commendable attempts to escape the orgy of ornamentation. A sanitary expert has intervened, or the designer of gas-ranges has tried to simplify the outside of his warehouse. I know that if during the next six months I go constantly armed with a notebook I shall accumulate a list of cleanly and respectable buildings erected, probably, during the last thirty years. The search has the proportions of a labour. I do not know that it is necessary. I would like to ask help from the readers, for it is impossible that *New Age* readers should need detailed guidance in such a matter. The case is so flagrant, the hideousness of the sham ornament so appalling. Have we not enough depressions as it is? Shall we leave the matter until after the war? Will anyone add to his mental burdens by looking at London buildings? I do not know.

I know there is great beauty in London. There are sky-lines fit for Haroun al Raschid, an Arabian Nights by Regent's Park, and looking east from the bridge in the St. James' Park, where there used to be a long pond for waterfowl and where there is now a huddle of temporary buildings, one had an enchanted country before one, that is, in early evening when there was a red glow under the arches in the Horse Guards.

There is the peculiar London architecture that has no popular name— St. Martins in the Field, the National Gallery, the Horse Guards. The period has probably a technical name, but I have met only one architect who professed any acquaintance with this particular style, or thought it had claims to attention.

I do not know that anyone has attempted to formulate an aesthetic of good city building. London is such a chaos, the task of reform looks so hopeless, but someone must make a beginning, and I should like to advance a few tentative and general principles.

I. Certain styles are suitable for the climate and for the general needs of contemporary city dwelling and business.

II. The unusual building, the freak building, the archaic reconstruction, must be much more carefully done than the building which conforms to the general style of its district. These buildings come under the same laws as ornament. They attract more attention and must be able to endure closer scrutiny.

To begin with the greatest caution, we may say that no dwelling-house built in the style of 18th-century brick, plain, restrained, in careful proportion, will be an eye-sore.

The pseudo-classical 18th-century to Regency style is pleasing where a block can remain uniform. But the old charm of the Regent Street crescent is fast perishing under the irruption of new imitation American structures. The pseudo-Hampton Court style is usually too-pseudo to be endured. There are various other styles which could be used and are not; there are good Italian models, and also the plain early Tudor, I think it is the Maison Henri Quatre on la Cours la Reine in Paris, that suggests this to me. It has been tried for a few district libraries in London, but, so far as I can recall, the execution has been nearly always contemptible.

The problem of larger shops, blocks of flats, and so on, needs more lengthy attention.

ART NOTES[30]
Kinema, Kinesis, Hepworth, Etc.

We hear a good deal about the "art" of the cinema, but the cinema is not Art. Art with a large A consists in painting, sculpture, possibly architecture; beyond these there are activities, dancing, grimacing, etc. Art is a stasis. A painter or a sculptor tries to make something which can stay still without becoming a bore. He tries to make something which will stand being looked at *for a long time.* Art is good in just so far as it will stand a long and lively inspection.

Photography is poor art because it has to put in everything, or nearly everything. If it omits, it has to omit impartially. It omits by a general

[30]*The New Age,* September 26, 1918, p. 352. Signed "B. H. Dias."

blurr. It cannot pick out the permanently interesting parts of a prospect. It is only by selection and emphasis that any work of art becomes sufficiently interesting to bear long scrutiny.

The best possible single exposure of a cinema film would be at most a good photo. It need not be even that, as it is designed to bear but the scrutiny of an instant.

Architecture has an aesthetic that one can base on principles similar to those effective in sculpture. The cinema is at the furthest possible remove from all things which interest one as an "art critic."

One could forgive the cinema for existing if one believed it would kill contemporary theatricals, but this hope no longer survives. It may cheapen the stage wages of actors, but it plays to the same type of slushy and sentimental mediocrity. Its one advantage is that it takes less time to convey to its audience the same amount of sentimental sensationalism. It emphasises and glorifies the cheap side of the modern theatre. It will educate the illiterate to a point, but it will not deliver us from anything whatsoever.

It is an excellent medium for news. News is the antipodes of literature, as the cinema is the antipodes of Art. The cinema is an excellent medium for Pathe's animated *Gazette*. It should be an excellent medium for instructing children in botany, physics, geography, zoology, the costume of foreign peoples, the appearance of foreign cities and the processes of manufacturing. It makes excellent "historic records"; it is also the medium par excellence for recording the present "aristocracy" which has few characteristics of aristocracy save appearance. The cinema is the phonograph of appearance.

But the cinema asks for "criticism," it asks to be taken seriously. It should apply to the "dramatic" or theatrical critic not to the Art critic. As much of the present theatre art as is dumb-show can be done on the cinema. It has two advantages: the actors need not be able to speak any language whatever, they need not have voices or suitable accents; and their work is international—one actor does for the Hottentot and the Lithuanian. And the audience does not have to listen to the rubbish that is talked and sung on the contemporary stage.

If the cinema really would kill the modern rubbishy theatre! But no, what does it give us? Plays with worse incongruities, more sentiment, "sob-stuff," so crass that it would be hissed even by Chas. Cochran's audience. The cinema has its public, its devotees who talk of cinema-technique.

Very well, its technique. The photographer's technique, and the actor's technique: the photographer's that of the snapshot; the actor's technique, but minus the necessity for memorising words or speaking them aptly. Let us grant that the pantomime of cinema actors is often quite as good as that of contemporary stage actors, perhaps better. In this pantomime and in nothing else has the cinema any technique that a serious critic can consider. The technique of the Palladium, of Dennis Eadie, of the Vanburgh family. Take it and welcome. One would rather see Mr. Temple Thurston's films that read his novels; but his making films will not stop his making novels. Mr. Cecil Hepworth with certain hyperbole asks us to consider the Thurston film. He is perfectly sound in saying that a cinema scenario should be made to be a cinema scenario and not an adaptation from a play or a novel. But what does he give us?

"Sob-stuff" on the cinema is no better than sob-stuff anywhere else. It consists in referring to some poignant situation in life. The clumsiness of the allusion or representation does not affect the poignancy. It is not the *quality* of the representation that moves one. People at theatres and cinemas weep over rubbish, and are irritated because they know it is rubbish.

Very well, take the two plays offered at a Hepworth private view. Take them for what the cinema is. *The Refugee* presents some admirably acted pantomime. But the refugee hidden in a Belgian garret continually sticks his head into the light of an attic window where it would presumably be visible from outside. The Hun finding more food and wine than he thinks a family of three would need, shoots the owner of the house but does not look into the loft for the English officer. Note that the old woman's pantomime is excellent. The English officer later escapes. There is a fine scene where he murders a German sentry with a jack-knife. He returns to England as a Belgian refugee; gets to his country place on Christmas day, is unrecognised by the butler, is unrecognised by his wife (he has been reported dead). He tells his adventures as a story to please the children, is recognised by his wife; alleged traces of hardship utterly disappear with a shave; he appears suddenly *in the same uniform* he had set out in, Sam Browne and all, in perfectly fresh condition.

The repetition of his original adventures on the screen while he is telling his story is a bore. It is shortened but not shortened enough. There is one close piece of scenario writing and excellent pantomime when the butler shuts out the dog, so that the wife will not have the sudden shock of the dog's recognising the officer too suddenly. The chance of allowing the dog to recognise the beloved master on later stretch of film is not taken.

In *Tares* we are presented with a very English newly married couple of Belgians—a baker and his wife who inhabit the same scenery as that used for the Belgian part of *The Refugee*. I note this only because it precludes the couple's being taken for Englished French people instead of Englished Belgians. We are asked to believe that suicide is the only means by which the woman can prevent giving birth to an illegitimate semi-Hun. Consistent as this view may be with life as permitted in English "best sellers" it is scarcely convincing as a portrayal of Continental thought. Mr.

80

Thurston should have read the discussions of this interesting problem as printed in the *Mercure de France*.

The French courts declined to convict, when a victim of similar outrage proceeded along different lines. I mention this only because Mr. Thurston has written a preface about "reality which war has brought home to the people of Belgium and of Northern France."

ART NOTES[31]
Parallelograms

The man in the street is neither called nor chosen to admire the works of Cézanne, Manet, Picasso, or even to applaud the effects of El Greco's astigmatism. With all due respect to his taste, it makes little difference whether he admires these highly specialised products of very rare temperaments. If he demanded Manets for home consumption there would not be enough to go round.

The health of a nation's fine art, or, let us say, of its finest art, depends on there being a few dozen people who have sufficient taste and foresight to buy enough contemporary work to keep the half dozen best contemporary painters and sculptors from starving. In the days of Rembrandt there were scarcely enough people to do this. In fact, the man of genius usually finds the state of a "nation's" art very unhealthy, and for himself in especial.

It is said that architecture is the first of the arts to arrive in a civilisation. In the middle of the last century architecture gave way to plumbing and sanitation. The best minds in the building trade were not builders but plumbers. An inspection of London's streets can lead to no other conclusion.

The day Queen Victoria married Prince Albert, of somewhere or other, the excellent Hanoverian tradition came to an end. The English automatically ceased to care what their town houses looked like. Forty years later the golden era of plumbing set in. Edward the Seventh, then Heir Apparent, discovered, we imagine, a plumber. The stationary bath-tub made its first bashful appearance. It was followed by the splendours of porcelain. Never since the days of the Roman decadence has the world known such plumbing as we in this era enjoy. But the art of making house-fronts has been wholly eliminated by drains.

From the charm of the old houses in Shepherd Street (W.1), with their mouldering dank basement areas, I ascend toward Marble Arch. No expense has been spared. I find hideous and expensive new houses, and I

[31]*The New Age*, October 17, 1918, pp. 400–1. Signed "B. H. Dias."

find the back of the new cinema at the Marble Arch corner an excellent piece of work. And so it goes. The cinema wants to be art, but there is not enough civic sense in this nation to inform people that it is a crime to put up visual abominations to last for ninety-nine years. English suburbs are nearly as bad as modern French suburbs, than which there is nothing worse, not even the German art nouveau houses on the Venetian Lido.

We are threatened with any amount of building and housing after the war. The daily Press is dealing with the matter, chiefly in relation to cottage building. Popular writers have the sense and decency to be crying out against ornaments. There are also the city house-front, the small city house-front, and the suburban house-front to be considered.

If the God of the English had any aesthetic sense, or if the Established Church wished really to save the souls of the people, there would be a crusade against "trade ornament"; against ornamentation by machine. Here, if anywhere, is employment for the Suffragettes' rusting hammers. Here, if anywhere, is a justification of sumptuary laws, and a provocation to violence. You have enough ornament in the judicial and political systems; why must we have it also on cornices, by the yard, by the rod, by the 10,000 roses and volutes?

I have looked carefully at over eighty old houses. It would seem as if almost any parallelogram front, punctuated by any arrangement of smaller parallelograms, could be beautiful *if* it was erected before 1840. It would seem almost as if no possible arrangements of such parallelograms could be beautiful *if* erected after 1875.

All the brains have gone into devising new and luxurious lines for bath-room fitting and for the bodies of automobiles. *Line* in automobiles has been for years magnificent and expressive. There is as much character as you like in some of the bull-nosed big cars. Each age has its qualities and its own particular blindness. *Yet* there are various publications devoted to architecture. The Olde Country House is an object of sentiment, and no country is richer than England in this form of elaborate ornament. Does the Englishman go automatically blind the moment he enters a city or the suburb of a city? It is, of course, a gentleman's country. Architecture is provided for gentlemen; the plebs have only got as far as pianos. Before the cities can have a decent appearance there must be a great popular rebellion, a board school rebellion against stupid building, and against hideous house-fronts. This is a form of art which does concern every man. Every man, or nearly every man, lives inside of something, and every man walks in the streets.

THE A.B.C.

"How to look at a house front." Architecture of detached buildings is akin to sculpture, as far as the exterior is concerned. The façade of a city house

set in a block is, however, a composition in two dimensions only, and one judges it by the same sense of composition used for a picture. Where one is dealing with a uniform row of houses, the individual front is a unit of the pattern.

As we said a few weeks ago, the old Regency pseudo-classic style serves very well in blocks. But whether one judges the single front in itself, or as part of the row, the question of its proportions is similar. And, to keep hammering on the most elementary points, it is (a) a matter of the composition of window parallelograms in the whole, (b) ornamentation.

Take the most hideous houses in London: the row of six story plus basement red striped with yellow abominations on Observatory Avenue, Campden Hill. No jerry-built horror of Clapham exceeds the rankness of these huge hideosities. They are so hideous that one remembers them above other hideous houses in London. We first perceive that ornament has a good deal to do with it. This thought gives way on more careful analysis to the perception that the actual mass of each house is not bad (not offensive unless one have a prejudice against mansards). The height of the windows has been graduated, but not their breadth, *and* the windows are set too close together. The whole effect is appalling. The process by which one discovers this, *despite* the bewilderment of bad mouldings, stripes of hideous colour, convolutions, and so on, is the same as the process whereby one determines that any picture in any sort of art show is well or ill composed.

If the public, or even a very limited and select portion of the thinking public, is to develop any better sense of art than it now has, it must begin by these very simple sorts of analysis, by these very simple but personal judgments about form, about shapes and proportions. I cannot see that it matters whether one begin in the street, or whether one disentangle the elements of a composition from the paint-smears of the Boldini school. One wants something "beyond" the general sloppy sentimental appraisements of *Colour* and the people who talk about the "soul of the artist."

ART NOTES[31a]
Super-fronts

I am more interested in the "normal" house or shop than in the occasional exceptional building. At least the multiplied unit is more important in city-building. And it is the subject on which the sense of composition should begin to exercise itself. Vitruvius begins, I believe, at the other end of the subject. If there are not prepared tables of the possible proportions

[31a]*The New Age*, October 24, 1918, p. 414. Signed "B. H. Dias."

of window parallelograms in larger parallelograms, there at least could be very serviceable tables of good proportion and they might almost be included in a shilling manual. Palladio began, I believe, by getting good façades, and much Italian renaissance work got no further. The façade is a two dimensional affair. I do not intend to imply that it is "all there is to architecture." It is simply the part of architectural art which comes first into the scope of this criticism and, being in the street, most concerns the man in the street.

Going on to the un-uniform or unusual buildings put up in London during the last ten years or so—buildings which we can take as examples of "what is being done"—we find some traces of intelligence, and a great deal of mediocrity and stupidity.

The Catholic Cathedral has an excellent exterior, and the interior was impressive until they began to encrust it with shamrocks in mother-of-pearl, and to put in too much soapy marble. The Methodist building by the Abbey is a good piece of structure utterly ruined by bad, I suppose Viennese, ornament. It had one virtue before completion, a virtue now obscured by the "finish." One entered through a small door, and as one proceeded one had gradually the sense of liberation, larger and larger doors and halls; this in contrast to many buildings where a mountain door opens into a mole-hill apartment.

There is a really fine pre-renaissance structure in Jermyn Street. Interest attaches to the Christian Science Church in Half-Moon Street, off Piccadilly. From Piccadilly one sees apparently the whole façade. The architect who won the competition in the plans for this church was the only one who looked first at the site of the building, and then made his plans accordingly. The lot on which the church is built extends some thirty feet further east. Other architects put the centre of their proposed buildings in the centre of the lot, *not* in the centre of the part of the lot visible down the length of Half-Moon Street.

The rarity of what would seem the simplest forms of commonsense in the arts is almost amazing. The curve of the girders or arches inside this church is excellent. The architect has shown a natural talent, or an acquired talent, or at any rate a fine feeling, for space. The steel window frames are not well set, and his sense of ornament is defective.

Automobile companies seem to show care for the appearance of their premises. Presumably their experts are continually thinking about structure, and they are also accustomed to steel. As we have said before, bad metal construction persisted as long as people tried to use metal as if it were stone. Metal has a binding as well as a supporting property. The pictures one sees of modern American building show that the better American architects have amply grasped this. In steel buildings the wall is not a support but a curtain. Wherever architects realise steel and its

84

possibilities and cease trying to disguise the medium, a new grace comes into the buildings.

Certainly there has been a limited attempt to attain severity in some contemporary buildings. Plainness would appear to be almost the sole road to health. The Ritz is not new, it is respectable and uninteresting, very ordinary pseudo-late-renaissance plus mansard. The sheltered space under its portico is useful in wet weather. Above this portico there is a line of carved faces. In any sensitive period the job of making these faces would have been given to a sculptor. Any sort of personal endeavour to make interesting faces on the keystones would have made the Ritz almost interesting as a building. There must be or must have been thirty or forty young sculptors who would have done this work almost for the fun of it, for the chance of putting their work in a relatively permanent position; for the chance of doing a good job. They would have done it just as cheaply as the four-by-six stone cutter.

When the official taste is as bad as it is at present, one would almost think that private building enterprise of this sort was the sole opportunity for architecture and sculpture to meet. There was a start in the right direction when someone whose name is now forgotten commissioned the Epstein statues in the Strand. Any active tendency of this sort is to be welcomed. One cannot say that the University of London has been felicitous, or that the new building on Marylebone Road has done well with its lions, though its general structure is good.

It is almost incredible that with some of the best sculpture in the world stored in the British Museum English sculpture should have stuck dead in the Albert Memorial period for so many years. One of my colleagues began an outcry against the allegorical figures of British sculptural building-ornament some years ago, and the question should not be allowed to lapse too completely. Even some of the people who exhibit in the Royal Academy are better than those who are permitted to set up figures over doorways of banks and of government departments, in public places, that is, where hundreds and thousands of people can and do look at them daily.

"But if there aren't the sculptors!" If there aren't the sculptors, if there is so appalling a dearth of talent; why the mania for completion? The cathedrals were often a long while in building. One could at least leave the blocks in the rough until the talent arrived. The unfinished blocks would serve as an incentive to young sculptors. When one thinks of Gaudier-Brzeska too poor to buy stone for his work, one can readily believe that had the Ritz blocks been left rough, he would have been often only too glad to carve them at a guinea a mask; and Piccadilly would have been that much the richer.

The Stones of Venice which gave such delight to John Ruskin must have been carved upon some such system. Are we never to escape from the dead hand of Monsieur Viollet le Duc?

ART NOTES[32]
Leicester Gallery, Etchings

The Leicester Gallery show is extremely interesting and the modern masters of etching are nearly all represented by at least one piece of their best work. It is not a show to be missed by anyone interested in "the not very interesting medium." No medium is of much interest in itself, and if etching has suffered more than any other from the work of cheap-jacks, other mediums have suffered and suffer.

Manet's dark-blotted "Olympia" is one of the gems of the collection; of the fifty Whistlers there are all sorts and conditions, the earliest of merely biographical interest, the last Amsterdam pair showing his final mastery.

There is the bare and definite in "Black Lion Wharf" (182) with its properly "Whistlerian" economy of line; the distinct, "Soupe à trois sours" (184a); the well-known dry-point portrait of himself, and the portrait of Becquet of about the same period. The Tanagra period, exquisite in his pastels, is indicated in 191, "Model Resting." "Tatting" (192) epitomises the Victorian hell, the Mrs. Meynell period with a touch of almost Balzacian fustiness.

"The Adman and Eve" (195) is well known. "Upright Venice" serves to remind one of the glory of all Whistler's Venice. It is a perfect etching, and one would perhaps be able to value it as such, but the memory of pastels and Whistler's Venetian colour comes upon one, and one is, perhaps too soon, discontented. The thing wants extension into colour. "Mairie, Loches" (200) deserves attention. But the utter mastery comes in "Long House" (202). One does not think about its being an etching; one takes it directly as a picture. It is last phase of Whistler, the important phase, or, rather, an important phase, more important than even the enthusiasts have agreed.

The Whistlers are well arranged. Roughly, one groups them as early and Victorian work, important; then the clear, hard, definite, one might almost say, Meryon manner, save that J. McN. is dead and should not be deprived of an answer.

These give great pleasure as etchings.

Then the dry-points, a progress, but not, perhaps, so satisfactory; then several periods where the etchings are rather a reference to his other work, as in "Model Resting," and even in the excellent "Venice." Then the "Balcony" (201), and more especially "Long House," where one does not

[32]*The New Age,* November 21, 1918, pp. 44–45. Signed "B. H. Dias."

think of the medium at all. It excels in suavity, by tone, and the ease in originality which is, in Whistler, the ultimate reward of a lifetime's uncontented continuous respect for all the details of his art.

No Whistlerian will, and no art student should, miss inspecting the West wall. The show in its entirety gives ample chance to study the whole matter of modern etching. It would be of interest even without the Whistlers.

7. O. Hall, technically good. 11. Glyn W. Philpot, Condering with a dash of Ricketts. 15. C. W. Cope, R.A., trial proof and finished state, excellent chance to see how the Victorian rot rotted. 22. Rops. No. There is, however, a good Rops of a satyr holding an image.

Mary Cassatt holds her distinction and originality, a little Hindoo in mode, both the strength and weakness of her talent are in 25. 50 is one of the few successful colour etchings, and the colour is superb. On the wall opposite the Whistlers her two prints hold attention; suavity in "Le Sein." "Maternité," 163, maintains the impression.

"Noctes Ambrosianae" (26), the blurry deep bit, and 132, "Old Hotel Royal," come as a much-needed reminder that Walter Sickert was an artist. "Legrand" (35) bad Degas. 47. M. Bauer, merit.

Berthe Morisot series of dry-points, worth looking at and of charm—both 60 and 53. Besnard has mood in "La Femme." 78. The series "Vie d'une Femme" has a narrative interest, a vigour in imagination, or recording of life, less interest as actual workmanship. Latouche, 81, excellent. Manet's "Les Chats" is interesting, but, as noted, the "Olympia" is the masterwork.

Meryon's architectural fidelity and charm show in 98, and the clear lining comes, I think, better in this than in the connoisseurshipist's preferred print on green paper; which loses much that is characteristic of this master.

Legros's 102 is clearly executed. Cameron's "Berwick" is charming. E. A. Cole, 109, swank. Degas shows levity in 110, but the "Au Louvre" is very important, both for the comedy of the female in the chair and for the Etruscan figures in the case. The drawing of these gives one a wink at certain more modern "innovations." Cassatt's distinct style I have mentioned.

James McBey has something to him. "In Moroccan Market" we find an interesting arrangement of triangles more or less isosceles. I found my eye coming to rest on other of his works, as "Gunsmiths, Tetuan." M. Bauer, "Kremlin," has an air—somewhat deceptive. Pissarro, in the main, a very much over-estimated artist, is quite good in 137.

The Forains are uneven in interest; his drawing can scarcely be without some attraction. He is excellent in "Maison Close." Besnard, again, has Iberian charm in "Pensive." Steinlen, from whom one must now and again demur, is good in "Bourg-Breton," 205. Meryon, à la Durer, 208.

C.R.W. Nevinson does very poorly in this august gathering; "The Estuary" is a composition which recalls the puppy and the damp umbrella, "On dira encore que c'est moi" picture, once so familiar in Paris.

Picasso is represented by two prints, the simple "Roi d'Yvetot" and "Femme au Miroir" representing an early period of his work too little known here in London; the inception of his cubism is indicated in the distinctive right-angle elbow of the male figure, to be found in his "Man at the Table," and other work of this period. This is, with the final Whistler, the Manet and the Degas, among the most interesting prints in the show.

I think the aesthetic of etching must make some sort of division, not merely a higher and lower, but a separation in mental approach, between "the Meryon sort of thing" which is delightful because it is good etching; and the late Whistler, Manet, and, even here, the Picasso, sorts of things which are delightful *irrespective* of their being etching at all. One wants to recognise a difference in kind.

LONDON GROUP, AT HEAL'S

Very much the same thing and same group as last year, all a year older, some a year wiser. Roman pavement by Anrep (once van). Bevan and Ginner, commendable. Wolfe, No. Portraiture by Hamnett and Allinson. Gaudier-Brzeskeque and Paris approximation of animal and vegetable forms shows up in Fry's caterpillar tree and in somebody else's duck-eye. Lessore, fading cubism. Allinson, "L. Gamallt," *mit seele*. Gertler, visible.

C. Billing is studying Matisse to advantage. Water-colours, in general perhaps better than the oils, etc. Refer to our last year's notice for general tonality and personnel of the group.

Gertrude and Harold Harvey (exhibition at Leicester Gallery) should have no difficulty in getting their work reproduced in *Colour*.

ART NOTES[33]
Jean de Bosschère, and the Less Fortunate

Art, as exposed in the shows opened during the past month, has been almost wholly lugubrious. M. de Bosschère is the best of it, but even his exposition at the Leicester Gallery must be viewed with mingled feelings of pleasure and bitterness. This artist is an excellent draughtsman, a draughtsman of unusual endowment; he has all sorts of technical skill: there is keen intellect in his eliminations in drawing *when* he is doing his own particular work, as in the black and white drawings and frontis-

---

[33]*The New Age*, December 26, 1918, pp. 126–27. Signed "B. H. Dias."

piece portrait for "The Closed Door." We note the admirable Cubing and analysis in the portrait of himself, the mastery of line and of composition.

But for the rest, the drawings appear as if made to order and in commerce's most shameful livery. They are an Albert Hall masked carnival with a job lot of costumes, à la Dulac, à la Rackham, à la Persia, à la China; with, perhaps, a trace of old Flemish influence almost wholly obfuscated. It is as if the artist had concealed his own honestly ironic and macabre countenance under the sloppily amiable mask, barber-pink cheeks and white wool whiskers of Father Christmas. Fortunately, the disguise does not wholly cover the actor beneath it. There are shown alternately an understanding of character, a perception of the ludicrous, deliberate slop, damned prettiness, technical skill, sometimes beauty. There is invention, a pot pourri, sometimes translatable into the bald English literality of the phrase. In "The Singer" there is excellent execution in the upper figures, and a memory of Stefano da Verona; "Two Friends," excels in the macabre. In the "War God," we feel that the artist might have taken long enough to eliminate the Mestrovic figure; 49-50-51 show him in his nudity; in the portrait we note the coffin-lid hat; all through the tragic-ludicrous presentations we feel what a fine book De Bosschère really could make if he were given a masterpiece, a great classic, to illustrate, and if he were set loose without some presumable publisher demanding the vendable.

The Etchings are still on show at the "Leicester" (vide my note of some weeks ago). I noticed, again, Belcher's "Mrs. Harris"; Besnard's "La Femme"; a pair of gaudy stockings, by Gaston Latouche; and a curious phase of Whistler in "La Marchandise de Moutarde."

The "Camouflaged Ships" pictures at the Goupil have no aesthetic value whatever. It is apparent that the camouflagers applied vorticism to the ships; vorticism being apparently the only art-theory in England which is based on the actual effect of form and colour on the human eye. Had the war come in the days of Manet, they would have used, or have tried to use, impressionism, and spotted the ships in small dabs. The stripe system must be easier to inculcate in port-painters and labourers. When dealing with actualities and necessities only these non-metaphysical systems of aesthetics are of any use. The metaphysics of the mangel-wurzel post-impressionist, Kandinskysts, Fryites, etc., have not availed during the war. Mr. Everett, however, confines his vorto-cubism to the representation of the ships. Backgrounds, etc., are filled in on the old *Pears' Annual* chromo system. It is difficult to focus Picabia and Poynter simultaneously. Some of the later "dazzle" designs, as shown in photographs and the manual of dazzle, are of aesthetic interest; Mr. Everett's paintings of none.

There is some sense of distortion in 24. 29 is à la Nevinson; 36 is simple oleo, and the ships are so far in the distance that their designs do not affect the splotch of the whole. 48 is pretty. 9 illustrates faintly the supposition that the design on the ship might confuse the man under the periscope.

F. Sancha's exhibit at the Twenty-one Gallery is plain and flat. There is no reason why he shouldn't exhibit with his contemporaries at Heal's. Bevan, Gilman, Ginner, on the other hand, might exhibit at the Twenty-one Gallery. One wonders that several of their group do not try to demonstrate their scope (if extant) by one-man shows in the smaller galleries.

The statuettes at the Fine Arts Society rooms in Bond Street are just academy stuff, boudoir and parlour-ware. There is a trace of ability in one thing by Bertram Mackenna. But they have the crust to show a small bronze of Watts' "Physical Energy," as if the minds of the citizens had not been sufficiently galled by the chryselephantine abortion of this composition which disfigures Kensington Gardens. Certainly, it proves that England suffered no metal famine during the war; but we are no longer in need of that stimulus.

Raemaekers' work is so important as political documentation that one does not wish to insult this great pamphleteer of drawing by discussing the ninth-rate draughtsman. As a man who has done fine political work against Germany Herr Raemaekers is worthy of every respect. The cartoons—there must be over a hundred—are on show at the Fine Arts Society.

The fine Canalettos, noted in these columns some months ago, are still to be seen in another Bond Street Gallery.

The "Author-Artists Exhibition" at the Little Art Rooms, Duke Street, shows that the Adelphi is swarming with small "galleries"; it also shows that a certain group of people who are, in writing, for the most part, unserious, have determined to be wholly unserious in the use of pencils and brushes. The exhibit is a tribute to the jolly English belief that it is better to be a duffer at several things than to do anything really well. It is the lovely amateur spirit that likes to think of the arts (or anything else that one can't excel in) as a species of joke. We believe from hearsay, and we, at any rate, hope that a novelist who enjoys so wide a popularity as Mr. Arnold Bennett, is more efficient with his pen than he appears to be with his brush. The bold Belloc exhibits one modest and neatly-drawn sketch of "Palace of the Hague and the Hotel de Ville, Louvain." The sketch is so small that probably only half the title belongs to it. Mr. Chesterton rollicks through a couple of book illustrations worthy of the worst Crystal-Palace period of illustration. Cora Gordon has some little pen jokes of babies and cats, Haldane Macfall shows some fuzz. Commander Dion Clayton Calthrop follows Conder at an almost incalculable distance in 48. Mr. Bennett's "Garden Cammarges" has really no merits whatever. Mr. Guthrie's "gesso" and oleos are uncalled-for. Calthrop is neat, almost gaudy in 39.

The proprietor of the Gallery assures me that he is going in for living artists of all save the most modern schools, and that he will have books on art for sale.

The Fine Arts Society should be thanked for the Raemaeker's exhibit, and also for an exhibit of Persian art, which, if I remember rightly, I had no space to mention at the time.

ART NOTES[34]
Canadian War Memorial: A commendation

The present Canadian war exhibit at Burlington House is a very pleasant surprise; for the first time in "history" or for at least the first time in one's memory quite a reasonable number of good paintings have been hung in these spacious galleries; and when one considers what official art is; when one considers the difficulties of gathering three hundred or four hundred pictures, painted to order, illustrating a given subject, one is more than ready to commend the work of the Canadian War Records office. The show is more or less what the "Academy" ought to be; that is to say, all schools of contemporary painting are represented without dogmatic bias. The gamut extends from the deplorable efforts of Mr. Bundy to the work of the moderns, John, Lewis, Turnbull, Kennington, Nash, and through various intervening schools, to the quiet paintings of Talmage, Gilman, Kerr-Lawson.

Mr. Bundy's canvases are the sort of coloured soap and scented dishwater which a discredited body like the Royal Academy might have been expected to unload on the Ottawa savages had no other force intervened; but these two horrors are exceptions in the exhibit.

Turnbull is the discovery of the committee. His pictures, painted as if from the actual airplane, combine designs good enough for the most abstract art with the "representation" demanded by Sir Claude Phillips and his unintelligent following. Apart from the fact that Mr. Turnbull's work can be demonstrated to show the wings, guns, etc., of the airplanes and patches of field beneath them, there is nothing to segregate it from the admiration of the advanced spectator who has already discovered virtue in Picasso, Matisse, the futurists, cubists and vorticists. In 77 he might have made the wing-outlines a little more definite; a matter simply of re-painting one or two lines with a little more smoothness and hardness. Nash shows four or five drawings which we have already commended in our note on his own exhibition. Mr. Kennington is very skilful, and the elephant huts is a good composition. Mr. Roberts' sort of SS (double s) melange is rather confused; there is flurry but no "dust of action," and the

[34]The New Age, January 16, 1919, pp. 179–80. Signed "B. H. Dias."

red of the Zouave uniforms is not quite satisfactory in relation to the rest of the canvas; it suggests the displeasing posterism of Byam-Shaw. Still Roberts' picture is one of the good pieces in the show, and one must consider that he had to make a greater break with his former work (vorticist) than let us say Sims or Gilman.

Mr. Lewis' picture will excite comment. Certainly many officials must have shuddered at the thought of having *Blast*'s editor thrust among them, and it is difficult to conceive what Mr. Lewis' mental attitude must have been while trying to meet official commissions. The picture has sinister tone, as befits a painting of war. The design is clean and apparent, and in this it contrasts most favourably with nearly all the other large canvases, its composition gaining by contrast with Roberts' curleycues shown beside it. The faces are intense and intent on the matter in hand, i.e. working the gun; the khaki and mud are held by the El Greco blue of the sky. The most interesting parts are the red leather waistcoat and the big pink-shirted nigger in the foreground, painted more nearly as one would imagine Mr. Lewis would have painted had he not been on an official job. Indeed, the feline Negro is quite up to Lewis' own standard, or at any rate worthy of the painter of "Kermess," the "Red Duet," the Timon portfolio.

John's panorama is not yet painted. One needs to get far back from the huge charcoal drawing to untangle it. At present it is of uneven interest, the drawing excellent in parts; presumably the colour will clarify the composition. It is now a promissory note; but it promises a good deal and bids fair to demonstrate the value of official encouragement of painting. I mean that John has been getting slacker and slacker for some years; he has been repeating himself; this chance to cover some hundreds of square yards of canvas with the surety that it will be properly hung in a suitable building and with proper perspective has evidently been the needed stimulus, and there is no reason why the result should not stand comparison with the Rubens room in the Louvre, the big Italian renaissance frescoes, or the mural work of Tiepolo.

One cannot see three hundred and fifty-five pictures in two hours and know all about all of them. I have mentioned the main points of interest. The Canadian artists: Varley, Gyrth Russel, A. J. Munnings, deserve commendation. Brangwyn's "Vimy" (278) is perhaps the best of the lithographs. Taking the pictures in detail, as far as fatigue permits, I found: Cameron (3) touch of quality; Nevinson (4) muzzy; Nevinson "Roads in France" worse than even I had expected of him; Gilman (5) Halifax Harbour, air and light, rather good; S. J. Soloman (7) Moroni, manqué; Gyrth Russel (9) good colour; Byam-Shaw (10) symbolic bluff; Anna Airy (17) Luxembourg, old Paris salon stuff; C. Sims "Sacrifice" (20) symbolic pseudo-impressiveness, well painted in parts; A. Atwood (23) granulated and blurred; Jack (28) certain amount of movement, but . . . ; Laura Knight (29) has learned nothing from Segonzac; on the whole rather deplorable; Forbes (31) granulated; N. Wilkinson (33) water questionable; Kerr-Lawson, Ypres cloth-hall, well drawn; Lavery (46 and 51) clear air; Kennington (63) skilful; Lewis (66) discussed above; Roberts (67) ditto; W. Rothenstein (68) washy; (71) "Whistlerian" pastel; Nevinson (78-81) bad, as noted; Varley (92) good, vide supra; B. Lintot (93) high class oleo; A. Barne (109) good portrait; G. E. Moira (96) post-Puvis prettifying, but probably well planned to fit into the well-designed building, painting as an adjunct of architecture; Ambrose McEvoy (102) better than usual, (111) slop; Bundy (116) soap, as noted; (123) comic effect, false colour à la 1871; A. Y. Jackson (122, 124, 125) good; Varley (131), Russel (134) merit, as noted; L. Weirter (135) nowhere in particular; Cullen (137) merit; Munnings (147) merit; Talmage, forestry corps pictures, (174) etc. merit. Derwent Wood handles his bronze well, and is, I think, the best sculptor in England after Epstein; one wishes he were less photographic, but in the "Golgotha" he has manipulated his medium well; the thing is not the horror the *Daily Mail* had led one to expect; the bricks of the wall are not spoiled sugar marble; he has skilfully avoided the fatal trap of the Cross which is so apt to ruin design, and gets an interesting composition by the obtuse V of the arms, against the two sets of beams in the wall, and the repetition of the V more acute in the grouping of the Huns; the treatment of the crucified officer's coat and collar in continuous loopline, contributes well to the composition. Moira (192) no raison d'être; J. W. Beatty (194) commendable try for stylization; L. Richmond (216) poor medium for subject, much better in smaller pictures (217), etc.; Armington (262) economy of pigment, clean; R. Jack (269) sort of thing to which he might confine himself with advantage.

In conclusion, one should say a word in commendation of the whole scheme, and of Rickard's admirable plans for the building which is to contain the collection. The architect has a fine flair for space. The presence of pictures in Burlington House naturally recalls the Academy. Last year we suggested a means of improving it; failing that or in addition to it, the present show leads one to suggest that Mr. Konody should be made a committee of one to select, hang, draw, quarter and otherwise manage the Academy exhibits until some more drastic measure can be provided. He has at least demonstrated that the action of officialdom in the arts need not be wholly malign. One does not know what resistance he has overcome, or how much further he would have gone if left to his own free will. Official art must, I suppose, be comprehensible to the majority of the electorate; that being so, the Canadian Committee may be felicitated on having done about as well as possible.

On the other hand: there was more war in the repeated V angles of the "Revolt" and in the funeral picture at Marinetti's pre-war futurist show than anywhere in this exhibition. The Canadians have given a black eye to the Tate and to the Chantrey Bequest, and the late boss of the Academy has passed into desuetude. One hopes some stir of movement has been made, but there is still plenty of room for advance, and one hopes, even though war is retrogressive in tendency, that some other Dominion or some other committee of Empire will go the whole hog, and commission the recording artists to paint the thing wholly as they have seen it and felt it; remembering that a "memorial" should speak not to the present but to the future, and that the revolution of to-day is the convention of to-morrow; and that no future generation would have blamed the French government if they had commissioned Manet in his lifetime. But when one thinks of what the Academy would have done to Ottawa, one must cordially compliment the officials and the critic who have prevented their doing it. The show is probably as good as circumstances permit; it is at any rate a move in the right direction.

All the commissioned pictures are not yet finished. I noted Wadsworth's name on the plans, and one hopes that work by Epstein, Bevan, Ginner, Hamnet, Haines, Bomberg, and a few others will be included.

ART NOTES[35]
Canada, and the Remnants

The problem is economic, and the Canadian War Memorial has proved that "official" art or official support of painting does, or at least can, pay.

"The whole of the great expenses incurred in the formation of the collection have been defrayed by other enterprises of the Canadian War Records Office." By running films, "publications," etc., in connection with painting, and apparently not counting the shillings about to be taken at the door of Burlington House, a large collection of paintings, including several works of art, has been acquired by the Canadian government.

The Mercure de France for January 1 opens with an "Appel aux poetes, aux artistes" to form a Grand Atelier in Paris to develop a communal style, and shoot the "rays and clarity of the flower of civilisation across a renascent world." Paris is firmly convinced that such a Grand Atelier would pay somebody, either the world, French artists, or both.

Having at bottom no interest in official art or official support of the arts save in so far as they might be used to produce a little (or even quite a lot) of good art, one begins to speculate. If the public will flock, at a shilling a head, to see three hundred and fifty pictures, containing only a few of what even the Evening News calls "oases," would it not flock in

[35]The New Age, January 30, 1919, p. 212. Signed "B. H. Dias."

equal numbers to see four hundred and fifty paintings containing at least fifty "oases"?

I do not believe that "under the circumstances" the Canadian government could have been persuaded to accept a more contemporary collection; but having broken the back of the Academy "old gang"; having really, by a triumph of tact, insinuated a few works of interest into an official collection, should not the promoters of the enterprise he cheered on, encouraged, prodded, threatened, cajoled, anything you like, into continuing the good work? Should not New Zealand, or Queensland, or the Maharaja of Molahawak be reminded that art has paid Canada; that Canada has got her money back, and has a collection of paintings beside?

A lot of money has gone to a lot of artists, some of whom ought to have it. There must be waste in the arts; you must have a huge flood of art in order to get a little good art. There must be "competition," both among artists, and among buyers. Some other Dominion ought to want a better collection than Canada's. (And it ought to be quite easy to get it.) Some other office ought to begin where the Canadians have left off. They should start with John, Gilman, Lewis, Turnbull, Kennington, Roberts, whose second war pictures would all, almost of necessity, be an advance on their first. The "of necessity" is not vague conjecture. None of these men are or were illustrators; every one of them went at a new job; each of them adapted his own means to new conditions, *on demand*. I imagine that most of them made concessions.

One would like to see an exhibit, the nucleus of a permanent collection, in which the artist should be asked to say exactly what he thinks of the war, regardless of what the general spectator of pictures is for the moment ready to "hear." The more I think over the Canadian exhibit the more I find it inferior in warlikeness to the futurist canvases "Revolt" and the "Anarchist's Funeral," though neither of these canvases was satisfactory, or, perhaps, very well executed.

In Jack's largest atrocity there is a suggestion of the rhythm of bombardment, inferior to that produced by some of the Italian cinema films, but still a suggestion. The stasis of painting is perfectly capable of showing the feeling of violence; the cinema is only more facile, not more capable or capacious.

PASTELS

One goes from the "advance" of Canadian officialdom, across Piccadilly to the "Institute," and one wonders if there is any use for tolerance; if there is any use trying to see the good in all schools. Hugh Williams alone of all the pastelists is good enough to hang in Heal's gallery along with the London Group. Anna Airy's drawing for her Canadian War Record's picture is rather better than the picture. It would be an exaggeration to say that any member of the society has gone so far as to attain even a passable mimicry of Whistler's pastels.

There are two kinds of painter's ability: the ability to copy a set mode with remarkable skill; and the ability to "do something new"; to "express," or to open the beholder's eyes to some visual (or, perhaps, even emotional or metaphysical) quality not before apprehended. (I do not want to enter endless quibbling over other than optical values in painting. At least the artist must use eye-language. He must speak with form and colour, whatever he may wish to convey.)

Detailed analysis of the pastels "yields": Bernard Partridge (still a malevolent force apparently, mortmain continuing) 18, stumpy, 19, Murillo, thoroughly damned; T. Williams, touch of impressionism; M. A. Cohen, probably got a likeness in 28; R. G. Eves, R.O.I. distressing as ever; F. D. Bedford, 48, curable only by annihilation; A. S. Bennett, 68, at any rate, the grass is green; Bethia Clarke, unspeakable; M. A. Eastlake, 99, rot; 100, wild plunge into post-impression of P.R.B.ism; 103, the tongue wearies of blaming. M. Harris, 110, record parody of Augustus John; A. Hope, more successful in the faces of 111 and 112; 114, record parody of Velasquez. A. Hitchens, 119, chromo; Aimee Muspratt, 123, demands amputation; E. Lawrence-Smith left over Mucha, 133, "Bacchante," with nothing Bacchic save, perhaps, the thick ankles; S. Dowie, 147, also calls for amputation; 157, ditto; R. C. Wilkinson, might take to painting china; F. F. Foottet, that blue of Tintagoel, old romance of the period; Shepperson, penny plain in *Punch*, and 2d. coloured; H. Bedford, meritorious photos. A. Wardle worst in 236, better in 237; J. R. K. Duff, R.I., 245, really the worst "Venice" I have ever inspected. M. Fisher, shows restraint in 248, and good photography in 253; J. Littlejohn, bright colour, pseudo-Pryde; plus Russian ballet, etc.; W. Rossiter, verging toward the careful; L. Richmond, R.B.A., R.O.I., shows our old friend romance; D. Lyster attempts to make the exhibit artistic, Chelsea hunch; T. B. Wirgman's portrait of "Comrade Graham" is just recognisable; T. Hughes needs annihilation; L. Baumer tries to bring the Whistlerian near enough to Kirchner to be practical.

ART NOTES[36]
NAVY, MOSTYN, Lithography, Etc.

Two respectable painters in a week is a bag as unexpected as pleasurable. The pictures in the Sea Power Exhibition, Grosvenor Galleries, are worth

[36]*The New Age*, February 13, 1919, pp. 240–41. Signed "B. H. Dias."

seeing because of Major Charles Pears, R.M. The canvases of Lavery, McEvoy and Philpot call for some new form of abuse, but are not worth the expenditure of energy necessary to devise it.

One R.M. is obviously worth two hundred and eighty "R.A.""s. Pears greets one in the corridor with excellent clean pastels (Note 305). In Room III we find his oil work, clean, conscientious, with a drive for veracity, the work of a man who has seen the sea; who has had his eye on the object; who has set out to put down various effects of sea and light which might be considered rather incredible. There is hard light on "Thunderstorm, Harwich"; and veracity in 129, the best painting of "dazzle" ships I have yet seen. (Note 133.) He has thought about his work.

Lavery opens fire with grease and mud, note 31 greasy; P. Connard shows some average colour prints; Philpot, distressing portraits; McEvoy disgusting portraits, general laziness for which there is no need for any sympathy or tolerance, simply a man slopping through a bad job in perfect complacency. "Society Portrait Painter."—Give a dog a bad name!

F. Dodd shows drawings at about the level of American magazine illustration; 122 coloured is "impossible." Cecil King, couple of clean water-colours in the corridor, along with Sir John Lavery's grease. Sir John deserves as little pity, mercy or sympathy as does McEvoy, or Mr. Philpot. Wylie, under the glare of special electric light, looks bearable; Robt. Smith presents an example of false colour.

Tom Mostyn has given the Fine Art Society (Bond St.) its best show since the Persian miniatures. He paints mostly in an impressionist-to-pointilliste manner, bright colour skilfully used, with a rather personal way of contrasting thick squirly curves of paint, somewhat Monticelli, in figures with thinly painted suave backgrounds. One would say there is kinship with, or influence from, Böcklin, Conder, Velásquez' pictures of the Villa Medici Gardens. No. 11 might be an early work or an experiment in archaism, reverting toward "old English" (XVIIth century) styles.

5, orange and dragon-blood; 10, won't do, despite well painted sky; 17, thin paint, satisfactory; 20 and 23 excellent composition; 26, difficult colour scheme cleverly managed; 31, thin paint, commendable; 33, I think a failure; 35, the Monticelli figures and thin background, better than 1. No. 40, water properly vitreous; 45, Brangwyn touch not to be commended.

Mostyn has a sense of romance and of the staginess of nature, if that term can be understood without opprobrium.

The Duchess of Rutland's little drawings with silver-point effect, in the next room, are quite as good as anybody else's little drawings, and much better than the crayons of Mr. Eves. They are really quite as good as Mr. Sargent's tossed off little charcoal portraits, but nobody will believe that of a Duchess. Has not Mr. Sargent painted the prophets for the centre of Boston Kultur?

(I meant to add here a little disquisition about the functions of "aristocracy," but there are other exhibits demanding attention.)

ACADEMY

Having no painters and only five centenarians among its members the Royal Academy has elected an architect for its president. As Sir Aston Webb is over seventy, and as he is naturally more interested in achitecture than in painting, and as architecture is supposed to be a conservative sort of business, it is generally hoped by the rank and file of the academicians that Sir Aston will not give too much encouragement to impressionism and other forms of modern pictorial eccentricity. It is also hoped that the age limit for admission to the Academy will be raised from 63 to 67.

CINEMA

The manner in which the Surrender of the German Fleet film was given at Queen's Hall (Jan. 22) was a disgrace to cinematography and to whatever Government department is responsible for the film. Low visibility during the surrender would account for the poor quality of the negatives, but to use a secondhand lantern, an amateur operator, a worn-out positive, to give the thing out of focus, with a shatter and shiver reminiscent of the experimental bioscopes of twenty years ago, is inexcusable impertinence, especially as it is a double price show. The film is by Gaumont: J. Tait manages the present exhibition, but he had fled from London: Gaumont's own operator was said to be in charge of the machine. The quality of the screen effects would have disgraced a 3d. house. All the more irritating when one considers the excellent quality of the Italian war films; or the clarity of the images given in the Hepworth impossible "drama." If melodrama is worth such technique, what is to be said for such public presentation of a great historic event (accompanied by sentimental songs and a cliché lecture)?

LITHOGRAPHS, DILAPIDATIONS, ETC.

At Heal's, Muirhead Bone's "Shipyard from Crane" is conscientious and thoughtful; No. 2, not quite so successful. Hartrick is bad, very bad Belcher. Nevinson's 5 is clearly done. He is better when restrained by some such medium as lithography; which is emphatically *not* Mr. Kennington's medium. Kennington's 3 is pure bluff. Clausen in 2 gets in a haystack, as usual, this time it "represents" a furnace. He is better in 3. Maj. Pears had better stick to paint, lithography is not his spiritual fatherland. Nicholson takes advantage of the medium, and his "End of the War" is about the best thing present. John's "Dawn" is a mess. Prof. Wm. Rothenstein's "Triumph of Democracy" is the worst possible rummage sale of theosophic babu mahatmas, plus decayed Orpen "Tommy" to the left, plus slightly John female. Why Mr. Ricketts, a man of some cultivation, should have produced "Italia Redenta" passes my comprehension. Shannon (Charles not J. Jebusha) shows the arts being reborn in full nubile femininity out of some heterogeneous wreckage. E. J. Sullivan gives a joke, infants and a rainbow. Moira is omissible, wholly omissible. Dulac has made rather good use of the medium, and his colour scheme is felicitous. The design is clear if quite simple, and there is less finnicking detail than one usually finds in his work. There is, in fact, no superfluous detail. Shepperson is at his best in "Clearing Station" into which he has got a good deal of quality. His other prints are not above his average. Nevinson's "Making Engine" is nearly good. E. Jackson has no reason to exist. Brangwyn is best in "Going Abroad." His big stuff looks better on the catalogue covers than on the wall. One wonders how many of these people really cut their stones, and how many simply send drawings to a workman.

The Senefelder Club (Leicester Galleries) maintains a much higher technical standard of lithography. The show is worth more detailed criticism than space permits. Note especially Pissarro (3), Whistler (6), Signac (74), Conder (77), Forain (78), Vuillard (84), Degas (86) and more especially 93; all the lithographs here are drawn on the stone by the actual artists. Whistler's 1 is not up to his pastels; C. Shannon 7, good Victorian; H. Paul's 18 is clean as an etching; Carrière was better as a painter than as a lithographer; Signac shows a good colour; Conder's draughtsmanship is more easily discernible in 77 than it was in most of his painting; Vuillard is emphatically in his element; Forain, magnificent; Veber, amusing; Legros, neat; E. Gabain, grace in 64; fine blacks in 65; J. Copley, interesting in 36, very inferior Picasso in 40; Forain, 56 and 28, to be noted; F. E. Jackson, simple academism in 54; show well worth a visit.

George Thomson, shows pleasant oil and water-colour in next room; still life not so good as Nicholson; 34, simple dignity; 37, 44, 53, 54, 57, worth inspection; 50, clean and well composed.

Wyndham Lewis' extremely interesting show at the Goupil Gallery now open, notice to follow.

WYNDHAM LEWIS AT THE GOUPIL[37]

Mr. Lewis' picture of the "Gun Pit" is one of the few outstanding works at the Canadian War Records exhibit, but his drawings now at the Goupil Gallery are an advance on the painting, or else the painting is a retro-

[37]*The New Age*, February 20, 1919, pp. 263–64. Reprinted in *Selected Prose*, London, 1973, p. 396; New York, pp. 426–28. Signed "B. H. Dias."

gression from the drawings, one of which appears to be a more personal study for the left lower corner of the big picture.

As Mr. Lewis implies in his preface to the catalogue, there are two ways of regarding "war paintings"; first, as paintings (*vide* Mr. Lewis' remarks about Uccello); secondly, as illustrations of war (*vide* Mr. Lewis' remarks about Goya); as "paintings" Mr. Lewis' drawings are about the most successful war show we have had. There are fragmentary drawings like the detail of mechanism of the camouflaged gun, a mere study; there are intermediary states, and there are fully finished works like the drawings of gun pits; works which can be submitted to all the criteria. These works are signally free from the violence which characterised Mr. Lewis' pre-war productions. The artist is the antidote for the multitude. At least, there is antidotal art, whether one approves it or no. There is also art which needs antidotes. Mr. Lewis' art does not. The drawings in this exhibit could, most of them, hang in one's study without palling. This means that they are well composed, well constructed, and harmonious in their colour schemes.

What are called the tactile, but should be called the lift-ile values are excellent. I mean there is definite proof of anatomic skill in the degrees of tenseness of the various figures: the men, particularly the centre man, lifting the short balks preparatory to building the gun pit; the men hauling the gun; the larger figures pulling on the rope (40) all display the different, the quite different mechanical or physical strain of their attitudes; and this expression or exposure of bodily capability is shown by the artist with the fine graduation of a master. The layman will be hard put to tell you just why each figure expresses such a strain: the per-kilo, per-foot pressure in each instance. That is to say, the strain is exposed with great economy of means. So also is the devitalisation of the wounded as they return over their duck-boards.

By subtle gradations we come out of the technical problems of composition into the problems of "drawing," and thence into the illustrational qualities: man the alert animal peeping dog-like out of his protective burrow, nosing danger.

Another property of Mr. Lewis' work is its "partialness." I mean that every series of the three series of Lewis' drawings I have seen appears to be the beginning of some exposition which might go on indefinitely for the rest of the artist's life. (In two cases it has been continued by imitators.)

There seems no reason why Mr. Lewis should not go on for years unrolling the panorama of artillery labour, phase by phase of the operations; there is a complete world of the matter; just as there was a complete possible world of violent or impassive forms suggested by his "Timon"; or by drawings at the old Doré Gallery in 1914. The present show is manifestly only one corner of Mr. Lewis. But it is no function of mine to speculate about potentialities. I am here merely to find the good in each show as it opens regardless of "school," whether it be Mr. Nicholson's conscientious still life; or Mr. Geo. Belcher's gratuitous labour in refining his tones for drawings that will be made mediocre in weekly reproductions. Mr. Lewis' show is of no particular school; it touches his vorticist work at one corner, and Uccello or Signorelli, or perhaps Kunisada at another. One should perhaps run over to the National Gallery to discover just which primitive it should "recall" to one's memory. There is, or was, the little Judas in or near the front hall; and various other scenes of the crucifixion. Before the renaissance there were simplifications and elimi-nations quite as "revolutionary" as any we shall find at the Goupil. But I cannot see that these early Italians were more satisfactory.

It also appears to me a sign of resource that a man known chiefly as a revolutionary inventor of forms, and what his adherents termed "forms in combination," should now appear as a narrative painter with an ap-parently unlimited subject-matter, a capacity for suggesting unlimited subject-matter. I think the readers of *The New Age* have by now become reconciled to Matisse, Brancusi, Picasso, or, at least, to Van Gogh, Gaudier, Cézannne. I do not think the majority will find the present work of Wyndham Lewis "too advanced." There is, from the purely aesthetic point of view, a calm pleasure to be derived from clear tones, the cold air, the desolation of the Ypres Salient, with the pyramidal arrangement of three men in the wilderness. The sketches in the entrance room lose nothing by comparison with Turner's water-colours. Those who ragged Mr. Lewis five years ago for his cubism, futurism, vorticism, and so forth, will vainly seek for the old points of attack in these drawings. My own preference is for the rough, spirited oil painting, "To Wipe Out"; here the purely optical effects of shell-burst and of battle are fused with emotional expression. The figures in the lower right-hand corner are, I think, more satisfactory than even the pink-shirted nigger in the Canadian War Records picture. I would draw attention to the forms in 11, to the "Walking Wounded" (No. 17), to the treatment of combined figures in 29, to the concentration of force, to the gun mouth in 19, to the detail of 52: and my aim in this article has been to suggest that Nos. 11, 17, 32, 36, 39, 40, 41, 43, 45, 47, 53, are the best art that has "come out of the war"; but they have come a good deal more out of art; out of art's resistance to war, than out of war's much-vaunted "effect upon art." Indeed, Mr. Lewis would seem to suggest that art is a cut above war; that art might even outlast it.

ART NOTES[38]

Sir,—What is the use of Mr. Dias' treading on eggs? Mr. Wyndham Lewis is one of the five or six painters in this country whose work has any

[38]*The New Age*, February 27, 1919, p. 283.

significance, or who would take any sort of rank among the French "Independents." Neither Mr. Dias nor anyone else is qualified to speak of Mr. Lewis's work unless they have seen both the Baker collection and the collection of fifty "drawings" (mostly in rich colour) which I sent to New York for the Vorticist Exhibition, at which they were all of them sold, the best of them being now in Mr. John Quinn's collection.

EZRA POUND

ART NOTES[39]

Mr. Pound mistakes both my tone and my attitude; but whatever I might think of Wyndham Lewis' work, I cannot, in fairness to other artists, use these columns for the criticism of any painting save that which has been publicly exhibited. I have, as a matter of fact, seen the Baker collection, but I can include neither that nor the works which Mr. Pound sent to New York in an estimate of Mr. Lewis' work unless I am also to include the unexhibited work of Mr. Lewis' contemporaries. I am, however, quite willing to admit that Mr. Lewis is one of the dozen, or perhaps even the half-dozen English painters, whose work merits international attention.

International standards are difficult to appraise, and all our knowledge dates from before the war. Contemporary Japanese art consists in imitation of American magazine covers, and imitation of Brangwyn; Viennese art consists or consisted of Zwintscher, a gentleman who imitated old masters; who never, I think, painted a whole picture well, but who inserted in nearly every canvas some patch of masterly workmanship; and Klimt, who imitated Beardsley in gilded and gaudy colours. In Paris there was a Russian lady who did tricky eyes in one or other of the old salons; and there were Picasso, Matisse, Derain, posthumous exhibits of Rousseau, Laurencin (who is no better than some people in London), Metzinger (ditto), Picabia (emphatically ditto), Gleizes, and there was somewhere a person called Kandinsky, and a fine draughtsman named Pascin. Matisse was chiefly to be valued for his innovations in pure colour. In America there is an elderly gentleman called R. Henri; and the more "advanced" painters: Arthur Davies, W. Kuhn, and, if we may judge from reproductions (which we can't), a master of water-colour called Demuth.

This list is, naturally, not complete. There is Signac, De Segonzac, probably Balla, Severini; it is possible Casteluchio is still in the running, though he probably belongs to a past era, and one forgets how bad a painter may be when one hasn't seen his work for five years. There was also a man who painted allegorical Greek subjects in blue and white and

[39]*The New Age*, March 13, 1919, pp. 310-11. Signed "B. H. Dias."

hung in the Independents. All of which, let me repeat, is not an attempt to give a complete catalogue of living passable painters, but simply an endeavour to find out what one means by international standards. Does one mean to count in only living painters, or is one's bogey the Cézanne collection outside the Port Maillot, and the massed work of Van Gogh and Gauguin?

Lavery and Lambert used to have their paintings hung in the Venetian International, but one will scarcely suggest that this is a claim to international importance. An ideal British Academy would include, I suppose:

Nicholson, who is a careful and conscientious and meritorious painter, and one who hasn't stopped trying to make each picture a work of art with its own proper and individual interest.

Augustus John, who was the best painter in England ten years ago: who is not very strong in composition, and rather tends to imitate himself, and to let a single figure float waftily about in the middle of a canvas, and who is getting less exigent of himself each year.

Orpen, purely on the strength of past work, and not in any way on account of anything he is now doing or is now likely to do.

Pryde, because he once painted some rather good pictures.

Sickert, a man of talent who has done a certain amount of experimenting, honest colour schemes, and courage enough to try the ugly. He has at any rate suited himself, gone his own way, not with great individuality or originality.

Chas. Ricketts, a very talented archaeologist, and possessed of genius for water colour.

And after these gentlemen it seems to me we must chronologically reach Mr. Wyndham Lewis, peer, at the most moderate estimate, to any of the foregoing. I am willing to hear further nominations from anyone who admires members of the Royal Academy, the Society of Twelve, or other painting organisations.

Coming to the London Group we must first express our sincere regrets for the recent death of Harold Gilman, a sober and earnest painter, whose work will be greatly missed from their shows. There remain Bevan, Nina Hamnett, Chas. Ginner. And Albert Rothenstein is a talented draughtsman, though not of this group.

I have been going patiently to art shows for some years, but I cannot at the moment recall the names of any other English painters whose work I should care to possess, save that of the very "advanced" group, Wadsworth, Etchells and Roberts, and in the cases of these three I should want to make a very rigorous selection. None of these men and none of the members of the London Group are in Mr. Lewis' class. In sculpture England is

103

beneath all forms of contempt. Both Epstein, the devastator, and Derwent Wood, the hidebound and purblind Academician, are Americans. They are both in their separate ways excellent sculptors.

As for the rest of the painting in England, it consists in the modest private diversion of several untalented painters; the expression of several forms of conceit; the deliberate attempt to make money without any concern for art, and the purely unscrupulous bluff of Messrs. X, Y, Q, M., etc.

There are also some honest tradesmen earning their weekly and monthly living by fulfilling contracts, making illustrations, etc. There is also the type of person whose work is published in *Colour;* this constitutes a lower level of the various classes I have mentioned.

I have omitted names quite well known to the so-called "public," but I trust I have committed no sins of forgetfulness. (N.B.—If I *have* forgotten anyone I will admit the fact on receipt of notification.)

NATIONAL PORTRAIT SOCIETY

A lady of established social position asks me not to slate Sargent's portrait of Mrs. A. "because every fool in London has done so"; unfortunately there is no other reason for ignoring the fact that No. 22 is an exceedingly bad picture of almost the worst possible sort; and as a little card informs us that it has never been exhibited before, one wonders at the reputedly modest perpetrator's having permitted its present exposure. I have no doubt that the great man did so out of charity to his younger competitors, and in the hope that they would shine by comparison. Several do, and the show is almost worth visiting.

Guevara's "Walter Taylor" is clever, a good likeness, in an excellent colour-scheme of somewhat Matisse-like tonality. It is the most interesting canvas in the building, though it has a poor cat in the background. Guevara's No. 1 is fancy work. Strang's (2) is carefully delineated, and the paint well put on. V. Forbes, No. 4, prize example of bold desperadism. McEvoy's (5) has no merit. His (12) is the "sweet-pretty," his (31) has some nice colour in the background.

Wolmark (7), is Munichism gone to seed. E. B. Johnson shows in (8) a presumable likeness; Philpot, in (11), pseudo-old-masterism with some *métier;* Lavery in (13), some pretty obscuration. Rankin (14) slops along in McEvoy's vestiges. D. Jagger's (15) is posed. F. Howard, in (20), has made an excellent picture, but left out the likeness to his sitter; Sickert shows a probably commendable dirtiness in (21). John has the likeness of Davies in (23); Rankin's (24) is bad colour. W. J. Leech has probably drawn the face well in (33), and used simple and pleasing colour. G. F. Kelly does not shine as a sculptor.

104

O. Gardner (71), more incompetence; B. Munns has been very careful about Sir T. Beecham's shirt-front and waistcoat; Stuart-Hill uses suave tone in the coat and velvet, but has skimped the pearls, and the fur of (80). One might dismiss most of the rest of the show as "the usual bluffs and incompetences"; F. Hodgkins needs firm negation; Tytgat ditto; Strang's (192) is bad imitation of himself. Miss Hamnett is Paris of six years ago, and rather too wooden in (223), but considerably more successful in (210); E. Sawyer (239) shows the usual colour photo with rather unusual care.

ART NOTES[40]

Sir,—We can readily understand that any inquiry into the details of art, any writing that should tend to concentrate the examining faculties of the spectator upon the actual workmanship, would tend also to upset Mr. C.R.W. Nevinson. In a world so abundantly furnished with clever counterfeiters of everything, from Treasury notes to old masters, we do not pretend to omniscience, nor can we tell how every duck emerged from a hen's egg. Yet, as one sitting apart humbly and in truly monarchical splendour, dependent upon "advisers" and acting only upon the recommendations of our Ministry, we express our willingness to learn whether Mr. Nevinson's lithographs are bit by a wholly new process of pyric acid through suet.

B. H. DIAS.

P.S.—To prevent needless discussion, your correspondent might be informed that the implications of the verb "cut" are not limited to incisions by chisel, "an instrument by which wood or stone is pared away."

ART NOTES[40a]

Sir,—Mr. Ernest Wilton Schiff's "sane individual" is, according to Mr. Schiff's own statement, a person who "would destroy" pictures and books when they do not happen to conform to said individual's theories. This form of sanity died late in Spain, and prevailed in Europe during the late Middle Ages and the counter-Reformation. My personal predilection is for a sanity which includes a shade more restraint and just a touch more of

[40]*The New Age*, March 13, 1919, p. 315.
[40a]*The New Age*, March 20, 1919, p. 331.

tolerance. I do not, however, wish to over-emphasise my own view, and under no circumstances would I consider destroying Mr. Schiff for any of his opinions whatsoever.

B. H. Dias.

Sir,—If we *must* choose between "impertinence" and burning books and works of art at the stake, give me, I pray you, O little gods and great editors, an impertinent cosmos without either Papal or Schiffal indices expurgatorii.

Ezra Pound.

ART NOTES[41]

In Capt. Baker England has lost one of her most intelligent art collectors, and the more advanced painters have lost their most stalwart English supporter. Baker began his collection with prints of Rowlandson and Hokusai; he bought Innes at a time when Innes was not widely known, but Innes is not so well represented in the Baker collection as in that of Mr. Horace Cole. The main interest of the Baker collection is the series of 40 or 50 Lewis drawings.

Capt. Baker, alarmed at the rapidity with which the best of Wyndham Lewis' work was being absorbed by America, determined to retain in England a collection of Lewis as representative as that possessed by the Quinn collection in New York. It was a patriotic labour on his part. On his return from Rumania, and before his departure for France in 1917, he left the nucleus of the Lewis series (twenty drawings in colour) and Wm. Roberts' best piece of work, "The Dancer," in care of Mr. Pound, with instructions that they were to be offered to the South Kensington Museum in the case of his death and that of the artist. The instructions specified that if the S. Kensington or other public institutions were not yet ready for such "advanced" work, Mr. Pound was to retain the pictures until the official eye had been educated.

After leaving hospital in 1918 Capt. Baker more than doubled the set of colour-drawings and added one of Lewis' three main large canvases, "The Crowd." This is the most abstract of Lewis' large canvases and of importance at least equal to that of "The Sailors" or "The Kermess." It is not known, however, whether Baker before his sudden and fatal pneumonia had drawn up any will or other formal instructions binding his heirs; but whether the collection go to the nation or not it is to be hoped

[41]*The New Age*, March 27, 1919, p. 342. Signed "B. H. Dias."

106

that, at any rate, some adequate and illustrated catalogue of the collection will be issued, and that at least a suitable record of Baker's patriotic endeavour will not be lost. There is a vast difference between the collector who acquires the work of living artists during their vital period and the dealer-collectors who only acquire work of aged and declining men, or of dead artists with established commercial accretion. A few works of Rodin's best period, for example, would outweigh the remnants of his old age, which he himself had to present to this country. The Lane collection of "Impressionists" was like a dealer's left-over stock. (His Goya was magnificent.) The collector who buys from young men, trusting to his own vision, partakes in their further creation; he is not a patroniser of, but a participant in, the arts, and his selective intelligence may be worth more to the arts than the work of a dozen dilettantes and inferior workers.

EXHIBITIONS

Winifred Cooper's "Russian Peasant and Bolshevik" pictures at the Goupil are that sort of painting which can only attract a moment's notice by having a particular subject-matter; as in the past: "Pictures of the Holy Land" or "Pictures of Arctic Exploration" by various now obsolete artists.

Capt. B. Bairnsfather's drawings at the Greatorex Gallery contain no qualities not observable in the fully familiar reproductions.

Mr. Rutter's new gallery at 9, Duke Street, Adelphi, makes happy debut with an excellent display of woodcuts by Edward Wadsworth. Cleanliness, efficiency, precision are first notes of the show, which reopens the whole question of processes. The first query concerning any process-produced work of art, etching, lithograph, woodcut, is whether the design is interesting, whether the artist has, in it, expressed anything worth delaying one's attention. The second question is whether the expression has been well carried out, and whether it has *gained any advantage from its particular medium.*

This second question hardly arises until the first one has been answered in the affirmative; though the prophesying commentator may be more inclined to prognosticate well of a workman who appears to be in earnest in matters of execution, even though his other powers be immature.

Processes are employed by good artists (a) when they want a number of copies of some design, and (b) when they find it possible to get certain effects by a process which they can get in no other way. The first of these reasons presents no aesthetic interest; it has the social and educative value of bringing beautiful designs within reach of a comparatively indigent public.

Bad artists take to processes from expediency, publishers' or governments' orders, etc., often regardless of the effects.

Some men indubitably find it possible to get a finer and firmer line

107

with an etcher's point than with pen or pencil; one does not doubt that Meryon could have been as hard and neat with a pencil as he is in his etchings. There is also the matter of permanence; an etching or lithograph does not rub and smear like pencil or charcoal drawing. The decision of means must be a matter of the artist's own *libido;* one's pleasure in seeing the work must be, in part, in feeling that the medium has been employed to advantage, that it has intensified some property of the work; that some hardness, or some clearness, some softness, some blurr, some simplicity, some complexity, has become more expressive by reason of the particular medium than it could have been, or would have been, had other means been employed.

Etching offers a chance to black line, where the paper is pushed into the inky groove of the plate; woodcut offers a great smoothness and evenness in the putting on of larger black or coloured surface, for the blacks and colour patches of the print come from projecting surfaces of the block, from the part which the artist has not cut away.

The fine even blacks of Wadsworth's woodcuts, as, for example, that of the engine-room, the big triangular composition (31), show that he has exploited this opportunity with great efficiency. In the later and smaller blocks of Greek towns and harbours (as in 9 and 11), we find an added interest in designs capable of application in various colour schemes, and a very considerable advance in the artist's power of form-arrangement.

The simple black cuts are the most uncompromising abstraction we have had since the Vorticist show of 1914. They are akin to the most cubic cubes of Picasso, to Picabia's weaker imitations, to the phase of Lewis shown in the "Plan of War," "Portrait of an Englishwoman," and "Timon," designs reproduced in *Blast.* The later black blocks of camouflaged ships, made presumably in anticipation of the Wadsworth official painting for the Canadian War Memorial, are of interest in lesser degree.

He is at his best in the colour-prints in the upright somewhat floral design (15), and in the Greek towns; these prints, demanding great care in registration, are each produced from several blocks by a series of printings; one should inspect the portfolios as well as the designs on the wall if one is to appraise the variety which can be got from the same designs by varying the colour mode.

Wadsworth is acquiring his place in contemporary art by cold-blooded persistence; the quiet assertion of his work, no piece of which ever pretends to be what it is not, is rather pleasing after the innumerable exhibits of bluff and pretentiousness; the innumerable canvases and drawings which all hope the beholder will take them for something more valuable than they are. A fake woodcutter would have given us fake Kunisadas and exploited the cult of Japan. Mr. Wadsworth has given us, in a few of his best designs, woodcuts which afford interesting comparison with the work of Japanese artists. And his craftsmanship is beyond question.

108

ART NOTES[42]

Although no further "nominations" for an ideal academy have yet reached me, I have been taken in argument. One man had a candidate but was not sure he had yet exhibited publicly. Another thought my just and righteous contempt for the British Academy harboured dangerous propaganda in favour of the French Salons. He said there was good academic painting in England. But I was unable to get a definition of "academic" from him before others had barged into our dialogue and diverted its course.

Whatever "academic" painting may be, British Academy painting, Tate, etc., is just the mechanisation, the discoloration, the general decadence of renaissance formulae, with nothing whatever to be said for it, save that some of its practitioners have showed a certain zeal for accurate representational drawing, though there has never been a first-rate intelligence among the lot of them. *But* the Old Salon and Beaux Arts contain painters quite as bad as those enclosed in the British Academy. The alliance with France is perhaps strong enough to permit me to say that there are French painters as bad, definitely as bad, as Mr. Bundy. No greater insult has ever, to my knowledge, been hurled at French painting, but the jibe is deserved and its justness will be granted by many who recall those foamy "creations" of bibulous monks being, in allegorical vision, confronted by ballet-girls (aspect à la J'hv to Moses on Sinai) and so forth.

The statement that influenza rages in England does not imply that the disease is not rampant elsewhere. The *Mercure de France* for March 16 brings evidence that Paris is as much plagued by doddards as we are. The Ecole des Beaux-Arts started a fund for assisting art-students who had been mutilated in the war, chiefly men so mutilated that there was no chance of their continuing their work. They asked Forain to design a poster for the fund. Forain, who had done a fine poster for the Prisoners of War fund, made them a grave and sober design of a one-armed artist holding one of his former pictures in his left hand, with the implication, "That's over."

The professors of the Beaux-Arts demurred, they thought the design inopportune. First the "administration" discovered that the drawing was not in "good taste." Then M. Cormon decided that it was "dangerous and discouraging." He said: "Our wounded have not this sadness."

"Et il ajouta ces mots qui résument mieux que tous les livres du monde ou tous les pamphlets l'art de l'Ecole des Beaux-Arts:

"Si encore il avait mis une allégorie . . . avec un casque."

No, London is not the only afflicted city. After several days of discussion, in which M. Bonnat took no part, the Beaux-Arts decided to refuse Forain's drawing and the thousands of francs it would have brought

---

[42]*The New Age*, April 10, 1919, pp. 378–79. Signed "B. H. Dias."

to the fund (for Forain had ceded all the possible profits from sales of reproductions). All this happened three years ago, but we are grateful to the *Mercure* for publishing the facts. Certainly, their correspondent is correct when he says: "Cette anecdote des mœurs artistiques de la France en guerre méritait d'être connue."

"Une allégorie . . . avec un casque." The Beaux-Arts will receive the firmest and most loyal support from *Punch*'s staff of cartoonists, from Mr. Simms, from the elders of our Academy, and from most of "those in authority." A mammal in the British postal or customs service has just burnt a consignment of Rops.

ART NOTES[43]
Rutter's Adelphi Gallery

In noticing Mr. Wadsworth's show of woodcuts I should perhaps have emphasised the importance of Mr. Rutter's newly opened gallery at 9, Duke Street, Adelphi. This gallery is intended to meet the "need" both of artists who wish to sell and of "consumers" who wish to purchase in-expensive pictures and drawings (i.e., definitely from 10s. to £10).

When one remembers Gaudier-Brzeska too poor to buy stone for carving; when one remembers how ready he was to sell drawings of animals at 10s. each (with presumably a reduction by the dozen), and to sell statues at what people would now pay for one of his drawings, indeed at half or a third of what some of his drawings now bring . . . and all this only five years ago, one readily sees what use some such artshop as Mr. Rutter's might have been at that time; and, denying that all art stopped with Gaudier's death, one is happy to think of the service the Duke Street room may perform for other young artists.

Judging from the few books exposed for sale on the window ledge, the Rutter-Reed taste has escaped from the Georgian fetters of Devonshire Street; and the more active literary as well as the more advanced artistic elements are apparently to have a boutique in which they will not be regarded with disparagement or embedded in quotidiana. At present the place seems to suffer from a constant absence of staff; but there is much to be hoped from the enterprise, and we wish it every success.

THE FINE ART SOCIETY

The Fine Art Society caters to a more opulent and conservative clientèle. Constance Rea, whose work is now to be seen there, is not a bad painter of the Manet-Chas-Shannon-J. J. Shannon-cum-even-Orpen consign-ment. Her "Lotus Eaters" is hampered with an unfortunate simple-life

[43]*The New Age*, April 24, 1919, pp. 411–12. Signed "B. H. Dias."

preraphaelite face; her 11 is extremely well painted. Such titles as "My Lady's Dress" and "Phillida Flouts Me" indicate the trend of her labours. "The Sentimentalists" remembers Manet not displeasingly. Mary Davis' silk painting is Conder that doesn't quite come off.

W. G. ROBB

But the gallery has scored in the Robb exhibit, perhaps the most interesting work they have shown since their Persian miniatures. The show is burdened, like many other shows, with a preface written in bilge of the purest water by Maj. Haldane Macfall: "Uttering the moods of nature, etc.," "cast upon his senses as Wordsworth aforetime sang such moods in verse," etc.

Now, it is to Mr. Robb's credit that he obviously paints to please himself. He appears to be of a single mood (about as much like Wordsworth as Diane de Poitiers may be said to be like Jane Austen). His "world" is unvexed by Bernard Shaw, by Marinetti, by any art-thought since Conder. I don't imagine he would be different if Conder had never existed. He goes in for delicate feminine robes, delicate half-lights, mists, gallantries. (All these things being, M. Macfall, the very gist and essence of Wordsworth?)

His (Robb's) nature is decked with artifice and with silks and satins tone Watteau-Fragonard, with general Corot-Conder sort of formula for the arrangements, technique, soft, faint colours with bright dashes of blue and orange. There are no cubes and no vortices, but there is a perfect veracity to his own intention, and his technique is in his own control; here we find a background in thin paint almost as simply applied as the flames in the background of Velasquez' "Don Juan de Austra"; in 31, trees flaked in a manner that might have been assimilated from Perugino. These "influences" are applied in the right way, and Robb has learned his traditional métier as traditional métiers should be learned.

We would mention particularly Nos. 3; 12; 13 for its fall of sunlight; the bright centre and pseudo-classic pavilions well arranged in 15; the blue skirt in 19, 31, 32 in which last the small delicate figures are done with pleasant suavity. No. 16 is, perhaps, earlier work; the rainbows and the oval are less convincing, the tall trees picture less convincing. On the whole the work is of "the summer of the mind," *galan, airoso*. No. 30 also has its merits, and 5 also; 8 is rougher. Almost any of the pictures would have a permanent charm in a boudoir or drawing-room.

EPSTEIN

To come nearer the popular heart and to borrow a formula from the *London Mail* or the *Sunday Evening Telegram*: "Is it not about time that" the country made some use of Jacob Epstein's indubitable sculptural genius? The plums are falling, they are falling large and luscious into various mouths of lesser distinction than Epstein's. I will grant any claim of the adversaries. I grant that Epstein is an artist as grumpy as he is great. I grant that he has not been to school with Baldassare Castiglione, *but* it is the function of an all-wise and beneficent administration to make use of the national resources, and Epstein's ability is definitely part of these resources. Personal considerations should not intervene. There are more memorials to be made than there are good sculptors to make them. They are not all of them national. With Epstein idle, there is a chance for some municipality to steal a march on the Empire. I, for one, hope some city will do it if the central administration does not.*

There are several other directions in which the war museums might show more zeal than they have. It would indeed be interesting to see a published list of the proportion in which the works of various artists have been acquired for these institutions. After all, we are les jeunes, we are the people who will live the rest of our lives in the face of these memorials. And it is even permitted one to hope that England will not lie permanently under the cloak of Bundy-ism or even of Orpenisation.

SIBYL MEUGENS

At the Goupil we find a room full of Oriental decorativism, escaped more or less by Miss Meugens in 12, rather overdone in 19; displaying pleasant humour in 3, à la C. Bax and Summerun, with a little too much of "that" angel and cup business in 4. We have Persia *vs.* China in 9; and considerable Turkestan feeling in 10 (about the best thing in her show). Dulac did it first with rather more technique and less godly sobriety. 14 is presumably a successful portrait.

W. DACRES ADAMS

"Old Bristol" in the next room is the usual representative painting, simply and cleanly done at its best, with grain of canvas left showing. Sunlight and hardish definition of the lines of buildings. 1, 3, 13, 25, 26, 27, 28 show about the best workmanship.

AT THE LEICESTER GALLERY

The Society of Twenty-five Painters need not detain us long. One of my advisers says: "There aren't 25 painters." Another is of the opinion that

---

*Frivolous correspondent suggests that J. E. should design (purely abstract) monument to transpontine finance. Soyons sérieux.

there are, but that they are not contained in this group. Even Miss Rea's work is not so convincing as that which she shows at the Fine Art Society. A little ink drawing of Manet's (no part of the exhibit) compensates one for one's 'bus fare.

ART NOTES[44]

1

A few weeks ago I declined to take count of work that had not been publicly exhibited. This is a fair rule for a writer of public criticism, and I am only moved to depart from it on learning of the comic pomposity of the London Group as displayed in their rejection (fine old term of the Salons!) of Stuart-Hill's landscapes.

I don't yet know just which landscapes were rejected, but after all, here is a man with a style of his own (in landscape, at any rate), and half a dozen pictures to his credit which are certainly out of the reach of this "group," and one wonders what these little self-named progressive secessions are worth if they do not mean more room for experiment and a wider opportunity for divergent inventions.

2

Having seen in one week these extremely interesting oils and encaustics of Italian towns, as well as a fine Picasso, of a period not at all known to the London public, and knowing of more modern art available to private inspection, but "unexhibitable" for various reasons, chiefly that a painter cannot have a one-man show unless he has a very considerable amount of *unsold* work, it strikes me that there might well be a loan exhibit of "Painting Since Gauguin and Cézanne," and that the public would profit by such an educational scheme.

It is only one of a hundred anomalies, of a hundred signs of the irreconcilability of art and commerce that the more or more rapidly a man sells, the less is his work made public, the less chance has the spectator to pay his humble shilling for looking at it, the more it becomes private property and ceases to be the artist's communication to the world, State purchase being damned in England by the Chantrey bequest which is unbalanced by any enlightened expenditure of any comparable sum.

One needs the vigour and the licence of a Synge for the ninetieth time to treat the Tate and the Academy.

[44]*The New Age,* May 8, 1919, pp. 29–30. Signed "B. H. Dias."

3

From art to splendours and regality. I learn that the exhibit of meticulous water-colour at the Greatorex Gallery is under the highest, or almost the highest, possible patronage. Mr. E. A. Rowe's "Old World Gardens" do no violence to Tate taste and tradition. To say that the work is very, very old-fashioned, is not to say that it has the classic calm of Perugino, it is merely to say that the colour is really false and pre-Manet; that the painting is as good as tight water-colour, with no blank paper to speak of and a surface suggesting painting on ground-glass or frosted porcelain, is likely to be.

THE LONDON GROUP

The London Group show at Heal's is nearly as gloomy as it was last season. It is almost as unalterable as the Academy. In fact, it is rather more sure of being without surprises, unless one can count E. Wolf's tent for boy scouts with a few pseudo-Gaudier animals disported upon it (as good as anything in the show), as a surprise.

Washed out "Liberty" or washed out Wm. Morris is the prevailing tonality. R. Fry has bucked up a little, and his decadence from Manet is less decayed than it has been for several seasons (*vide* 25, where the light is rather good).

The pathetic thing is the assumption of modernity, the faint camou-flage of the novel. Thus, the poster by Kauffer, a cross between pseudo-Lewis and Teddy Tail; and the infinitely despicable imitation-dilutions of Lewis by Atkinson, without doubt the most supine of supine imitators, a painter with less invention, positively with less invention than anything I can think of at the moment. There is also an A. N. Lewis who signs modestly and simply "Lewis," without any initial. (At the present time of writing I have not heard of anyone's having mistaken No. 78 for the work of "the other Lewis"; the gentleman who did the "Guns.")

The London Group is Hamlet (spelling please) with Hamlet left out since it ceased to be the Camden Town, or something of that sort with several distinguished artists included. It is indeed the "rump" of the modern movement. Phases which once were interesting because they were full of venture and experiment are here dignified, moribund, stereotyped.

Walter Taylor is an honest and industrious painter; he keeps to his own modest style; his work is recognisable and his own, and usually enjoyable. Bevan is just the Bevan d'antan; ditto Karlowska. Gertler vies with the "Herald" rooster poster; but has merit in the portrait of "Gabriella." We doubt if Rupert Lee has ever seen solferino trees or his apes save in atavistic vision. Kauffer manages his light decently in 26. J. F. Porter is

114

possible in 31; the dishes of Miss N. Hamnett in 61 are free of all trammels and bound by no stale conventions of gravity. D. Fox Pitt uses a style that amateurs used in Paris about 1907, and with a remarkable lack of skill, a great superabundance of strokes, while pretending to clever elimination, a really remarkable skilfulness.

R. Lee's gun team is another dilutation. In fact, the whole show is in the spirit of "borrow but do not admire"; of "go behind," "follow in the track of," but "do not be led." So far as is known these people have no admirations. If they have any admiration it is wholly undiscoverable, and, in consequence, there is a pervasive lack of that tensity which even a poor artist may occasionally attain in a desperate struggle to equal or come near to a fine model.

We are told in the prefatory note on Gilman that he was enthusiastic about Van Gogh. Let it go at Van Gogh; Van Gogh had intensity. I would almost say that any inventor has intensity. The statement is an exaggeration, but an inventor is often driven into invention by a disgust with prevailing slop, and the pressure of the disgust breeds intensity. The London Group invents nothing whatever; it appears to admire nothing very much; if it hates, it does so in a personal manner, which adds nothing to its work. An *impersonal* hatred of some quality or thing is or may be an artistic asset. Personal hatreds are of no value whatever. If anything accrues from them it is fortuitous by-product. Here we have the general école de goggle-woggle, cream-ice and stucco tonality; the arty, the sloppy.

ART NOTES[45]
Five Ordeals

BY WATER

The Royal Institute of Painters in Water-Colour presents the accustomed expanse of cotton-wool, of pseudo-imitators of Meissonnier, of, for the presumably 110th time, fake Alma-Tademas, the Hydrotherapic nudes, the sub-why-you-need-Sanatogen-ads, et cetera.

Miss D. W. Hawksley leads, in the wake, or if not in the wake in the manner of Russell Flint. Her 56 is much better than Flint, and less fussy and detailed than the accustomed Dulac or Rackham illustration: a nearly-nude on a vermilion couch in suave colour and suave outline, with the hollow cubicity of the room-space, is well rendered, and there is no inconsiderable charm in the subdued May-Fairish sort of pearl-grey shirt-studs harmony of bright pigments flatly and quite ably and smoothly

[45]*The New Age*, May 29, 1919, pp. 88–89. Signed "B. H. Dias."

applied. Her other two pictures are less interesting, a mild Flint in 417, and a mild approximation of abstract patternism in 423.

The clear light of Van Anrooy's 2 disposes one favourably amid so much cotton batting. J. B. Mathews, Tadema rubbish. H. Ryland, Tadema, very sub-. B. Pittar, economy, but not much else. J. Finnemore, more of these betagged and beribboned cavaliers, monks, jesters, etc. "That's what we are up against," said the owner of a "gallery," pointing to the window of an "art shop." Ryland (24), Tadema outrage, as above.

Harold Copping, in 70, further abuses a very long-suffering figure. Hal Hurst's "Tears" call for a remedy. Montagu Barstow presents "Bacchantes and Fauns: a frieze"—i.e., the classics revamped for the cake-tin. William B. E. Ranken, R.I., R.O.I., presents a highly desirable residence, not despicably done, but the house is worth more than the picture. Fredk. Whiting's "Salmon Fishers" are broad but not goodly. Hester Margetson shows Peter-Panism in the last, the very last leaf. Wynne Apperley shows "The Mirror," pre-Raphaelitism (i.e., worst phases of D. G. Rossetti), aspiring toward nudity, the "art-element" present in the abnormal elongation or out-jut of scoop nose and jaw. Probably a bold innovation to compensate for Gabriel's necks.

Lieut. Christopher Clark in "Wartime on the Clyde" tries to exploit vorticist patterns of ship-camouflage without leaving the safe haven of academic water-colour. F. Matania has netted a porpoise (definitely netted in fish-nets) for his "Dancing Sirens," the main obesity should have *danced* in the distant room instead of sitting it out in the foreground.

C. Whymper, ghosting, we presume, the lamented humanitarian and animalitarian Landseer, presents (title): "The Stalker; bother the grouse, where's my stag?" Bother the picturist, where have we laid the harpoon?

Matania (308), "Balnearia," hydrotherapy definitely labelled and acknowledged, even if in a "furrin" dialect.

Fred Roe quotes three lines of somebody's translation of Villon. He can't even paint silk stockings up to the Kirchner texture. He adds also the Bishop of London or sentimental moralist element, trying to make the best of both abysms, to lascivise the eye with the scarlet fascinator and sermonise the befuddled soldier all at once. "Sermons in stone, books in the running brooks"; and a good place, too, not only for most current publications but for some pictures.

333, wash. 341, portrait, but not much other merit. Hal Hurst (354), cotton-bale parody of the worst botches Rodin ever committed during his senility; unspeakable fuzz; mushy dabble in allegories. Fred Taylor, "An Italian Nocturne," not unornamental, "mystery" à la Don Giovanni, etc. Ranken in 374 attempts to have a technique. Sir David Murray continues to exhibit the false colour which undistinguishes his long habitual products. O. Moser's 408 calls for extreme measures, abysms below

116

"Bubbles." Miss E. Lord, tries an etiolation of our before-observed first parents—need we say Adam and Eve?—with bodies pumiced down to Rue de la Paix tactility. L. Walker, fusses and feathers in 415.

LEICESTER GALLERY

Three bad shows all at once, and a few rather able drawings by M. A. J. Bauer (59, 60, 62, and 63, I think), some attempt at elimination of unnecessary strokes.

T. C. Dugdale shows water-colours possibly rather above Royal Institute average, but of no real skill, or personal style, or originality.

Capt. W. G. De Glehn, in contrast to Dugdale's quietness, splashes and splotches with magentas and general swash and underlying commonness; 112 is a disgusting violation of Conder.

The cool restraint of Oliver Hall is at first, for about three minutes, pleasant after De Glehn's noise; 135 and 137 are not so very bad, but 131 exhibits all the weaknesses of his school and convinces one that Hall is really a bad painter who has done the few better things more or less by chance. Weakest possible Turnerism in 159.

Thence fleeing to

THE ADELPHI GALLERY (9, Duke St., W.C.2) we find Mr. Carlo Norway in an aggravated state of utter uncertainty, hoping to please everybody at once or at least to put into the show something, anything, one thing at least which will *be bound to "appeal"* to every possible entrant. Sic: Russian Balletism in 1; ecclesiastical windowism in 2; bilge sans adjective in 3; society decorative portraitism in 8; muzzy paint in 9; plain water-colour in 10. No. 14 is labelled "Panchronist" (?? panchromist??), apart from which it looks like a bad design for stained-glass window without need of further adjectives or other supposed theory of construction. 17 hopes towards Beardsley "decay." For 18 *vide* 10. 21 is not bad; 22 is possibly the best in the room; the artist might settle or at least perch for a few weeks on this genre; 23 for *Vogue;* 26 fake orientalism; "Resurrection, 1919," appliqué feltism, wobble-goggle symbology; 31 blue beard; and then, bless us and save us!—is the man going to omit no chance of ultimate immortality, whatever weather-vane of fashion point to whatever undiscovered North?—the mildest possible vorticist-vortexette (rather as in 1915) in "L'Ecrivante." 34, 35, 36, in the playful mood of the scout's text at Heal's. For 43 *vide* 3.

Thus we spend our hours. The Eldar Gallery has also had a show of mixed drawings by all the great masters from del Sarto to Chas. Shannon, from Taylor (W.) to Tiepolo, from Goya to Hope Read (whoever he may be), etc. Terms for Mr. Norway's decorative portraits and painted bowls can be had on application. Such is his versatility that I dare say he will,

117

for a little encouragement, do the prospective sitter on a pipe-head or a lamp-shade. Apart from this he has a quite nice, normal talent.

ART NOTES[46]
Capt. Guy Baker's Collection at the
South Kensington Museum

The New Age "representative was this day permitted" to inspect the drawings from the Guy Baker Collection now at the South Kensington Museum, and he can now firmly compliment England on having the most fecund and inventive draughtsman in Europe and on *not* having the public control of her galleries entrusted to an hopeless atavism like M. Leonce Benedite (of the Luxembourg).

The French have recently been with us; M. Benedite has long, alas, been with the French; so have the Beaux Arts; and Paris *was* the artistic capital of Europe; Paris is, perhaps, the artistic capital in so far as she contains (possibly) a greater number of good artists than London. Derain is perhaps a little effeminate; Marchand is an excellent portrait painter with abundance of technique; Vlaminck can be most briefly described to an English public by stating that he does, really *does*, what the London Group tries and fails to accomplish. Vlaminck is an excellent painter, in and out of the dynasty of Constable and Corot, whom he does not resemble. He does not paint in pretty-picture colours, but colours solidly comparable to chairs and doors and other objects. His white is white, his green is green, as pillar-box red is red. Our contemporaries would go to some length in describing the psychological rapport between M. Vlaminck's temperament and his landscapes. I can but suggest that M. Vlaminck is a lyrist and that his chief technical interest, merit, lies in his colour and in the stern, broad application of it, and in a much more skilful "decomposition" or dissection or dissociation of colour than was to be found in the pointillistes. He is one of the most formidable painters in Paris at the moment.

Picasso is in London, is Spanish, and is by no means as fecund or as vigorous as the creator of the twenty-seven coloured drawings by Wyndham Lewis which I have just examined. And I think it is only with the final cataloguing and exhibiting of these drawings that the public, the limited public which has already seen Mr. Lewis' war show and his "Timon," will be in a position to judge Mr. Lewis, if not in entirety, at least with some adequate data.

The drawings are as follows:

[46]*The New Age*, September 25, 1919, pp. 364–65. Signed "B. H. Dias."

CACTUS: three green figures, mood lyric, horn-player and figure leaning on pole.

EARLY MORNING: two dark figures, tropic sun, simplicity but skill in the conveyance of bright light unsurpassed so far as I know.

FIRST IMPRESSIONS: dramatic interest, black and white.

GOSSIPS: shows the Rowlandson attitude of mind, depiction of character, blue ink and green.

MOONLIGHT: musicians in the mode of the horn-player in "Cactus," the hollow moon, sylvan profusion.

COMBAT: massiveness of the two central figures, energy not to be found in Picasso, wholly different from Blake, who is the one English predecessor of Lewis in presenting dynamic energy, as is Rowlandson the one British forbear of Lewis in social satire.

THEATRE MANAGER: very early Lewis (drawn in 1909); it has Daumier for its grandfather, but I doubt if Daumier has done anything better.

AT THE SEA-SIDE: calm blue.

Ninthly and tenthly, two satires on the human animal, the cat in man (and woman); the chicken in man (and woman). There is super-irony in the cats.

PROSCENIUM: note the spectators.

BABY'S HEAD: excellent, and contains nothing that cannot be grasped by even the most general public.

GROUP OF TWO (DEMONSTRATION), among the best of Lewis' developments in his vitreous mode.

THREE PHILOSOPHERS, in the mode of "Gossips."

Late head, "A GREAT VEGETARIAN"; early head, "ANTHONY," blue and orange.

VITREOUS FIGURE, delicacy of colour.

A FEMALE, obviously of the thinner and "lower" classes.

MARKET WOMEN, DIEPPE: The Queen Vic. type and another selling apples (1917).

THE DOMINO: two figures, cat formula, discover a mask.

COMBAT 3: thin, insect-like figures at prise, part of the combat series, with thin piston-energy in contrast to the weight-energy of the other "Combat."

SUNSET AMONG MICHELANGELOS. The chief piece of the collection, four Titan figures against dull flush crimson-to-vermilion background.

SECOND MOVEMENT, depiction of animal, aimless exuberance, yellow figures.

THE COURTESAN, shows Wyndham Lewis' mastery in the use of chalks, soft effects in rich colour, scale and modus of colour very different from his vitreous gamuts.

PASTORAL TOILET, on the other hand, illustrates his peculiar and personal use of inks; half satire and rural disinvoltura.

RUSSIAN MADONNA contains parody of all pseudo-Italian old-masterism in the little background landscape.

THE LABOUR DEPUTATION should be reproduced broadcast for popular education. It would not help the Conservative Party, but it would protect us from half-baked excesses.

I have given this list in detail because no one drawing by Lewis is convincing in the degree that two dozen of his drawings are convincing. Some critic has said that the evidence of a great poet is not to be found in any single line, but in an undercurrent or element everywhere present. We have here twenty-seven drawings in almost as many different modalities, each representing a phase and a movement of the artist's development; the first public document of his existence between the "Timon" period and the transient phase of the war drawings.

This collection or at least some part of it will be open to everyone in a few weeks; it is worth the detailed enumeration I give it, because the work of a nation's few best artists is worth infinitely more attention than the work of the two hundred second-bests, and because out of each generation of painters only a few have anything to say to the day after to-morrow.

Wm. Roberts's "Dancer" is also contained in the Baker bequest. Among other modern things to be seen at the South Kensington (other wing) are Epstein's infant head, the torse by Gaudier-Brzeska, and an early "Dancer," slim and with raised arms, by Gaudier-Brzeska; also an unfortunate "Christ" by Gill.

All these things should be borne in mind by people who are wont to sigh after Paris and to suppose that all advances, artistic and bureaucratic, proceed from the left bank of the Seine.

Admitting that we have no Renoirs to speak of, admitting that art from 1880 to 1905 is almost wholly absent from English galleries, let us also note that art since 1905 is almost wholly absent from French public galleries; and therefore mix with our envy of one fact a little pity for the other, with thanks to the South Kensington and to Captain Martin Hardy, of the Department of Drawings, who has braved, possibly, the furies of Bloomsbury and of the "Omega" by an acceptance which should encourage other men, interested in the present, to revive or to initiate an interest in the permanent public collection of modern art as distinct from Chantrey Bequests and other public misfortunes. Here, at least, British official receptivity has attained a higher plane than the French.

There are two channels open to the public; one, and the simpler, to insist that adequate space be provided at South Kensington for permanent open exposition of the best work in the collection, not only of drawings, but of sculpture and contemporary painting; secondly, to defeat the malign intention of the Chantrey Bequest by opening the British Academy to works of art. (In which there is, alas, small hope of signal success.)

120

ART NOTES[47]

It is not every man who can die regretted by his friends and acquaintances, leaving comfortable memories. Harold Gilman is definitely regretted by the London Group and by a wide circle outside it; the memorial exhibition of his works at the Leicester Gallery adds little to what we know of him. He was a sober and industrious artist with none of the excess of genius. We live in an overpainted age; Gilman's work was not in the realm of the superfluous; it is well that in the welter of sham some men should be earnest; but it might be even better if all or most of this serious labour—which does not partake in the excess of gift and inspiration—were bent in some less aimless endeavour. Given application, let us say, to some corner of permanent building, Gilman might have left a distinctive work, as distinctive, perhaps, as that of Nicolas Bachelier or Tullio Lombardo. As it is he leaves some meritorious pictures, in the mode known now in Sickert, now in Walter Taylor, now in Ginner, once even in Rackham, and in drawings which have only to be placed next a Gaudier to display their lack of élan.

Twenty Gaudier drawings are now available in an excellent portfolio published by the Ovid Press (43, Belsize Park Gardens, N.W.3), at 15s.; one might carry them to various art-shows as a touch-stone.

The Press has done its work remarkably well; the drawings are of various periods ranging from Gaudier's very early work; unfortunately, the prints on vellum are undated, but the progress is easily discernible if one take the trouble to range the drawings, all but three or four of which are of interest apart from that of biographic documents. A Press willing to undertake this sort of work has long been a desiderium, and we wish it every success.

The most hopeful sign in current shows is the great improvement in Nina Hamnett's work instantly visible on entering the exhibit at the Eldar Gallery (40, Great Marlborough Street). The characterisation in the portraits is excellent. Miss Hamnett has at last escaped the greenery-yallery, or, perhaps, we should say the grayery-fryery, of the London Group; she with Guevara whose portrait is the star exhibit at the Grafton "International" has succeeded in bringing a touch of life into British portraiture.

Miss Hamnett's portraits of Messrs. Gilson, Butts and Sitwell are, in the Bloomsbury phrase, "amusing," but the work does not end there. The Hope Johnson in an earlier mode is good in its flatter way, but with the Stuart Hill, Miss Price, and infinitely better in the Mrs. Reavis, Miss Hamnett attains a three-dimensional structure and much greater vitality.

[47]*The New Age*, November 6, 1919, pp. 13–14. Signed "B. H. Dias."

The portrait of E. Lacey is perhaps best in its relation to background, and the artist has been admirable in rendering her subject's "boxing" eye and the knotty muscles of the somewhat scraggy athlete. "Louise" is perhaps the best modelled of the earlier manner. In the blotchy water-colours like 44 and 45 we have very great competence, and in some of the drawings Miss Hamnett shows that she has profited by Gaudier's example more than any other artist in England; there is great gain of freedom over her earlier drawing.

On the whole, it is no small comfort to the critic to find a couple of "younger artists" emerging from the wash and waste of the London Group dreariness, and to find some portraiture which definitely portrays the sitters in some other manner than that of the Boldini-ex-Sargento-McEvoistic nougat.

The International has considerably cheered up. Guevara's painting is, as indicated above, the chief interest. There is no pleasure or exhilaration in praising an artist whom even Sir Claude Phillips has got round to "discovering"; but, on the other hand, it is perhaps worthwhile to defend a good painter from journalists' froth and little jokes about the canary-bird-cage. Guevara has got a likeness of his sitter, an excellent likeness; he has put in a great deal of colour, rather prettily, but well; he has also introduced some pleasures of composition and pattern, and this by no means eccentric or even vigorously Matissean arrangement is quite enough to set tittering the little men who, while they don't buy the *Pears' Annual Gallery of Art*, think it neat to pretend that art should have stopped where it was in the heyday of Poynter.

The International is disfigured by the worst Whistler yet discovered. Christabel Dennison, Gladys Baker, John D. Revel, emerge amid Ambrosiana with the usual Philpotts', etc. Mr. Cole favours with a selection from Mestrovic. For the rest, the usual trade-show of parlour decorations, there is nothing new to be said about this sort of thing, and we have probably devoted too much space to it in the past.

Brown and Phillips are having their usual show of modern etchings, Meryon, Legrand (132), Courbet, Pissarro's portrait of Cézanne, Forain "Pietà," Degas "Au Louvre," Forain (181), Steinlen (194). Good portrait of R. Schwabe by F. Dodd, Wm. Walcott (205), and a Derain which shows that he is better as a painter of stage scenes and a designer of ballet costumes than as an etcher.

Alfred Wolmark is exhibiting at the Hampstead Gallery. The work doubtless shows vigorous, or, at any rate, violent colour; we shall be glad to inspect it when it has been brought south into the metropolis.

The Old Dudley Art Society, founded in 1861, still bears the stamp of its era (Mill Street, Conduit Street, W.1, can be found with a map). Here we find water-colour as Ruskin conceived it. L. Burleigh Bruhl still contends for true representation of nature, the "impression." Chas. Spenclayh contributes a large miniature with meritorious drawing, but done in the illusion that floorboards, etc., gleam and glisten with great altitude of "finish." The kindly mentor who accompanied my inspection of this show gave away a good deal of the "modern trouble"; he said Spenclayh's work had merits but that it had taken a month to do, whereas it would "have tired him in half an hour."

There is a great deal to be said for the continual practice which enables an artist to paint a picture in a few hours; but there is everything to be said against an almost inherent and cognate vice of this system, namely, the unwillingness to spend a month or so on one painting. This is a kind of impatience bred of impressionist habit, bred of the attention to light, which never rests the same, *rather than* to structure which does not alter.

If we return to the Hamnett portraits we find that Miss Hamnett's progress is really the progress precisely from attention to impression, in the earlier work, to attention to structure in the later. And if there were anything to be said against Guevara's portrait; or perhaps not against, but simply in qualification, we might say that it is "very contemporaneous"; it does pay equal attention to arrangement and to the character impression of the sitter, and more to both of these than to the actual structure of the sitter's face and head. It has no Cézanne in its make-up; it has kinships with Matisse and with the best Sargents; this in laudable contrast to the McEvoys whose difference one from another is, in kind, the sort of difference between solio and velox, between carbon and platinum finish as ordered from the photographer.

ART NOTES[48]

London's first important exhibit of Matisse's work is now open at the Leicester Gallery. There is "very little to say about it" because it is in itself so conclusive. The public should know that the show is open, and they should go and look at the pictures. Prejudice against advanced and even wildly experimental work should fade in the face of this exhibition. Gleizes, Boccioni and the rest are justified, apart from any merits they themselves may possess; they are justified because the shows of cubism and even of futurism have made it possible for even a fairly wide public to look at Matisse in simplicity; to look at Matisse without having to climb hurdles of "strangeness."

The eye which has seen any modern work at all finds nothing in "Portraits de femmes" more startling, more "eccentric" than it would find in Moroni or Gozzoli. It is a great blessing that fortuitous accidents should be cleared away, and that by having got used to "very advanced

[48]*The New Age*, November 27, 1919, pp. 60–61. Signed "B. H. Dias."

work" one can now look at the essential qualities of Matisse's work without adventitious distraction.

This portrait of three women is great painting; it is akin to Moroni and the Old Masters; it reminds one, in the treatment of eyes, of Gauguin and of the encaustics from Egyptian mummy cases, and these three diverse "associations" are not in the least contradictory. Neither is the contender for "pure form" and for "forms in relation" stumped by the traditionalism or the "psychology." The eight pair of eyes in the six pictures clustered on the west wall of the gallery do, indeed, express a deal of psychology, variants in the temperaments of the sitters; the geometric means is simple; the geometric means is no more than the relation of a disc to the two concave curves above and below it, tangent or almost tangent to the disc, but like all simple means used by an artist, the artistic depth, as in contrast to the mathematical plainness, is due to great subtlety in the use, ergo, to great sensitiveness in the user; and, in the end, sensitiveness plus experience and perseverance is great knowledge.

Eyes looking out of a picture are a catch-penny dodge and one easy to use cheaply; Matisse has not used them cheaply. Eyes looking out of a picture are not a catch-penny dodge; they are a legitimate means for a portrait painter, and a means which only a snobbish desire to avoid interesting the public will lead him to neglect. Eyes looking out of a picture are a common ground for good artists and for tricksters. Let us take the eyes in Matisse's portraits at their just value. Matisse is a great draughtsman; the nude (19) makes interesting contrast to Gaudier's drawings; it has the suavity of maturity, whereas Gaudier's work has the attack and invective of youth in it. The big portrait of three women is admirable in composition; it has the apparent, and probably real effort-lessness in originality which is one of the signs of mastery.

The character in "à la Toque de Joura" is, like the eyes in the companion pictures, due to great knowledge of structure. It is not necessary, either in the young or in the mature artist, that all the geometry of a painting be tossed up into the consciousness and analysed by the painter before he puts brush to canvas. *The genius can pay in nugget and in lump gold; it is not necessary that he bring up his knowledge into the mint of consciousness, stamp it into either the coin of conscientiously analysed form-detail knowledge or into the paper-money of words, before he transmit it.* A bit of luck for a young man, and the sudden coagulation of bits of knowledge collected here and there during years, need not for the elder artist be re-sorted and arranged into coin. This sort of lump-payment is not mediumistic or psychic painting; it is mastery, and Matisse displays it.

I have said often enough in these columns that Matisse, perhaps more than any other man living, has given us a renewal of colour-sense. One had but to see a Matisse in "Les Indépendants" to see the surrounding pictures painted in mud. In a show consisting entirely of Matisse one might not be very much aware of the colour achievement; indeed, one takes the pictures quite easily and as a matter of course. They are not a matter of course, but they are in the true sense classic. There is no attempt either for novelty or for the avoidance of novelty.

It is very hard on Therese Lessore, whose show at the Eldar Galleries synchronises with the Matisse show, that she should be the butterfly broken on the wheel of comparison with the integrity of Matisse. But the demonstration is too apt. Before the Lessore pictures one feels that the artist, with perfectly conventional mind, has in each case, with perfectly conventional perception of scene, decided to "do it" in modern manner; we have all sorts of old pictures re-done in the mode of 1919, the result being thinness.

In Matisse the style rises out of the subject; the treatment, given Matisse himself, is inevitable; the result is profundity. One finds nothing whatever to question. No one else has painted these pictures; no one else in all time has painted the composition of form and colour to be found in the chair-back and environs of the portrait of three women. The eyes are Gauguin or Egyptian coffin lids without in the least disturbing the oneness of the picture. The oldest of old dodges is here and without being a detriment.

One feels in the Lessore show that there is not one picture which would be what it is *unless* someone else had painted some other picture, eighteenth century classicism or early nineteenth century prints; or Degas theatre scenes, or Manet, etc., with a thin coating of Lessore 1919, i.e., a sort of super or superior London Groupism on top. One is not convinced that Lessore before the child swinging on the fence-chain has seen anything which would not have been seen by any Tate Galleryist, or that there is any reason deeper than that of the calendar, i.e., deeper than the accident of its having been July, 1919, rather than July, 1870, when she painted it, to have caused it to be as it is.

Before the Matisse one feels the exact opposite; one feels that if Matisse had lived in 1870 or in 1570 he would have painted his three women in exactly the way that he has. This feeling may be quibbled about, but at bottom is very nearly justifiable. In the essentials nothing would have been altered; minutiae of the pictures would, let us admit, have been different had Matisse lived in another century, but the main drive of the canvas would have been the main drive as we have it.

The antithesis is very hard on Miss Lessore, but one cannot help it; the catechumen seeking enlightenment as to the difference between masterwork and not-masterwork has a very convenient chance of finding it out, not by reading what a critic can tell him, but by going from one gallery to the other and employing his eyesight. Lessore is modern and Matisse is of the eternal. Lessore is clever; the difference between Lessore and Sickert, between Lessore and Manet, between Lessore and any other known artist lies in a purely conscious effort to be different. Matisse's mastery lifts him above any attempt to be different.

In the end the critic can do no more for his public than try to persuade them to fill their eyes with good work, to fill their visual memories with the effects of good work. You cannot explain to a man that a drawing is bad or indifferent or "uninspired"; you can only show him good drawing often enough and hope that in time he may come to know the difference.

Matisse is art, and his show demonstrates inevitably that Lessore is only top-dressing; but Miss Lessore may comfort herself with the reflection that Matisse's work has and would have exactly the same effect on the work of many other artists with greater reputations than her own. There is proof of this at the Leicester Gallery itself, where the work of various other well-known artists is "also hung."

ART NOTES[49]

Wyndham Lewis' portrait of Ezra Pound rises with the dignity of a classic *stele* to the god of gardens amid the bundles of market-garden produce at the Goupil Gallery "salon" (5, Regent Street).

Bond Street (148, The Fine Art Society) presents Russell Flint's most serious assault on our attention to date; he has some technique and an effective use of wet water-colour. "Lochaber" is good in the old way. Flint is flanked by some pictures by C. A. Hunt, whereof the archaeology reaches back to the Turner mode; and by a stirring exhibit of William Walcot's mixed media. Walcot's larky and apparently swift embellished water-colour cum oil cum gouache, etc., is really very enjoyable. He is full of vivid contrasts. The "Venice Market" is clean and spirited; the style in "Loggia" is admirable; he comes near to pure form in "Bernini's Colonnade"; displays bravura in "Baths of Constantine," and, throughout the show, a very successful elimination of the unnecessary. Walcot is also a bold etcher, and the more conservative public can be safely recommended to inspect his pictures.

The stir and hullabaloo of the month is not, however, among painters, but among architects. Following their perturbation over the "Caliph's Design," and their natural defence—i.e., that the pamphlet was merely destructive—Mr. Wadsworth has had the temerity to exhibit a plaster model of a vorticist building. To the trepidation of the *Daily Mirror* and the architectural trade, an idea has launched itself against British architecture, placid since Wren carefully placed his epitaph *inside* St. Paul's Cathedral for fear some literate person should look at the external "sculpture" and "ornaments" of that edifice (i.e., outside, where the light is better).

[49]*The New Age*, December 11, 1919, pp. 96–97. Signed "B. H. Dias."

Apart from our natural horror that any man should think of designing a building unlike Messrs. Lyons' Corner House, or the dwellings in Observatory Gardens, or any other of the only too numerous monuments of the Albert Memorial era, we remain calm enough to observe that Mr. Wadsworth's model, presumably for an eight-storey building, is covered with curious ridges and excrescences; this is, we presume, an attempt to fit the architecture to our climate and to provide means for catching such light as there is; for catching much more of it than is possible by presenting all windows on a flat surface. This aim is commendable. For years intelligent people have, in vain, objected to the English use of an architecture designed for a warm and sunny climate. Even the fine-looking Italian, or Ferrarese, buildings in Jermyn Street suggest the exclusion rather than the invitation of light.

Wadsworth's model (at the Twenty-one Gallery, Adelphi) has likewise the virtue of considering the properties of his material; the structural laws of ferroconcrete differ from those of stone construction. We have before now commented on "architects" who use steel as if its chief virtue were to be the imitation of stone.

However, a break with building tradition should look farther ahead than to the construction of one building block. Paris has already its terraced house—i.e., a house of which each floor recedes successively from the street front and from the lower storeys. The loss of space in this construction is more than compensated by the gain in brightness of interior. Not only should London houses be terraced to admit light, but they should be oriented. How many dozens of corner houses have I not seen with blank walls to the west and windows facing north!

Also, for the crowded districts, for Piccadilly Circus, Ludgate Circus, the Bank, Liverpool Street, etc., we should seriously consider the traffic question. The sane solution lies in two levels; not an elevation of trams such as makes parts of New York and Chicago uninhabitable, but in the elevation of footway; cantilever side-walks; buses boarded at roof-level, not from underneath the spatter of mud and petroleum; bays for vans and goods delivery from the big stores; bridges for footway around the circuses. No one will *mount* a bridge to cross a road, but the continuation of elevated side-walk is a vastly different matter from a bridge over the gap between two street-level pavements. There should also be bays for females who wish to lose themselves in the ecstatic contemplation of Messrs. Selfridge's and Messrs Otherbody's front windows. A two-level system permits these innovations. It also permits the widening of streets without the tremendous expense of buying miles of private property in the most expensive districts of London. One would leave but a very narrow street-level kerb for entering taxis, etc., etc.

The Ovid Press (43, Belsize Park Gardens, N.W.3) again challenges our attention, following the excellent Gaudier-Brzeska portfolio with a still ample Wyndham Lewis mounted portfolio. Given the "Timon," Mr.

Lewis' exhibition of artillery drawings and the collection of his work at the South Kensington, the public has now a chance to judge Lewis as an artist, not merely as a volcanic and disturbing "figure."

The nudes I, II, and III of this portfolio give interesting points of comparison with the Matisse lithographs, or the Gaudier studies, or the John etchings now at the Chenil Gallery. We observed in the Matisse work a suavity and maturity in contrast with the youthful "attack" of the Gaudiers. In the second nude of the Lewis portfolio we find a very great vigour of design, a bolder treatment of the anatomy as design. And certainly qualities perhaps less analysable which neither Gaudier nor Matisse has presented.

In the "Group" (soldiers) we have Cézanne's structure made angular, and, I think, cleaner cut. The "Pole Vault" gives the transition from the "Timon" to the "Gun Drawings." Lewis becomes increasingly more menacing to the earlier British standards of acceptability. This is no longer due to his accessory literary ability. The time is past when artists could refer to him as a "mere man of letters." He is, needless to deny, our most searching and active art critic. Few people noticed his serious analysis of art in 1914; the periphery disturbances of *Blast* were too numerous; but the pitiless analysis of Picasso and of contemporary fadism in the "Caliph's Design" (*Egoist*, 3s. net) are worth very serious consideration.

Since Whistler's "Ten O'clock" no man actually a painter has been able to present thought about painting; and treatises from the actual workman have always an interest unattainable by aesthetes and men who analyse from the outside. The man who spends the whole or even the half of his life actually applying colours to paper and canvas must both know and care more for that process than the man who only looks at the final results.

When a critic is mere critic he is so for one or two reasons: either he cares more for ideas and discussion than for the art he criticises; or, secondly, he is so sensitive to excellence that he would rather not paint (or compose or sculp) than compose, paint or sculp like so-and-so. This second state is preferable to the state of the bad artist; but it implies a certain faintness of vitality. This second sort of critic *would* be a good artist *if* he had the energy, the patience of the good artist. And this very energy, this very patience, which inhere in the successful maker *are bound* to add something even to the critical side of his intellect.

The "Caliph's Design" is a fine curative and purgative against all the titter of Frys, Bells, Lhotes, etc., and as such it should be taken and administered in the cause of public health and morality.

The Ovid Press is to be complimented for the excellent quality of its coloured lithographic reproductions, and, in the cases of both of the Gaudier-Brzeska and Lewis portfolios, for offering the public excellent value for its money.

128

The Chelsea Book Club Gallery, 65, Cheyne Walk, opens with an excellent show of French drawings and water-colours; notice to follow.

ART NOTES[50]

"The Nation's War Paintings and Other Records, Imperial War Museum," are fittingly exhibited on the premises of the Royal Academy; the Royal Water-Colour Society, the Ducal Paste-board Society, the Imperial Papier-mâché Company, Inc., etc., all have a look in; the nine hundred and twenty exhibits plus the unnumbered "models" afford a prime opportunity for one of those circumambient pieces of tact made familiar in contemporary columns; it is such a chance to say the right thing by refraining from saying anything; and the labour of picking the good from the rubbish is thankless, *in the extreme.* As a popular beanfeast it is suitable that all tastes should be represented; and to find the art in this heap longa et ardua.

One may begin by eliminations, for there are the usual "marine pictures" in oily and soap-surfaced blue, with a few water-spouts added to label them "war"; there are the merely decorative efforts; the pseudo- but smartened Millais (383); the flagrantly missed opportunities, as the ship in dry-dock (389). 377 is just decorative; Jan Gordon's 374 looks as if it were by the same hand as 377, but it *has* the atmosphere of its subject, possibly attained by the masks on the operators; yet there are bandages in 377, and the feeling of eeriness, of the uncanny and unusual *could* as well have been produced by bandages as by masks. No, the first real demarcation we find in this show, apart from all questions of decent and indecent, honest and filthy painting, apart from difference of "school," is just this question of getting the feel of war, the feel of the evil and uncanny: some of the pictures are full of it, others are just attempts to evade the issue; to pass off what might have been an old landscape painted in 1898 for a fulfilment of the nation's commission to paint a picture of war.

Pass the rural in 388, the journalese in 389, fuzz in 395, pointillisme in 398; Nevinson in his big picture has at any rate painted mud that clings to the boots, and corpses that are not mere bright spots of decorativity; the body in the foreground is not only *nass und tot*, it has been *nass und tot* for some time; apart from the picture being, to my mind, a bad painting, it is uncontestably a representation of reality and an excellent record of war, and it gains honour by much of the frivolity in the exhibit, Orpen's, for example. Orpen has a nice little Dutch-like bit of prettiness, excellent objet d'art, all the crinoline of war, in fact, in his Dear Tommee inside the window; he has his bit of real stuff in the loony chap who has just

[50]*The New Age,* January 1, 1920, pp. 145–46. Signed "B. H. Dias."

been blown up, and for that drawing we commend him, in spite of his portraits, etc.

James McBey comes well out of the matter (drawings 819 and near that part of the exhibit) and Richard Carline, especially in "Samorra," shows a touch of the real thing; these men have done their jobs honestly. John Nash attracts perhaps more attention with his painting 72 and drawings; at least 72, Oppy Wood, is the first picture to draw attention. It is well hung and shows well from the full length of the room; on closer scrutiny we find the man in the trench is ill-painted, but if the canvas is intended to be placed high in some large decorative scheme this does not greatly matter; the main disposition of the picture is very good. W. P. Roberts has the place of honour, perhaps justly, but the composition does not carry, and at close range the Hollandy convention is questionable. Still, the picture is among the three or four best; Paul Nash's "Menin Road" is somewhat rhetorical; Roberts' drawings are excellent, though one is mildly frivolous; the Nash brothers seem to have attained official favour, and their drawings are strewn through all the rooms. Henry Tonks' 77 displays every despicable quality that we can imagine; it is as if various indiscriminate soups had been palely poured from a dozen tepid soup plates, amorphous, soggy, in short, what might have been expected, but more so, really more so; and low as has been my opinion of Mr. Tonks' work, this canvas has served to depress it. Mr. Spencer has been bent on decoration and composition, the prettier side of the shambles.

Glyn Philpot does the best of the official portrait paintings, with Admirals Tyrwhitt and Keyes. The pictures are what they should be, personality of the sitters conserved; though, of course, the work does not compare with Epstein's superb bust of Lord Fisher. This alone is worth the horrible boredom of searching through the thousand exhibits; and apart from his great abstract works, this is perhaps Epstein's best work; it is one of the durable achievements in closely representative portrait sculpture. One can set it next the Caesar in the long gallery of Roman heads in the British Museum (among which the Caesar is perhaps the one great work of art, if not the only important work). Needless to say, the Epstein head is not starred by the hanging committee or put where any undue attention will fall on it. Likewise the Wyndham Lewis gun-drawings are represented by only one specimen, this *given* by Muirhead Bone; yet all the silly lithographs of the propaganda department are spread out in serried array; Mr. Bone has also presented some John S. Sargent watercolours, possibly to get rid of them, for they represent a further state of Mr. Sargent's decline than we had yet been made aware of. Lewis's large picture will not add much to his reputation, although there are several things in it which only Lewis could have done (*first*). The back of the smaller figure in the left middle lower part of the picture, the grouping

130

and arrangement of the whole, the sinister grey lighting of the main figures at the left; the green and suggestive light on the far hill—it is difficult to see, where the picture hangs, as it needs distance, just as the Roberts' rather suffers from distance. Both pictures would gain by an exchange of position. We suppose, however, that the ideas which might have arisen had the Lewis been hung where it could naturally and would readily have incited the spectator to comparisons, did not appeal to the hangers. The abstraction of the moving smoke is of interest; at the same time the ensemble is rather a subject for study, an incitement to close thought about art than a wholly convincing performance.

Philip Connard gives an amiable and commendable whimsical portrait of Admiral Gough-Connard (27); McEvoy's portraits are bad, as usual, and in the usual way. Gill (83) goes in for the decorative; L. C. Taylor in 126 at least uses a decorative motif *inherent* in his subject. Bayes' 237 appears designed as a tribute to our Japanese allies; his underground station commends him to us more favourably. "Tunnel Mouth" (365) is just landscape. F. Dobson presents stylisation à la Van Anrep in 404; Revel is decorative in 457; Paul Nash good in 460 and 467; Roberts especially good in 489; Will Dyson is well represented by Ordinance Workshops, and 630.

Adrian Hill has drawn well in 858, Bone is at his best in "Sunset, Scapa," McBey in "Desert of Sinai," Will. Rothenstein presents the national characteristics in 893, Nelson Dawson in 918 shows an appropriate decorativeness as distinct from inappropriate decorativeness.

The large bas-reliefs seem to imply that pseudo-Mestrovic is to be the decreed mode of the "suggested frieze." If it can't be done by a great sculptor, why not come nearer home and have at least pseudo-Epstein?

ART NOTES[51]

The Chelsea Book Club Gallery (65, Cheyne Walk, S.W.3) opens auspiciously with an excellent show of French drawings; the press of fashion-plate females, the lack of a complete catalogue and the absence of numbers from such drawings as were listed in the catalogue such as it was, made the critic's job, and still make critical reference to specific works, rather difficult.

One noted especially the wet washy water-colours of Vlaminck. The Cézanne portrait might possibly have attracted less attention had it not been for the awe-hushed whisper that a Cézanne was in the room. Within seven minutes I heard all the great phrases applied to this small canvas, all,

[51]*The New Age*, January 8, 1920, pp. 159–60. Signed "B. H. Dias."

that is, of the great phrases now current concerning Cézanne; and I have heard them recurrently since; "so massive," "so simple," "such quality in the paint," "such interesting, etc. . ."

This Cézanne is no better than any one of half a dozen pictures by Matisse now at the Leicester Gallery, yet the clichés applied to Matisse will be from a different series. M. Lhote's drawings (at the Chelsea Book Club) are as vacuous as his writing might lead one to expect. Picart LeDoux is agreeable, and one wonders what has become of the placid blue and white Dianas and Pans which used to hang in the "Indépendants," and whether his two styles are successive or simultaneous.

The Chelsea Book Club, in excellent situation, offering an open market for all contemporary literature and for all schools of art, influenced, so far as we can observe, by no clique tendency, and certainly more artistic than commercial in its aim, should be extremely useful to the arts; there is but one caution arising from the exotic nature of the opening exhibit. It is a good thing to import the best foreign work (as, for example, in the augmentation of the Matisse exhibit); it may even be advisable to import other foreign work; but the managers of this gallery should remember that there is no closer ring than the ring of the Paris art-dealers; they are doubtless quite ready to "unload" on the London market; M. Lhote is even in movement for unloading the excess stock of David; we should prefer to see an exchange both of works and of knowledge. We have local products quite as good, and, in some cases, better, than the work now at the Book Club; and its managers would double their effectiveness if they would stipulate a foot per foot and week per week exhibit of English works in Paris in return for London exhibit of French works here. We believe, from present indications, that the Book Club could do this, and that it would be impartial in its selection of English work.

Mr. Campbell Dodgson, C.B.E., is about to issue a catalogue of the etchings of Augustus E. John, a royal quarto, in which every known etching (134 in number), frequently in more than one state, will be illustrated. In view of this impending inclusiveness, any comment one might now make on the 127 John etchings now at the Chenil Gallery might seem to be supererogatory. John has had a remarkable career. Known even as a Slade student, his maximum impact upon the public sensibility was achieved when he was about 28 or 30 years of age, at which time he was indubitably the finest painter in England and his success wholly deserved; as a confrère remarks, "he had made so close a study of Rembrandt's method," etc. John had made a close study of various artists. He led the anti-Academy party for some years, for no man of so great a talent who had studied any great masters whatsoever could possibly have *complied with* the Academy party. A sight of Velásquez in Whistler's case, or of Rembrandt in John's, was enough to make an "irreconcilable."

When our eminent contemporary calls Rembrandt John's only master

132

in etching, we must, however, suppose that he refers solely to questions of craft, for etching would seem to have been John's medium for imitation and experiment. By "imitation" I do not mean anything derogative, nor does the term necessarily imply want of inventiveness; every good artist, or, at any rate, every very comprehensive artist must be filled with curiosity about the works of his predecessors; he will want to "see if he can do it," he will wish to make analyses more minute than can be made by any means save that of doing the thing with his own hand. Thus, in John's case we find Rembrandt, Goya, Chardin, Millais, the Pre-Raphaelites, allegories, possibly Blake, and even a Belcher charwoman in the etchings, just as we find Botticelli and the Italian primitives in his painting; much of this must be counted as study, as beneficent and praiseworthy study. There remains the distinctively "John" draughtsmanship (more apparent possibly in some of the unnumbered and vigorous drawings in the upper rooms, than in the etchings now at the Chenil).

The possible limitation of John, seeing that his success was the initial launch-out of indisputable talent for draughtsmanship, may lie in an insufficient regard for the maturer faculties, for the labour of great construction, for intellectual reinforcement; after ten years of zenith it is difficult to say whether, if one had seen three hundred Matisse heads all with Egyptian or Gauguin eyes, one might be too familiar with them to "have an opinion"; one is now very familiar with the John style in painting and etching.

One goes from the Chenil to the Leicester Gallery and receives great impact from the new picture by Matisse, a black-haired woman in white. One finds "La Villa Bleu" (No. 5) to be all that a landscape should be. It has a vitality not in Constable. The "Paysage" (30) and "Viaduc" (31) are like unto it. "Intérieur" (10) is mere colour. "Intérieur" (15) is colour plus the indefinable; it is the apogee of decorativeness, "La Liseuse" (21) is like unto it. It would be highly instructive to see an array of John paintings and an array of Matisse paintings hung on the opposite walls, a challenge which neither artist should shrink from. Would Matisse's colour prove the "phantom antagonist"?

The Matisse work at the Leicester has been shifted from one room to another, and the new lighting enforces a different set of values. The Rousseauesque "Etude Jeune Fille" (25), and the "Femme Orientale" (27), show to particular advantage, as also the lithographs 1 and 7 in the new hanging.

Maillol's faintly obese Tanagras do not excite much comment; they are obese Tanagras; it is faintly interesting that one should be able to combine the grace of Tanagra with this somewhat Gallic or slightly bourgeoise or peasant obesity; it is, possibly, a demonstration that the grace of the objet d'art is not quite the grace of the subject; it is possibly only an implicit art treatise on relativity in the nubile. Tanagra held for fausse

133

maigre, the gentleman from the Midi inclines to the opposite structure. His drawings have an eighteenth century grace, though no very personal or distinctive characteristics; they might be by Chardin.

Mr. Sheringham sinks far below Maillol; he is decorative; he has not sought a subtle commentary on familiar things, or not on things so familiar as Boucher; he has brilliance and oriental exoticism; his silks and satins are part of the artistic furbelows of the era; there is nothing in his work to put off the most opulent lover of luxurious boudoir furnishing, and there is probably no house in Mayfair where his work would be out of place. Mr. Rackham declines to the status of a children's entertainer, though his drawing, No. 1, is carefully executed.

Mr. Walter Bayes exhibits at the Hampstead Art Gallery, 345, Finchley Road, N.W.3.

ART NOTES[52]

The exhibition of drawings by Wyndham Lewis, now at the Adelphi Gallery (9, Duke Street, Adelphi) should finally and ultimately wipe out the last trace of "husky man-in-the-street" jabber about "these new men doing stunts because they can't do anything else." I write this recalling the genial statement made to me a few weeks ago at Burlington House, sic: "Aw! nobody would know anything about 'em, nobody would see anything in it, if it weren't for a few critics tellin' 'em"—the "popular psychology" in this case being apparently, "Don't go to anyone who knows anything about it." This new show of Lewis' drawings strikes a very serious blow at the prestige of John and of Matisse. The nude (7) will probably convince any impartial observer where the highest skill is to be found. The eyes in the portrait drawing of Major Windeler show a vast deal more artistic concentration than do Matisse's derivations from Egypt and from Gauguin.

If mastery in drawing means absolute obedience of the pencil to the will of the artist, then mastery is indubitably here; and in comparison both with Matisse and with John we have a deal more focusing of mentality upon the matter in hand. A few devotees will regret that Mr. Lewis shows none of his more abstract compositions, yet his control over the elements of abstraction was hardly ever greater than in some of these present drawings, and his independence of the actual never more complete than in his present subjugation of it to his own inner sense.

We note particularly the palpable flesh quality and texture in the black nude in 6, the sense of certitude and simplification of the facial elements in 7, the grace and ease in 4, mood in 13, severity in 5, economy not stint

[52]*The New Age,* January 29, 1920, pp. 205–6. Signed "B. H. Dias."

in 9, and, throughout the series, consummate ability to define his masses by line and to express the texture of soft substance without sacrifice of an almost metallic rigidity of boundary.

Edward Wadsworth (Leicester Gallery) has found a curious ally in Mr. Arnold Bennett, who, according to the introduction, has "never yet seen anything more 'advanced' than the Elgin Marbles." We know all about the Elgin Marbles and David and the last decision of the Paris (strictly informal) arts fashion committee; and Mr. Bennett is right up to time (last despatch left six weeks ago). Matisse also looked at the Elgin Marbles in the British Museum; they "couldn't get him away" (ssh! "distortion," we must have our bit of aaartistik slang). Well, Mr. Bennett has written quite a nice introduction, warning us that the Black Country isn't the Five Towns (nor the Cinque Ports, neither), and it is the best thing Mr. Bennett has done for some time.

Mr. Wadsworth, to come back to our business, has found in the Black Country slag-heaps a content just suited to his particular talent; all the care he spent a few years ago in abstract stripes now bears fruit in more animated compositions. He is the fortunate man who first made a map of the country he intended to find and then gone out and found it; it is vorticistic high-handedness, but it works. Here are slag-heaps and factories, very like—in fact, unmistakably like—slag-heaps and factories, and unmistakably like Mr. Wadsworth's own abstract painting. He has, in full sense, incorporated or given a body to an idea. We note especially the curvilinear 37, the space in 38, calm of 29, vivacity of 33.

As for the other shows at the Leicester, the less said about Lanteri the better; the Gaudier fawn and even the Reid Dick mask plant the last funereal stone on Lanteri's Westminster Abbey traditions. There are some porcelain flowers—quite competent—by Beatrice Bland, and some water-colours by William T. Wood, sometimes tasteful and sometimes false. The superb Gauguin double portrait of child full face and profile, with its reserve, dignity, and sense of volume, is a masterpiece not to be missed by any art-lover.

The New English Art Club show (at 5a, Pall Mall East, S.W.) is dominated by Augustus E. John's portrait "Iris" (patronymic to be divined). This picture is brisk and well painted; it is hung in atrocious light, and one has to dodge all over the gallery to make out its points; but it is manifestly John at his best, the figure well poised and well accommodated in the canvas. The main disposition of the show is cheering, in antithesis, somewhat, to the yield given by examination of individual pictures in it. Thus, Mooney shows us the usual paradise (1) that we have been led to expect, perhaps over often; and M. Milne gives us sham-modernised Watts with a coating of Russian-toy-ism; and Stanley Spencer and Gilbert Spencer burgeon into pseudo-sanctimoniousness (repeatedly) ("la littérature religieuse est morte"). However, we have Christ looking like a Café Royal drunk, aetatis suae LVI, being hoisted upon his cross by four huskies in pants, who hang upon the bar of the implement instead of lifting (if pants, we query, why not an electric chair or a gibbet or a guillotine? this charming naiveté!). Of course, it may not be Christ at all, but only our old friend S—— from the café; but "The Sacrifice of Zacharias" and stray bits of sham Pre-Raphaelitism in the vicinity lead one to suspect that the Spencer family has a penchant for "sacred subjects." R. Ihlee shows pleasing still life (10); C. J. Holmes honest landscape (11). G. Spencer is hopelessly affected in 16; M. Jeffries in 21 paints like De Smet; it is not a very nice thing to say about him; David Bomberg in 31 has carefully made use of the abstract forms used some time ago by W. Lewis in his picture "The Crowd"; Lessore shows pale post-Sickert; Wheatley is sentimental in "Edith"; H. Squire shows a Wadsworthian 40. F. H. S. Shepherd falls into hopeless pseudo-Italian sentimentalism in "La Poveretta"; C. M. Gere carefully enamels 48; E. Darwin shows spiritual affinity with R. Flint; Wm. Shackleton shows a Victorian portrait (53). Then there is more buncombe Pre-Raphing. G. Raverat makes some exaggerated remarks about "Pietà"; Morley's Apollo is "In Exile," and a long, long way into it at that. B. Meninsky shows Teddy Bear in the burning bush, quite in keeping with his religious co-hangers; O. Gardiner gives us more jokes about the "bloomin' Boible"; faced with her C. in Temple, it is impossible to refer to the "Scriptures" as anything save "the bloomin'," etc. Maresco Pearce's 74 is, very considerably, more than a good poster; J. E. Southall rather good, if he can keep from playfulness; M. S. Florence shows more Pre-Raph. hurly burly (89).

The general decorativeness of the walls is probably due to that fact that the New English Art Club painters have mastered the problems of spacing; that their pictures are "good arrangements," however obsessed they may be with a desire for "amusing" subject-matter. (Word "amusing" used in sense now current in Bloomsbury's tittering argot.)

Of the drawings we can say simply that they are not up to Lewis, and anyone with lingering superstitions or a desire to clear his own mind can learn a great deal about the gap between the two qualities by walking from Pall Mall to Adelphi. A. Davies is spirited in "Peace Night," and Albert Rutherston displays Botticellian grace in 113 and 130.

Some of Wyndham Lewis' drawings, from the Guy Baker Collection, and a few charcoal studies by Gaudier-Brzeska, are now on view in the East Hall at the South Kensington Museum.

ART AND LUXURY[53]

"Art" which means for many people "painting" or "painting and sculpture" flourishes as a luxury trade, in comparison with literature, or

[53]*The New Age*, February 12, 1920, pp. 238–39. Signed "B. H. Dias."

poetry, "the consolation of the poor," which merely "exists." Music flourishes in large cities when it provides a circus for the display of osprey plumage, etc.

This is no new thesis, and whatever virtue these notes on art may have had, they have always aimed at sorting out the art which is discovery, invention, clarification, analysis of perception, expression; from the "art" which is adjunct to the various luxury trades.

It is, possibly, to the advantage, and certainly to the disadvantage, of the painter and painting, that "art" should be capable of this ambiguous blending and borderland; but there is always this difference between the ignominy of bad art and that of bad literature, that, whatever crapularity may be displayed by the writing pander, he does not produce an article which can be bought by the general public to be stored and made a matter of profit.

The rewards for "incidental lyrics" in musical comedy, for bad novels, etc., are monetarily considerable, but the temptation before the writer is different in kind from the temptation of the maker of pretty objects. A painter creates objects of cash-value in a way wherein a poet or musical composer cannot. The slight exceptions made by rare sale of original mss. and first editions do not invalidate this statement.

If the painter has not more chances of selling his soul twice over from Saturday to Monday, he has, at any rate, more chances of being paid cash on the nail for such transactions.

It is the dignity of the poet or of the composer that his product is immaterial. What he makes can go direct to the poor, to any poor man with wit to understand it. Whether it be the young Masefield treasuring his copy of *Paradise Lost* in a shoddy American boarding-house, or the Arab in an unfurnished desert carrying his songs, which the Emir Feisul has promised Colonel Lawrence to collect for the benefit of the Occidental student, or the Irish peasant, reputedly revelling in the beauties of exuberant language, we do not lack proofs for the democracy of the art of fine speech, as contrasted with the luxury of the painter's wares.

In the case of poetry it is the thing itself, not an oleograph or a photo-reproduction which goes to the man on the veldt, to the Ceylon planter, to the errand boy in a Manchester slum. Given the love of the thing, given an inclination to care for the best, poverty is no bar, remoteness is no bar, to possession.

On the other hand, a knowledge of pictures is confined to the people who live in a few great cities or who can afford visits to great galleries and current exhibits. All of which creates a modus of appreciation and appraisement for painting very different from the usual modus of appreciation of literature.

There are any number of minor quibbles; one may point out that reproductions of pictures figure in fashion papers, that "art" is seduced into them as an extra spice, as a subtle flattery to the luxury-instinct, that fashion cribs from new painters; superficially one may point a parallel in the poems printed in fancy type in *The Sphere,* poetry dragged in to flatter the readers of that sheet that their taste is a taste for literature.

But one does not get round the fact that Mr. Schwartzbaum, Mr. McPherson, Mr. Blood, Mr. Biebenstein cannot buy up the original mss. and "make a good thing of it" in any way even approaching the way in which even the best painting may be made a matter of commerce.

The writer may be "tempted," but he is tempted to reach a large audience, the painter is tempted to appeal to the taste of a few luxury lovers, or a few dealers. The pull is different; the writer, one may say, is tempted to appeal to the no-taste of the multitude; the painter to what may be the remains of a somewhat decaying but refined taste of a few opulent "lovers."

The declivities lead on the one hand toward the demagogue, and, on the other, to the maker of sofa cushions. These diatribes are prompted partly by a show of pictures at a dealer's. Last year I found two fine Canalettos; this year, I find almost without exception, a set of oils, having no artistic merits of any sort, but which offer, perhaps, as great a margin of profit to the dealer as did the masterwork which he sold last season.

I do not believe that authors have quite this sort of thing to struggle against. True, Mr. Dent can undersell living authors by his cheap reprints of work on which he does not have to pay royalties, but the Temple Classics and Everyman are a public benefit, and nearly all of his volumes tend to breed a finer taste in the reader.

My second irritation with the luxury-sense comes from a matter, perhaps, at first sight, outside the proper scope of these notes, but it is so interwoven with the much-praised "sense of beauty," that I cannot keep from it; more especially as the "Ed. 'Observer'" states that he "cannot publish further correspondence on this subject." I refer to the Plumage Trade. Mr. Hamel Smith has had the insolence to defend this infamy. I can do no better than quote from several of the letters to *The Observer.* First, Mr. H. J. Massingham:—

> So it is my "lively imagination" which borrows untruthful facts about this vile traffic from others. Would Mr. Smith like to know where I get my facts from—not only the U.S. Government and the exact and carefully corroborated evidence of naturalists who witnessed the atrocities committed on the birds, not only from the evidence of the House of Lords Committee in 1908, etc., but from the catalogues of the feather merchants themselves. Here is an extract from one of them:—
>
> 75,000 egret skins, December, 1912; 77,000 ditto, June, 1913; 7,395 bird of paradise skins (exchanged, according to Mr. Walter Goodfellow, F.Z.S., M.B.O.U., with the natives for rum and opium), May,

1911; 10,700 crowned pigeons, February, 1908; 5,140 ditto, February, 1913; 6,328 ditto, June, 1913; 24,800 humming birds, February, 1911; 18,000 sooty terns, February, 1908; 5,321 white terns, February, 1913; 162,750 Smyrnian kingfishers, June, 1913; 1,233 emu skins (smuggled), February, 1913; 16,211 white crane wing quills, February, 1913; 19, 125 osprey ("mullet hawk") wing quills, February, 1913; 10,800 bustard quills, February, 1913; 8,321 condor quills, February, 1913; 40,000 ditto (one firm only), June, 1913; 1,203 greater bird of paradise skins, October, 1913.

Here is a handful of species out of hundreds and hundreds savagely massacred in the breeding season by these advocates of preservation, for naturalist after naturalist bears his testimony that in all the vast districts desolated by them they go for every bird that flies, whether great or small, of dull or brilliant plumage.

Secondly, Mr. Willoughby Dewar, from whom *The New Age* heard on the same subject a few weeks ago:

Sir,—Mr. Smith asks that persons concerned in the plumage trade should be heard. I agree with him. The evidence of Mr. A. H. Meyer, for nine years a plume collector in South America, is valuable. Mr. Meyer has made the following statements on oath:—

(1) That "picked up" plumes are of small value owing to poor conditions. That egrets, etc., have their plumes only in the mating season, and that it is the custom to shoot them while the young are in the nests.

(2) That wounded birds are often left to die of starvation with their young when the plumes have been pulled from them.

(3) That wounded birds are tied up and used as decoys until they die from their wounds or are eaten by ants. He has seen the red ants eating their eyes.

Thirdly:—

Sir,—Can Mr. Hamel Smith deny that every "osprey," pair of wings, or bird of paradise tail in a hat or a shop window means a bird dead instead of alive? Or that such spoils of the dead are to be counted in London alone by thousands?—Yours, etc.,

CLEMENTINA BLACK
22, Westmoreland Road, Barnes, S.W.13.

There is the case, with some brevity. I present it because this trade is a by-product of the degradation of the sense of beauty into a sense of luxury. And in so far as it concerns the sense of beauty it is a commentary, and no

139

irrelevant commentary on the public attitude toward art; a commentary on the loose thinking displayed in much contemporary art talk and art criticism. The kind of "appreciation" which makes this trade possible, is the kind of "appreciation" which militates against the creative element in painting, and is, therefore, part of my subject-matter.

It is also worthy of note that the Plumage Trade works through the very trade and fashion papers with which *The New Age* has at no time shown any sympathy. I go so far as to express a doubt whether any member of a staff or any owner of a fashion journal will take any strong stand against aigrets; reason being discoverable, where much else is discoverable, namely, in the advertising columns.

ART NOTES[54]

Epstein is the greatest sculptor in Europe. This statement needs no qualification whatsoever. The death of Gaudier-Brzeska robbed the world of his only possible contemporary peer. Of the "Christ," of the "Mrs. Epstein," of the "Gabrielle Saonne" bronzes, now at the Leicester Gallery, one can only say that they are equal to any sculpture that has ever been in Egypt, in Assyria, or in the Congo. The critic is permitted his preference for Epstein's "abstract" work, but is compelled to admit that in the three above-mentioned works Epstein the representative has equalled Epstein the maker of strange images.

A process of "abstraction" or synthesis has, however, occurred. Egypt, Greece, Africa, Assyria, Mongolia have lent racial qualities to different busts in this exhibit, so that at least six of the bronzes are not merely portrait busts, but the concentration of race into; the expression of race by means of; the single head. This occurs in slighter degree in the very American soldier.

The world's better intelligences gave up what is called Christianity during the Renaissance, and since that period there has been no religious art in Europe north of the Pyrenees. There has been propaganda; there has been sentimentalisation about religious subjects (so recently as Eric Gill); there have been Sunday-school illustrations of the Bible and innumerable paintings of religious subjects. ("Christ and the Boy Scout," for example.) But there has been no religious art.

"The Guardian" will cite Bougereau as a refutation of this statement, and is perfectly welcome to do so. Epstein's "Christ" is a break in this order of things; it is, emphatically, religious art. This figure would arrest and hold attention, it would convey the full blast of its sculptural and emotional content, were it found in the desert by tribes who had never

[54]*The New Age*, March 4, 1920, pp. 291–92. Signed "B. H. Dias."

heard of the Christian religion. It is, that is to say, an *expression*, not a mere *reference to a known legend or "history."*

There is not the faintest trace of dogmatism in this work. One cannot restate it in language. The Gospels are an adequate footnote; they would explain various artistically irrelevant facts *about* the statue to the above-supposed "tribes"; but these facts are sculpturally no more necessary to the statue than a philological note about Venus or Victory is necessary to the statues of Milos or Samothrace.

The statue is not translatable into the phrases: "I have behaved in a perfectly reasonable manner, and my hand has been pierced. I refused to be intimidated by imbeciles, and my hand has been pierced. I have also been interred, but you have not seen the last of me. Two and two make four, and the sealing me into a sepulchre will not alter the sum of two twos." The statue expresses all this, but does not end with that expression.

Ce bonhomme n'est pas très agréable. An unkind photographer has suspended his camera from the chandelier and taken a distorted photograph which brings out a resemblance to the heavenly twins, President Wilson and Sir A. Geddes. This is a slander on the bronze, and the degree of distortion may be gauged by the transformation of the rectangles of the base into obtuse and acute angles.

This sort of contretemps may befall any work of art; one may disregard it, as one disregards other irrelevancies. The "Mrs. Epstein" and the "Gabrielle" are on a par with the "Christ." The other heads are excellent, but the present critic is inclined to think that they are in a different category. They are, like the head of Admiral Fisher, good Epstein. They are what we can count upon Epstein doing when in form. But the "Gabrielle" is Epstein's skill and experience, plus inspiration, plus the unpredictable élan. There is a grace and poignancy in it which was not in his abstract work.

Over and above the personalities of contemporary art squabbles, over and above the discussable personality of the sculptor, there rises this triumph of his genius. The jests of the gutter-critics, the small-talk of exasperated acquaintances, should count for a very slight patter of sound, a passing sprinkle of rain which will wear away nothing of the bronze. And in an age where, as in all other ages, there is little lasting merit, we can give unqualified praise and unqualified thanks for such work as is here presented.

The Senefelder Club (Leicester Gallery) shows, as usual, some excellent lithographs—Goya, Gauguin, Daumier, Fantin-Latour, and one very good Guevara, "The Turn's End," Wadsworth's "Ladle Slag," a Matisse study, Bonnard's "La Rue." One notes that the Goyas carry with great efficiency, despite the closeness of detail; Lautrec is clever; the Daumiers, 128–31, merit special attention; J. McL. Hamilton shows grace; H. E. Cross, pleasing pointillism.

It is probably a little late to note the meritorious January show at the Eldar Gallery. It contained a Forain, showing utter mastery of water-colour, atmosphere, and real knowledge; and various works by great names, of diverse interest—a Ziem, à la Monticelli, a K. X. Roussel, a Vuillard in dull granulation.

The Chelsea Book Club exhibits the child-naïve manner in Nicola Galante. Their Renoir exhibit contains the good "Jeune Garçon" (No. 4) sort of hard woodenish manner, an interesting piece of work, the one "modern" canvas in the room, distinct from the rest of the crushed fruit which Mr. Fry explains to us, in a foreword, that we should enjoy, not because Renoir painted well (which he did on numerous occasions), but chiefly because Renoir liked passionately the good things of life; because his art is "almost as simple a matter as the enjoyment of good food"; because "Renoir trusted implicitly to his own sensibility." Mr. Fry seems to think that Renoir was very daring in saying "how much he loved a pretty sight." But a reference to chronology might almost lead one to believe that Renoir was young and impressionable at a time when nearly everybody did like pretty sights ("Bubbles," etc.), and when this simple predilection for pink cheeks, chromatic flowers, etc., would have aroused no very acrimonious protest. However, it is very, very hard to write convincing forewords for collections of not quite the best work of artists who have a deservedly large reputation. One might almost venture the formulation that these canvases of Renoir's show the effect of impression-ism upon a fundamentally nineteenth-century personality, who happened to be a good painter, with no psychology whatsoever.

At the Goupil, Professor Frederick Brown shows some goodish water-colours, but the Monarro group seems to have no reason for existence; the backwash of Monet's and Pissarro's imitators, resulting in a sort of Lon-don Groupishness sans the Fry pallor or the sickert fog-an'-sootism. (Note that this fog-an'-sootism is Sickert's own, and worthy of praise in Sickert, in whom it did indicate a certain courage, a certain courageous realism, a certain search into ugliness for the possibilities of new harmony.)

Pissarro has provided one woman with a horse's tail without convincing us that the effect is intentional. C. H. Hassell's 32 is not so bad. E. M. Henderson tries the Gauguinesque, not unpleasingly, etc. Even Monet's own "Les Nymphes, paysage d'eau," might be almost Stephen Crane after Turner. One penalty for greatness is that all one's side-slips are destined for garish publicity. Amen.

We note with some amusement that the Society of Modern Portrait Painters have failed rather lamentably in an attempt to insult Mr. Gue-vara and modern painting in general. They tried a spoof show of new geniuses, and failed to take in even the most hasty of our contemporary pressmen. Mr. Konody has given them what they deserve in the *Sunday*

Observer for February 15, and we need not continue the story. We trust they will go away and lie down until they learn better. Of course, if the poor old dears were in earnest—i.e., if they wanted to begin Vita-Nuovas— to see if they could earn better livings by trying to follow new masters (however ineptly). . . . Still, that is an economic question which they should refer to their agents. (N.B.—We do not think this latter hypothesis is correct, but if they want to bring off this sort of thing they should not hang their efforts on the same wall with Guevara.)

ART NOTES[55]
The Functions of Criticism

Criticism of painting should imply not only that the paintings criticised are worthy either of praise or blame, but that there is some way of saying so which will tell the readers or hearers something which they would not have found out for themselves. In an ideal state of society, adorned by a great galaxy of active artists, such criticism might be possible once a fortnight.

In the case of Mr. Augustus John it is, now, nearly impossible to say anything which the literate public does not already know. Ten years ago John was probably the best painter in England, the knutocracy babbled of his "wonderful drawing." Nothing is changed, nothing is altered in that drawing. So far as we can make out, John is still himself, his old Bohemian self. It is extremely doubtful whether I shall learn anything more about him by going to the Alpine Club Gallery, Mill Street, Conduit Street, W.1, where his work will remain on show until April 29.

On the other hand, it is obvious that Mr. John has every right to two columns of *New Age* publicity; he has every right to have his show announced in some sensible and visible form in numerous periodicals and dailies. His work is much more worth seeing than much which one has "noticed" in these Notes. On the other hand, for our monster must be multimanuous, we cannot hope to increase Mr. John's market, or his glory, or anything that is his. My impression is that he is an artist to whom justice is and has for some time been done.

The critic's function is, when possible, to see that justice is done and to prevent or to put an end to various forms of injustice. John is in a state of equilibrium, and we can therefore pass by, our services being supererogatory.

Coming to Frampton (I believe it is Frampton) we find injustice. Here

<hr>

[55]*The New Age*, April 8, 1920, p. 372. Signed "B. H. Dias."

is the offical artist, the nation's choice. The monument does not dishonour Miss Cavell, but it is an example of art existing as a parasite on heroism, on the heroism of someone else. This is the opposite of creation. But for a deed of heroism (I am saying nothing concerning the wisdom of it) the sculptor would not have had the chance to perpetrate this monstrosity, the pussy-cat lion, the cheap symbolism, etc. Mr. Frampton (it was, I believe, Mr. Frampton) is better placed in doing the squirrels and mice on the base of the "Peter Pan," where he had Mr. Rackham's Hodder-and-Stoughton illustrations to jog his imagination.

Turning to another public institution, *Punch*—the publisher's poultice of C_3 humour—we find a caricature of the modern sculpture. As the text is in English and as there is only one non-academic sculptor in England we presume one of Sir O. Seaman's officeboys is having a shy at Jacob Epstein. It has, however, escaped the eagle-eye of the chief poulticer that the statue caricatured is very, indeed very, like the "Cenotaph," and the "Cenotaph" is the work not of a sculptor, but of an architect, the *daahling* of the official and of the knutocrat. And therefore it must be a mistake, this caricature, for in all its long life *Punch* has never once lifted his bauble against the preferred and the accepted. Miss Marie Corelli has been more courageous. She has burst out of Stratford to protest against there being sculpture in England. We may refer her to Butler's poem on the "Discobolus."

The "Cenotaph" is in itself sufficient confession of official terror and of the bankruptcy of British sculpture. Admiral Fisher may not have been always right, but, judging from the one point where he crossed a field really known to us, we are inclined to accept his opinions. He did have his bust done by the best sculptor available. This shows a better intelligence than any of his colleagues have displayed in the same field, although some of them do paint (école de Lavery) in their spare time. In short: Fisher goes to Epstein. The discreet officials go to an architect for a nullity which "does not offend." The enthusiasts go to Frampton, though they might have followed more barbaric tradition and imported a few thousand Teuton monstrosities, save that this would have been a kindness to Germany, where more than one Siegesdenkmal has elicited "Avenged at last" from vanquished and visiting opponents. After all, a "monument" has two chances of being ridiculous, either by form or by occasion, and Landor is perhaps the only man who ever got anything good out of any of these mementos in London, with his lines on the Duke of York's statue:

Enduring is the bust of bronze,
And thine, O flower of George's sons,
Stands high above all laws and duns.

As honest men as ever cart
Convey'd to Tyburn took thy part
And raised thee up to where thou art.

In the present cases the tragic subjects of official recognition deserve a better mnemonic effort than official art-substitute seems able to provide.

THE EVIDENCE

Analysis of the current expositions yields:

Alpine Club Gallery, more dangerous than one would have supposed, the idol in worse condition. No man can make forty works of art in a season. With the exception of "La Veilleuse," where there is a resorgimento of fantasy, a good figure, and a pleasing background, the whole show might almost be by Sargent, Boldini, and even, in the case of the Maharaja, by some anonymous member of the Pastel Society. "Portrait of a Boy" is rather better. "La Veilleuse" is excellent.

Fine Art Society: A. R. Smith and W. J. James, neither having any merit to speak of. Ditto for Messrs. S. and R. Carline at the Goupil.

Women's International: One clean picture by M. McDowall; P. Sutton, two etchings; H. Henderson (88), badly done but with permissible ambitions. N. England, "decorative."

X Group, at Heal's: Mr. Wadsworth, as per his last show plus "Tipton Furnaces" and "Metal Runs," new compositions of merit. W. Roberts not at his best. Handsome catalogue with wood-cut portraits of the artists. Mr. Wyndham Lewis represented at time of press view, by strong appeal to imagination, sixteen hanging chains of doubtless excellent brass, and by a reflection of some of his former phases in the work of the lesser members of the group. Hamilton alone preserves the simon-pure abstraction of 1912–14.

Nicholson: The real pleasure at the end of a wasted and weary day is to be found at the Goupil, where we find Wm. Nicholson's "Silver Box," with beauty of low tones, deep lake and "morocco leather" orange, carefully done, dignified, as is also "The Glass Bowl." The Nicholson water-colours, "The Mistral," "Le Sportif Bar," are in a class with Whistler, and "Les Baux," an excellent invention. Pryde exhibits a piece of Italian magniloquence (22) and a Rembrandtopolonaise head. There is a magnificent Walter Greaves, wood-tone with an inflow probably of Uccello. At last a sip of nectar, at last after a weary pilgrimage, the evidence that one man once wanted to paint an enjoyable picture, and that one man still enjoys putting paint on canvas.

CREDIT AND THE FINE ARTS[56]
A Practical Application

"Considering the impossibility of getting a discussion of *Credit Power and Democracy* in the British press at the time of its first publication"; yes, my first review of the book appeared in Belgium, my second in New York, my third, carefully "toned," in the then *Athenaeum* presumably incomprehensible to its editor, my fourth or fifth in *Les Ecrits Nouveaux*, an arty sort of French magazine having no actual equivalent in the England of 1922, but being rather like the old *Blue Review* and of no more importance or significance. The point of interest is that this article was quoted almost entire, fairly quoted, with all its essential points—and if anything improved by the cuts—in the *Progrès Civique* of the week after. The *Progrès Civique* is a popular weekly for sale on all the kiosks, and no more highbrow than *John Bull*. That gives you a fair measure of the comparative receptivity of France and England.

Yeats says "England is the only country where a man will lie without being paid for it." When I mentioned that to a Frenchman here, and went on to discuss the abolition of free speech, or at any rate the uncensored publication and circulation of ideas in England, he said, "Yes, we have the same thing here, I mean they know they ought to keep quiet, but they just can't. *Le français est trop bavard.*"

Discussion of the *Progrès Civique* article by a group of French and Americans here has led to the following experiment (Bel Esprit), à propos the Douglas text, "Release of more energy for invention and design."

One recognises that there is no functioning co-ordinated civilisation in Europe; democracy has signally failed to provide for its best writers; aristocratic patronage exists neither in noun nor in adjective. The func-

---

[56]*The New Age*, March 30, 1922, pp. 284–85. Reprinted, in part, in *Impact*, Chicago, 1960, p. 217. Signed "Ezra Pound." See *The Selected Letters of Ezra Pound*, ed. D. D. Paige, London, 1951, pp. 241–42; New York, 1970, pp. 174–75. As Donald Gallup notes in *A Bibliography of Ezra Pound*, London, 1969, p. 380, "The first year's funds [for the Bel Esprit project] were to be used for T. S. Eliot, so that he might be able to leave his position at Lloyd's Bank; when T. S. Eliot refused to accept the money, the funds were returned to the subscribers and the project was abandoned."
Virginia Woolf's comment at the time may be of interest. In *The Letters of Virginia Woolf, II: 1912–1922*, eds. Nigel Nicolson and Joanne Trautmann, New York and London, 1977, p. 572, she writes:

> Tom's psychology fascinates and astounds. There he has let us all go on writing and appealing for the past 6 months, and at last steps out and says he will take nothing less than £500 a year—very sensible, but why not say so at first; and why twist and anguish and almost suffocate with humiliation at the mere mention of money? . . . Very American, I expect; and the more I see of that race the more I thank God for my British blood, which does at any rate preserve one from wearing 3 waistcoats; enamel buttons on one's overcoat, and keeping one's eyes perpetually shut—like Ezra Pound.

tion of an aristocracy is selection; illiterate motorowners are incapable of that function.

The rewards of writers are in inverse order of merit. That is to say, the worst work usually brings the greatest financial reward. Current systems of literary prize-giving are not much more satisfactory. They occasionally reward merit, or advertise it. A carefully specified prize like the Goncourt may "work" several times; often the first two or three awards of a prize are "good"; after that the conditions change, and a third-rate author receives what might better have gone to the upkeep of someone whose work escapes the specifications (or had appeared on January 7, 1922, instead of on December 30, 1921). Anatole France may well have "deserved" the Nobel Prize, but no one will claim that his reception of it in the hundred and first year of his age is likely to increase his production or improve its quality.

The only thing one can give an artist is leisure in which to work.[57] To give an artist leisure is actually to take part in his creation. It is a question of making freemen, in the only sense that that word is worth while. It is NOT a charity. Bel Esprit is definitely and defiantly not a charity. It is not based on pity for the human recipient: it has nothing to do with Manchester Liberalism. Civilisation has got to restart. The rich are, with the rarest exceptions, useless. One cannot wait until the masses are "educated up" to a fine demand. There is no sign whatever that they are tending in that direction. Even the *Daily Mail* is losing influence.

Bel Esprit proposes simply to *release more energy for invention and design;* the practical way (Douglas' scheme does include a man's beginning on his own doorstep, and his own job) is to release those artists or writers who have definitely proved that they have something in them, and are capable of its expression. What we want is not more books, but a better quality of book; and the modus is (1) to find the man; (2) to guarantee him food and leisure, by a co-operation of subscribers (individuals or groups) pledging themselves to give £10 per year "for life or for as long as the artist needs it."

It will be noticed that this reduces the urge to write for money to a minimum. The writer is given a bare living, he is allowed a certain leeway to earn his comforts. Say that honest work under present conditions brings in about £100 a year. At any rate when the author's earning capacity reaches a certain point his subsidy diminishes proportionately, so there is as much reason for him to suppress a faulty but vendible piece of work as to print it. This solves the age-old problem of paying a man to keep quiet.

[57]From Rome, Pound wrote to John Quinn: "By 1978 all the bum artists will be supported . . . ." Not quite an exact prophecy, but at least in 1978 there is the National Endowment of the Arts, and many state councils of art.

The artist's circumstances are considered. That is to say, the action of the society is strictly realist. It recognises an individual need and an individual qualification. In commerce one does not expect copper from an iron mine. The scheme permits the hypothetical individuals whom one has for years heard saying that "they would like to do something" but cannot afford £300 a year, to "do something." In that sense it is a showdown. The aesthetic admirer can now "put up or shut up." The gauge of a given interest in literature or the fine arts is set. Choice of the artist is important, the *esprit* is more or less *bel* according to the artist he chooses. If he does not like the choice of the Paris group of the Bel Esprit, he is perfectly free to start a group of his own, backin' 'is local fancy.

The supposed danger of the individual patron is eliminated, there being 30, 20, or in the case of very young men, even so few as ten backers required. There would in any case be enough difference of taste among them to prevent their trying to force the artist's work into any mould or modality not his own. If one of them tried to make him write or paint in one way, presumably some other would counteract this; and in any case no one donor would be sufficiently essential to the artist's welfare to give him an inconvenient hold. As the selection of the artist is made by the people most interested in art or literature it may reasonably be taken as an honour by the recipient.

It may be of interest to note that in this group of Parisians and Americans the first choice fell on T. S. Eliot, some of whose work has already appeared here in French. The Parisians supported the decision because it seemed more probable that we should find enough backers, having three countries to draw from, and because they thought it would be much easier to arrange for their French candidates if they had a model in actual operation. Also the other cases were not as clearly defined. Rightly or wrongly some of us consider Eliot's employment in a bank the worst waste in contemporary literature. During his recent three months' absence due to complete physical breakdown he produced a very important sequence of poems: one of the few things in contemporary literature to which one can ascribe permanent value. That seems a fairly clear proof of restriction of output, due to enforced waste of his time and energy in banking. Mr. Eliot's own wishes have *not* been consulted. There were four people present at the discussion capable of subscribing instanter; the number of "moral certainties" increased the list to ten; with a problematical fringe; other members have undertaken further organisation, private and public.

It now remains to be seen whether Mr. Eliot's English admirers will subscribe heavily enough to leave him with any feeling that his continued residence in that island is morally or sentiently encumbent upon him. My personal feeling is that the British literary imperium began its decline when Landor departed for Italy. The subsequent history is: Byron,

Keats, Shelley, Beddoes, in Italy or Germany, Browning in Italy, and Tennyson in Buckingham Palace. And later, the dispersal of men of letters from London, Swinburne in Putney, Hardy in Dorchester: the Irish and American use of the English capital giving it a deceptive appearance of life until . . . . until even that faded from it.

I expect to meet Mr. Eliot in Sienna before I meet him in Piccadilly; but the Londoners still have their chance. (Perhaps he would stay there anyhow. It is not my affair, but I *am* concerned for his leisure. I consider it "economic.") Pending arrangements for permanent quarters and secretarial address, communication may be sent to Bel Esprit, care of *The New Age.*

2
Vorticist Publications

BLAST[1]

Bearing the date of June 20th, 1914 the first issue of *Blast*[2] appeared. The term vorticism was a last minute invention as can be seen from the earlier announcements of *Blast* as a paper intended for discussion of half a dozen heteroclite contemporary movements. One needed a name to distinguish the qualities of Lewis' work from the nature mortisme of Picasso's cubism and more generally to distinguish what was being done in London from continental work, if there were any such dividing line. Etchells had an idea that a couple of poems in *Ripostes* had something or other to do with what he was attempting in paint, or that there was a common base for the elimination of some sort of padding from all the arts. No one was expected to recede from his own personal position in favour of a formula. Three of us wrote Vortices, they do not very exactly coincide. They were research, intended to discover wherein we agreed. So far as I know none of the attacks on vorticism paid the least attention to *any* one of the Vortices or showed the least knowledge of the work of Gaudier or of Lewis or of myself. Six months later a bright spark in Liverpool or Manchester discovered that the intention of *Blast* was satiric. For confirmation of which I must refer the reader to the editor's opening pages, let us say those headed *6* on pages 18 and 19. My own Vortex was as follows, and my note on Lewis appeared in the *Egoist* for June 15, 1914.

[1]"Collected Prose," p. 434 (unpublished). Yale University Library.
[2]"Lewis is starting a new Futurist, Cubist, Imagiste Quarterly. . . . it is mostly a painters magazine with me to do the poems," wrote Pound to Joyce. See *Pound/Joyce: The Letters of Ezra Pound to James Joyce*, Forrest Read, ed., New York, 1967, p. 26.

VORTEX.

POUND.

The vortex is the point of maximum energy,

It represents, in mechanics, the greatest efficiency.

We use the words "greatest efficiency" in the precise sense—as they would be used in a text book of MECHANICS.

You may think of man as that toward which perception moves. You may think of him as the TOY of circumstance, as the plastic substance RECEIVING impressions.

OR you may think of him as DIRECTING a certain fluid force against circumstance, as CONCEIVING instead of merely observing and reflecting.

THE PRIMARY PIGMENT.

The vorticist relies on this alone; on the primary pigment of his art, nothing else.

Every conception, every emotion presents itself to the vivid consciousness in some primary form.

It is the picture that means a hundred poems, the music that means a hundred pictures, the most highly energized statement, the statement that has not yet SPENT itself it [sic] expression, but which is the most capable of expressing.

THE TURBINE.

All experience rushes into this vortex. All the energized past, all the past that is living and worthy to live. ALL MOMENTUM, which is the past bearing upon us, RACE, RACE-MEMORY, instinct charging the PLACID, NON-ENERGIZED FUTURE.

The DESIGN of the future in the grip of the human vortex. All the past that is vital, all the past that is capable of living into the future, is pregnant in the vortex, NOW.

Hedonism is the vacant place of a vortex, without force, deprived of past and of future, the vertex of a stil [sic] spool or cone.

Futurism is the disgorging spray of a vortex with no drive behind it, DISPERSAL.

EVERY CONCEPT, EVERY EMOTION PRESENTS ITSELF TO THE VIVID CONSCIOUSNESS IN SOME PRIMARY FORM. IT BELONGS TO THE ART OF THIS FORM. IF SOUND, TO MUSIC; IF FORMED WORDS, TO LITERATURE; THE IMAGE, TO POETRY; FORM, TO DESIGN; COLOUR IN POSITION, TO PAINTING;

151

FORM OR DESIGN IN THREE PLANES, TO SCULPTURE; MOVE-
MENT TO THE DANCE OR TO THE RHYTHM OF MUSIC OR OF
VERSES.

Elaboration, expression of second intensities, of dispersedness belong to
the secondary sort of artist. Dispersed arts HAD a vortex.

Impressionism, Futurism, which is only an accelerated sort of impres-
sionism, DENY the vortex. They are the CORPSES of VORTICES.
POPULAR BELIEFS, movements, etc., are the CORPSES OF VOR-
TICES. Marinetti is a corpse.

THE MAN.

The vorticist relies not upon similarity or analogy, not upon likeness or
mimicry.

In painting he does not rely upon the likeness to a beloved grandmother
or to a caressable mistress.

VORTICISM is art before it has spread itself into a state of flaccidity, of
elaboration, of secondary applications.

ANCESTRY.

"All arts approach the conditions of music."—*Pater.*

"An Image is that which presents an intellectual and emotional complex in an instant of time."—*Pound.*

"You are interested in a certain painting because it is an arrangement of
lines and colours."—*Whistler.*

Picasso, Kandinski, father and mother, classicism and romanticism of
the movement.

POETRY.

The vorticist will use only the primary media of his art.

The primary pigment of poetry is the IMAGE.

The vorticist will not allow the primary expression of any concept or
emotion to drag itself out into mimicry.

In painting Kandinski, Picasso.

In poetry this by, "H. D."

> Whirl up sea—
> Whirl your pointed pines,
> Splash your great pines
> On our rocks,
> Hurl your green over us,
> Cover us with your pools of fir.

152

ET FAIM SALLIR LE LOUP DES BOYS[3]

I cling to the spar,
Washed with the cold salt ice
I cling to the spar—
Insidious modern waves, civilization, civilized hidden snares.
Cowardly editors threaten: "If I dare"
Say this or that, or speak my open mind,
Say that I hate may [sic] hates,
   Say that I love my friends,
Say I believe in Lewis, spit out the later Rodin,
Say that Epstein can carve in stone,
That Brzeska can use the chisel,
Or Wadsworth paint;
                 Then they will have my guts;
They will cut down my wage, force me to sing their cant,
Uphold the press, and be before all a model of literary decorum.
                                 Merde!

Cowardly editors threaten,
Friends fall off at the pinch, the loveliest die.
That is the path of life, this is my forest.

DOGMATIC STATEMENT ON THE GAME
AND PLAY OF CHESS[4]
Theme for a Series of Pictures

Red knights, brown bishops, bright queens
Striking the board, falling in strong "L's" of colour,
Reaching and striking in angles,
           Holding lines of one colour:

---

[3]*Blast No. 2* (July 1915), p. 22.
[4]*Blast No. 2* (July 1915), p. 19. Pound in a letter to Harriet Monroe (April 10, 1915) explained that the poem was not futurist but the "concept of arrangement is vorticist." See p. 290.
   In an interview with Donald Hall (*Writers at Work*, Second Series, New York, 1963, p. 44), Pound comments: "'The Game of Chess' poem shows the effect of modern abstract art, but vorticism from my angle was a renewal of the sense of construction. Color went dead and Manet and the impressionists revived it. Then what I would call the sense of form was blurred, and vorticism, as distinct from cubism, was an attempt to revive the sense of form—the form you had in Piero della Francesca's *De Prospettive Pingendi*, his treatise on the proportions and composition. I got started on the idea of comparative forms before I left America."

153

This board is alive with light
These pieces are living in form,
    Their moves break and reform the pattern:
Luminous greens from the rooks,
    Clashing with "x's" of queens,
    Looped with the knight-leaps.
"Y" pawns, cleaving, embanking,
Whirl, centripetal, mate, King down in the vortex:
Clash, leaping of bands, straight strips of hard colour,
Blocked lights working in, escapes, renewing of contest.[5]

THE VORTOGRAPHS[6]

This note concerns only the vortographs and not the paintings in this exhibition. Mr. Coburn's paintings were done before the invention of the vortoscope. He has attached no label to them, but they are, roughly speaking, post-impressionist. It should be quite clear that the paintings were not done in agreement with the work of the "Vorticists," and that there is no connection between Mr. Coburn, as painter, and the group known as the vorticist group.

I am concerned here solely with vortography. The tool called the vortoscope was invented late in 1916. Mr. Coburn had been long desiring to bring cubism or vorticism into photography. Only with the invention of a suitable instrument was this possible.

In vortography he accepts the fundamental principles of vorticism, and those of vorticist painting in so far as they are applicable to the work of the camera.

The principles of vorticism have been amply set forth by Wyndham Lewis, Ezra Pound and Gaudier-Brzeska. The immediate ancestry is given in two quotations in *Blast:* Pater's "All arts approach the conditions of music"; and Whistler's "We are interested in a painting because it is an arrangement of lines and colours." Cézanne began taking "impressions" of masses. The term "mass" or "form" has been more prominent than the term "line" in recent discussions.

The vorticist principle is that a painting is an expression by means of an arrangement of form and colour in the same way that a piece of music

[5]"Contes" in *Blast No. 2.* Corrected here as in Pound's *Personae*, New York, 1949, and London, 1952, p. 120.

[6]Notes written anonymously by Pound in the catalogue for the exhibition at The Camera Club during February 1917 of *Vortographs and Paintings* by Alvin Langdon Coburn. Reprinted almost in its entirety in *Pavannes and Divisions*, New York, 1918, pp. 251–55.

is an expression by means of an arrangement of sound. In painting the form has only two dimensions (though it may suggest or "represent" a third dimension). In sculpture one uses three dimensions.

Or to put it another way: Painting makes use of colour arranged on a surface; Sculpture of masses defined by planes.

In vortography colour is practically excluded. There can be suggestion of colours. There can be a variety in the colour of the paper on which the vortograph is printed. But the medium of the vortographer is practically limited to form (shapes on a surface) and to a light and shade; to the peculiar varieties in lightness and darkness which belong to the technique of the camera.

THE CAMERA IS FREED FROM REALITY

A natural object or objects may perhaps be retained realistically by the vortographer if he chooses, and the vortograph containing such an object or objects will not be injured if the object or objects contribute interest to the pattern, that is to say, if they form an integral and formal part of the whole.

The vortoscope is useless to a man who cannot recognise a beautiful arrangement of forms on a surface, when his vortoscope has brought them to focus. His selection may be *almost* as creative as a painter's composition. His photographic technique must be assumed. It does not form a part of this discussion, though it is extremely important, and all, or most, of the qualities of the black and white, of light and dark, will depend upon it. These things, however, can be discussed by any intelligent photographer, assuming that such persons exist. There is no need of any special foreword about this part of the technique.

VORTICISM has reawakened our sense of form, a sense long dead in occidental artists. Any person or animal unable to take pleasure in an arrangement of forms as he or she takes pleasure in an arrangement of musical notes, is thereby the poorer. People are sometimes tone-deaf and colour-blind. Other people, perhaps more numerous, are form-blind. Some ears cannot recognise the correct pitch of a note, and some eyes get no pleasure from a beautiful or expressive arrangement of forms.

Until recently people enjoyed pictures chiefly, and often exclusively because the painting reminded them of something else. Numerous contemporaries have passed that state of development.

The modern will enjoy vortograph No. 3, not because it reminds him of a shell bursting on a hillside, but because the arrangement of forms pleases him, as a phrase of Chopin might please him. He will enjoy vortograph No. 8, not because it reminds him of a falling Zeppelin, but because he likes the shape and arrangement of its blocks of dark and light.

155

Obviously vortographs will lack certain interests that are to be found in vorticist paintings. They bear the same relation to vorticist painting that academic photography bears to academy painting. Almost any fool can paint an academy picture, and any imbecile can shoot off a Kodak.

Certain definite problems in the aesthetics of form may possibly be worked out with the vortoscope. When these problems are solved vorticism will have entered that phase of morbidity into which representative painting descended after the Renaissance painters had decided upon all the correct proportions of the human body, etc., etc., etc. That date of decline is still afar off. Vorticism and vortography are both at the beginning of their course.

Vortography stands below the other vorticist arts in that it is an art of the eye, not of the eye and hand together. It stands infinitely above photography in that the vortographer combines his forms *at will.* He selects just what actuality he wishes, he excludes the rest. He chooses what forms, lights, masses, he desires, he arranges them *at will* on his screen. He can make summer of London October. The aereën and submarine effects are got in his study. All these vortographs were done in two or three rooms. The dull bit of window frame (vortograph No. 16) produces "a fine Picasso," or if not a "Picasso" a "Coburn." It is an excellent arrangement of shapes, and more interesting than most of the works of Picabia or of the bad imitators of Lewis.

Art photography has been stuck for twenty years. During that time practically no new effects have been achieved. Art photography is stale and suburban. It has never had any part in aesthetics. Vortography may have, however, very much the same place in the coming aesthetic that the anatomical studies of the Renaissance had in the aesthetics of the academic school. It is at least a subject which a serious man may consider. It is not for me to decide whether there can be a mathematical harmony of form, angles, proportions, etc., arranged as we have had a mathematical "harmony" arranged for us in music.

I am not concerned with deciding whether such a mathematical schedule is desirable or would be beneficent. But if it is *possible,* then the vortescope could be extremely useful, and may play a very important part in the discovery of such a system.

Such a system would be of aesthetics and not merely of physics and optics. It would "depend" on the science of optics as much and as little as musical harmony depends on the physiology of the ear.

Impressionism sought its theoretic defence in, if it did not arise from, Berkeley's theory of the minimum visible, i.e., of the effects of points of light and colour on the retina.

Pleasure is derivable not only from the stroking or pushing of the retina by light waves of various colour, BUT ALSO by the impact of those waves in certain arranged tracts.

This simple and obvious fact is the basis of the "modern" "art" "revolution."

The eye *likes* certain plainnesses, certain complexities, certain arrangements, certain varieties, certain incitements, certain reliefs and suspensions.

It likes these things irrespective of whether or no they form a replica of known objects.

3
Selections from Miscellaneous Publications

THE CURSE[1]

Museums are the pest of our age. They are its highest achievement. There is a good deal to be said for the museum as a school. There is a good deal less to be said for it as a tomb. And the utter condemnation of today's British civilisation, if any more condemnations were needed, might be found in the fact that uncountable excellent things are housed in a horror like the Victoria and Albert.

For the *contents* of this architectural iniquity, we may be, and are, duly thankful. For the one institution in England which is not *by charter* inhibited from possessing works of art regardless of age or origin; which can, let us say, *receive* a drawing by a living artist regardless of whether he was born in Madrid or Pretoria, or whether he has exhibited at the Royal Academy, let us be thankful—deploring the limitations of floor space, etc., but still thankful.

This has no particular bearing on the *"curse of museums."* The curse is not of "a museum," but of *museums*, it is the pest and epidemic of museums. I have one at my elbow, my right elbow, a few perfect pieces of jade, an ivory "museum piece"; and at my left elbow, a portfolio that I have just shared with the public. Mr. X. and Mr. Z., of my acquaintance, almost as poor as I am, have both of them their little section of museum, better than the similar sections of any public institution. And as for the "bloated capitalists"—the bloat need be very modest, London is crammed with museums, and is "a splendid city to loot."

[1]*Apple (of Beauty and Discord)*, January 1920, pp. 22, 24.

158

It is also a hideous city to look at. We have ten thousand people ferreting little bits of art into drawers, into glorified what-nots; bustling about to old curiosity shops in search of "virtue," and into second-rate, and even first-rate studios in search of "Art" with the capital letter, or in search of "Name" or of "something that's going up." Yet there is not enough public taste to ensure one building that is not an eyesore; there has not been a decent doorway constructed for eighty years.

And Paris is worse than London. Since the assassination of architecture by the Beaux Arts, Paris has been under the curse. Take, for example, the slimy figures ornamenting the Lutetia (hotel, etc.), a prize example of the idiocy that comes from treating stone as if it were not a hard and brittle substance, but a sloppy matter like stucco.

Some matoid technician and self-styled materialist will rush in, and say that the Parisian stone comes soft from the quarry and is, when new, "so easy to cut." So much the worse for Paris. The French have less excuse than the English for their putrid present building, in so much as France teems with fine models of houses, from the few very old ones left in Toulouse (13th century), from St. Bertrand de Cominges to Sarlat, from Brive to Beaucaire there are the grave models of excellent building.

The waste and the curse in London is that the taste, which should keep the streets fit to walk, leaks away into the album, the portfolio, the plate-glass cabinet in the drawing-room; so atrophied are we to the untried and the living; so normally and hourly insensitive. I mean that we have lost the faculty to perceive beautiful form save at the set moment when we are ready for the aesthetic tickle.

It is a variation on the century-old jibe that the Englishman wants his joke in *Punch,* if he sees it in *Punch* he knows it is "funny." Half of us are as badly off for art as the traditional bull is for humour; we must have it served on a platter.

Result: the cast-iron pseudo-gothic ornamentation on the law courts; the horror of the last "front" in Bond Street.

I am not raving or in sudden explosion. For weeks last year I searched the streets for well-proportioned facades, for well carved wood-work over doorways. I know the pleasure of rare discovery, and I know the extent of the desert, the abysms of the ignominious.

Instead of a bit of jade in a box, why should I not have a doorway fit to look at? Price absolutely the same. I, alas, share my doorway with twenty other heads of as many households; I do not even own the twenty-first part of my doorway.

For a facade lovingly made, one goes to the Oriental Section of the "V. and A."; not because English facades were not once lovingly made. There are, indeed, a few still left in London as a monument to the ages, but it is easier to go to the museum where one is sure to find something than to search miles of abominable street.

The curse is not wholly due to the landlord and flat system. Leave the "economist" to blame lack of wit on a system. What we have lost is the ability to apply intelligence. The taste that enables us to find the choice bit in the second-hand shop is utterly incapable of *getting anything done*, we are impotent either to make our own doorways or *to get them made*. Our taste now serves only as a servant to acquisitiveness, it is incapable of translating itself into action.

When Gaudier was too poor to buy stone he would gladly have made door-heads and capitals, and no man offered him a stone door-post. So terrified are we of a man with an unusual faculty, or of a man "burning to speak." Against this set an age that built the Maison Carrée instead of making horrible buildings to hold beautiful odds and ends; and let us try to remember that when the Florentines needed a new gateway, Donatello was sixteen years of age. Yet the city council recognised that the intelligence of one man of genius, of one boy of genius, was, in its own particular groove, worth the caution and education of a whole County Council, and Donatello was made sole chooser of the plan.

The British are the most timorous people on earth in any matter of aesthetics. And the nation will get no buildings worth seeing, it will have no "new age of cathedrals" until it takes a chance on the "maniacs."

True, it might take a bold government or a bold private firm to entrust its choice of buildings to Wyndham Lewis or to myself. In practice they do not even employ the taste of their more alert departmental heads (let us say of the departments of sculpture or drawing at the South Kensington Museum); yet all "styles" in architecture, all vivifications of architecture come from "turning some one man loose." I add the words "private firm" with intention, for our streets owe more to private firms than to the main administration and it is an insular habit to attribute all ills to a government. And the present government is probably better than "representative" of the general taste. The curse is not in an administration, but psychological; we can absorb, acquire, to any extent; but we can get nothing made.

DEMARCATIONS[2]

Leisure is necessary to any form of civilization higher than that of ants, apes, Kipling and his cousin Stan Baldwin.

H. E. Pacces had written ably against bureaucracy and against the almost unavoidable tendency of efficient governments to increase the gross and damned number of government servants.

The dilemma is this. Men must have time to do their best work.

[2]*British Union Quarterly,* January/April 1937, p. 40.

You "employ a man" to do a given job; it develops into routine. He has no time to stand back and observe its relationships to the total social order.

OR in trying to avoid this you multiply sinecures.

This is really the lesser evil. But anyone who has been near a government office in time of stress knows that the only men who have time to think are the unemployed. That is, a peculiar type of unemployed, those who do not have to worry about where they are to eat and how they are to pay their rent or hotel bills.

The fatty degeneracy of ruling classes, miscalled aristocracies, etc., has manifestly and demonstrably bred FROM NECESSITY one-party governments, parties with a sense of public responsibility, composed at least in part of men who weren't tied to desks and who didn't have to spend six or ten hours a day "performing functions."

You have, almost, to go to active artists to get the sense and the feel of such action. I would put up a dozen brass tablets to one phrase of Constantin Brancusi's:

ONE OF THOSE DAYS WHEN I WOULD NOT HAVE GIVEN UP FIFTEEN MINUTES OF MY TIME FOR ANYTHING UNDER HEAVEN.

There speaks the supreme sense of human values. There speaks WORK unbartered. That is the voice of humanity in its highest possible manifestation.

THAT AUDIENCE, OR THE BUGABOO OF THE PUBLIC[3]

The curse of a large audience is not its largeness but crassness of its criteria. A painter or writer who paints or writes for the multitude is, or becomes, a bad painter or a bad writer not because masterwork is incapable of wide distribution, but because masterwork is incapable of wide recognition *immediately* after its birth.

The artist must work for the few because there are only a few for whom he can really work. There are at no time more than a few hundred, or perhaps a few dozen, men who know at first sight whether a given work of any one living artist is that definite artist's best; whether it is actually the finest thing he can do or whether it represents a bad moment, a tired hour, a day when his head or his hand or both was, or were, being lazy.

[3]*Colour*, September 1919, p. 42.

When the artist ceases to work for this vigorous circle of harsh friends and priceless "enemies"; when he begins to work for the public who will buy his canvas or his copy for his name, careless of quality, incapable of knowing the quality, his work begins to decline.

He may have as much critical sense as you like, but little by little the effects of this living among profits and contentments will show itself in his work.

Pretentious people tell you that a work of art should give *them* pleasure; I once met a barrister who really thought I wrote with the express desire of arousing his approbation. The man has since "taken silk," but he is still incapable of learning that I am as indifferent to his opinion of my works as he would be to my opinion of the next probable winner of the Derby, or as an engineer or mathematician would be to my opinion on some technical matter of turbines.

Even a stupid man who had carefully looked at pictures, or turnips, or fat cattle for fifteen years, would probably know more about pictures, or turnips or fat cattle, than a clever man who had devoted only fifteen minutes to any one of these matters; yet you still find people who do not believe in the existence of experts.

EPSTEIN, BELGION AND MEANING[4]

I

One cause of tedium in contemporary aesthetic discussion is that the critic's critic persistently insists on "disagreeing" with the critic's "meaning" when in most cases he has not tried to understand it and is merely disagreeing with the verbal formulation.

Any verbal formulation is sufficiently difficult and I think the mathematicians probably set us a good example. They are more often content to seek the right answer and spend less time demonstrating the minute errors in the equations of unsuccessful scientists.

When a practitioner of one of the plastic arts has been forced into a supplementary verbal formulation I doubt if the "critic" performs any great service in finding the discrepancies of this verbal formulation unless he is able to find thereafter or thereby some verbal expression which will satisfy the artist himself. Only on such basis can one proceed to any lucid discussion of the validity of the artist's intentions.

As far as *verbal formulation* goes Mr. Epstein's statement as to the "meaning" of "Night" as quoted by Mr. Belgion (*Criterion,* January

[4]*Criterion,* April 1930, pp. 470–75.

1930) might leave that work open to the same criticism one would launch against the baroque rubbish on the roof of St. Paul's.

The question of what the curved lines express lets in the full flood of irrelevance that is always let in when one starts discussing a "plastic idea" in non-plastic terms.

Mr. Epstein knows this perfectly well, as I think adequate reference to his context (i.e., various remarks forced from him during the past twenty-two years) would show.

Ultimately a plastic work has to be judged by its plastic. The goodness or badness of the combined curves and straights, etc., masses, combinations of same, etc., will be a matter of their form and even their expressiveness will depend on this and not on what the sculptor says he intended to express.

Few critics are sufficiently pure-minded to grant this and few plastic artists have been strong enough to depend on form alone, dispensing with the stimulus or support of a literary content. Brancusi still keeps this faith. In England the courage reached its known maximum in the period 1911 to 1914 as shown in the work of Wyndham Lewis, Gaudier, and in a few works of Epstein (those with the suavest outlines, the simplest combinations of mass). In drawing, this movement, so far as the general public knows, passed out of English work with Lewis' artillery designs, where he was forced to include a narrative or at least literary content but still held firm the original direction of his will. (His present work is not sufficiently known either to me or to the public to serve me as illustration.)

In fact I for the moment aim only at possible rectification of Mr. Belgion (not qua rectification *of* Mr. Belgion, but as rectification).

The error of making a statue *of* "Night" or *of* "Charity" lies in tautology. The idea has already found its way into language. The function of the artist is precisely the formulation of what has not found its way into language, i.e., any language verbal, plastic or musical.

When Mr. Epstein says "Night" is the subject he means rather more. Everybody knows what "Night" is, but Mr. Epstein or Mr. Phidias or whoever, is presumably intent on expressing a *particular* and definite complex (ideas, emotions, etc.,) generally oriented by a rather vague concept already mapped out. The difference is as great as that between firing a bullet in a generally easterly direction and hitting a particular bird.

II

Mr. Belgion again fails in a necessary dissociation of ideas in his use of the term "skill."

163

Brancusi has said, "Non, les choses ne sont pas difficiles à faire, mais nous, de nous mettre en état de les faire."

The difference between the great artist and the poor artist and then down to the casual observer is that the first of these has so vigorously or so persistently, so clearly, or in such sudden and violent light dissociated some concept in some particular tone, shade, and set of implications that his expression becomes a new noun.

And these nouns will be found mainly, I think, in works that can be judged according to their own particular idiom, i.e., as to form, as to sound, or as to literary style (i.e., as to the unforgeable properties which distinguish a statue by Brancusi or a novel by Henry James).

III

The question of self-expression as raised by Mr. Belgion against Epstein's *verbal formulation* is example of the general fault mentioned in my first paragraph.

The artist, if he is any good, expresses his own dissociated concept (his truth or the something which he prizes above something associated in his own mind with a word called "truth"). He puts forward this concept as distinct from the blurred, messy, less defined or by-the-public-demanded formulation of the to-the-public-familiar.

There is no need to shift the "criticism" out of aesthetics and into metaphysics or to postpone a lucid aesthetic discussion until one has written ten volumes on "the self" the "self and the etc." und so weiter.

IV

As to surrealism, Pater and Co. mixed up artistic discussion (we may as well recapitulate). There was a period when the symbolistes, etc., discussed each art in terms of some other. There was (under various names) a puritanical period (call it that to forestall abuse) when some few dozen men agreed to discuss, or tried to discuss the separate arts in their own terms. As far as this concerned the plastic arts, few painters and sculptors were strong enough to meet the (perhaps excessive) demands.

A traditional hunger for literary values returned. As conversely a great hunger for formal excellence has emerged in the most concentratedly literary periods of painting (videlicet my own beloved and never surrendered Quattrocento). The two things are not mutually exclusive. Perhaps both gain by clear demarcation.

There is a Cosimo Tura in Bergamo which Arp has probably never seen. Arp's admirers will probably admire it more than any spectators have during the intermediate period.

164

I am not making that statement in a fit of irrelevance. I mean to imply that anyone who has for a quarter of a century held to an admiration for thirteenth-century poetry and fifteenth-century painting has very little difficulty in adjusting himself to surrealism—surrealism that comes after a period of aesthetic purism (Picasso, Picabia, Marcel Duchamp, Wyndham Lewis, Gaudier, Brancusi).

I cannot conceive a surrealist objecting on aesthetic grounds to Cavalcanti's

> Veder mi par de le sue labbia uscire
> Una si bella donna che la mente
> Comprender non la puo che'mmantenente
> Ne nasce un altra di bellezza nuova
> Da la qual par ch'una stella si muova.

Though Luigi Valli intent on making Guido into a protagonist of a forbidden sect has nothing but contempt for the obvious statement and wants to translate it by a secret "code."

One could, I think, consider Guido surrealist, in a sense that Bertrand de Born was not.

Guido came, let us admit, into a world that seems to us very highly conventionalized. His wildest statements, let us say concerning the emergence of spirits one from another, seem perhaps orderly in comparison with surrealist expression, but they probably did not seem so in A.D. 1284. They were probably as little concerned with supporting the hierarchy of thrones as are Mr. Aragon's verses with proving the divinity of the Third Republic.

The surrealists are making a fresh start with a hitherto undigested content. "I saw three angels," wrote Swedenborg, "they had hats on their heads."

The mystics have always annoyed the enchaired professors. There is no reason why MM. Breton, Péret, Aragon and company, should have their subconsciousness decorated with the universe of Avicenna or with the more Mosaic religious background of Blake.

They may or may not want to own an ancestry or to co-ordinate themselves with precursors or with other art of similar phase.

> Fuor di salute giudicar mantiene
> Che l'intenzione per ragione vale, etc. . . .

occurs in Guido's triumph of melodic symmetry, and, let us admit, does not go quite so far as to deny reason altogether. It asserts a reality outside the scholastic logic.

The surrealists also assert an external reality. In the morass of Berkeley-ian-Bergsonian subjectivo-fluxivity they have perhaps chosen a good moment to do so.

They will probably be all the better for not knowing their ancestors. It does not in the least matter whether they hang their family-trees in their halls or hall-bedrooms, or whether they claim immediate descent from non-being.

As far as writing goes we are laggards, I mean in relation to scientists; we still cling to modes of expression and verbal arrangements sprung from, and limited by, scholastic logic. French suffers from a worse paralysis than English. The verbal stirring of Apollinaire and Cocteau is not yet comprehended. (This is not the moment to examine it or to isolate instances, ref. Cocteau, "Poésies 1920," etc.)

The biologist is familiar with, and capable of distinguishing, an infinite number of states, things, differences for which there are no verbal equivalents. Berman goes as far as to deny real understanding even to men who have had laboratory experience if they have not also had experience as medical practitioners. In a general sense the quarrel is as old as Hippocrates, but in a particular sense it has a new application not to science but to verbal manifestation.

We no longer think or need to think in terms of monolinear logic, the sentence structure, subject, predicate, object, etc.

We are as capable or almost as capable as the biologist of thinking thoughts that join like spokes in a wheel-hub and that fuse in hyper-geometric amalgams.

The difficulty of the layman who wishes to distinguish research from fumisterie is not our primary concern. Perhaps sobriety and goodwill are the layman's best divining-rods in such matter.

The defect of monolinear sentence structure in so far as it concerns criticism, as distinct from art, is that the critic using the tradtional forms is so often constrained to contradict (or to appear to contradict) someone who is only five points off the critic's truth and to ally (or appear to ally) himself with an undefined vulgus which is ninety or more points off the same "truth."

Which same property of traditional language is, of course, most useful to politicians, organizers of hate, etc., in almost exact ratio as it is useless and offensive to anyone concerned with accurate thought or discussion.

Even now nineteen readers out of twenty will receive the impression that I am expressing an opinion about Mr. Epstein's statues "Night" and "Day" which I have seen only in photograph and which I have no intention of discussing.

This note concerns language, the use of language, and refers to a rectification of critical method.

STONES OF RIMINI[5]

Adrian Stokes. (Faber and Faber.) 12s. 6d. net. With 48 illustrations in half-tone

Whether one accepts Frobenius' hypothesis as fact or as an indisputably advantageous means of synthesis, the sense of personal property in art is, I think, breaking down.

The idea of "style of a period" takes on a new significance. In criticism of honest work we need rather a collaboration than mere destructive picking at another man's work, whether or no such collaboration fall definitely in the domain of book reviewing.

With his *Quattro Cento* Mr. Stokes demonstrated to the satisfaction of at least a few readers that, despite the superficies of his writing, he was not merely another follower of Walter Pater. He got down "to bedrock" in using STONE as the basis for his criticism of certain qualities of Quattro-centro architectural ornament. He quite astutely refused to be entangled by a set of axioms which my decade, or the period from Brancusi to Gaudier-Brzeska, had erected for the totally different problem of SCULP-TURE 1910 to 1930, in an attempt to interpret the use of stone in fifteenth-century building.

He gave his own personal colouring to the work with the term "stone-blossom," where another might have stuck to the more usual "emergence." Whatever reminiscences showed in the manner of his own verbal manifestation, he had been to the places, he had LOOKED at the stone, and the whole of his verbal floridity had at any rate that unity of source.

He has been right in zoning his work. The present volume seems perhaps a link between two larger works, it contains technical material that he obviously had to deal with were he to escape charges of superficiality. He has relied on his halftone reproductions very greatly, but without giving the duller reader a lead, which would have been useful self-protection. You cannot so greatly trust readers to understand that certain effects of a book are not merely fortuitous.

Say that the present reviewer knows the TEMPIO as perhaps not another dozen men, apart from professional architects and conservators know it. He has learned quite a good deal from the shock of seeing the, as it were microscopic, slides of the detail in this particular juxtaposition. He does not therefore think this due to undesigned chance.

Results:

I. What a medley! The "Tempio" in Rimini would have been a far less

[5]A review of *Stones of Rimini* by Adrian Stokes. *Criterion*, April 1934, pp. 495–97.

daring synthesis had all its details been fully digested and reduced to a unity of style, à la Palladio. As a human record, as a record of courage, nothing can touch it.

As to the medley—looking straight at it: Buddhism, the far east, as distinct from any scheme of composition you could identify with the near east. Always the perfect Hellenism of the straight columns and non-representative features. Very late clumsy Roman forms. In plate 33, a pattern sense unrivalled or unsurpassed out of Africa, and as it were digesting the very snappy and forth-going Hercules (lower right).

In all of which Stokes has found at least one basic unity or antithesis: Water and Stone.

For that alone the book is worth printing. For wisdom to unhorse the whole gnat-tribe of ergoteur logic-chopping "critics": (p. 25)

"The writer is a fool . . . who formulates a definition when his whole book is intended as such."

II. The jacket design seems to me anything but fortuitous, but the key not quite distinctly indicated. Another principle of unity seems to me to exist, and to be given not by the building, but by Pasti's medal of intention.

I believe the construction to have a spherical basis—fortunately foiled in the effect, but there always as principle and as cause of a solidity, a satisfaction which no other base-form could have attained.

Take a full set of photos of the Tempio and start counting the CIRCLES. Reverse, for a moment, Stokes' stone-blossom criterion or rather augment it by the idea of the flattened sphere.

Again and again we find the sphere squashed down. Whereas Greek sculpture is weak in comparison with the best African work, because the latter is conceived solid as mass, and the Greek so often as merely a profile on a pivot, or the set of profiles taken by someone walking around the subject, the Rimini bas relief is conceived in three dimensions and then squashed. I mean at its best.

That seems to me the "formal" adjunct which might aid in pursuing Mr. Stokes' analysis further.

As to sources and conjectures of what was in Sigismundo's mind etc., etc. There is Gemistus Plethon's Greek manuscript in Florence; someone should check up on Schulze or whatever his name was, who dealt with Plethon in German. The seven side arches, three front arches, in relation to the basic sphere; the clear lead to metempsychosis in Basinio's Isottaeus are all indispensable elements in any conjecture that is to be taken seriously, and are all more intimately connected with Rimini than is Pontano's "Urania."

Stokes' "water" concept is, whether he remember it or no—in harmony with the source of all gods, Neptune, in Gemistus's theogony.

168

As for the triumph of Agostino di Duccio, the actual work has gamut from registration of, so far as I am concerned, a concept of absolute physical beauty, achieved in its proportion, having nothing to do with Milos or Greece, say Italic beauty and sanity. This at its apex, down to simple botch, and physical figures so defective that they wouldn't get by a simple Atlantic City or Ziegfeld judging committee.

And thank heaven, there is nothing, utterly and completely nothing that theory can now do to it; or about it.

PARIS LETTER[6]

December, 1921

If the term "letter" at the head of this rubric is to be anything but a mockery it should imply not only communication but answer. To form any sort of porch, vortex, academia, agora there must be at least five or six people sufficiently interested in one another's ideas to wish, one need not say, to correct, but to bring them into some sort of focus; to establish not a foot-rule but some sort of means of communication, and some under-standing of how a given idea, emitted from the left side of the table (Rome, Paris) may strike someone seated at the other end or opposite side of the board (Denver, London, Rio de Janeiro).

Thus "one" is a little surprised to find his Excellenza the Italian Minister for Education still "going on about" Balzac. "One" had sup-posed that Balzac was a local French necessity; that the search for inter-national literary standards had ceased to find him thereto pertinent. "One" observes with approbation that Excellenza Croce discusses Balzac's art, or lack of it, and not the shape of his bathrobe, herein differing from the present or London *école de Ste Beuve*. One offers the suggestion that Croce is indulging in a bit of purely local propaganda when he compares Balzac to Manzoni in order to glorify Italian genius. An impartial non-national critic would have set Manzoni against Flaubert and found the former, I think, inferior, his chief and perhaps only demerit being that he is rather dull, though eminently meritorious, unless my wholly untrust-worthy memory is more than on occasion at fault.

Mr. Wright is, surely, a little hard on Propertius and Ovid or else a little careless in his manner of stating a wholly apposite and commendable appreciation of Petronius; and when Señor Santayana says that he likes "to hear and to see what new things people are up to," someone in the company should be permitted to wink, to wink audibly but respectfully, and to cite, perhaps, the Diana of Montemayor.

[6]*Dial*, January 1922, pp. 73–78.

If the "Letter" is to show even approximately "where in a manner of speaking" its author or the *milieu* which he attempts to communicate "has got to" it can hardly confine itself to jottings on the five or six latest books, even when there are so many in a season; it should at least try to dissociate certain ideas moving in the ferment or sediment beneath or upon current work. For some years "literature" or at least the "movement" has been more or less regarded as a sort of parasite on the new painting, magazines if at all renovatory were usually "magazines of *Art* and literature," the phrase goes without needing comment, there is now nothing more to be said *about* a Braque than about a Nicholson picture; an abstract mode, or several abstract modes have been established and accepted. I mean that a cubist picture is now an accepted sort of painting, distinct, as say a flower piece or a Dutch interior is distinct from a Raphael or Murillo "Holy Family," or an English "Historic." Faced with a given example of any of them, the critic can only say: this is well or ill executed. The mark of the shop is upon a great deal of current production; Picasso experiments, but, lately, in the mode of Michael Agnolo or of Ford Madox Brown. Marie Laurencin's rather "eighteenth-century" charm persists.

The main interest is not in aesthetics; certain main questions are up for discussion, among them nationality and monotheism. I mean that there is a definite issue between *inter*nationalist and *de*nationalist thought, and a certain number of people believe that it is a calamity to belong to *any* modern nation whatsoever. I suppose the present phase of the discussion began with the *heimatlos* in Switzerland, during the war. It is not a matter of being anti-French or anti-German or anti-patriotic, it is a question of disapproving fundamentally of the claims of the modern state. Stephen Decatur's words nobly reproduced with the morning Paris issue of the *Chicago Tribune* referred, let us say, to a group of ideas "my country," that is to say the liberty of thirteen colonies and the right to think and act as one pleased. The modern state has been defined economically as "The difference between the credit a nation possesses as an aggregate and the sum of the credits possessed by its individual members"; and that tough nut the "intellectual" begins to ask himself at what point this difference in credits has a right to interfere with his thought, his expression, his liberty, his freedom of movement, et cetera.

Economics are up for discussion not in their technical, Fabian, phases, but in the wider and more human phases, where they come into contact with personal liberty, life, the arts themselves, and the conditions aiding or limiting their expression. Back of it all is the Confucian saying, "When the Prince shall have called about him all the artists and savants, his resources will be put to full use."

I take it these questions are discussed, at least in their philosophic phases, more freely in France than elsewhere; the French have not the

English hatred of ideas, they have not the English instinct warning them against the possible material commotions which may pursue the functioning of a given idea, and even if an idea is labeled "dangerous" the French will go on discussing it, *"parce qu'ils sont trop bavards."*

Denationalism is Athens against Sparta, or, better, Athens against Rome; all empires are in the nature of things a little pompous and ridiculous. Greece, as I think Maine says, never managed to give laws, for the Greeks were always more interested in the exception, in Phryne for example, than in the flat average; Athens had a civilization, Rome had an empire, and the greatest virtue of that empire was to act as a carrier for Athenian civilization. Athens consisted of an open square, a few groves and porches where men met, talked ideas to death, but also talked them into form and into precision; and where . . . and so forth . . . the dream has been too often attempted . . . or perhaps not sufficiently often . . . the reader may try it for himself.

As for monotheism, it is a philosophic shallowness and frivolity to accept monotheism as fact, rather than as a perhaps interesting, at any rate to some temperaments convenient or plausible and to other temperaments sympathetic or apathetic, hypothesis. *Convenit esse deos,* says Ovid, using the plural. Monotheism is unproven, the Catholic church itself has accepted a paradoxical compromise, and any philosophy which does not begin with a doubt on this point is, to put it mildly, presumptuous. In practice monotheistic thought leads to all sorts of crusades, persecutions, and intolerance. If one is forced by one's reason to accept this hyperunity as a probability one can also accept it as a nuisance, and the moon is twelve miles out of its course, or else the Paris edition of the *Daily Mail* is in error; this latter is, of course, highly improbable.

Above or apart from the economic squabble, the philosophic wavering, the diminishing aesthetic hubbub, there rests the serene sculpture of Brancusi, known, adored, also unknown.

Rodin, let us say, broke the academic ("Florentine Boy") tradition; Epstein and Gaudier-Brzeska in England instituted a new conception, or reintroduced an old conception of, or appreciation of, form; Brancusi, contemporary of Epstein or somewhat older, is in many essentials in agreement with the best work of Epstein and of Gaudier; he is distinct from the futurist sculptors, and he is perhaps unique in the degree of his objection to the "Kolossal," the rhetorical, the Mestrovician, the sculpture of nerve-crisis, the sculpture made to be photographed; and I think I am quite safe in saying that he is unique among living sculptors in his devotion to and research for an absolute formal beauty. That is a large order, and any general sentence falls short of real meaning in dealing with a question of plastic.

In writing of work like Brancusi's for numbers of readers who have not seen the work itself, one is stumped; the formula for exposition is to proceed from the known to the unknown; and one doesn't in the least know what *is* known. A certain number of photos of modern sculpture of ten or twelve different schools have been reproduced in books having a moderate circulation; there are books on Gaudier, Epstein, and every other modern sculptor of note, save Brancusi. I doubt if even good photos would emphasize Brancusi's distinction. For those who know Gaudier's work, let me put it that Gaudier, killed at twenty-three, never had time to repeat a given composition; he saw, often, chances of improvement, but never had time to put them into execution. Brancusi has had, and taken the time. Gaudier was a genius beyond cavil. From the people I have taken to Brancusi's studio I have collected reactions, bewilderment, admiration, admiration not in the banal degree of tolerant dilettantism; "But he is upsetting all the laws of the universe," or "But it isn't like work of a human being at all"; some of it is indeed like the work of a natural force acting with extreme certitude and felicity, producing the form which is the sort of Platonic quintessence, let us say the "that which is birdlike in all birds," *oiseau qui chante la gloire.*

Brancusi, in so different a way from Proust, has created a world, or let us say Proust has created a somewhat stuffy social *milieu,* and Brancusi has created an universe, a *cielo,* a Platonic heaven full of pure and essential forms, and a cavern of a studio which is, in a very old sense, a temple of peace, of stillness, a refuge from the noise of motor traffic and the current advertisements. . . .

PARIS LETTER[7]

December, 1922

. . . Experimentalism leaves perhaps more modes than men desirous of perfecting any one mode. Fernand Léger is industrious. Taking his work retrospectively one knows of the time he stopped painting and for some years puzzled over the problem of ideal machines, three-dimensional constructions having all the properties of machines save the ability to move or do work. This is a perfectly serious aesthetic problem; Léger comes to a provisional answer in the negative, not convinced, but wondering whether the *objet,* the real machine, won't in the end be more interesting to look at, and *better aesthetically.*

The struggle is interesting, at least as a symptom of sensitivity, and an evidence of his being aware of the much discussed and deplored gap between "art and life" in our time.

Léger returns to painting and finds the easel picture a constriction. Many of his designs only become effective when one imagines them forty feet by sixty, instead of the twelve by fifteen demanded by studio limits.

[7]Dial, January 1923, pp. 85–90.

Ghirlandaio wanted to paint the town walls of Florence. Léger would be perfectly happy doing the outside of a railway terminal, or probably doing an ad on the slab side of a skyscraper.

Through it all is the elegy, the lament that we lack a *"chef d'orchestre"*; that painting ought to be part of architecture; that there is no place for sculpture or painting in modern life; that painters make innumerable scraps of paper. This is true. The stuff is vendible or non-vendible, it is scraps, knick-knacks, part of the disease that gives us museums instead of temples, curiosity shops instead of such rooms as the hall of the Palazzo Pubblico in Siena or of the Sala di Notari in Perugia.

A rising painter said to me last week, "In a few years my worst competitors [in the job of making a living] will be the people who have bought my early work." This bogy did not weigh on the man who painted his masterpiece on an irremovable wall. He could *afford* to work for his bare board and keep.

In the midst of which let me come out "strong" for Miniver Cheevy, let me once more profess a love of the Medici. Cosimo was a pawnbroker, three of his golden balls still hang over every pawnshop in Manhattan. I wish his successors would hang out the rest of the six and paint the fleur-de-lis on the top one.

His friend Battista Alberti gives me a clue which twelve years among contemporary artists had not offered me. Miniver knew something the neighbours didn't. Alberti, a very great architect and not particularly well-known painter, says in his praise of painting in the *Trattato della Pittura* that the architect gets his *idea* from the painter, that the painter stirs the desire for beautiful building. One has but to recall the backgrounds of Quattrocento painting to see the sense of the remark. The painter begins with himself. Pinturicchio, whomever you like. If he cannot build he at any rate registers a precise ideal of beauty. This passion ran on into, I think, the eighteenth century. One finds rare collections of huge engravings, architectural designs no one could possibly pay to build, but which the designer hoped to see at least on the theatre stage.

It is very simple, we have got to make up our minds what we want, we have got to form a precise and positive desire, not flop about in a vague dissatisfaction. Ten years ago I was with Edgar Williams in San Zeno, and he came on Adamo San Guglielmo's signed column. Adamo was the architect, and is said to have cut some or most of the stone himself. Williams looked at the two simple spirals of red marble cut in one block, and burst out, "How the hell do you expect us to get any buildings when we have to order our columns by the gross?"

It is a very pretty economic problem. Paris is irritating to anyone who has ever seen any real architecture. A real building is one on which the eye can light and stay lit. The detail must bear inspection. The French had some stone-cutters once, *long* ago.

173

The lament for apprenticeage is hackneyed. It is also true that every art student wants to do a Venus de Milo or a Victory or a war memorial at the age of sixteen or eighteen, and that neither *maestria* nor titanic inventiveness is found, *d'habitude,* in adolescents. Mastery has usually risen from craft. I suggest that if art schools get their infant sculptors to making columns instead of drawing-room ornaments, the limiting of the field might produce something very satisfactory. Gaudier-Brzeska was the only young sculptor I ever met who was willing to do building ornaments. I have since known two older sculptors who had the necessary modesty.

If a number of schools could agree on a uniform size or several sizes of column, there would be a supply available, which could be sold at a possible commercial price; it would bring in something to the school or to the student instead of the usual nothing; and the town would have or could have a few agreeable façades.

I know that the contemporary tendency to look at all things from the point of view of paper credit makes this idea "difficult." The idea that the existence of a good building is a gain even to people who haven't a mortgage on it is dangerous, revolutionary, offensive both to unitized socialists and to the owners of munitions works. I accept the necessary exile.

It is not outside our tradition. Jefferson sent over for the measurements of the Maison Carrée. He did this as a private and civilized person, not as an elected magistrate. One doesn't need to relinquish the beautiful inutility of the Tempio merely because there is a new aesthetic of factory architecture. There was a new aesthetic of steel, there is a new aesthetic of reinforced concrete . . . mostly botched, incomplete, unaccomplished, unrealized by constructors. The great architect will always welcome an actuality. For the ass who built the Madeleine and the nincompoops who imagined that mere multiplication of some "classic" proportion would make a larger building more . . . Heaven help to an adjective, more shall we say, imposing, rather than more of an imposition . . . there is nothing but contempt. As for the studied aesthetic of factories, I have heard that an American began it, but his work is only published in Germany, and it has thence descended on Turin for its material realization. The general and generic ignorance of architects is beyond measure. The softness of the Paris stone invites every abortion; the boudoir and the curves of domestic plumbing seem to have set the Beaux Arts ideal of form. Throughout the rest of Europe the architects seem to have forgotten that the ordinary house façade is an oblong pierced by several small oblongs beside and above an oblong or arched door. The proportion of these oblongs can attain "the qualities of music," it does in any number of *palazzi* in Verona. You can't blame a botch in proportion on "building conditions," the responsibility here lies with the architect. I am still waiting to find a practising architect who has thought of the subject; or of the corresponding fun to be had in planning twenty-eight stories in place of the old three to six.

PARIS LETTER[8]

February, 1923

Consortium (cinema) invitation card showing several people being broken, roasted, rolled down hill on "the wheel," La Roue; also posters, nude figure on flaming ditto. Adaptation Musicale d'Arthur Honegger; "everything possible" done to make art a commercial proposition that must fundamentally remain a commercial proposition and please the million. Thanks, we presume, to Blaise Cendrars, there are interesting moments, and effects which belong, perhaps, only to the cinema. At least for the sake of argument we can admit that they are essentially cinematographic, and not a mere travesty and degradation of some other art. The bits of machinery, the varying speeds, the tricks of the reproducing machine are admirably exploited, according to pictorial concepts derived from contemporary abstract painters. The thing takes place on the railway, the driving wheels of the locomotive, et cetera, et cetera, the composition of the photos of the actual machinery, are interesting; and Mr Honegger's programmatic music accompanies them. Thus far the high-brow urge has carried the matter. These details are interpolated in a story (of sorts); and the rest of the show remains the usual drivelling idiocy of the cinema sentiment and St. Vitus.

Any amount of careful thought has been spent on making the good part good; I dare say we should laud the experiment; but am not quite sure on what grounds. As experiment, yes; as publicity for cubism, i.e., to lead the low-brow toward the art of abstract composition, possibly; to settle the question (in the negative) i. e., to satisfy us once and for all that the cinema is no use as art, very probably.

You test a picture by its powers of endurance. If you can have it on your wall for six months without being bored, it is presumably as good a picture as you, personally, are capable of enjoying. Even if the individual photo, in cinema-photography is good, as those in Cendrars' films presumably are, one is never given time to be sure of it.

Also there is the dilemma; the instant that slap-stick comedy, personal touch, tender infancy, puppy dogs, "humour," "drammer," et cetera enter, the whole question of visual effects, composition, et cetera is chucked overboard. *Inévitablement.* Yes, I think we may as well say, *inévitablement.* Ineluctably.

[8]*Dial,* March 1923, pp. 273–80.

With the progressive weakening of the popular mind, we may be subjected to a club-sandwich, an alternation of visual effects, photo-cinematographic effects, and the agile-flea melo-comic sentimento-kinesis. In passing, the French seem rather weak on continuous action in their films; lack of plot, or lack of transitions; giving us, not an action, but a poorly joined series of moving tableaux.

One must distinguish La Roue from Caligari. La Roue is honest, and the "art" portions frankly in debt to contemporary art. Caligari cribbed its visual effects, with craven impertinences, and then flashed up a notice, "This film isn't cubism; it represents the ravings et cetera." Precisely, ravings the inventors couldn't have thought of without the anterior work of new artists.

I should like to stigmatize a parallel impertinence: a recently pirated translation of Gourmont bears the legend "authorized translation." The hypocrisy of Prof.——can go no further. We salute this triumph of parsi-mony.

Man Ray's album (published by Léonce Rosenberg, 19 rue de la Baume) is interesting; although the reproductions do not carry the full force of his experiments in "painting with light," nor have any other reproductions yet succeeded in doing so. Ray's process is not involved in any mystery, it is misleading to call it "photography without a camera." Instead of placing a flat object on a piece of sensitized paper, he places a solid object before the paper, and shoots his light from various points, for various lengths of time, in varying intensity. (This is quite different from vorto-graphy, where the subject was selected and developed into a composition by the vortex of mirrors, and then carried through the lens onto a sensitized plate, from which any number of prints could be made.) Ray's process produces only one picture, with effects he cannot get by taking a negative.

Coburn went out of photography into painting, *via* vortography; Ray beginning as excellent painter, has eliminated his interest in colour in his search for the immaterial (intermediate stage represented by his picture of fans). He stopped wanting to "bring everything to the surface of the canvas." His work, to which *he* attaches no label, may be termed ex-pressionism, and it is a combination of forms in varying light. His defence, or explanation, is that the history of painting shows a series of swings from monochrome to strong colour; that people no longer com-plain of the lack of colour in etching; that white is all colours and black, the absorption of colour; and that, in fine, he is not destroying anything, he is adding something. He and Marcel Duchamp[9] have carried their art

[9]Pound realized Duchamp's dilemma. The artist's readymades had already denied a distinction between art and life, and his glass painting, "The Bride Stripped Bare by Her Bachelors, Even" (1915–23) had been the culmination of his search for an antiretinal art. In 1961 Duchamp declared that "the great artist of tomorrow will go underground." He himself from 1946–66 had been working secretly on his last major work, *Given: 1. The Waterfall, 2. The Illuminating Gas.*

to a point where it demands constant invention, and where they can't simply loll 'round basking in virtuosity. (That I get more pleasure from Man Ray's painting in colour, than from his admirable graduation of black and white, has nothing to do with the matter. A determined series of experiments persisting through a number of years deserves recognition, and one should do one's best to present the artist's own view with the maximum clarity.) Man Ray wants to express certain properties of light. He believes he can do so more effectively by a control of chemical reactions than with a brush; there is no divine ukase forbidding the artist to attempt employing one corner of chemistry as a fine art. . . .

TOTAL WAR ON "CONTEMPLATIO"[10]

(The following important note on art was printed as an introduction to *La Martinelli,* a small book of reproductions of the paintings of Sheri Martinelli, published by Vanni Scheiwiller, Milan, in February 1956.)

It cannot be denied that some of the paintings here reproduced fall into a category the title of which is already worn out and an annoyance at least to the present writer: work in progress. On the other hand: art is what the artist produces and the yatter of critics is powerless to blot a single line of that production. Two great phrases ring in my ears: Manus animam pinxit, taken as theme by D. G. Rossetti and the paradisal "melodia . . . piu a se l'anima tira."

During the past half century I have fought for three artists none of whom was making the art that I, personally, wanted for more than, say, 15% of his time. It was my duty to recognize their integrity and their merit, and to the best of my ability I did so. Gaudier-Brzeska, Wyndham Lewis, Brancusi. My volume on Gaudier is out of print. It has taken 50 years to get Brooks Adams into a cheap edition (Knopf. N.Y. 95 cents). I do not know how long the Douanier was considered merely a freak, or Cézanne admired for his persistence "à faire de la mauvaise peinture." Colour was dead, and Manet revived it. A new technique came into being, Manet and Degas remain. The sense of form died, it took Wyndham Lewis and Picasso, in his earlier phase, to remind men that Clouet and Piero della Francesca had known quite a good deal about it. Frank Harris animadverts somewhere on those who always deal "in something the value of which is unknown". As with "vers libre," so with what was called "abstract" painting, hundreds of crab lice or potato bugs crawled over the small amount of painting which had revived the sense of occidental

[10]*Edge*, October 1956, [pp. 19–20].

composition. An era of technique set in. Lewis said something about art not having any insides, not meaning what several misinterpreters have assumed. I had a word in the early preface to some studies of Cavalcanti. Frate Egidio had already written against those who mistake the eye for the mind. What Yeats called the "pragmatic pig" had so triumphed and the filth of hell, the squalor of degradation, had so overflowed the world that I have been credited with reviving a *lost* form of sensibility. The expertise of recognized "art-experts" is mostly limited to knowledge of market prices. Parisians speculated in Utrillo as in "actions" on the bourse de Paris. Marin is magnificent, but the human heritage is present in his work only in so far as it, MAGNIFICENTLY, don't let us minimize the magnificence, is present only in capacity for selection of what would strike with equal clarity the eye of a cow or a squirrel. Picasso's last published volume shows marvellous technique and total lack of human value, in fact it shows only depravity. The ground tone of one world-famous sculptor, whose technique must be universally recognized, is plain IGNO-BILITY.

And we turn, a few of us, or perhaps a still smaller number have never turned. Lewis once went into the needlessness of following a fad. He said: "Wait. If you mean it, the fashion will come round with the clock's hand." Léger refused to follow the African fad which had been perverted away from Frobenius who STUDIED Africa, to what Paris satirized on the cover jacket of *Les Folies Bourgeoises*. "Mais non! Non, c'est du sadisme, etc.," said Fernand dans la Rue Notre-Dames des Champs. Three years before that Picabia: "J'attends le jour qu'on offre au public une merde sur un plat."[11]

By 1937 or '38, whichever year they held the Biennale, it had been done in every pavilion save one, which no journalist ventured to mention. Gourmont long before that: "The essence of a religion is its art. Or l'art religieux est mort".

By 1954 that was no longer true, as shows in the "Ursula"; in "Lux in Diafana," both unfinshed. What the occident has was in Giotto, I mean as distinct from what we could learn from China. The unstillness that delayed my recognition till quite a while after that of my less restless contemporaries runs parallel with the unstillness in the work of la Martinelli, who is the first to show a capacity to manifest in paint, or in la ceramica what is most to be prized in my writing. The pressure at the pivotal point on which any art changes or swings into direction is tremendous. The American milieu is filled with poison that did not get there by accident. Since 1927 I have known that.

---

[11]Picabia anticipates perhaps the waste imagery of such artists as the contemporary German Joseph Beuys, whose exhibition at the Guggenheim Museum in 1979 drew large crowds.

Lewis has remarked that Michelangelo fled from Firenze to escape daggers, but that Florentine situation was comparatively simple at that time. They make total war on contemplatio.

*"Di star con nessun'huomo ti commando
Il qual vuol usar l'occhi per la mente."*

THE NEW SCULPTURE[12]

I

Some nights ago Mr. T. E. Hulme delivered to the Quest Society an almost wholly unintelligible lecture on cubism and new art at large. He was followed by two other speakers equally unintelligible. With the artists themselves fighting through the obscurities of a new convention it is foolish, or very nearly so, to expect a critic—even an amateur critic—to put forth generalities which shall wholly satisfy both artist and public.

One may stand and say "I believe." One can say with equal dignity "This stuff is a d——n sight more interesting than Rodin at his plaster-castiest or than the 'Florentine Boy.'" But whether one can lay down axioms of criticism that will not only *have* but *convey* a meaning is a thorny outrageous question.

The Greeks!!! Even the Greeks whose sculpture reminds all rightly constituted young futurists of cake-icing and plaster of Paris; even the Greeks had one ideal for their drama and another for cutting stone. They had Praxiteles to make them super-fashion plates; immortal and deathless lay-figures, and they had tragedy to remind them of chaos and death and the then inexplicable forces of destiny and nothingness and beyond.

Their sculpture has at certain recurring periods been an ideal for super-aesthetes and matinee girls. The placid have excused the Greek drama by the Aristotelian fable that it was made for purgation, that you beheld Clytemnestra and then retreated home to do differently. You exhausted your unseemly emotions by the use of vicarious horror and returned to an orderly life.

Of course the Greeks never did return to an orderly life. They were addicted to more disreputable vices than can be mentioned in modern society or even in "Modern Society." With the exception of a few plausible writers they were probably the most unpleasant set of people who ever existed, so that taking it all in all, it is not necessary to believe that the Aristotelian theory is pragmatical.

Mr. Hulme told us that there was *vital* art and *geometric* art. Mr. Lewis compared the soul to a bullet. I gathered from his speech that you could

[12]*The Egoist*, February 16, 1914, pp. 67–68.

set a loaf of bread in an engine shop and that this would *not* cause said loaf to produce cubist paintings.

A third speaker got himself disliked by saying that one might regard the body either as a sensitized receiver of sensations, or as an instrument for carrying out the decrees of the will (or expressioning the soul, or whatever you choose to term it). These two views are opposed and produce two totally opposed theories of aesthetic. I use the word aesthetic paradoxically, let us say two theories of art.

Finding this statement unfavourably received and wishing to be taken for a man of correct and orthodox opinions; trimming his words to the wind, he then said that you could believe that man was the perfect creature, or creator, or lord of the universe or what you will, and that there was no beauty to surpass the beauty of man or of man as conceived by the late Sir Lawrence Alma-Tadema; or that on the contrary you could believe in something beyond man, something important enough to be fed with the blood of hecatombs.

This last seemed to cheer the audience. Mr. Hulme had also expressed it.

II

Humanism having had no chance in the occident, in life, I mean, save for an occasional decade which has usually been followed by some pest like the counter-reformation or Praise-God Barebones or the most estimable S. Webbs & Co., Humanism has, I was about to write, taken refuge in the arts.

The introduction of djinn, tribal gods, fetiches, etc. into the arts is therefore a happy presage.

The artist has been for so long a humanist! He has been a humanist out of reaction. He has had sense enough to know that humanity was unbearably stupid and that he must try to disagree with it. But he has also tried to lead and persuade it; to save it from itself. He has fed it out of his hand and the arts have grown dull and complacent, like a slightly uxorious spouse.

The artist has at last been aroused to the fact that the war between him and the world is a war without truce. That his only remedy is slaughter. This is a mild way to say it. Mr. Hulme was quite right in saying that the difference between the new art and the old was not a difference in degree but a difference in kind; a difference in intention.

The old-fashioned artist was like a gardener who should wish to turn all his garden into trees. The modern artist wishes dung to stay dung, earth to stay earth, and out of this he wishes to grow one or two flowers, which shall be something emphatically *not* dung, *not* earth. The artist

180

has no longer any belief or suspicion that the mass, the half-educated simpering general, the semi-connoisseur, the sometimes collector, and still less the readers of the *Spectator* and the *English Review* can in any way share his delights or understand his pleasure in forces.

He knows he is born to rule but he has no intention of trying to rule by general franchise. He at least is born to the purple. He is not elected by a system of plural voting. There has been a generation of artists who were content to permit a familiarity between themselves and the "cultured" and, even worse, with the "educated," two horrible classes composed of suburban professors and their gentler relations.

This time is fortunately over. The artist recognises his life in the terms of the Tahitian savage. His chance for existence is equal to that of the bushman. His dangers are as subtle and sudden.

He must live by craft and violence. His gods are violent gods. A religion of fashion plates has little to say to him, and that little is nauseous. An art of the fashion plates does not express him.

There is a recognition of this strife in the arts—in the arts of the moment.

Those artists, so called, whose work does not show this strife, are uninteresting. They are uninteresting because they are simply insensible. And being insensible they are not artists.

One therefore says that Epstein is the only sculptor in England. One hears whispers of a man called Gill (the present author knows nothing about him). And more recently one has come into contact with the work of a young sculptor Gaudier-Brzeska (reproduced in this issue).

It is not to be denied that Mr. Epstein has brought in a new beauty. Art is to be admired rather than explained. The jargon of these sculptors is beyond me. I do not precisely know why I admire a green granite, female, apparently pregnant monster with one eye going around a square corner.

When I say that I admire this representation more than an earlier portrait of the same monster (in the shape of a question mark) I am told "It is more monumental."

These men work in an unchanging world. Their work permits no argument. They do not strive after plausibility. I think we are sick to death of plausibilities; of smooth answers; of preachers who "prophesy not the deaths of kings."

It is easier to get at our comfort, our exultation, our quiet in this new sort of sculpture, it is easier, I am trying to say, to get at or explain this by negative statements. We are sick to death of the assorted panaceas, of the general acquiescence of artists, of their agreement to have perfect manners, and to mention absolutely nothing unpleasant. We are equally sick of the psycho-intellectual novel—the analytical method of pretending that all hateful things are interesting and worthy of being analysed and recorded.

Therefore this sculpture with its general combat, its emotional condemnation, gives us our strongest satisfaction.

A sculpture expressing desire, and aware of the hindrance, a sculpture recognising inertia and not trying to persuade us that there is any use in analysing that inertia into seven and seventy sorts of mental and temperamental debility, such a sculpture has come to us in good hour and all one can say is that one is grateful and that it is very difficult to express this gratitude.

Realism in literature has had its run. For thirty or more years we have had in deluge, the analyses of the fatty degeneration of life. A generation has been content to analyse. They were necessary. My generation is not the generation of the romanticists. We have heard all what the "realists" have to say. We do not believe in Eutopias, we accept all that the realist has said. We do not think his statement complete, for he has often dissected the dead and taken no count of forces. To the present condition of things we have nothing to say but *"merde";* and this new wild sculpture says it.

The artist has been at peace with his oppressors for long enough. He has dabbled in democracy and he is now done with that folly.

We turn back, we artists, to the powers of the air, to the djinn who were our allies aforetime, to the spirits of our ancestors. It is by them that we have ruled and shall rule, and by their connivance that we shall mount again into our hierarchy. The aristocracy of entail and of title has decayed, the aristocracy of commerce is decaying, the aristocracy of the arts is ready again for its service.

Modern civilisation has bred a race with brains like those of rabbits and we who are the heirs of the witch-doctor and the voodoo, we artists who have been so long the despised are about to take over control.

And the public will do well to resent these "new" kinds of art.

EXHIBITION AT THE GOUPIL GALLERY[13]

The exhibition of new art now showing at the Goupil Gallery deserves the attention of everyone interested in either painting or sculpture.

The latter art is represented by the work of Epstein and of Gaudier-Brzeska. I endeavoured to praise these men about a month ago and shall again so endeavour.

Jacob Epstein has sent in three pieces: a "Group of Birds" placid with an eternal placidity, existing in the permanent places. They have that greatest quality of art, to wit: certitude.

[13]*The Egoist,* March 16, 1914, p. 109. See the reprint under "Ezra Pound's Estimate" in Jacob Epstein, *Let There Be Sculpture: An Autobiography,* London, 1940.

"A Bird Pluming Itself" is like a cloud bent back upon itself—not a woolly cloud, but one of those clouds that are blown smooth by the wind. It is gracious and aerial.

These things are great art because they are sufficient in themselves. They exist apart, unperturbed by the pettiness and the daily irritation of a world full of Claude Phillipses, and Saintsburys and of the constant bickerings of uncomprehending minds. They infuriate the denizens of this superficial world because they ignore it. Its impotences and its importances do not affect them. Representing, as they do, the immutable, the calm thoroughness of unchanging relations, they are as the gods of the Epicureans, apart, unconcerned, unrelenting.

This is no precious or affected self-blinding aloofness. Mr. Epstein has taken count of all the facts. He is in the best sense realist.

The green flenite woman expresses all the tragedy and enigma of the germinal universe: she also is permanent, unescaping.

This work infuriates the superficial mind, it takes no count of this morning's leader; of transient conditions. It has the solemnity of Egypt.

It is no use saying that Epstein is Egyptian and that Brzeska is Chinese. Nor would I say that the younger man is a follower of the elder. They approach life in different manners.

Brzeska is in a formative stage, he is abundant and pleasing. His animals have what one can only call a "snuggly," comfortable feeling, that might appeal to a child. A very young child would like them to play with if they were not stone and too heavy.

Of the two animal groups, his stags are the more interesting if considered as a composition of forms. "The Boy with a Coney" is "Chou," or suggests slightly the bronze animals of that period. Brzeska is as much concerned with representing certain phases of animal life as is Epstein with presenting some austere permanence; some relation of life and yet outside it. It is as if some realm of "Ideas," of Platonic patterns, were dominated by Hathor. There is in his work an austerity, a metaphysics, like that of Egypt—one doesn't know quite how to say it. All praise of works of art is very possibly futile—were it not that one finds among many scoffers a few people of good will who are eager for this new art and not quite ready.

It is perhaps unfitting for a layman to attempt technicalities, the planes of Mr. Epstein's work seem to sink away from their outline with a curious determination and swiftness.

Last evening I watched a friend's parrot outlined against a hard grey-silver twilight. That is a stupid way of saying that I had found a new detail or a new correlation with Mr. Epstein's stone birds. I saw anew that something masterful had been done. I got a closer idea of a particular kind of decision.

183

II

It is much more difficult to speak of the painting. It is perhaps further from one's literary habit, or it is perhaps so close to one's poetic habit of creation that prose is ill got to fit it.

Wyndham Lewis is well represented, especially by his "Columbus."

One can only pause to compliment the Countess Drogheda that she has set a good example to London.

Mr. Etchells has gained greatly in strength.

Edward Wadsworth has shown a number of canvases with brilliant and interesting refractions. I would mention especially the moods "Scherzo" and "Vivace," and his "Radiation" which is the "pictorial equivalent" of a foundry as perceived—and there is no need to ridicule these terms before having considered them—as perceived by the retina of the intelligence. It is expressed in terms of arabesque.

In general one may say to the uninitiated curious that cubism is an art of patterns. It differs from the pre-renaissance Italian patterns, and from the Japanese or from the pattern of art of Beardsley in that these arts treat a flat space. They make a beautiful arrangement of lines or colour shapes on a flat surface. Their first consideration is the flat space to be used.

Cubism is a pattern of solids. Neither cubism nor these other arts of pattern set out primarily to mirror natural forms. Thus one is removed from Andrea del Sarto and Carlo Dolci and from the discussions of art in *Il Cortigiano* and from all those people who are preoccupied with mimicry.

It is difficult to speak of the rest of this exhibit in detail, one may as well fall back upon impressionism as some of the painters have done.

There were so many pictures and so many people. They were a glittering confusion. There was someone after Van Gogh. And someone doing music halls not quite à la Degas. And there were people complaining about the Camden Town group and people very much relieved to find that there was still something which didn't threaten their early habits of thought. And it was—I mean the private view was—as they say in the *Times,* "A very brilliant occasion."

THE CARESSABILITY OF THE GREEKS[14]

To the Editor, *The Egoist*

Madam,

Your correspondent, Auceps, complains that I have not stopped to quote the whole of Reinach's "Apollo" in my 1000-word article on "The

[14]*The Egoist*, March 16, 1914, p. 117.

New Sculpture." He is angry because I have not filled my page with ideas out of Pater and the *Encyclopaedia Britannica*. He is more interested in preserving the label "Hellenic" than in the vitality of the arts. The difference between serious controversy and journalistic controversy is that, in the former, one is seeking a precise definition and, in the latter, one is trying to "do in" one's opponent.

I will therefore try to restate the disputed passages of my article rather than spend space in the analysis of the young Auceps, who is sufficiently apparent in his letter.

I

The gods forbid that I should set myself up as an art critic. I do not much believe in any criticism of the arts save that which is made by artists, that is I want a painter on painting, a poet on verse, a musician on music. Their criticism can be technical and exact.

Beyond this there is a realm of opinion. The layman can say that he likes or that he dislikes. He may explain his reasons. They may be interesting. If he is a thoughtful man or a man skilled in some other art they very probably are interesting. They are NOT, or in most cases they are not in the least likely to be the artist's reasons.

I say for instance that Epstein is a very great sculptor and that after him Brzeska is more interesting than any other sculptor in England. I don't in the least suppose that I like a work of Epstein's for the same reasons that he likes it. If I were more interested in form than in anything else I should be a sculptor and not a writer. Epstein working in form produces something which moves me who am only moderately interested in form. Rummel who is interested in sound produces a composition of sounds which moves me who am only moderately sensitive to sound. I, if I am lucky, produce a composition of words which moves someone else who is only moderately interested in words.

This faculty for being moved is not criticism but appreciation. There is no need to confuse them. It interests me to find that my surest critic is a contemporary painter who knows any good work from my bad—NOT by a critical process, at least not by a technical process. It is interesting philosophically or whatever you choose to call it. Anyhow it indicates a "life" or a sameness somewhere that we are both trying with our imperfect means to get at.

Our alliance must be with our own generation and usually with workers in other arts. No two of us have precisely the same function, and it is certain that the universe will not so suddenly alter its method that any two of us will suddenly come into complete understanding or accord.

185

II

Regarding this pother about the Greeks: Some few of us are at last liberated from the idea that "THE BEAUTIFUL" is the caressable, the physically attractive.

Art is not particularly concerned with the caressable.

The modern renaissance, or awakening, is very largely due to the fact that we have ceased to regard a work of art as good or bad in accordance with whether it approaches or recedes from the "Antique," the "classical" models.

We have come to recognise that that Greek work was not a uniform and unattainable perfection, but that out of a lot of mediocre work; out of a lot of remnants and fragments there remain certain masterpieces to be set apart and compared with other masterpieces from Egypt and from India and from China and possibly from the South Seas and other districts equally remote from Victorian or Pateresque culture.

Let us confess that we have derived more pleasure from the works of Wyndham Lewis than from the works of Poussin or of Apelles.

Let us take note that the Hellenist no longer takes his stand upon Tadema and Praxiteles.

Let us confess that we admire some Greek works more than others. Even the young Auceps may do some service in defending specific Greek works from the general contempt which is beginning to be hurled upon "the Greek," the Greek "as a whole," the Paterine sentimentalesque Hellenism. But he will not perform this service by refusing to see the force of other conventions, by resolutely entrenching himself in prejudice. By limiting his perceptions.

London.

EZRA POUND

WYNDHAM LEWIS[15]

Mr. Wyndham Lewis is one of the greatest masters of design yet born in the occident. Mr. Lewis has in his "Timon"[16] gathered together his age, or at least our age, our generation, the youth-spirit, or what you will, that moves in the men who are now between their twenty-fifth and thirty-fifth years.

---

[15]*The Egoist*, June 15, 1914, pp. 233–34.

[16]"In the series of six piano pieces called "Sonates Sauvages" Antheil gives us the first music really suggesting Lewis "Timon" designs (*Ezra Pound and Music*, ed. R. Murray Schafer, New York and London, 1977, p. 259). Pound searches for vorticist principles in each art form though he adheres to his vorticist demand, as stated in *Blast* No. 1, that "Every concept, every emotion presents itself to the vivid consciousness in some primary form. It belongs to the art of this form.

It is no easy matter to express the Zeitgeist nor even immediately to comprehend it when we find it laid forth before us in word or in diagram.

The "man in the street" cannot be expected to understand the "Timon" at first sight. Damn the man in the street, once and for all, damn the man in the street who is only in the street because he hasn't intelligence enough to be let in to anywhere else, and who does not in the least respect himself for being in the street, any more than an artist would respect himself for being hung in the Royal Academy.

But the man whose profoundest needs cannot be satisfied by Collier or by Mr. Sargent's society pretties, the man who has some sort of hunger for life, some restlessness for a meaning, is willing to spend six months, any six months, in a wilderness of doubt if he may thereby come to some deeper understanding; to some emotion more intense than his own; to some handling of life more competent than his own fumbling about the surface.

So it is amply worth while taking half a year to get at the "Timon," fumbling about, looking at Matisse and Cézanne and Picasso, and Gauguin and Kandinsky, and spoiling sheet after sheet of paper in learning just how difficult it is to bring forth a new unit of design.

As there is poetry which is creation and not merely a spreading of Keatsian decoration over different but similar surfaces, so is there design which is creation and not merely applying the formula of Manet to different vistas.

So one throws these two accompanying blocks at the spectator. The flying harp and the tom-cat or whatever it is. One throws them with the same confidence and with the same indifference that Giotto sent back his circle to the pope or whoever it was who wanted a sample of workmanship. Maestria is evident in small works as in great ones. If you cannot see the control and skill and power in these two designs, God help you.

"But what are they?" "What is it?" etc. When Ruskin was telling Oxford and the wives of the Oxford dons about the effects that could only be got with the pallet-knife, Pater was learning "that all the arts approach the conditions of music." It is therefore to be expected that lovers of mediocrity will object to any art that attains to the conditions of music.

The rabble and the bureaucracy have built a god in their own image and that god is Mediocrity. The great mass of mankind are mediocre, that is axiomatic, it is a definition of the word mediocre. The race is however divided into disproportionate segments: those who worship their own belly-buttons and those who do not.

There are some of us who do not need to be told that it is a nasty thing to marry off a young girl to a diseased old gentleman whom she dislikes, and who therefore have no need, no profound spiritual need of Mr. Collier's presentation of that fact.

If a man have gathered the force of his generation or of his clan, if he has in his "Timon" expressed the sullen fury of intelligence baffled, shut in by the entrenched forces of stupidity, if he have made "Timon" a type emotion and delivered it in lines and masses and planes, it is proper that we should respect him in a way that we do not respect men blaring out truisms or doing an endless embroidery of sentiment.

In Mr. Lewis' work one finds not a commentator but a protagonist. He is a man at war. He has, in superlative degree, a sense of responsibility and of certitude. He does not declare gaily that the intelligence can exist without aid of the body. He declares sombrely, if you will, but indubitably that the intelligent god is incarnate in the universe, in struggle with the endless inertia.

Our life has not the pageantry of Waterloo to give us a send-off for the beginning of a new *Chartreuse de Parme*. This is no cause for complaint. From the beginning of the world there has been the traditional struggle, the struggle of Voltaire, of Stendhal and of Flaubert, the struggle of driving the shaft of intelligence into the dull mass of mankind.

I daresay one's own art seems always the hardest. One feels that Mr. Lewis has expressed this struggle. One feels that in literature it is almost impossible to express it for our generation. One has such trivial symbols arrayed against one, there is only *The Times* and all that it implies, and the *Century Magazine* and its likes and all that they imply, and the host of other periodicals and the states of mind represented in them. It is so hard to arrange one's mass and opposition. Labour and anarchy can find their opponents in "capital" and "government." But the mind aching for something that it can honour under the name of "civilisation," the mind, seeing that state afar off but clearly, can only flap about pettishly striking at the host of trivial substitutes presented to it. One's very contentions are all in the nature of hurricanes in the traditional teapot.

The really vigourous mind might erect *The Times*, which is of no importance, into a symbol of the state of mind which *The Times* represents, which is a loathsome state of mind, a malebolge of obtuseness.

And having done so, some aesthete left over from the nineties would rebuke one for one's lack of aloofness.

I have heard people accuse Mr. Lewis of lack of aloofness, yet Mr. Lewis has been for a decade one of the most silent men in London.

Whenever a man finds the accepted media of an art insufficient or unsuitable for expressing his particular content, and having found them inadequate develops new media of his own he is accused of "trying to attract attention" by strangeness. Any man who uses a means of expression which Lord Haldane cannot understand must naturally be trying to appeal to Lord Haldane's particular mentality.

I have also read in some reputable journal that one shouldn't use irony in England, because it wouldn't be understood.

188

Therefore I will not use irony, I will say quite squarely and openly that Mr. Lewis is a great artist. I suppose that I am writing for the few people who no longer expect one to argue about cubism and expressionism. I suppose that everyone save Sir Claude Philips has ceased to take Picasso as a joke.

I sit here at my typewriter with two little black designs on the wall before me; they give me pleasure.

I have here also the design out of "Timon," marked Act III, and a Japanese print which is curiously cubist. Plenty of people admire the latter and I am at a loss to know why they cannot admire the former. I have also another "full-sheet" black and white design out of the "Timon," the one with the big circular arrow, and that seems to me the strongest of them all, the one that has most moved me to this rhapsody.

I think if anyone asked me what I mean—not what I mean *by* any particular statement, but what *I* mean, I could point to that design and say "That is what I mean" with more satisfaction than I could point to any other expression of complex intense emotion. I mean that Mr. Lewis has got into his work something which I recognise as the voice of my own age, an age which has not come into its own, which is different from any other age which has yet expressed itself intensely. We are not *les jeunes* of "the thirties" nor of "the nineties" nor of any other decade save our own. And we have in Mr. Lewis our most articulate voice. And we will sweep out the past century as surely as Attila swept across Europe. We can therefore be content to live in our own corner, and to await to be pleased by the deaths of survivors of an age which we detest. That is not, I suppose, a courteous remark but it is a quite true one. Whatever energy may have been in the Victorian age, and whatever may have been the virtues of distinct individuals who reached towards ours, it is certain that the voice of Victorianism is now only the meowing of understrappers and subeditors and survivors and that one need not profoundly mind it. It is an annoyance to see water-logged minds in administrative positions, but it is no more than an annoyance. It is a bore that the present members of the Royal Academy cannot go with their works to Buenos Aires and New Zealand, and that space and air should be occupied by the remnants of divers aesthetic movements. We who are not yet thirty or forty are ineffably bored by these anomalies. There is no reason why we should not say so, or why we should not deride young men who still prowl among the marcescent remains. All of this boredom and derision and so on, being quite distinct from the very sincere respect we feel for any man of ourselves who brings great art to the world, and very distinct also from the respect which we feel for great artists who expressed the life of their times in the past. This is not futurism. The futurists are evidently ignorant of tradition. They have learned from their grandfathers that such and such things were done in 1850 and they conclude that 1850 was all "the past."

We do not desire to cut ourselves off from the past. We do not desire to cut ourselves off from great art of any period, we only demand a recognition of contemporary great art, which cannot possibly be just like the great art of any other period.

At no time in the world has great art been exactly like the great art of any other time. A belief that great art will always be like the art of 1850 is "pastism," a belief that great art will always be like the art of 1911 is "futurism." One hopes that one is not afflicted by either of these diseases.

One hopes that one likes Confucius, and that one has faith in a sort of germinal perfect.

It is one of the hardest things in the world to say anything sensible about works of art at all.

Mr. Lewis has said what there was to say. He has expressed great things in the "Timon." He has presented cool beauty in his later "Portrait of a Typical English Woman." There is no doubt whatsoever about his mastery over his craft.

One can only stand by and say "Credo," and the cursed thing is that one cannot make even the statement of one's belief in the form one would like to make it. One can't "get the punch" into one's article, because of "the pressure of time," from the sheer and damnable fact that if "I," in the present case, take time to go back and rewrite this article in the way, or in approximately the way, it should be written, it means a shortage in my accounts.

EDWARD WADSWORTH, VORTICIST[17]
An authorised appreciation by Ezra Pound

I

"It is no more ridiculous that one should receive or convey an emotion by an arrangement of planes, or by an arrangement of lines and colours than that one should convey or receive such an emotion by an arrangement of musical notes."

That proposition is self-evident to all save the more retarded types of mentality.

Programme music is, for the most part, inferior music. Painting that relies on mimicry rather than on "arrangement" is for the most part inferior painting.

Innocuous people come to me and tell me that all vorticist painters are alike, or that they are like modern painters of other schools, etc. They say with fluttering voices, "I don't see where this new art is *going*," etc.

[17]*The Egoist,* August 15, 1914, pp. 306–7.

The new art in so far as it is the art of Mr. Lewis, Mr. Etchells and Mr. Wadsworth *is*. If you want art that is "going," go to the Royal Portrait Painters' show, that art is *going*, passing, marasmic. The futurists had a good painter named Severini, they still have a good painter, an expressionist named Balla. The vorticists have at least three good painters and more coming on.

These painters are not all alike, they are none of them like Balla. One of them agrees with what Kandinsky has written, but his work is not in the least like Kandinsky's. The new painters are no more "all alike" than Chinamen are "all alike." To the unobserving or untrained mind all Chinamen may look alike. A good vorticist painting is more likely to be mistaken for a good expressionist painting than for the work of Mr. Collier. I trust no one would mistake the work of even a vorticist student for the work of any R.A. or A.R.A. or R.P.P. or anything of that sort.

A Zulu might be unable to tell the difference between a Lavery, a John and a Sargent. They are "all alike," yet even George Moore could tell the difference between them. These men all work "on more or less the same principle." You would explain their differences partly in terms of technical efficiency, partly in terms of taste and personality. A good John is something different from a good or a bad Sargent. Even a good Lavery is something different from a mediocre Sargent.

These statements are absurdly simple, but they are no more simply absurd than the general talk one hears about the new art, and the general tone of the press thereanent.

II

The vorticist movement is a movement of individuals, for individuals, for the protection of individuality. If there is such a process as evolution it is closely associated with the differentiation of species. Humanity has been interesting, more interesting than the rest of the animal kingdom because the individual has been more easily discernible from the herd. The idiosyncracy is more salient.

The vorticist movement is not less unanimous because its two best known painters, Mr. Lewis and Mr. Wadsworth, are quite different, both in their works and in their modus vivendi.

Mr. Lewis is a restless, turbulent intelligence bound to make himself felt. If he had not been a vorticist painter he would have been a vorticist something else. He is a man full of sudden, illuminating antipathies. I remember a remarkable study by him in the *English Review* (before it fell into its present condition), I remember his comments, years ago, of some French story or other, a mind always full of thought, subtle, swift-moving.

A man with his kind of intelligence is bound to be always crashing and opposing and breaking. You cannot be as intelligent, in that sort of way, without being prey to the furies.

If, on the other hand, Mr. Wadsworth had not been a vorticist painter he would have been some other kind of painter. Being a good painter, born in England in such and such a year of our era, the time, the forces of nature, etc., have made him a vorticist. It is as hard to conceive Mr. Wadsworth expressing himself in any other medium save paint as it is to conceive Mr. Lewis remaining unexpressed.

This almost too obvious difference in temperament has, naturally, a resulting difference in the work of these two men. One's differentiation of the two groups of pictures arranges itself almost as a series of antitheses. Turbulent energy: repose. Anger: placidity, and so on.

It is natural that Mr. Lewis should give us pictures of intelligence gnashing teeth with stupidity, that he should choose "Timon" for a subject, and that he should stop design and burst into scathing criticism, as in his drawing of centaurs and sacred virgins.

It is equally natural that Mr. Wadsworth should take his delight in ports and harbours and in the vernal processes of nature; and that even his machinery should tend toward an oriental angular grace.

I cannot recall any painting of Mr. Wadsworth's where he seems to be angry. There is a delight in mechanical beauty, a delight in the beauty of ships or of crocuses, or a delight in pure form. He liked this, that, or the other, and so he sat down to paint it.

I trust the gentle reader is accustomed to take pleasure in "Whistler and the Japanese." Otherwise he had better stop reading my article until he has treated himself to some further draughts of education.

From Whistler and the Japanese, or Chinese, the "world," that is to say, the fragment of the English-speaking world that spreads itself into print, learned to enjoy "arrangements" of colours and masses.

(A word here about representative art: At the vorticist dinner, a large gentleman inclining to futurism said that some tell you they "represent" and some that they "don't represent," etc. The vorticist can represent or not as he likes. He *depends*—depends for his artistic effect—upon the arrangement of spaces and line, on the primary media of his art. A resemblance to natural forms is of no consequence one way or the other.)

I have hanging before me one of Mr. Wadsworth's arrangements in pure form, called (simply because it is necessary to call pictures something or other for ease of reference in conversation) "Khaki." It happens to have a khaki-ish sort of colour for ground and is therefore easy to remember as "Khaki."

This picture does not "look like" anything, save perhaps a Chinese or Japanese painting with the representative patches removed. The feeling I get from this picture is very much the feeling I get from certain Eastern paintings, and I think the feeling that went into it is probably very much the same as that which moved certain Chinese painters. It is a feeling that moves them to paint in periods before their form or "school" of art has decayed and become sentimental.

I have at my right an amazingly fine line block of "Vlissingen." The "motif" is ships in a harbour. It is a very fine organisation of forms. That is to say, there are a whole lot of forms, all in keeping, and all contributing to the effect. There is no use saying that the masts and sails are like the lances in a Paolo Uccello. They are not. Yet one might say that the organisation of forms was good in Wadsworth's drawing and in the well-known Uccello for somewhat similar or even for the very same reason. This is a bad way to criticise. One only refers to some old picture for the sake of getting the reader or the spectator who is hostile to, or unfamiliar with, the new painting to consider it from an impartial position.

There is a definite, one might say a musical or a music-like pleasure for the eye in noting the arrangement of the very acute triangles combined like "notes in a fugue" in this drawing of Mr. Wadsworth's. One is much more at ease in comparing this new work to music.

I recall a black and white of Mr. Wadsworth's, a thing like a signal arm or some other graceful unexplained bit of machinery, reaching out, and alone, across the picture, like a Mozart theme skipping an octave, or leaving the base for the treble.

It is possibly wrong to try to find names for one's pleasures. The pleasures of any one art are best rendered in the terms of that art, yet one may perhaps "talk around them"—one cannot help it, in fact. It is impossible to hear a fine musician without saying later that one has heard him, and without making comments, ending, of course, with "but what is the use in talking." One doesn't talk while the music is going on. One doesn't pretend that one's comments have the value of painting. When one sees some form of beauty attacked, some beautiful form uncomprehended, one takes up its defence, automatically almost. It is natural to praise and defend those who have given us pleasure.

GAUDIER: A POSTSCRIPT 1934[18]

For eighteen years the death of Henri Gaudier has been unremedied. The work of two or three years remains, but the uncreated went with him.

There is no reason to pardon this either to the central powers or to the allies or to ourselves.

[18]*Esquire*, August 1934, pp. 73–74; *Gaudier-Brzeska: A Memoir*, New York, 1970, pp. 140–45.

I dare say there was never a man better fitted to serve in trench warfare, and his contempt for war is a message. A contempt for war is by no means a contempt for physical courage.

"I seen so many better guys bumped off!" said Mr. Hemingway in the face of a minor author's obituaries. Than Henri Gaudier no better guy was bumped off.

With a hundred fat rich men working overtime to start another war or another six wars for the sake of their personal profit, it is very hard for me to write of Gaudier with the lavender tones of dispassionate reminiscence. The real trouble with war (modern war) is that it gives no one a chance to kill the right people.

William Hohenzollern was never in personal danger, the Baron de Wendel, Zaharoff, the brothers Schneider were never in personal danger, nor were the Krupp and Vickers directors. Hence the stink of the shambles. They say the ancient Serbian custom was to send the old men first into the battle. I could nominate nearly a full regiment.

The art of a period is what the artists make during that period, apart from that there are, in Foch's magnificent phrase "merely verbal manifestations."

Good sculpture does not occur in a decadence. Literature may come out of a decadence, painting may come out of a decadence, but in a decadence men do not cut stone.

A few blocks of stone really carved are very nearly sufficient base for a new civilization. The garbage of three empires collapsed over Gaudier's marble. And as that swill is cleared off, as the map of a new Europe becomes visible Gaudier's work re-emerges, perfectly solid. The last country to be seen collapsing is his own. The real France of the banks and gun works shows in Stawisky. I suppose he, Stawisky, was a great minor crook and owed his immunity to his knowledge of the real ghouls and wreckers.

Having said what I knew about Gaudier in my memoir of him I should have very slight excuse for restatement unless I could now show the same facts in some other light or perspective.

An artist's statement is made in and by his work. His work is his biography, and the better the artist the more this applies. "There *is* my autobiography" said Jean Cocteau one day when we were expressing mutual annoyance with the series of importunates who return again and again to requesting it.

The significance of Gaudier's sculpture is now granted, so far as I know, without demur by any person of the slightest competence. In 1916 it wasn't. The work was done from 1912 to 1914 with perhaps a little preliminary skirmishing in 1911, it was done against the whole social system in the sense that it was done against poverty and the lack of materials.

All our work was the work of outlaws and the significance of that fact is now, with the passing of two decades, effulgent. . . . I stated in my memoir that this fact had a meaning. I stated the meaning: Namely that the upper strata of society was rotten. I don't mean sexually fantastic, but that the whole mind of the exploiting class was trivial, idiotic, and that the best conversation was found *in quadriviis et angiportis.*

The white-gleaming intelligence in Gaudier's studio (half the space under a railway arch in Putney with the sides boarded up) in comparison with the podgy and bulbous expensiveness of Schonbrun, the tawdry, gummy, adhesive costliness of the trappings of the bourgeois drawing-rooms of the period, had a meaning.

And that meaning is now written into history. You can't keep a good man down, you can't keep the *beau monde* under, and the *beau monde* is the "world" with the most beautiful mind.

The "revolution in the arts" was quite distinctly revolution. The social revolution was coming, that is to say the most intelligent young ladies of Mayfair were spending their time in Tottenham Court Road to escape from society boredom. The young women with lesser mental equipment were seen *only* in their hereditary surroundings.

The key word of vorticist art was Objectivity in the sense that we insisted that the value of a piece of sculpture was dependent on its shape.

It is probably difficult for the contemporary (1934) reader to conceive any other position, yet if the last snippet of newspaper concerning London speaks the truth, the ineffable Britons have recently elected a director of their National Gallery who doesn't yet know this, and whose views on painting are equally stupid.

Pre-war Europe was guttering down to its end. One tried to persuade it to make a "good end." One may even have thought one was in the act of succeeding. In any case the years immediately before the great slaughter were full of exhilaration for those in the middle of the action—I suppose one must call it the intellectual scene—it was rather like a battle between a weasel and a cow with all the fun for the weasel. Whether we supposed we could trans-animate the cow and produce a miraculous superantelope or springbok, I doubt. At any rate capitalist society refused to make a good end. They hadn't the theatrical elan supposed to have been present in the aristos during the French revolution.

Even in this vicinage I don't know that we understood Gaudier's "Vortex." I mean we, a few of us, saw that it was a damn fine piece of writing, tremendously condensed. But if he had then heard of Frobenius, he was the only man in London who had, and, as nearly as I remember, he had forgotten the names of the authors of whatever he had read about art's archaeology.

But you can't even now get an English translation of *Erlebte Erdteile,* or even of *Paideuma,* and if you could there would still be more of Frobenius' essential knowledge in Gaudier's four pages than would go into any translator's forty.

"Sculptural feeling is the appreciation of masses in relation."

"Sculptural ability is the defining of these masses by planes." And that was 1914.

We have gradually learned that the best African sculpture is conceived as a mass, and that inferior sculpture has been seen as silhouettes in succession.

Epstein was already talking about form. And in twenty years I suppose a number of people have gradually got round to understanding the apparently simple and apparently platitudinous statement that a sculptor *expresses* his meaning *by* form.

A sculptor is a bloke that cuts stone (with the kindred arts of modeling in clay or wax and having bronze cast into forms). Mr. Adrian Stokes has thought a great deal about sculpture, about carving, modeling, meaning, but he is not thereby a sculptor.

People will sometimes admit this, but I am not wasting either your time or my own, when I try to induce you really to think about this distinction.

For eighteen years after Gaudier's death no one showed the least chance of succeeding him. Epstein had already done his most satisfactory work, and Brancusi alone continued the conquest of marble. Brancusi alone continued to use form to express a reality with greater precision, with greater knowledge than his contemporaries or predecessors had possessed.

Cubism has not decayed. Concepts do not decay, but inferior minds and inferior artists waddle about in dilutions of concepts, and exchange weak or faulty imitations.

Gaudier's meaning is expressed in his work. There is no use in anyone's thinking they can explain that meaning by mere talk about the work. If you can't get to the actual three-dimensional objects, the photographs will give you an approximate idea of his *meaning*, as they give you an approximate idea of his work. It is even possible that a well-meaning spectator with limited perceptions could study a statue by photographs, as he might find a dictionary useful in studying a foreign language. Stokes' photos, in his "Stones of Rimini," may help a man who has seen the original to see *more* of it. But no one will ever see all of it from the photos. Neither will the present reader get the full measure of the distance between Brancusi and Gaudier and inferior sculptors merely from looking at photos.

Any more than you can get an idea of Dante by reading some bloke's essay about him.

John Cournos said at the time (1914):

"Gaudier's Vortex is the whole history of sculpture." It is also the history of Kulturmorphologie, it is also . . . (and herein is the justification of my writing a new article on the subject), it is also the proclamation of a new birth out of the guttering and subsiding rubbish of 19th-century stuffiness. A volitionist act stretching into the future. The "fall of impressionism," the "Untergang" you can't call it sunset, but the moon-set or the slopset of a period that had included the whole three or four preceding centuries, in which expensiveness had usurped the place of design.

It meant a complete revaluation of form as a means of expressing nearly everything else, or shall we say of form as a means of expressing the fundamentals of everything, or shall we say of form as expressing the specific weights and values total consciousness?

Or would it be better to say simply "form as a means of expression?"

At any rate it was three-dimensional assertion of a complete evaluation of life in general, of human life in particular, of man against necessity, by which I include social and physical necessity and there is, of course, in the long run no social necessity. What we call social necessity is nothing but the temporary inconvenience caused us by the heaped-up imbecilities of other men, by the habits of a dull and lazy agglomerate of our fellows, which sodden mass it is up to the artist to alter, to carve into a fitting shape, as he hacks off unwanted corners of marble.

In this field Gaudier did his bit. Magnificently did it, in two or three years, getting rid of no end of superfluous nonsense in his immediate field, which was perhaps fifty dollars' worth of marble, and ten dollars' worth of paper and ink. (I am here making a maximum estimate.)

There is still enough energy even in what I was able to get into my memoir of his (i.e., all his own writing and 40 half-tone reproductions) to modernize Russia, to bring communism to date, I mean into harmony with the best thought of the occident, and to make America fit to live in. By modernizing Russia I mean that the trouble with Russia is the trouble with a smoky locomotive. When they get to dividing the cultural heritage, and to seeing that this heritage is the actual source of value they will have arrived at a state of understanding which will make them good neighbours even though Russian. And if we could do likewise we would also be good neighbours for them.

People talk about "abstract sculpture" without realising the various degrees of abstraction which can obtain and have obtained in great sculpture. We will never have active sculptural criteria until more critics understand the extent to which a good sculptor "abstracts" form, takes form from natural objects, and puts it together again in his work.

Gaudier's Vortex was so brief that very few people saw its profundity. John Cournos saw that it contained the whole "history" of sculpture, but it also contained pretty much the whole "Euclid." I mean the whole layout of the fundamentals. The real sculptor "sees" or is aware of, not only all the sides of his work, but of the "through," that is the diameters that can be passed through it from any angle.

Plates XIII, XXIX, "Hieratic Head" of E.P. The only large block of marble Gaudier ever had at his disposal. The work represents two months' actual cutting, and was preceded by a hundred drawings, many of which could be recognized as portraiture, and any one of which might serve as sculptural education. Like Henry James' prefaces, they indicate what the artist has in his head before he starts on the final manifestation.

THE PUBLIC CONVENIENCE[19]

. . . The capitalist imperialist state must be judged not only in comparison with unrealized utopias, but with past forms of the state; if it will not bear comparison with the feudal order; with the small city states both republican and despotic; either as to its "social justice" *or* to its permanent products, art, science, literature, the onus of proof goes against it.

The contemporary mind will have to digest this concept: the state as convenience.

The antithesis is: the state as an infernal nuisance.

As to our "joining revolutions" etc. It is unlikely. The artist is concerned with producing something that will be enjoyable even after a successful revolution. So far as we know even the most violent bolshevik has never abolished electric light globes merely because they were invented under another regime, and by a man intent rather on his own job than on particular propaganda.

(Parenthesis: a great deal of rubbish is emitted by "economists" who fail to distinguish between transient and permanent goods. Between these there are graduations.

1. Transient: fresh vegetables
                  luxuries
                  jerry-built houses
                  fake art
                  pseudo books
                  battleships.
2. Durable: well-constructed buildings
                  roads, public works, canals
                  intelligent afforestation.
3. Permanent: scientific discoveries
                  works of art
                  classics.

That is to say these latter can be put in a class by themselves, as they are always in use and never consumed; or they are, in jargon, "consumed" but not destroyed by consumption.

[19]*Exile*, Spring 1927, pp. 91–92; *Impact*, Chicago, 1960, pp. 219–20.

Note: the shyster is always trying to pass off class 1 for class 2 or 3. This is, naturally, bad economics. Just as the writings of Keynes, Pigou, and the rest of their tribe are bad economics.   end of parenthesis.)

The artist, the maker is always too far ahead of any revolution, or reaction, or counter-revolution or counter-re-action for his vote to have any immediate result; and no party program ever contains enough of his program to give him the least satisfaction. The party that follows him wins; and the speed with which they set about it, is the measure of their practical capacity and intelligence. Blessed are they who pick the right artists and makers.

VORTICISM[20]

"It is no more ridiculous that a person should receive or convey an emotion by means of an arrangement of shapes, or planes, or colours, than that they should receive or convey such emotion by an arrangement of musical notes."

I suppose this proposition is self-evident. Whistler said as much, some years ago, and Pater proclaimed that "All arts approach the conditions of music."

Whenever I say this I am greeted with a storm of "Yes, but . . . ." "But why isn't this art futurism?" "Why isn't?" "Why don't?" and above all: "What, in Heaven's name, has it got to do with your Imagiste poetry?"

Let me explain at leisure, and in nice, orderly, old-fashioned prose.

We are all futurists to the extent of believing with Guillaume Apollinaire that "On ne peut pas porter *partout* avec soi le cadavre de son père." But "futurism," when it gets into art, is, for the most part, a descendant of impressionism. It is a sort of accelerated impressionism.

There is another artistic descent *viâ* Picasso and Kandinsky; *viâ* cubism and expressionism. One does not complain of neoimpression or of accelerated impressionism and "simultaneity," but one is not wholly satisfied by them. One has perhaps other needs.

It is very difficult to make generalities about three arts at once. I shall be, perhaps, more lucid if I give, briefly, the history of the vorticist art

[20]*Fortnightly Review*, September 1, 1914, pp. 461–71; *Gaudier-Brzeska*, pp. 81–94.

"In September, 1914, I had an article in the *Fortnightly Review*, which was for the most part a closer form of a rather informal lecture given at the Rebel Art Centre in Ormond Street the preceding spring." (*Gaudier-Brzeska*, p. 81)

Richard Cork (*Vorticism and Abstract Art in the First Machine Age*, I, London, 1976, p. 257) calls this article "the most positive single essay ever written to expound the meaning of the Vorticist aesthetic." It also shows the relationship between imagism and vorticism.

with which I am most intimately connected, that is to say, vorticist poetry. Vorticism has been announced as including such and such painting and sculpture and "Imagisme" in verse. I shall explain "Imagisme," and then proceed to show its inner relation to certain modern paintings and sculpture.

Imagisme, in so far as it has been known at all, has been known chiefly as a stylistic movement, as a movement of criticism rather than of creation. This is natural, for, despite all possible celerity of publication, the public is always, and of necessity, some years behind the artists' actual thought. Nearly anyone is ready to accept "Imagisme" as a department of poetry, just as one accepts "lyricism" as a department of poetry.

There is a sort of poetry where music, sheer melody, seems as if it were just bursting into speech.

There is another sort of poetry where painting or sculpture seems as if it were "just coming over into speech."

The first sort of poetry has long been called "lyric." One is accustomed to distinguish easily between "lyric" and "epic" and "didactic." One is capable of finding the "lyric" passages in a drama or in a long poem not otherwise "lyric." This division is in the grammars and school books, and one has been brought up to it.

The other sort of poetry is as old as the lyric and as honourable, but, until recently, no one had named it. Ibycus and Liu Ch'e presented the "Image." Dante is a great poet by reason of this faculty, and Milton is a wind-bag because of his lack of it. The "image" is the furthest possible remove from rhetoric. Rhetoric is the art of dressing up some unimportant matter so as to fool the audience for the time being. So much for the general category. Even Aristotle distinguishes between rhetoric, "which is persuasion," and the analytical examination of truth. As a "critical" movement, the "Imagisme" of 1912 to '14 set out "to bring poetry up to the level of prose." No one is so quixotic as to believe that contemporary poetry holds any such position. . . . Stendhal formulated the need in his *De L'Amour:*—

> "La poésie avec ses comparaisons obligées, sa mythologie que ne croit pas le poète, sa dignité de style à la Louis XIV. et tout l'attirail de ses ornements appelé poétique, est bien au dessous de la prose dès qu'il s'agit de donner une idée claire et précise des mouvements du coeur, or dans ce genre on n'émeut que par la clarté."

Flaubert and de Maupassant lifted prose to the rank of a finer art, and one has no patience with contemporary poets who escape from all the difficulties of the infinitely difficult art of good prose by pouring themselves into loose verses.

200

The tenets of the Imagiste faith were published in March, 1913, as follows:—

I. Direct treatment of the "thing," whether subjective or objective.

II. To use absolutely no word that does not contribute to the presentation.

III. As regarding rhythm: to compose in sequence of the musical phrase, not in sequence of the metronome.

There followed a series of about forty cautions to beginners, which need not concern us here.

The arts have indeed "some sort of common bond, some interrecognition." Yet certain emotions or subjects find their most appropriate expression in some one particular art. The work of art which is most "worth while" is the work which would need a hundred works of any other kind of art to explain it. A fine statue is the core of a hundred poems. A fine poem is a score of symphonies. There is music which would need a hundred paintings to express it. There is no synonym for the *Victory of Samothrace* or for Mr. Epstein's flenites. There is no painting of Villon's *Frères Humains*. Such works are what we call works of the "first intensity."

A given subject or emotion belongs to that artist, or to that sort of artist who must know it most intimately and most intensely before he can render it adequately in his art. A painter must know much more about a sunset than a writer, if he is to put it on canvas. But when the poet speaks of "Dawn in russet mantle clad," he presents something which the painter cannot present.

I said in the preface to my *Guido Cavalcanti* that I believed in an absolute rhythm. I believe that every emotion and every phase of emotion has some toneless phrase, some rhythm-phrase to express it.

(This belief leads to *vers libre* and to experiments in quantitative verse.)

To hold a like belief in a sort of permanent metaphor is, as I understand it, "symbolism" in its profounder sense. It is not necessarily a belief in a permanent world, but it is a belief in that direction.

Imagisme is not symbolism. The symbolists dealt in "association," that is, in a sort of allusion, almost of allegory. They degraded the symbol to the status of a world. They made it a form of metronomy. One can be grossly "symbolic," for example, by using the term "cross" to mean "trial." The symbolist's *symbols* have a fixed value, like numbers in arithmetic, like 1, 2, and 7. The imagiste's images have a variable significance, like the signs a, b, and x in algebra.

Moreover, one does not want to be called a symbolist, because symbolism has usually been associated with mushy technique.

On the other hand, Imagisme is not Impressionism, though one borrows, or could borrow, much from the impressionist method of presentation. But this is only negative definition. If I am to give a psychological or philosophical definition "from the inside," I can only do so autobiographically. The precise statement of such a matter must be based on one's own experience.

In the "search for oneself," in the search for "sincere self-expression," one gropes, one finds some seeming verity. One says "I am" this, that, or the other, and with the words scarcely uttered one ceases to be that thing.

I began this search for the real in a book called *Personae*, casting off, as it were, complete masks of the self in each poem. I continued in long series of translations, which were but more elaborate masks.

Secondly, I made poems like "The Return," which is an objective reality and has a complicated sort of significance, like Mr. Epstein's "Sun God," or Mr. Brzeska's "Boy with a Coney." Thirdly, I have written "Heather," which represents a state of consciousness, or "implies," or "implicates" it.

A Russian correspondent, after having called it a symbolist poem, and having been convinced that it was not symbolism, said slowly: "I see, you wish to give people new eyes, not to make them see some new particular thing."

These two latter sorts of poems are impersonal, and that fact brings us back to what I said about absolute metaphor. They are Imagisme, and in so far as they are Imagisme, they fall in with the new pictures and the new sculpture.

Whistler said somewhere in the *Gentle Art:* "The picture is interesting not because it is Trotty Veg, but because it is an arrangement in colour." The minute you have admitted that, you let in the jungle, you let in nature and truth and abundance and cubism and Kandinsky, and the lot of us. Whistler and Kandinsky and some cubists were set to getting extraneous matter out of their art; they were ousting literary values. The Flaubertians talk a good deal about "constatation." "The 'nineties" saw a movement against rhetoric. I think all these things move together, though they do not, of course, move in step.

The painters realise that what matters is form and colour. Musicians long ago learned that programme music was not the ultimate music. Almost anyone can realise that to use a symbol *with an ascribed or intended meaning* is, usually, to produce very bad art. We all remember crowns, and crosses, and rainbows, and what not in atrociously mumbled colour.

The Image is the poet's pigment.* The painter should use his colour because he sees it or feels it. I don't much care whether he is representative or non-representative. He should *depend*, of course, on the creative, not

---

*The image has been defined as "that which presents an intellectual and emotional complex in an instant of time."

upon the mimetic or representational part in his work. It is the same in writing poems, the author must use his *image* because he sees it or feels it, *not* because he thinks he can use it to back up some creed or some system of ethics or economics.

An *image*, in our sense, is real because we know it directly. If it have an age-old traditional meaning this may serve as proof to the professional student of symbology that we have stood in the deathless light, or that we have walked in some particular arbour of his traditional paradiso, but that is not our affair. It is our affair to render the *image* as we have perceived or conceived it.

Browning's "Sordello" is one of the finest *masks* ever presented. Dante's "Paradiso" is the most wonderful *image*. By that I do not mean that it is a perseveringly imagistic performance. The permanent part is Imagisme, the rest, the discourses with the calendar of saints and the discussions about the nature of the moon, are philology. The form of sphere above sphere, the varying reaches of light, the minutiae of pearls upon foreheads, all these are parts of the Image. The image is the poet's pigment; with that in mind you can go ahead and apply Kandinsky, you can transpose his chapter on the language of form and colour and apply it to the writing of verse. As I cannot rely on your having read Kandinsky's *Ueber das Geistige in der Kunst,* I must go on with my autobiography.

Three years ago in Paris I got out of a "Metro" train at La Concorde, and saw suddenly a beautiful face, and then another and another, and then a beautiful child's face, and then another beautiful woman, and I tried all that day to find words for what this had meant to me, and I could not find any words that seemed to me worthy, or as lovely as that sudden emotion. And that evening, as I went home along the Rue Raynouard, I was still trying, and I found, suddenly, the expression. I do not mean that I found words, but there came an equation . . . not in speech, but in little splotches of colour. It was just that—a "pattern," or hardly a pattern, if by "pattern" you mean something with a "repeat" in it. But it was a word, the beginning, for me, of a language in colour. I do not mean that I was unfamiliar with the kindergarten stories about colours being like tones in music. I think that sort of thing is nonsense. If you try to make notes permanently correspond with particular colours, it is like tying narrow meanings to symbols.

That evening, in the Rue Raynouard, I realised quite vividly that if I were a painter, or if I had, often, *that kind* of emotion, or even if I had the energy to get paints and brushes and keep at it, I might found a new school of painting, of "non-representative" painting, a painting that would speak only by arrangements in colour.

And so, when I came to read Kandinsky's chapter on the language of form and colour, I found little that was new to me. I only felt that someone else understood what I understood, and had written it out very clearly. It seems quite natural to me that an artist should have just as much pleasure in an arrangement of planes or in a pattern of figures, as in painting portraits of fine ladies, or in portraying the Mother of God as the symbolists bid us.

When I find people ridiculing the new arts, or making fun of the clumsy odd terms that we use in trying to talk of them amongst ourselves; when they laugh at our talking about the "ice-block quality" in Picasso, I think it is only because they do not know what thought is like, and that they are familiar only with argument and gibe and opinion. That is to say, they can only enjoy what they have been brought up to consider enjoyable, or what some essayist has talked about in mellifluous phrases. They think only "the shells of thought," as de Gourmont calls them; the thoughts that have been already thought out by others.

Any mind that is worth calling a mind must have needs beyond the existing categories of language, just as a painter must have pigments or shades more numerous than the existing names of the colours.

Perhaps this is enough to explain the words in my "Vortex":—*

"Every concept, every emotion, presents itself to the vivid consciousness in some primary form. It belongs to the art of this form."

That is to say, my experience in Paris should have gone into paint. If instead of colour I had perceived sound or planes in relation, I should have expressed it in music or in sculpture. Colour was, in that instance, the "primary pigment"; I mean that it was the first adequate equation that came into consciousness. The Vorticist uses the "primary pigment." Vorticism is art before it has spread itself into flaccidity, into elaboration and secondary applications.

What I have said of one vorticist art can be transposed for another vorticist art. But let me go on then with my own branch of vorticism, about which I can probably speak with greater clarity. All poetic language is the language of exploration. Since the beginning of bad writing, writers have used images as ornaments. The point of Imagisme is that it does not use images *as ornaments*. The image is itself the speech. The image is the word beyond formulated language.

I once saw a small child go to an electric light switch and say, "Mamma, can I *open* the light?" She was using the age-old language of exploration, the language of art. It was a sort of metaphor, but she was not using it as ornamentation.

One is tired of ornamentations, they are all a trick, and any sharp person can learn them.

The Japanese have had the sense of exploration. They have understood the beauty of this sort of knowing. A Chinaman said long ago that if a man

*Appearing in the July number of *Blast*.

204

can't say what he has to say in twelve lines he had better keep quiet. The Japanese have evolved the still shorter form of the *hokku*.

> "The fallen blossom flies back to its branch:
>   A butterfly."

That is the substance of a very well-known *hokku*. Victor Plarr tells me that once, when he was walking over snow with a Japanese naval officer, they came to a place where a cat had crossed the path, and the officer said, "Stop, I am making a poem." Which poem was, roughly, as follows:—

> "The footsteps of the cat upon the snow:
>   (are like) plum-blossoms."

The words "are like" would not occur in the original, but I add them for clarity.

The "one image poem" is a form of super-position, that is to say it is one idea set on top of another. I found it useful in getting out of the impasse in which I had been left by my Metro emotion. I wrote a thirty-line poem, and destroyed it because it was what we call work "of second intensity." Six months later I made a poem half that length; a year later I made the following *hokku*-like sentence:—

> "The apparition of these faces in the crowd:
>   Petals, on a wet, black bough."

I dare say it is meaningless unless one has drifted into a certain vein of thought.* In a poem of this sort one is trying to record the precise instant when a thing outward and objective transforms itself, or darts into a thing inward and subjective.

This particular sort of consciousness has not been identified with impressionist art. I think it is worthy of attention.

The logical end of impressionist art is the cinematograph. The state of mind of the impressionist tends to become cinematographical. Or, to put it another way, the cinematograph does away with the need of a lot of impressionist art.

There are two opposed ways of thinking of a man; firstly, you may think of him as that toward which perception moves, as the toy of circumstance, as the plastic substance *receiving* impressions; secondly,

---

*Mr. Flint and Mr. Rodker have made longer poems depending on a similar presentation of matter. So also have Richard Aldington, in his *In Via Sestina*, and "H. D." in her *Oread*, which latter poems express much stronger emotions than that in my lines here given.

you may think of him as directing a certain fluid force against circumstance, as *conceiving* instead of merely reflecting and observing. One does not claim that one way is better than the other, one notes a diversity of the temperament. The two camps always exist. In the 'eighties there were symbolists opposed to impressionists, now you have vorticism, which is, roughly speaking, expressionism, neo-cubism, and imagism gathered together in one camp and futurism in the other. Futurism is descended from impressionism. It is, in so far as it is an art movement, a kind of accelerated impressionism. It is a spreading, or surface art, as opposed to vorticism, which is intensive.

The vorticist has not this curious tic for destroying past glories. I have no doubt that Italy needed Mr. Marinetti, but he did not set on the egg that hatched me, and as I am wholly opposed to his aesthetic principles I see no reason why I, and various men who agree with me, should be expected to call ourselves futurists. We do not desire to evade comparison with the past. We prefer that the comparison be made by some intelligent person whose idea of "the tradition" is not limited by the conventional taste of four or five centuries and one continent.

Vorticism is an intensive art. I mean by this, that one is concerned with the relative intensity, or relative significance, of different sorts of expression. One desires the most intense, for certain forms of expression *are* "more intense" than others. They are more dynamic. I do not mean they are more emphatic, or that they are yelled louder. I can explain my meaning best by mathematics.

There are four different intensities of mathematical expression known to the ordinarily intelligent undergraduate, namely: the arithmetical, the algebraic, the geometrical, and that of analytical geometry.

For instance, you can write

$$3 \times 3 + 4 \times 4 = 5 \times 5,$$
$$\text{or, differently, } 3^2 + 4^2 = 5^2.$$

That is merely conversation or "ordinary common sense." It is a simple statement of one fact, and does not implicate any other.

Secondly, it is true that

$$3^2 + 4^2 = 5^2, \ 6^2 + 8^2 = 10^2, \ 9^2 + 12^2 = 15^2, \ 39^2 + 52^2 = 65^2.$$

These are all separate facts, one may wish to mention their underlying similarity; it is a bore to speak about each one in turn. One expresses their "algebraic relation" as

$$a^2 + b^2 = c^2.$$

That is the language of philosophy. IT MAKES NO PICTURE. This kind of statement applies to a lot of facts, but it does not grip hold of Heaven.

Thirdly, when one studies Euclid one finds that the relation of $a^2 + b^2 = c^2$ applies to the ratio between the squares on the two sides of a right-angled triangle and the square on the hypotenuse. One still

206

writes it $a^2 + b^2 = c^2$, but one has begun to talk about form. Another property or quality of life has crept into one's matter. Until then one had dealt only with numbers. But even this statement does not *create* form. The picture is given you in the proposition about the square on the hypotenuse of the right-angled triangle being equal to the sum of the squares on the two other sides. Statements in plane or descriptive geometry are like talk about art. They are a criticism of the form. The form is not created by them.

Fourthly, we come to Descartian or "analytical geometry." Space is conceived as separated by two or by three axes (depending on whether one is treating form in one or more planes). One refers points to these axes by a series of coefficients. Given the idiom, one is able *actually to create.*

Thus, we learn that the equation $(x - a)^2 + (y - b)^2 = r^2$ governs the circle. It is the circle. It is not a particular circle, it is any circle and all circles. It is nothing that is not a circle. It is the circle free of space and time limits. It is the universal, existing in perfection, in freedom from space and time. Mathematics is dull as ditchwater until one reaches analytics. But in analytics we come upon a new way of dealing with form. It is in this way that art handles life. The difference between art and analytical geometry is the difference of subject-matter only. Art is more interesting in proportion as life and the human consciousness are more complex and more interesting than forms and numbers.

This statement does not interfere in the least with "spontaneity" and "intuition," or with their function in art. I passed my last *exam.* in mathematics on sheer intuition. I saw where the line *had* to go, as clearly as I ever saw an image, or felt *caelestem intus vigorem.*

The statements of "analytics" are "lords" over fact. They are the thrones and dominations that rule over form and recurrence. And in like manner are great works of art lords over fact, over race-long recurrent moods, and over to-morrow.

Great works of art contain this fourth sort of equation. They cause form to come into being. By the "image" I mean such an equation; not an equation of mathematics, not something about *a, b,* and *c,* having something to do with form, but about *sea, cliffs, night,* having something to do with mood.

The image is not an idea. It is a radiant node or cluster; it is what I can, and must perforce, call a VORTEX, from which, and through which, and into which, ideas are constantly rushing. In decency one can only call it a VORTEX. And from this necessity came the name "vorticism." *Nomina sunt consequentia rerum,* and never was that statement of Aquinas more true than in the case of the vorticist movement.

It is as true for the painting and the sculpture as it is for the poetry. Mr. Wadsworth and Mr. Lewis are not using words, they are using shape and colour. Mr. Brzeska and Mr. Epstein are using "planes in relation," they are dealing with a relation of planes different from the sort of relation of planes dealt with in geometry, hence what is called "the need of organic forms in sculpture."

I trust I have made clear what I mean by an "intensive art." The vorticist movement is not a movement of mystification, though I dare say many people "of good will" have been considerably bewildered.

The organisation of forms is a much more energetic and creative action than the copying or imitating of light on a haystack.

There is undoubtedly a language of form and colour. It is not a symbolical or allegorical language depending on certain meanings having been ascribed, in books, to certain signs and colours.

Certain artists working in different media have managed to understand each other. They know the good and bad in each other's work, which they could not know unless there were a common speech.

As for the excellence of certain contemporary artists, all I can do is stand up for my own beliefs. I believe that Mr. Wyndham Lewis is a very great master of design; that he has brought into our art new units of design and new manners of organisation. I think that his series "Timon" is a great work. I think he is the most articulate expression of my own decade. If you ask me what his "Timon" means, I can reply by asking you what the old play means. For me his designs are a creation on the same *motif*. That *motif* is the fury of intelligence baffled and shut in by circumjacent stupidity. It is an emotional *motif*. Mr. Lewis's painting is nearly always emotional.

Mr. Wadsworth's work gives me pleasure, sometimes like the pleasure I have received from Chinese and Japanese prints and painting; for example, I derive such pleasure from Mr. Wadsworth's "Khaki." Sometimes his work gives me a pleasure which I can only compare to the pleasure I have in music, in music as it was in Mozart's time. If an outsider wishes swiftly to understand this new work, he can do worse than approach it in the spirit wherein he approaches music.

"Lewis is Bach." No, it is incorrect to say that "Lewis is Bach," but our feeling is that certain works of Picasso and certain works of Lewis have in them something which is to painting what certain qualities of Bach are to music. Music was vorticist in the Bach-Mozart period, before it went off into romance and sentiment and description. A new vorticist music would come from a new computation of the mathematics of harmony, not from a mimetic representation of dead cats in a fog-horn, alias noise-tuners.

Mr. Epstein is too well known to need presentation in this article. Mr. Brzeska's sculpture is so generally recognised in all camps that one does not need to bring in a brief concerning it. Mr. Brzeska has defined sculptural feeling as "the appreciation of masses in relation," and sculptural ability as "the defining of these masses by planes." There comes a time when one is more deeply moved by that form of intelligence which can present "masses in relation" than by that combination of patience and trickery which can make marble chains with free links and spin out bronze until it copies the feathers on a general's hat. Mr. Etchells still remains more or less of a mystery. He is on his travels, whence he has sent back a few excellent drawings. It cannot be made too clear that the work of the vorticists and the "feeling of inner need" existed before the general noise about vorticism. We worked separately, we found an underlying agreement, we decided to stand together.

THE DEATH OF VORTICISM[21]

The Kaiser has gone, or at least we hope he will have gone before this article reaches the press room; the Papacy is on its way to commendable desuetude, with lamentable slowness; vorticism has been reported dead by numerous half-caste reporters of Kieff, by numerous old ladies, by numberous parasites who having done their best to prevent the emergence of inventions later find it profitable to make copy out of the same, etc., etc. Mr. George Moore has fled to the scriptures for inspiration and come back without it, but with serious damage to his style,—a style once so pellucid in its description of bed-room furniture and of his whilom friends' dirty linen.

Gaudier-Brzeska's life work was, we admit, stopped by a German bullet. It may be remembered as significant of the way in which the English press welcomes the work of genius that Mr. James Douglas of the *Star* commented on the death notice of Gaudier by writing that the perpetrators of *Blast* carried a joke too far in printing pretended death notices of these invented madmen. It is also significant of what the American "aesthetic public," as engineered by the relics of "the nineties," will swallow that the celebrated aesthetic publisher and book-pirate Mr. Tom. B. Mosher of Portland, Me., has published Mr. James Douglas as the fine flower of British aestheticism.

NOTE. I am often asked whether there can be a long imagiste or vorticist poem. The Japanese, who evolved the *hokku,* evolved also the Noh plays. In the best "Noh" the whole play may consist of one image. I mean it is gathered about one image. Its unity consists in one image, enforced by movement and music. I see nothing against a long vorticist poem.

On the other hand, no artist can possibly get a vortex into every poem or picture he does. One would like to do so, but it is beyond one. Certain things seem to demand metrical expression, or expression in a rhythm more agitated than the rhythms acceptable to prose, and these subjects, though they do not contain a vortex, may have some interest, an interest as "criticism of life" or of art. It is natural to express these things, and a vorticist or imagiste writer may be justified in presenting a certain amount of work which is not vorticism or imagisme, just as he might be justified in printing a purely didactic prose article. Unfinished sketches and drawings have a similar interest; they are trials and attempts toward a vortex.

[21]*The Little Review,* February/March 1919, pp. 45, 48.

When one mentions simple facts of this sort, idiots say that you are "embittered"; and when you call a block-head a block-head he can not believe you, he usually says that you are clever but insincere. Indeed I find it harder to convince a man that you really think him an ass, no matter how obvious his inanity, than to convince him of any other proposition whatsoever, Et pourtant there are people whom one does quite quietly and sincerely and placidly believe to be thoroughly stupid, inane and insipid.

And vorticism has not yet had its funeral. Gaudier was killed at Neuville St. Vaast in 1915. The memorial exhibition of his work in London last summer received from all quarters the appreciation due in his lifetime.

It may be said that after all kinds of naval camouflage without satisfaction the government has at last put a vorticist lieutenant in charge of the biggest port in England; that the French aesthetic camouflagists working on theory and at a distance from the sea-bord, are unsatisfactory and that their work has to be corrected.

I shall not go into detail of the vorticist improvement of the earlier impressionist systems; suffice it that in dealing with actual modernity the new art has proved its contentions, and that where actual knowledge of *how the human eye is affected by colours and patterns in relation,* where there is some standard of judgment other than that of half educated dilettanti, vorticist hard-headedness has made good.

After trying all kinds of war painters, with, for the most part, lamentable or at any rate negligible results, the government has taken on Mr. Wyndham Lewis; and after irritating delays, such as may be expected of an artist who waits to know his own mind before rushing into expression, the government is now getting its finest war pictures. The elderly are content to compare them to Luca Signorelli, but those who really knew Mr. Lewis' mastery of his medium, before 1914, are perfectly content to see in them nothing more than the continuation of Lewis.

Mr. Roberts, the youngest member of the *Blast* group, is also doing work for the government, and "giving satisfaction."

Obituary notices from New Zealand, Oregon, Bloomsbury and other suburbs will be read with interest by *i vorticisti,* communications via Amsterdam and the Wolff bureau will also be read with interest and with reserve.

SCULPSHURE[22]

My Khrist Kant somethin' be done about this man George G. Barnard. It aint Mikel Angerlo, an' it aint even Rodin. It's just mashed popatoz and

[22]Signed "Abel Sanders." *The Little Review,* January/March 1921, p. 47.

the fog end of the last century's allegory. Before he spoils all that good marble can't somebody tell him about Egypt and Assyria, or pay his ticket so he can go look at some sculpshure made by someon' who had some idea of stone as distinct from oatmeal mush an molarsses. Hasn't even the sense of stone one finds in Barroque.

BRANCUSI[23]

"I carve a thesis in logic of the eternal beauty," writes Rémy de Gourmont in his *Sonnets à l'Amazone*. A man hurls himself toward the infinite and the works of art are his vestiges, his trace in the manifest.

It is perhaps no more impossible to give a vague idea of Brancusi's sculpture in words than to give it in photographs, but it is equally impossible to give an exact sculptural idea in either words or photography. T. J. Everets has made the best summary of our contemporary aesthetics that I know, in his sentence "A work of art has in it no idea which is separable from the form." I believe this conviction can be found in either vorticist explanations, and in a world where so few people have yet dissociated form from representation, one may, or at least I may as well approach Brancusi via the formulations by Gaudier-Brzeska, or by myself in my study of Gaudier:

> "Sculptural feeling is the appreciation of masses in relation."
> "Sculptural ability is the defining of these masses by planes."
> "Every concept, every emotion presents itself to the vivid consciousness in some primary form. It belongs to the art of that form."

I don't mean to imply that vorticist formulae will "satisfy" Brancusi, or that any formula need ever satisfy any artist, simply the formulae give me certain axes (plural of *axis*, not of *ax*) for discrimination.

I have found, to date, nothing in vorticist formulae which contradicts the work of Brancusi, the formulae left every man fairly free. Gaudier had long since revolted from the Rodin-Maillol mixture; no one who understood Gaudier was fooled by the cheap Viennese Michaelangelism and rhetoric of Mestrovic. One understood that "Works of art attract by a resembling unlikeness"; that "The beauty of form in the still stone can not be the same beauty of form as that in the living animal." One even understood that, as in Gaudier's brown stone dancer, the pure or unadulterated motifs of the circle and triangle have a right to build up their own fugue or sonata in form; as a theme in music has its right to express itself.

[23]*The Little Review*, Autumn 1921, pp. 3-7; *Literary Essays*, New York and London, 1954, pp. 441-45.

No critic has a right to pretend that he fully understands any artist; least of all do I pretend, in this note, to understand Brancusi (after a few weeks' acquaintance) even as well as I understood Gaudier (after several years' friendship); anything I say here effaces anything I may have said before on the subject, and anything I say the week after next effaces what I say here—a pale reflection of Brancusi's general wish that people would wait until he has finished (i.e., in the cemetery) before they talk aesthetics with or about him.

At best one could but clear away a few grosser misconceptions. Gaudier had discriminated against beefy statues, he had given us a very definite appreciation of stone as stone; he had taught us to feel that the beauty of sculpture is inseparable from its material and that it inheres in the material. Brancusi was giving up the facile success of representative sculpture about the time Gaudier was giving up his baby-bottle; in many ways his difference from Gaudier is a difference merely of degree, he has had time to make statues where Gaudier had time only to make sketches; Gaudier had purged himself of every kind of rhetoric he had noticed; Brancusi has detected more kinds of rhetoric and continued the process of purgation.

When verbally intelligible he is quite definite in the statement that whatever else art is, it is not *"crise des nerfs"*; that beauty is not grimaces and fortuitous gestures; that starting with an ideal of form one arrives at a mathematical exactitude of proportion, but *not by* mathematics.

Above all he is a man in love with perfection. Dante believed in the "melody which most in-centres the soul"; in the preface to my Guido I have tried to express the idea of an absolute rhythm, or the possibility of it. Perhaps every artist at one time or another believes in a sort of elixir or philosopher's stone produced by the sheer perfection of his art; by the alchemical sublimation of the medium; the elimination of accidentals and imperfections.

Where Gaudier had developed a sort of form-fugue or form-sonata by a combination of forms, Brancusi has set out on the maddeningly more difficult exploration toward getting all the forms into one form; this is as long as any Buddhist's contemplation of the universe or as any mediaeval saint's contemplation of the divine love,—as long and even as paradoxical as the final remarks in the *Divina Commedia*. It is a search easily begun, and wholly unending, and the vestiges are let us say Brancusi's "Bird," and there is perhaps six months' work and twenty years' knowledge between one model of the erect bird and another, though they appear identical in photography. Therein consisting the difference between sculpture and sketches. Plate No. 5 shows what looks like an egg; I give more photos of the bust than of this egg because in the photos the egg comes to nothing; in Plate No. 12 there is at the base of the chimaera an egg with a plane and a groove cut into it, an egg having infantile rotundities and repose.

I don't know by what metaphorical periphrase I am to convey the relation of these ovoids to Brancusi's other sculpture. As an interim label, one might consider them as master-keys to the world of form—not "his" world of form, but as much as he has found of "the" world of form. They contain or imply, or should, the triangle and the circle.

Or putting it another way, every one of the thousand angles of approach to a statue ought to be interesting, it ought to have a life (Brancusi might perhaps permit me to say a "divine" life) of its own. "Any prentice" can supposedly make a statue that will catch the eye and be interesting from *some* angle. This last statement is not strictly true, the present condition of sculptural sense leaving us with a vastly lower level both of prentices and "great sculptors"; but even the strictest worshipper of bad art will admit that it is infinitely easier to make a statue which can please from *one* side than to make one which gives satisfaction from no matter what angle of vision.

It is also conceivably more difficult to give this formal-satisfaction by a single mass, or let us say to sustain the formal-interest by a single mass, than to excite transient visual interests by more monumental and melo-dramatic combinations.

Brancusi's revolt against the rhetorical and the kolossal has carried him into revolt against the monumental, or at least what appears to be, for the instant, a revolt against one sort of solidity. The research for the aerial has produced his bird which stands unsupported upon its diminished base (the best of jade carvers and netsuke makers produce tiny objects which also maintain themselves on extremely minute foundations). If I say that Brancusi's ideal form should be equally interesting from all angles, this does not quite imply that one should stand the ideal temple on its head, but it probably implies a discontent with any combination of proportions which can't be conceived as beautiful even if, in the case of a temple, some earthquake should stand it up intact and end-ways or turned-turtle. Here I think the concept differs from Gaudier's, as indubitably the metaphysic of Brancusi is outside and unrelated to vorticist manners of thinking.

The great black-stone Egyptian patera in the British museum is perhaps more formally interesting than the statues of Memnon.

In the case of the ovoid, I take it Brancusi is meditating upon pure form free from all terrestrial gravitation; form as free in its own life as the form of the analytic geometers; and the measure of his success in this experiment (unfinished and probably unfinishable) is that from some angles at least the ovoid does come to life and appear ready to levitate. (Or this is perhaps merely a fortuitous anecdote, like any other expression.)

Crystal-gazing?? No. Admitting the possibility of self-hypnosis by means of highly polished brass surfaces, the polish, from the sculptural point of view, results merely from a desire for greater precision of the form, it is also a transient glory. But the contemplation of form or of formal-beauty leading into the infinite must be dissociated from the dazzle of crystal; there is a sort of relation, but there is the more important divergence; with the crystal it is a hypnosis, or a contemplative fixation of thought, or an excitement of the "sub-conscious" or unconscious (whatever the devil they may be), and with the ideal form in marble it is an approach to the infinite *by form*, by precisely the highest possible degree of consciousness of formal perfection; as free of accident as any of the philosophical demands of a "Paradiso" can make it.

This is not a suggestion that all sculpture should end in the making of abstract ovoids; indeed no one but a genius wholly centred in his art, and more or less "oriental" could endure the strain of such effort.

But if we are ever to have a bearable sculpture or architecture it might be well for young sculptors to start with some such effort at perfection, rather than with the idea of a new Laocoon, or a "Triumph of Labour over Commerce." (This suggestion is mine, and I hope it will never fall under the eye of Brancusi.—But then Brancusi can spend most of his time in his own studio, surrounded by the calm of his own creations, whereas the author of this imperfect exposure is compelled to move about in a world full of junk-shops, a world full of more than idiotic ornamentations, a world where pictures are made for museums, where no man has a front-door that he can bear to look at, let alone one he can contemplate with reasonable pleasure, where the average house is each year made more hideous, and where the sense of form which ought to be as general as the sense of refreshment after a bath, or the pleasure of liquid in time of drouth or any other clear animal pleasure, is the rare possession of an "intellectual" (heaven help us) "aristocracy."

HISTORICAL SURVEY[24]

. . . The strength of Picasso is largely in his having chewed through and chewed up a great mass of classicism; which, for example, the lesser cubists, and the flabby cubists have not. . . .

The work of art is not a means.
The work of art is an end.

It is the result of an act or actions commuted to please the artist and for no other reason. . . .

The work of art is an end. When he has done it the artist is *as* artist through with it. If he remembers it—if it is good enough to give him pleasure when he next sees it, when he sees it after a lapse of ten years, he

[24]*The Little Review*, Autumn 1921, p. 42. Paragraphs excerpted from a longer article.

then approaches it as the admiring spectator; or if he has pride in it, if it serves to lift him out of a grutch, he approaches it merely as the proud parent, or in some such sentimental, human relation.

THE BIENNALE[25]

Sir,—Mr. Porteus was a little hard on pore ole Marinetti and the Biennale. But he is right in saying the Biennale is a poor show. There are two chief causes of this. First, and lasting, is the system of organisation. Each nation has a committee, that is to say, it sends usually official art—I never can remember the names of curators of the Luxembourg Gallery, so I can't list those characteristics which would lay me open to libel charges. The nasty frogs pick frog artists: the frog pavilion is NATIONAL, so that Picasso or any foreigner in Paris is omitted *on system*. The best American painting is, in great part, done in Paris. Naturally the local halfwits in New York don't see it; and send the parish prize doilies instead.

The second reason is Maraini, backed up by Ojetti. These people are Italy's Murray Butlers. They are clever at short range. Until people like the directors of Il Milione and P. M. Bardi are put in charge of the Biennale, or until order comes from "above" to get the best painting and damn the bureaucracy and the dealers, the Biennale will stay what it has been. No Brancusi, no Picasso, no Douanier, or at any rate none of the first rate painters, until they are matters of history. Venice had a memorial show of Boldini, who is what Ojetti probably LIKES.

E. P.

MACHINES[26]

Introductory Letter

Dear Samuel, Respected Editor:

By yet another of those chains of circumstance etc. which shelter the never eager public from most of my cerebral activity my notes on machinery have remained in typescript until

---

[25]*New English Weekly*, May 30, 1935, p. 140.

[26]*The New Review*, Winter 1931/1932, pp. 291–92. Pound's enthusiasm for machines was characteristic of the age. See the poet's "Affirmations" article in *The New Age*, February 11, 1915, in which he writes that "a feeling for . . . machines" was "one of the age-tendencies, springing up naturally in many places and coming into the arts quite naturally and spontaneously in England, in America, and in Italy." For the different attitudes toward the machine of the vorticists and futurists, see Wyndham Lewis, *Wyndham Lewis the Artist, from "Blast" to Burlington House*, London, 1939, p. 79, quoted in Cork, *Vorticism*, II, Berkeley and Los Angeles, 1976, p. 326.

I shd. prefer an immediate imprint of Terra Italica to resurrecting even a part of them.

I do not propose to go into an explanation of the reasons for the delay (tragedy of X., idiocy of Y., etc.).

The progress of the cinema, the vast improvement in gen. standard of photographs of machinery make it desirable to relegate to scrap heap a good deal of what I wrote four years ago. This dissociation however remains and the reader will waste his time unless he grasps it firmly. I am not talking about the aesthetic of *photographs* of machines; but about the aesthetic of the machines themselves, the formal beauty of the machines themselves, not any question of how you can get a camera squirted at a bit of machinery and a bit of lighting.

This ought to be just as clear as the idea that a bit of sculpture has a certain formal beauty quite distinct from the cleverness or art of some chap in utilizing that formal beauty in making a pretty photo.

The photos used to illustrate my points have been taken with the intention of introducing the minimum of accessories, and of concentrating the attention on the actuality of the machines and their parts.

E. P.
Oct. 1931.

POSTSCRIPT

As I am now this day the 2nd. Oct. 31 unable to find the ms. of my original essay, the reader will be spared a good deal.

1. Formal beauty of machines, distinct from lighting, photography, etc.

2. Might be supposed to conform to proportions of architecture and sculpture.

"A small machine is never the miniature of a large machine of the same type." (Dexter Kimbal, *Industrial Economics.*)

Definition of beauty as fitness to a purpose possibly in conflict with strict question of plastic beauty.

Sticking to question of pure form there might be a best size for a machine of a given type.

The great sculptor however seeks scale; not the only quality but a very important one, that is to say a proportion that gives a small statue the rights of a large one.

For example, one feels that Gaudier's "Boy with Coney" might be very much larger in the same shape.

I am not being "coherent" or making statements in simple sequence. If the reader is going to think at all about the question he will have to start with a lot of disparate, disproportionate, possibly contradictory facts and feelings and try to sort them into shape and coherence.

216

When Fernand Léger and Co., years since, tried to make "ideal machines," three dimensional compositions of machine forms that wd. simply look pretty but do no work, they found that they cd. not come up to the *plastic* excellence of actual machines.

Now look at the photos. There were about 60 in my collection but these 15 will do. Also try to remember machinery you have seen; I conclude:

1st. The plastic beauty of machinery reaches its maximum in the mobile parts and in the parts where the maximum power is concentrated. (Vorticism, confirmation of the 1914 manifestos.)

Much lower plastic standard in the immobile parts or casings etc., where the form is arbitrary and not imposed by the necessities and efficiencies of the machine. (Where it is mere question of the "taste" or half educated or uneducated form sense of the designers, mechanical aesthetes, etc.)

Damn sentimentalizing about machinery.

II. Inferiority in plastic of early farm machinery, formal uncertainty in machines that are composite of several simple machines, or a congeries of machines of same function, though the latter may tend to "repeats," pattern, etc.

(Definition: pattern, a design in which certain elements, simple or compound, occur repeatedly and in a determined order.)

Reader note particularly plate no. 6 for sculptural value. Plate 9. The gothic, architectural and having defects of the gothic, I mean *as* machinery also.

My thanks to Bliss and Co. in particular, to Wellman Seaver Morgan, and Shepard Co., also to F. S. Bacon for rustling the photos.

So much for the "plastic." For remarks on the acoustics of machinery, see second edtn. of my *Antheil* pubd. by Covici, Fried, who have recently atoned for many crimes by pubctn. of "March 1917."

TO WHISTLER, AMERICAN[27]
On the loan exhibit of his paintings at the Tate Gallery

You also, our first great,
Had tried all ways;
Tested and pried and worked in many fashions,
And this much gives me heart to play the game.

Here is part that's slight, and part gone wrong,
And much of little moment, and some few
Perfect as Dürer!

[27]*Poetry*, October 1912, p. 7; *Personae*, New York, 1949, and London, 1952, p. 243.

"In the Studio" and these two portraits,* if I had my choice!
And then these sketches in the mood of Greece?

You had your searches, your uncertainties,
And this is good to know—for us, I mean,
Who bear the brunt of our America
And try to wrench her impulse into art.

You were not always sure, not always set
To hiding night or tuning "symphonies";
Had not one style from birth, but tried and pried
And stretched and tampered with the media.

You and Abe Lincoln from that mass of dolts
Show us there's chance at least of winning through.[28]

EZRA POUND FILES EXCEPTIONS[29]
London, Eng., July 30, 1916

Editor of Reedy's Mirror:
   In the interests of accuracy:

1.

I was not born in Utah, "it is immaterial," but still I am not to be
confused with "Ezra, the Mormon," however charming and sympathetic
or fictitious he may have been. I was born in Idaho, in Hailey, in "the
residence now occupied by Mr. Plughoff" (unless he has moved). There is,
so far as I know, no memorial tablet.

2.

I am not the "head of the vorticist movement." I said quite clearly in my
memoir of Gaudier-Brzeska that the vorticist movement implied no series
of personal subordinations. The pleasure in the vorticist movement was
to find oneself at last *inter pares.* Mr. Wyndham Lewis is a man of so

---

*"Brown and Gold—de Race."
   "Grenat et Or—Le Petit Cardinal."
   [28]In an article of Rémy de Gourmont in the *Fortnightly Review*, December 1,
1915, and reprinted in *Selected Prose: 1909-1965*, ed. William Cookson, London,
1973, p. 388; New York, p. 418, Pound writes: "Just as there is more wisdom,
perhaps, more 'revolution,' in Whistler's portrait of young Miss Alexander than
in all the Judaic drawings of the 'prophetic' Blake, so there is more life in Remy
than in all the reformers."
   [29]*Reedy's Mirror*, August 18, 1916, pp. 535–36.

marked a genius, of such swift and profound intuitions that it would be ridiculous to speak of anyone else as being his "head." I cannot picture either Brzeska or Etchells considering himself as anyone's elbow or shin-bone. As an active and informal association it might be said that Lewis supplied the volcanic force, Brzeska the animal energy, and perhaps that I had contributed a certain Confucian calm and reserve. There would have been no movement without Lewis.----

At any rate, if you are irrevocably wedded to the phrase, "head of the movement," you would be more correct in applying the title to Lewis than to anyone else.

3.

Let us come to your remarks about Gaudier-Brzeska's sculpture in your issue for July 14:

A.

You say it seems to you "a new language known only to the sculptor."

Has any new light ever come in the arts or in the sciences save through a new speech known, *at first,* only to the artist or the inventor?

There was a language known only to abstract mathematicians (I believe to the men who experimented in "determinants"). This language grad-ually became known to physicists, or to a physicist, and you have now the very popular wireless telegraph, which is still "incomprehensible" to a very great number of people.

The intelligent man will learn as much as he can rather than pretend to be more ignorant than he is.

B.

You ask: "What is formless form?" And then you rush on to talk about *"mutually agreed upon symbols."* I have not talked about "formless form." But try to follow me for a moment.

A circle or a triangle has just as much form as the Albert Memorial. Its form is simpler, to be sure.

Some centuries ago John Heydon professed to derive aesthetic satisfac-tion from the perfection of simple geometrical forms. There is the fable of Giotto's circle. I do not base an argument on these records. I adduce them simply to persuade you that it is possible to distinguish between a simple form and a "formless form." The latter term is your own. I do not profess to understand it.

Now it is manifestly ridiculous to say that you cannot take pleasure in a form *merely because* it is not the form of a man, an animal or a bunch of asparagus.

Many forms, such as those of the stone zoological garden on the Albert Memorial, are incapable of delighting us by the mere fact that they portray easily recognizable flora and fauna.

The perspective of arches as one looks toward the Koran *niche* in the Mosque of Cordova gives one infinitely more pleasure than the idiotic representative slush which "ornaments" St. Paul's Cathedral. The so-called ornaments obviously *represent* certain "saints" (behold your "mutually agreed upon symbol." The damn things are "saints," models of virtue, sacred effigies of deceased Orientals). The *form* of this statuary suggests nothing so much as plates of decomposed ice cream on a warm day, or soiled clothes dumped out of a hamper.

The arches in Cordova have, however, no form save the form of very beautiful arches. They do not *represent* anything else. The combination or composition is interesting. It required more skill to arrange this series of arches than to make one beautiful arch. If I claim an architectural pleasure in seeing this series of arches no one will call me fanatic or even fantastic. Yet this pleasure is a pleasure in form, in unadulterated form.

Ultimately all sculpture is judged by its form. As music is judged by its sound.

If sculpture were judged by the closeness with which it copies pre-existing material objects, the plaster cast or mould of the object would be the apex of the achievement.

You do not demand that the musician copy natural sounds. You permit him to start with a simple melodic form and develop his fugue, his harmony, or whatever he chooses.

In the case of Gaudier's "Dancer," you find your "themes given you" with the utmost clarity and distinctness. You have the circle on the breast and the triangle on the face. These two forms become animate, move, interplay, an increasing suggestion of power and movement in their various positions, distortions, culminating in the great sweep of the shoulders, the back of the statue, the arm thrown over the head.

It seems to me foolish to talk of this as the "powerfully crude suggestions of the beginning of sculpture." If, however, it did not suggest even to you the adverb "powerfully," I would think it failed through being over-intellectual, over-civilized in its concept, lacking in the emotional energy of great art.

There is in this work nothing of the "Rodin impression of emergence" theory.

C.

When you write, "Without interposition of symbol, without ornament," you are right. When you add "without proportion or form," you are in error.

220

Brzeska's statues have form. No material object can escape it. My contention is that they have very interesting and expressive forms. It is not necessary that one should associate their form or forms with the forms of anything else. It is for the spectator to decide whether the forms of this sculpture are in *themselves* delightful. There is no need of referring the form of the statue to the form of something extraneous.

As to proportion: "The Boy with a Coney" has "scale." Perhaps I had better define that last term. Scale is a very skillful sort of proportion. We say that a statue or a painting has "scale" when its proportions are so finely arranged that it might be reproduced in various sizes without the destruction of its beauty. This process is not infinite. It is not necessary that every work of art should possess it.

Still, when a novelist says by way of praise that a six-line poem has the "form of a novel" or that it "is like a good novel" or "contains" a novel, he is making an interesting criticism of the poet's sense of proportion and balance and "form" (if one be permitted to use the word as it were metaphorically).

When a statue one foot high could be reproduced at forty times that size and still remain finely proportioned, this possibility is an interesting commentary on the sculptor's sense of "proportion."

D.

So let us leave Hamlet's clouds which were so "like" something or other. The musician Erik Satie once wrote a prelude which he called "Prelude in the Shape of a Pear." It served as a designation.

E.

As for understanding and "mutually agreed upon symbols" and the general "intelligibility," I open a weekly abomination and find a reproduction of a piece of sculpture labeled, "Figure Representing Aspiration." It displays a plump, lolling female and an infant deficient in the spankable parts. One can go down to the "Tate" in peace time and see messy pictures by the late Mr. Watts called "Hope," "Love," etc. These works do not please me. I never see why "Hope" mightn't just as well be something else. And as for the figure "representing" Aspiration. Does it represent "Aspiration?" I never saw aspiration looking like that. But I have seen spaghetti piled on a plate and the *form* was decidedly similar. A great deal of "representational" sculpture is, *in form,* not unlike plates of spaghetti.

In conclusion, I would advise the patient to look carefully at the illustrations to the Gaudier-Brzeska. I would then advise him to get the local art gallery to provide him with Wyndham Lewis' "Timon" portfolio. I would then ask him to go forth again into the world and see what he can see where before he saw little or nothing.

The great mass of mankind are ignorant of the shape of nearly every-thing that they see or handle.

The artisan knows the shape of some of his tools. You know the shape of your pen-handle, but hardly the shape of your typewriter. The store of forms in the average man's head is smaller than this meager verbal vocabulary.

Yours,

EZRA POUND

THE SYMPOSIUM[30]
Adrian Stokes, The Quattro Cento *(Faber & Faber. 1932) 21s.*

Quakers in the north of England use the word "concern" in a peculiar, probably correct and certainly forceful sense, meaning not inactive worry but a state of mind intending, or feeling constrained to, action. A very real undercurrent of such "concern" carries Mr. Stokes through two hundred and more pages of purple language and finally justifies his writing.

Pater had an equally floribund vocabulary, but the renaissance served him as an excuse. Mr. Pater meant to write essays. He liked the renais-sance, he, you might almost say, salivated at the thought of the renais-sance. It more than gave him a subject, and once started he did not greatly care whether he overdid it.

Mr. Stokes is not merely looking for a subject. He has a *concern* for fifteenth-century stone cutting and for the shape of Italian buildings.

You can justify Pater by saying that he wasn't trying to tell facts about the renaissance but was trying to find and to make intelligible the sources of its enthusiasm. Pico della Mirandola, often very stupid, has, to that end, to be exhibited in a favourable light, mainly by his one most exalted paragraph.

Stokes has not only picked the best period, defined it, limited his definitions, but he has for a number of years ransacked Italy not as archaeologist, but as looker. He has carried his eyes about and made them work. He has very definitely scrutinized the shapes. One might suppose that this is what all art critics would naturally do. The value of a piece of sculpture depends on its shape. The architectural value of a building depends on its shape, that of architectural ornaments on their shape and their disposition. All of which is vastly too simple for people to under-stand.

If you concede that the finest criticism is that which expresses the most profound and complete understanding of a subject, the finest criticism of

[30]A review of *The Quattro Cento* by Adrian Stokes. *Symposium*, Concord, N.H., October 1932, pp. 518–21.

the Quattro Cento is contained (so far as I know) and is almost wholly contained in a small bas relief by Gaudier-Brzeska. So far removed is that complete knowledge which enables a man to act, from that partial knowledge which enables him to talk, even in an interesting manner, about any matter.

It is almost incomprehensible that any man can have as great a concern for the shapes and meanings of stone beauty as Stokes has, without its forcing him to take the tools in his hands. In fact one can only suppose that he in some way regards himself as the forerunner of some sort of sculptural amelioration, or at any rate is trying to clear up incomprehensions and to establish the relations between pure and mixed sculptural values.

There is no doubt that the Quattro Cento values emerge from a compost of literature and carving. The incontestable interest of Stokes' work lies in his not having started from a theory (even from a correct one). His concern has led him to objective facts and he has compared them, correlated them, setting shape against shape and gradually arriving at much better "taste" than he had a few years ago.

To a vorticist and to several kinds of cubist that means simply that what Mr. Stokes now likes is more nearly justifiable on grounds of form alone than it was a few years ago.

BUT (majuscule) the Quattro Cento did not act from pure formal desire. Nobody can understand the Quattro Cento, feel with the Quattro Cento, on a stripped-bare cubist basis. Valid dogmatic criticism can perhaps do little more than create enough open space around the best work to permit our seeing it clearly.

Possibly the dogmatic element in Stokes' book comes from his ambience. He has loved this mixed product of literature and stone and has felt constrained to justify it against the incult, the squalid, the half-baked flux which in our day obscures the work of the few really first-rate makers.

We shall never, for writing, painting or stone cutting, get a better demand than Dante's for results "quae totam artem comprehendunt." There is no doubt that the ruck of pavement artists, post cubists, post impressionists, post pointillistes, etc., etc., post academicians, etc., leave out a great deal too much, and that they do this without the faintest intention of concentrating on some great or principal element that is being, or has been, mislaid by almost everyone else. Stokes' book is a book against squalor, a book against paucity. It is a book for the "whole life," it is very much a book for "stone alive." He has invented the term "stone bloom" from inner necessity and from the manifest quality in his subject (as for example the well curb, Verona marble, Plate VII). He has carried as much of his fact by collotype illustration as any publisher would permit. He has not (like the typical and foul bloomsburger critics) tried to slip something over on the reader by talking of things that would not wholly support his statement. The truth in regard to Quattro Cento sculpture is florid. Even the term "sculpture" is almost a distortion. Stokes is, and the period was, concerned with ornate building. There has been very little tolerable ornament since 1500. The Greek workmen whom a Roman emperor got to make a temple in Nimes, cut stone as stone should be cut. The Quattro Cento had an analogous though different passion, it found a material to which certain finnikin faults were uncongenial, and in which several were almost impossible to commit. When Stokes gets down to this perception he is very nearly down to pure sculptural values. Verona marble could not have been used in pure geometric demonstrations. When there is nothing but geometry left, sculpture is absent. I am not trying to be funny in setting down these so obvious truisms. I have lived through an age of muddle when very few people understood anything about sculpture. Sculpture is shape *and* stone, Stokes in getting down to stone has got down to a fundamental, whereas he might perfectly well have been simply "boggit" in fifteenth century allegory. His book is the tale of his own endeavour to find out what the makers and orderers of this Quattro Cento cut stone felt and thought. It is rightly labeled "Quattro Cento" (orthography explained by the author) and not "Study of the geometrical value of stone cutting during part of the fifteenth century."

I am, of set purpose, defending the book against a few people who have considerable intelligence but who are afflicted by fixed ideas. The secondary public, the hysterical ladies, the hysterical aesthetic, in the old sense, gentlemen are doubtless lapping it up and rolling around in its succulence.

Eliot is right in asserting (privately to me) that the book contains nonsense as well as sense. Wyndham Lewis years ago described the succession of fashions in art with an analogy to a clock whose hands revolved ever faster and faster. No man need cut out his own tongue or dispense with his own nostrils. Idiots like Prothero couldn't see Lewis and Gaudier in 1913. A few people who "saw" cubism but refused to excerpt their own eyes have been justified by the arrival of Salvador Dali. The permanent bases of art do not dry up and vanish. It is better to comprehend one fine work than to swallow a catalogue. Stokes has inserted collotypes of the best and the second best and the bad. There is infinite wisdom in Plate VII. I don't honestly know whether the "reader" can learn more from Stokes' printed text than he can from that illustration. And you might, on the other hand, maintain that sculptural rot came in with Donatello.

The grace and wisdom of an age has gone into the well curb at Terracina. The Quattro Cento abounded in partial works, time and again a bas relief contains one or two figures illuminated by the artist's contact with the deeps, and beside these figures are others that are nothing but a recollection or botch of some Greco-Roman *porcheria*. The highest highbrow will do no better than the old *custode* in Santa Maria dei Miracoli saying, "There it is. For four centuries they have been trying and they cannot get anything as good as these mermaids."

Some day we may have the true story of the legendary meeting between the young Stokes and Berenson in the temple at Rimini, the young man telling his elder "where to git off at," much, I should imagine, to the delight of the latter.

One man knows wine so that he can write down names of the vintages, Mr. Stokes knows his epoch as if he had drunk a great deal of Burgundy.

THE WAR AND DIVERSE IMPRESSIONS[31]
Mr. Nevinson Thinks That the Public Is More Interested in the War Than It Is in Art

Mr. C. R. W. Nevinson has seen the war. He has seen it, he tells us, "anywhere and everywhere between the coast and Ypres, along the French, British, and Belgian lines," as private in the R.A.M.C., as ambulance driver, as hospital orderly.

Philip Gibbs is telling us of the war day by day, very eloquently and quite vividly. The "Battle of the Somme" film told us much. Mr. Nevinson, being neither writer nor cinema expert, but a painter, has set out to tell us of the war as he saw it.

His exhibition at the Leicester Galleries should attract a wide public. Connoisseurs will speak with reserve, but then connoisseurs always do speak with reserve, and no one likes connoisseurs. Mr. Nevinson's show is really full of all sorts of interest.

Mr. Nevinson is the son of a distinguished war correspondent. Training must count for something, and Mr. Nevinson is full of exuberance. He is going to tell us about the war—"a fig for aesthetics and theories." At least, I construe his "Note by the Artist" to mean: "A fig for your theories, a fig for your friend Marinetti; I am going to paint about war." War is the thing.

War Versus Art

Or as the expositor told me. The expositor? Yes, all really modern picture-shows have an expositor to tell you what the artist is driving at, because a really modern artist always is driving at something; and if you are over forty you're quite sure to know what it isn't.

The expositor does not always expose what the artist would wish. I cannot guarantee the reader that the expositor in this case spoke from the heart and mind of the artist. I can only record his utterance. He said, "Mr.

[31]*Vogue*, London, October 1916, pp. 74–75.

Nevinson thinks that the public is more interested in the war than it is in art."

This impression must be common to all of us. I, for instance, think the public is more interested in the war than in art.

Those who hate the art of the younger generation may complain, and those who care very intensely for *some* phase or phases of the most modern art will certainly complain, that Mr. Nevinson has been in such haste to paint about the war that he has not stopped to choose his idiom. That is to say, he has painted about the war in a half-dozen different styles, dating from any period during the last twenty years. We have impressionism pure and simple, and we have the well-known brand of futuristic kaleidoscope, and we have Mr. Nevinson in his rough lump-sugar surface, and Mr. Nevinson smooth, and the bewildered but fundamentally conscientious critic may search in vain for a unity or for any reason for all these changes.

IMPRESSIONISM RATHER "SQUARED UP"

Mr. Nevinson says, in his "Note," that the results represent "abstract, dynamic, mental" impressions. And we must conclude that some of the subjects struck or impressed the smooth, and some the lump-sugar, and some the futuristico-kaleidoscopic facets of his volatile mind.

But the result is interesting. You have here a hospital ward to compete with the best horrors in the Wiertz Gallery; you have a pretty fragment of face in the peaceful Piccadilly of the "Return to London." You have a really fine energy and brute force in the mass and angle of the heavy machine-gun.

You have a very good picture in "Bravo"; it is impressionism "rather squared-up."

It is manifestly an exhibition for the wide public, and not for the connoisseur in new movements. There are troops on the march, rather than new discoveries in form and form-composition. There are "Sprucers" lolling on their bales in the bright sunlight, there are disconsolate refugees, and men resting massed up with cubistic tin pans. No one has yet achieved a calm and unified conception of the war. Is it any surprise that Mr. Nevinson, painting just after the heat of the thing, should not yet have hit on a simple single and masterly style which would render all his impressions?

IMPRESSIONS "DYNAMIC, ABSTRACT" AND OTHERWISE

The show has the confusion of war—of war striking on an impressionable painter, on a temperament which feels a hurrying necessity to record what

226

it feels on the instant, or at the first opportunity. Troops diminishing into the distance, wounds, searchlights, aeroplanes passing through cloud, a flooded trench on the Yser. All of them real and insistent, bounding off the mind of the artist.

A motor-ambulance driver, "1914," and so on and so on. They tell me, "Oh, he sees the mechanical side of war!" I should not have thought so. I should have said he sees the war as human and horrible and very much sprawled over everything. And, on the whole, he sees it much better than that other painter who "did" the war, or at least one corner of it, as if it were a sort of stained-glass window occupied by a group of young men with Italian-primitive faces. If Mr. Nevinson went to, or returned from, the French lines with no particular artistic convictions, at least he took with him no prejudices as to what he would see there. He has seen timbers being loaded at Southampton in the manner, more or less, of a Wadsworth wood-cut before it is simplified. He has seen some things *pointilliste,* some romantic, and some horrible. And he has used whatever style of relatively modern painting has seemed to him fitting to convey his impression—his "dynamic, abstract" (not very abstract after all), a mental, as opposed to concrete, static, or "optical" impression.

COMPARATIVE EXPRESSION

By sheer accident there was in the corner of the Leicester Gallery room a little nude figure cut in the real stone of the trenches. It bore the legend, "Cabaret Rouge, Souchez," and an added label stating that W. Reid Dick had made it during a heavy bombardment. It is exquisite; it shows a fine sense of form. It has no convention more new than Tanagra. It is the work of a man under fire, of one who is not an impressionist.

I am not going to draw any moral. Two kinds of temperament are impelled to artistic expression. One of these kinds is impressionist. One creates out of itself from the fruit of many impressions, of meditation, of analysis.

It is curious that the statuette should have been there. It hurls so many questions at Mr. Nevinson's show. Or rather it does not hurl any. Mr. Dick was expressing himself; Mr. Nevinson was conveying impressions.

And yet how unstable words are! Mr. Nevinson is also expressing his personality. First, in the choice of his school; for of the various brands of really active new art—post-impressionism, cubism (assorted brands of cubism to the number of seven indistinguishable outside of Paris), expressionism, vorticism, Matisseism or rhythmism, futurism—Mr. Nevinson chose the latter; and futurism, alone of them all, insists on the present, on the "impression." The rest, rightly or wrongly, are all searching for some stable verity, or at least for some "principle," for something which makes art "good," "bad," or "indifferent." Mr. Nevinson might call this search "academic," or he might dismiss it as "obsolete symbolism." He is at present concerned with his subject. He has even "chucked" futurism, or at least there is no mention of the futurist sect in his "Note by the Artist." All this expresses his temperament. But the main expression is in the pictures—the vivid, roughly painted, various, confused, confusion-transmitting pictures. There are also dry-points, rather like other men's dry-points, and more pleasing than most of the pictures. I say "more pleasing" advisedly, for they are just that—"more pleasing"; BUT not more garish, more lurid, more war-like. And I must presume, as Mr. Nevinson makes the small drawings first, or the small designs and pastels first, and then the larger pictures, that it is his intention to represent the war as he sees it, and not to paint pleasing pictures.

THE CRITIC HAS TWO COURSES OPEN TO HIM

He has given up painting enlargements of wounds, possibly because the photographs in Crile's "Mechanistic View of War and Peace" have shown wounds more thoroughly.

The critic of the exhibition who would constitute himself an appraiser has two courses open to him. He may compare Mr. Nevinson with other modern and ultra-modern painters—Balla, Severini, Lewis, Picasso—or he may compare him with past painters of war like Vereshchagin.

But the result is of interest only to a few buyers of pictures. The public should see, in the painting, Mr. Nevinson's record of the war, the war set down as he saw it, a personal record. And the pictures are certainly worth more than his note; for they are particular statements—statements of concrete facts, such as the pain of wounds, the movement of men, the brutality of the guns, the mechanical activity of men and machines loading timber. The note is full of vague generalities.

4

Selections from the
John Quinn Correspondence

UNPUBLISHED LETTERS TO JOHN QUINN[1]
The John Quinn Memorial Collection, New York Public Library

London, 18 April 1915

Dear John Quinn: You will think I have been an age getting your photos. of Brzeska's stuff but he is, as you know, in the trenches, and Mrs. Finch, in whose studio he left most of his stuff, has gone to Norway.

Hence I enclose under sep. cover photos of the *Dancer*, and the *Stags* (*Blast* reprod.). I think he asked £30 for the *Dancer*, and £60 (probably would take £50 for the *Stags*).

I have had the *Dancer* here for a month and have grown to like it, especially the heroic feel of the back view, arms slung over shoulder. The front is grotesque, the face a triangle, and the two nipples a circle and ellipse. If you want an extreme work it is a good sample. And you can get a bas relief of a cat, or something else that will illustrate his other faculty, that of feeling animal life. The *Dancer* is a fine mass (red stone, dark).

The *Stags* are in veined alabaster.

You will notice that I send also a portfolio of Lewis' *Timon*, for you to get used to. I send also my article on him, which you may think

---

[1]Deletion symbols follow those established by D. D. Paige in *The Selected Letters of Ezra Pound*, London, 1951, New York, 1971, i.e., - - - - indicates that one to twenty-five words or so have been dropped; –/–/indicates that more than fifty words have been dropped. Only material irrelevant to art or more clearly presented elsewhere in the text has been omitted.

229

extreme. I have thought so myself, but still when I came back to the things after having been away two months in the country I was ready to take oath on it over again. I admit it took me six months before I *got* them first. But if any man is to bring into Western art the power of Chinese painting it will be Lewis. And there is nevertheless an almost solid opposition to him, buyers and editors, even those who admit some or nearly all of the other moderns . . . an opposition due in part to the fact that he suffers fools badly . . . in conversation.

I enclose also a copy of an Etchells' drawing. Etchells has been driven back from the Balearic Islands by the war. Lewis has lent him his kitchen to live in and asked me the other day if anybody would give £4 for the original of Etchells' drawing, the rest of E's possessions being apparently in the Balearics, and E. supposedly destitute.

I will send more Brzeska photos as soon as I can break into Mrs. Finch's studio. Sorry I can't get a reverse of the *Stags*. Also that I can't be absolutely sure of prices. He wrote me from the trenches that he had forgotten what price he had set on various things, but he won't be unreasonable.

The *Dancer* is 17 inches high, base 9 inches diameter. *Stags* must be about same height, no, a bit lower, and base about 14 by 12, as I remember.

As to Lewis, I think his prices will soar like Matisse's when once they start. Anyhow your collection is not complete until you have a few of his best things.

London, 11 August 1915

Dear John Quinn: It's a man's letter, and I thank you for it.

I have spent the entire day rushing from Fulham to the French Embassy etc. etc. etc. with the net result that I find it harder than I ever thought to spend money.

Gaudier, intestate, his position with regard to the French army irregular, his "sister" illegitimate *at least*, his mother in the wilds of the French provinces, the Embassy working with reduced staff.

However, I shall get you some sculpture if I have to use half your advance on side arms and a maxim gun. The *Dancer* is in my care so that piece you can be certain of. The *Stags* and heaven knows what else are still locked in the studio of that woman who is in Norway. I suppose she will return. They say "September." The *Cat* is held by Fry's "pincushion and curtain factory," they asked £20 this morning. I suppose that means £15.

I must see what things there are altogether before I decide what's the most worth buying. Fry has four things and a cast on sale.

There is an *Imp* now at our show at the Doré which may be better value than the *Cat*. Until I see all the work, and until the Embassy appoints some proper person to receive the payments I don't know that I can conclude any purchases.

I don't think there can be much question about your getting the stuff as the deal had been, as it were, opened during his lifetime and he had written to Mrs. Finch; to me about Mrs. Finch; and to me asking if you had decided.

I heard this afternoon that *a* Mrs. F. was a scoundrel, but I do not think it the same woman, however the whole day has been exciting and entertaining.

B.

Etchells has been in bed for two months and was thankful for the £5.

Lewis is away for a week (it is London and August, you know). I will get a drawing from him, and that and the Etchells *Head* can start West at once.

I will send the twenty new *Blasts* tomorrow, and the twenty first *Blasts* as soon as Lewis returns.

C.

Your offer *re* the exhibit in N.Y. is very sporting. Of course I can't answer that until I get at the stuff and I think the stuff should be exhibited here and then sent over.

Of course you can have the vorticist show, now at the Doré, at once if you like, but I think it would be better to wait until you can have the full Gaudier show.

Your letter is just the least bit ambiguous. You make a flat offer for "a" show, but does that refer to a Gaudier memorial show, or a memorial show plus the painters.

I take it that the sculpture would be the part that would cost most to ship. At first reading I thought you meant the full vorticist (Gaudier, Lewis, Wadsworth, Etchells, Roberts) show, and I dare say you do, but the "legal phrasing" don't precisely warrant that assumption on my part.

D.

Now about such of Gaudier's things as I know to be on sale.

At Fry's this a.m. there was no one who could give me the prices. (You understand that Fry, or the official receiver for the other stuff, may jump the price up now that Gaudier is dead.)

Anyhow at the Omega shop there are

1. *Cat* . . . supposed price . . . £20
   (bas, or rather, high relief)
2. A torso of a flat-chested woman, naturalism, very beautiful from certain points of the compass, even to admirers of "THE GREEK," in fact VERY like the Venus de Milo from certain angles. He did two or perhaps three of these torsoes all at a stretch as a sort of experiment.

He later condemned the one my mother-in-law has, as being "insincere."

Still, it, the flat one, is a charming "object" about nine inches high, not counting pedestal. It is better than the plump one my *belle mère* has.

3. A figure in alabaster with arms locked over the head, right arm up so that the elbow forms a very sharp right angle. Done I should think some time ago. The alabaster is very transparent, or translucent. The thing is very much his own without being very "modern" or without being cubist or vorticist at all. The stone[2] itself is so fine.
4. A figure, sort of bullock-god-human, in exquisite soft marble (possibly a very opaque white alabaster but I think soft white marble, rather ugly. This is newer, he had no more of the first marble to go on with.
5. A plaster cast, modern, not interesting, at least not particularly interesting.

I suppose they'll swot on the price for 2, 3, and 4. They are all things one could take pleasure in. They are nearly all, I dare say, *all*, things that an admirer of Rodin *at his best* might admire. ??? The torso is interesting because it shows how original Gaudier could be even within such narrow limits when doing an, at first sight, conventional piece of work. I think one needs a variety of his stuff to realize the scope of his powers, his promise. There is not one of the four things that I wouldn't buy like a shot if I could afford it. But . . . but . . . but . . . (and of course I hate the thought of Fry making profits, but it don't really worry me.)

The *Imp* now at our show is almost the last thing he did, and no one but a vorticist (or my mother-in-law for god knows what reason) or a lover of the grotesque could abide it. I think it was left in Wadsworth's or Hulme's care. Proceeds would go to artist's heirs, whoever in hell they may be. I really don't care who gets the cash now. It would be fine thing to have a decently representative collection of Gaudier kept together.

But then a well illustrated memoir will keep alive some memory of his versatility.

The torsoes are useful, controversially, because they DO put the blocks to the fools who say he did "vorticism" because he couldn't do anything else.

In plaster that he broke up he used to tie knots in Rodin's tail.

For the rest of the things mentioned in the vorticist show catalogue, I think the *Singer* is too placid to please you much. Fox Pitt once made an offer for it, and but for the stupidity of the Goupil Gallery it would have been sold.

[2]Probably "stone." The handwriting is difficult to decipher here.

Caritas is not particularly beautiful save from one angle. It is interesting, savage, unwieldy, it is in dull stone. So is the *Singer*. They were both intended for garden ornaments, I believe. In fact I know they were.

To give you an idea of my "idiom," let me take the current number of *Blast*.

The things I personally would buy if I had the cash are. Saunders' *Island of Laputa*. (Tendency to placidity in upper right ¼ of picture counteracted by great energy in her waves convention. This is Miss S. with Lewis, so to speak, "sitting on her head.") Still it is her picture.

The only other thing in the magazine I should want to own is Lewis' *Kermess* (p. 75), now, I think, two years old.

(I of course leave out of consideration the head of me by Gaudier which can't be judged by a reproduction.)

I simply insert this example of my vocabulary so that you can tell what I mean when I say "I would buy" or "I think interesting." I *want* the five little statues infinitely more than I could want the drawings mentioned. I think any one of them would *make*[3] a room.

It may interest you to know that I took Miscio Itow[4] to see the big bust of me in F.M.H.'s[5] garden where I keep it, and he was very much impressed, stayed and stayed and said, "He is better than Epstein?" Itow is the most intelligent jap I have ever met. The most intense. Also I think he is friend of Jacob, so it makes the statement all the more interesting. It was most unexpected. "Strong, strong" he kept saying. Blast the bloody printer anyhow. The half-tone has spoiled the bust, but I think I sent you a kodak shot of it.

In brief the things of Gaudier's that I have found lying about apart from *Stags* (supposed to be at Mrs. F's), and the *Dancer* are (it is damn difficult to put them in the order of importance, in fact one simply has to stab. Anyhow here goes):

Imp   ???? £15 or £12
Cat (relief)   £20
Water Carrier (figure with pot or cup on its head, white stone—
     this is possibly the most interesting of the lot. It *is* so hard to
     tell.)   Probably more than £20
Torso   ////////////////////////////
Alabaster figure   ////////////////////////////

[3]Probably "make." Illegible.
[4]Japanese dancer who interested Pound and Yeats.
[5]Ford Madox Hueffer.

On these last four things I of course don't yet know what Fry will drop to.

Nor do I know how I shall be able to treat with whoever is appointed to represent the family. The French ambassador would take ten bob for the lot, and the first secretary of the legation is a man of intelligence and wouldn't.

I have never had the spending of any one else's money before and I don't want to make a botch of it.

There is nothing in the above lot that I wouldn't like to have here in this room. However, they are all gentler, and with the exception of the *Imp* all "prettier" than the *Dancer*. They are all small objects. The *Imp* probably would not go into an overcoat pocket, the rest would, making a weight and a bulge.

No, the *Cat* wouldn't, and the alabaster just would. The *Water Carrier* might annoy one very much because of the difficulty of considering pure form when part of the form is put on in a different piece of marble. It is very intriguing.

AND

There is still that enigma of Mrs. F's studio. Of course the Fryshop prices are just about double, not quite double, what Gaudier would have asked, but now we are thinking of saving stuff from scattered oblivion, not about feeding the artist. It's his *gloire* not his stomach.

Another point. You must not corner the market against yourself. Against which is the fact that the executor, when he is appointed, will want cash and not works of art. -/-/

London, 23 August 1915

Dear John Quinn: -/-/I have spent a most interesting morning going over all the stuff Lewis has accumulated since Augustus John used to admire him, and when he bought his *Sailors*. Lewis would have had a big one man show here had it not been for the war. And I am not sure it would not, or rather I am pretty well sure, that the proper approach to a vorticist show *is* via a Lewis show, with some of the earlier work (say ten things) thrown in. At any rate the result of this morning's research in his studio I found 30 drawings, of great variety, so that there would be no effect of monotony or repetition if they were shown in one room. All, I should say, quite as interesting as the one I am sending you and all different. 12 or 15 different phases of Lewis. A portfolio of stuff that I shouldn't hang in a show but that the curator could have to show to people worth while or interested. 13 more drawings, smaller. 12 sketches of sailors, sort of preliminaries to the big picture which John now has.

THESE DRAWINGS COULD BE SHIPPED OVER TO N.Y. UN-FRAMED for almost nothing, if that were convenient. It would be almost like sending them over for you to choose from. The 30 drawings run from about the size of the one I am sending to about four times that size (i.e. double each way), a few are smaller. I suppose there'd be 40 drawings by the time he has remembered where they are. (This is of course his and my *selection* not an exhaustion.)

Then there are big pictures which would be more expensive to send, but there ought to be at least five and possibly ten if it is to be a real Lewis show. We thought this morning of *The Crowd* (on loan), *Kermesse, Plan of War, Christopher Columbus* and other undecided. (This *Kermesse* is not the same as the drawing in the second *Blast*.)

Mind you, the drawings alone would make a fine room and to my mind a most fascinating exhibit, but I think Lewis would be rather reluctant to send them without *some* paintings (under the term drawings he includes stuff with colour, oh I suppose water colour, and chalk, and various mediums). The "printings" are oil (one or two tempera but not in the list I have given).

I swing onto this proposition, rather than hammering on "vorticist show," because of the indefinite and aggravating and uncertain nature of the delay about the Brzeska stuff.

And so far as I am concerned "VORTICISM," and the reason why I embroiled myself with a tribe of former friends etc. etc. etc. ad infinitum has been solely Brzeska and Lewis.

Wadsworth does occasional good things, Etchells does desultory good things, Miss Saunders has done one, but I can't say that they *feed me* (i.e. my mind). And I can most certainly say that without Lewis there would be no vorticist school, no vorticist painting (and even, in infinitely less degree, no gay and irritant *Blast*).

At the present Doré show he has simply stood aside. He did all the work of getting it up, gave Wadsworth *the* wall, persuaded a few things out of Etchells and hung his own stuff on a screen.

Proper proportion would have been 40 things by Lewis and 30 by all the other contributors. Most of whom have simply built on one or another corner of his work, and done things "which he hadn't happened to do." I think even that a Lewis show might raise up in New York an equal number of vorticists quite as good as the rest of the crowd here. (For god's sake keep this opinion to yourself, I don't want another imagist rumpus.) -/-/

Also I think it fairer to Lewis to show his sweep than to put him in on an equality with others.

To have him balanced by Brzeska was another matter entirely.

London, 7 September 1915

Dear John Quinn: -/-/???? Do you realize how many Brzeska drawings there are? I don't know myself how many there are. Your pace is a bit

235

alarming to me for I have always had to bite twice on a sixpence before parting. I suppose 50 drawings will do ????????? (I don't know what they are going to charge per drawing.) I should rather have Lewis' drawings myself. And I should rather see you buy Lewis' drawings. The collection I spoke of in the letter I sent after your cable arrived. Roughly speaking Brzeska's drawings are all the same, i.e., there are about two drawings done over and over, simply as studies and experiments for his sculpture. (Line drawings only with a very few exceptions.) Lewis' collection is, I think, unique in its scope and variety.

I'll get the *Kermesse* drawing and the *Island of Laputa* this week. Though, again, if I may be permitted to put an oar in, you ought to have the big *Kermesse*, i.e. the big painting not this ink study. Aug. John was very enthusiastic over the picture in the days when he flocked with Lewis.

In a collection like yours, seeing that you can afford the big things, I should think you would want the monumental single works, and that you would do well to guard against loading up with too much small stuff.

(Don't mind my fussing, only I can't help seeing pictures as if in a gallery with the need of variety, with the need of distinct and different impressions . . . any more than I can think of literature save as comparative or international literature. I.e. eliminating duplications and works in one language not quite so good as works of essentially the same sort in another.)

As for the present instance, the *Kermesse* drawing, it won't reduplicate. (i.e. the drawing might be an interesting accompaniment to the big picture, if you decide to get it later.) I just throw in this thought as a general maxim. −/−/

London, 21 October 1915
Dear John Quinn: Don't wait until the magazine affairs are settled to send me definite instruction re/Brzeska drawings.

I have said that it is out of the question to get you all of his stuff, also it would be foolish for you, and would cause no end of hard feelings here. God knows there is row enough on already.

I send two proofs of the illustrations for the book.

The *Stag* drawing loses most of its force by being reduced. You can get a fair idea of the strength of the pen-strokes if you will look at the thing through a strong magnifying glass. The original sheet is about four times the size of this block.

All the good drawings are priced at £5/. As you know, I've copped eight, about the best.

There are very few of the newer drawings like the one in the lower left hand corner of the photo of Gaudier standing by his *Bird Swallowing Fish*.

Of *The Animals* in line drawing the tigers and birds are about the best. How many are you likely to want?

Of course you recognize that the line drawings aren't particularly "modern" or "vorticist" or anything except rattling good drawings. 30, 40, or even 50 ought to be enough for any single collection. But I am at your orders.

Various people will be about with little lumps of money trying to get first smell. The South Kensington is getting about a dozen but the man who came to select 'em hadn't the seein' eye. And besides I had had my first pick and Miss Brzeska was holding out her favorites for Paris.

Not that the S. Kens. wanted the latest work, or that Paris is likely to either.

These animals in thin line are amazingly skillful, as are also some of the nudes. They are not as interesting to the mind as Lewis' solid drawings though of course there are many more people who admire them at first sight.

The other animals are one to a sheet, not a whole gallery, like the *Stags*.

London, 17 November 1915

Dear John Quinn: -/-/I think I sent you cut of Gaudier standing by his *Bird Swallowing Fish*. I have had further chance of examining this work and think it very excellent. I should advise your having it cast in bronze here and shipped in bronze. Plaster is not very tough.

The bas-relief made from another design of wrestlers, not so good as the drawing reproduced, is of much less worth than the *Bird Swallowing Fish*, but I don't think a cast of it in metal would cost much. -/-/

London, 26 May 1916

Dear John Quinn: -/-/Saw old Yakob a week or so ago. He says the flenite you have is the same as the one I saw at the 21 Gallery. In which case you have, I think, about the best thing in modern sculpture. Epstein hasn't Gaudier's intelligence, but in that flenite and in the *Sun-God* he has got more intensity than Gaudier had managed to put into any one piece of work.

I haven't seen the *Sun-God* for some years but I thought it damn fine when I saw it. ----

Dear John Quinn: –/–/I am glad you don't think me a fool about the dynamics of Lewis' stuff. I don't think it is futurist. At least I hope not. Certainly we hold that the *form on the canvas* is the thing that matters. This seems to me the age-old fundamental of the art.

Dulac also called the things "literary," which term in the mouths of painters interests me, though I'm hang'd if I see what they mean. They seem to apply it to what might be called either "non-representative," "non-mimetic," "non-photographic" or in a sense "musical," but which certainly isn't "literary," and which most certainly isn't "literary painting" as that phrase has been used.

The split from the cubists is, as Lewis has written somewhere, because the cubists are always doing things "mort," "dead." Lewis is all motion and vitality, but I can't see that it is ever the simple painting of the same object in two places at once on the canvas, as some of the poorer futurists do.

On the other hand, I must grant that Balla (who might just as well call himself an expressionist) isn't very unlike. And the "Revolt" [Severini's][6] also is not very different. Perhaps it is only the Marinetti part of futurism that one need very greatly object to. Still the whole creed IS diametrically opposed. (For whatever that's worth.) –/–/

Dear John Quinn: –/–/I think I have said all along that Lewis was "the life of the party." I did even suggest a show of his drawings alone.

Though this might have led to some personal discontent among the rest of the circle, and probably wouldn't have satisfied the general (or your particular) curiosity, for perhaps it isn't general.

Etchells is desultory and intelligent. Wadsworth industrious and careful. ——The Roberts' drawing is a good one. He is still exceeding young, but habile. Lewis is the genius of the protoplasm. –/–/

The *Red Duet* is the one I want back, if you ever get tired of it and if I ever (which at the moment looks damn doubtful) am in a position to buy another painting.——

About Lewis colour, I think for quite a while he was intent almost wholly on form. Then there came an almost deliberate, perhaps wholly deliberate research into ugly colour. I don't think we have any of us mentioned colour in any of our talk or writing, or hardly at all. I think however that Lewis with his fundamental realism has been trying to show the beauty of the colour one actually sees in a modern brick, iron, sooty,

[6]Illegible. Probably the futurist "Severini."

238

railroad yarded smoked modern city. I think his revelation, or his training of the beholder or whatever we are to call it, is very largely in an investigation of drab colours which we ordinarily look away from in so far as it has to do with colour at all. All this as distinct from the pretty brightness of Picabia or 1910 Paris.

His things wear awfully well, at least I sit here with them opposite me and don't get bored with them.

Of course I don't know Davies new stuff. The one or two things I have seen reproduced seemed to me weaker than Lewis, in design, i.e. rather fluid and inexpressive, or expressive of a not very intense emotion. An emotion about the intensity of Lewis' "Joyeuse" with rather that sort of ease and grace and naturalness.

For god's sake don't think I am crabbing Davies, or even attempting to criticize on a couple of reproductions. That's simply my present state of ignorance regarding him.

Lewis seems to me *the* inventor. THE organizer of forms, at the present moment. *The* fecund mind with any amount of form-organizations fermenting in it.

Again, I don't see why he should paint pictures, his gift as I see it is so much in invention, it is so much a matter of almost speech in form, that I myself should probably keep him at drawings if I had any control over him.

He himself is very apt not to finish or not to fill in the colour of drawings. I think this is a real indication that the job is finished, that the creation is finished when he has drawn in his figure, or indicated a few tones.

Again, I haven't seen Davies things, and can therefore make no sensible comparison. There is a deal of force in the *Kermess*. I wonder has Davies the perception of humanity (literary talent?) which keeps leaking into Lewis painting, or rather drawing? (that is a matter outside questions of paint, but damn it all it does make the man's work interesting). -/-/

London, 19 July 1916

Dear John Quinn: -/-/Have been seeing a good deal of Dulac, who is much more interesting than his published works. I wish to God he would get uncoiled from his contracts and publishers and illustrations in batches of fifty and over elaborations and in general take art a little more seriously. It seems a shame to have so much technical faculty running almost wholly to waste. I don't think the idea of being a great artist has even occurred to him. He is much younger than I or anyone else had thought so perhaps there is time, in fact there IS time. IF there's the spirit. -/-/

Oh yes, about colour and colour-sense. I think *Lewis* has got a colour sense. Though a couple of years ago he seemed possessed to paint in nothing but shit colour of one sort or another. That phase is over. Also a phase of screamingly funny morbid pen and ink obscenities OF a vigour!!!!

I think he is often experimenting in "unaccepted" colour, in colour that is often, at first sight, unacceptable. Just as he is often working in "unaccepted" form. I am fairly certain that he doesn't care about using anybody else's colour OR colour-sense. On the other hand, "we" have been mostly interested in form. When I say "we" I mean Lewis and I, Gaudier and I as we have talked about art. Whether Lewis would say he was more interested in form than in colour I do not know.

I do know that he is very contemptuous of people who will look at nothing but a *certain sort* of technical ??? excellence ???? or finish.

I was a bit shocked at his first denunciation, and stayed so until I found out what he was driving at.

It is part of his general surge toward the restitution of the proper valuation of *conception*, i.e. CONCEPTION then finish.

Whereas the journalistic attitude at present is concerned solely with brush strokes and colour, NEVER with conception.

That is I dare say a clumsy way of saying it. Still you may get what I mean. *By conception* I mean *conception in form and colour*. I don't mean a desire to paint something expressive of faith, hope and charity, (this is merely inchoate babble) which IS what I should call in the bad sense "literary" painting, though it is a degradation of the word literature to apply it. ---- Wadsworth and Roberts certainly aren't literary in ANY sense. Couldn't possibly write anything.

London, 27 July 1916

Dear John Quinn: Macmillan affair very much as I should have expected. I thought you would find a snag as soon as the anonymous blackmailer in their office warned them that I was myself. So we will weep no salty tears.

I think you will find a certain amount of real opposition to me. I don't think it is all my eye. I am even less acceptable than Lewis. And there is sense in the opposition. Business sense. If all your capital is sunk in Leighton and Tadema you don't encourage Cézanne and Picasso. The minute people begin to realize a few simple facts which my work reveals they cease to swallow a lot of Victorian slosh. That cessation will be very bad for certain ancient publishing houses. I quite recognize hatred and terror. -/-/

London, 26 August 1916

Dear John Quinn: -/-/ I propose also [in addition to a book on Wyndham Lewis] to back up the Gaudier book by a monograph on Greek sculpture

240

before Phideas. H. Watt, the agent, has the profuse illustrations now in hand and is hunting an English publisher. Text would be very brief. Tracing the development of forms (vorticistically) in early Pisistratan stuff and before then. The *Moscophoros is* good. Greece had one really fine sculptor and has carefully forgotten his name. Encyclopedia Britannica on Greek sculpture is the "Aunt Sally."

By the way, Flinders Petrie has just brought out a book on Egyptian sculpture that you will want. I haven't yet read it but he must *know* or he couldn't have chosen his illustrations so well. -/-/

London, 3 September 1916
Dear John Quinn: -/-/ I should like to see China replace Greece as the body of antiquity, and Egyptian sculpture (roughly) put in the place of the Farnese bull in the academic curriculum, since curriculums must deal with the past they may as well see a good past as a fifth rate imitation. Etc. and provincialism be damn'd.

London, 9 September 1916
Dear John Quinn: -/-/Despite Picasso etc. I don't believe that you will ever regret having a good collection of Lewis' drawings. I am not wild about *Workshop* and I differ from you on one or two, or perhaps four of the drawings, but there must be at least that amount of margin for personal preference or we should all be wearing a Prussian uniform or some other badge of complete standardization. The Dismorr purchase is pure ability. I am glad Miss Saunders is to get something as she has been a very good fellow and worked hard *pour le mouvement.* I think the *Island of Laputa* much her best, despite its being all pasted over with strips of second layer of paper. -/-/

London, 13 October 1916
Dear John Quinn: ---- Don't know that there is much to report save that Coburn and I have invented the vortoscope, a simple device which frees the camera from reality and lets one take Picassos direct from nature. Coburn has got a few beautiful things already, and we'll have a show sometime or other.

I think so far as design and composition are concerned we'll be able to pretty much do what we like. Select the unit of design, cut out everything we don't want, and build the result. First apparatus clumsy, second one

241

rather lighter. Coburn don't want much talk about it until he has his first show.

One should see the results first, and then have explanations. At any rate it's a damn'd sight more interesting than photography. It would be perfectly possible to pretend that we'd discovered a new painter, only one's not in that line. ----

London, 17 December 1916

Dear John Quinn: -/-/The show of vortography comes off next month. I don't know that it is in your line, but it is a new plague for the laggards, and not wholly lacking in interest. The results are at least better than bad imitations of the few inventive painters. ----

London, 19 April 1917

Dear John Quinn: -/-/Grosvenor Gallery private view Royal Portrait Painters yesterday. London in much gayer mood than since the beginning of war. The advance has cheered everyone.

Epstein, Yakobb, exhibits a *painting*, a portrait, a *merd*itious, excrementitious, Matisse and shitsmearish portrait.

I shall be writing about Derwent Wood as the SCULPTOR, if this sort of thing continues. At any rate his meticulous head of somebody rather like Henry James did look as if it was made of stone.

To think that I should have lived to see another Boldini hung upon a wall, a pink-shaving-lather-safety-razor Boldini. And works of Augustus,[7] and Yakobb therewith hanging in consort and company. And a real if dilapidated duchess just leaving, and a full length smear of Lady D. and seated in profile Lady M. both by the rising smearer McEvoy, one yellow, and light, the other red and dark with large earrings.

The same that I tried to write of.

The Stalls

Her face was almost Italian
But her voice Covent-Garden Spanish

"Oh, my *dearh*, have you ever observed such ear-rings?"
"No, my dearh," I have never observed such ear-rings."

And a red, i.e. polish and chalk line, pseudo-Raphael-at-his-best-period-demi-Kricher-in-the-"Sketch," line portrait of the same Lady D. with a tragic, or at any rate concentrated expression of countenance.

[7]Augustus John.

Dear John Quinn: -/-/Greek art is about as fine an example of UNINTERRUPTED decadence as one could want and its decay keeps pace with the advance of popular power. -/-/

The vortographs are perhaps as interesting as Wadsworth's woodcuts, perhaps not quite as interesting.

At any rate, it will serve to upset the muckers who are already crowing about the death of vorticism.

The vortoscope will manage any arrangement of purely abstract forms. The present machine happens to be rectilinear, but I can make one that will do any sort of curve, quite easily.

It ought to save a lot of waste experiment on plane compositions, such as Lewis' *Plan of War* or the Wadsworth woodcuts. Certainly it is as good as the bad imitators, Atkinson, possibly some Picabia, and might serve to finish them off, leaving Lewis and Picasso more clearly defined. -/-/

London, 29 December 1917

Dear John Quinn: -/-/Captain Baker has just cleaned up the best of the remaining Lewis drawings. He has now about 35, they will be kept together. Probably all hung in one room near British Museum. Fine room for the display, where people can be taken privately to see them. And ultimately they go to the nation.

Baker is a chap of about 38, "old army" captain, younger son. He has been in hospital for nearly a year and it is that money (pay during that period) that has gone on the new lot of Lewis. He is not a man with money. When he went to the front, he was to leave some sort of last request to his brother to finance large colour plate edition of book on Lewis, to be done by me in case both he and Lewis were wiped out.

There are a few white men in the world. -/-/

London, 25 June 1918

Dear Quinn: ---- I, of course, thought Leicester Galleries had sent you a catalog. ---- I didn't ask prices at show, now over. I still think the *Red Stone Dancer* about the best, and my *Boy with Coney* a close second. And if I were buying anything myself it would be the *Dancer,* and a bronze of the *Bird Swallowing Fish.* This is not adequately shown in the book. Plate XXVI shows it, but doesn't give its quality (amateur photo, used because it shows Gaudier).

The big head of me also has a good deal to it, but it is a sort of monumento nationale, and not for sale until the bribe is really colossal. I

243

might give it to the Luxembourg if they ever progressed to the point of acceptance, but avarice also grows against this impulse to the grande geste. It is certainly a bloody sight finer than the monstrosity of Verlaine in Luxembourg Gdns. -/-/

London, 10 October 1918

Dear Quinn: -/-/It was certainly remiss of me not to write you about the "crack" in *Stags*. If I did not do so, I certainly took count of it in the valuation, and would have argued on it against doubling, trebling, octupling the price.

It don't show save as a line of red in the veining of the brown-red veined alabaster (cloudy soapy alabaster, same piece of stone, *Boy Coney* and *Imp*).

The thing is as Gaudier first exhibited it. I think the whole knob of one of the stag heads or tops, the whole mass of one animal to one side of the main cleft between the two heads, came off in the carving. The stone is very grainy, and given to these land slides. So far as the eye is concerned, and therefore so far as one's aesthetic pleasure is concerned, the break (I believe it to be a break. IF it were a "crack" it couldn't have been stuck back on with the red waxy cement or whatever it is), so far as aesthetic pleasure is concerned it don't matter. But so far as the thing is reckoned a valuable object, it must affect the value.

The Fawn, marble. 98. in Leicester catalogue, property of O. Raymond Drey (male wife[8] of Anne Estelle Rice) is an exquisite carving. The bronze cast don't quite get there. Your *Water Carrier* rather represents the style of the thing, that peculiar softness. I don't think the cast is one of the first things to acquire. The thing depends so much on "feel" (effect of *surface* to the eye) rather than form, and don't get into the metal.

I should plug first for *Red Stone Dancer,* or a good bronze of it. I think it would be quite as pleasing in bronze (only you wd. have no real control of the number of other bronzes made later).

Bird Swallowing Fish (presumably the sea bird) wd. I think be fine in bronze. £60 wd. be I think ample, or at any rate £60 plus cost of casting and agents' commission.

I can't sell the *Boy with Coney*. My wife owns part of it, and wd. be the "dissolution of the home" if it were taken to market. The furniture wd. go first.

I once thought of giving the *Embracers* to the S. Kensington, and then discovered that she was *really* opposed to letting it out of the house, (even though it is my own entirely).

[8]*Sic.*

244

What she would feel about the stone in either case *after* a cast had been made, I don't know. Suppose it wd. depend on the cast. I think a cast of the *Embracers* should be as good as the original, as the *Princes in the Tower* (copy of a celebrated Acad. pict.) and is spotted with trace of drill.

I think £260 for the *Stags* decidedly high. -/-/

The *Russian Ballet* is a charming *early* thing, rather in the French parlour ornament [tradition] OF THE VERY BEST taste. At first sight, might be by various Salon sculptors or men with Paris market twenty years ago.

There are marks of Gaudier's skill in it. I had not seen it before the show, nor had I seen Drey's *Fawn*. It (*Ballet*) is a good thing, but there are plenty of people who don't admire Picasso who might get it. I can't see that it would jarr the admirateurs of Ricketts and Shannon.

The *marble* of the *Fawn* lying down (Drey's) is certainly worth £100 or more I should think.

I should rather have the marble than most of the other things.

The *Ballet* must be worth the £105 they ask. But it is not dynamite for a museum of modernity.

Sepuchral Monument I just don't remember at all. I should rather have the *Dancer* than the *Stags*, I think. Though Gaudier priced the *Stags* higher.

I don't, in some ways, think £165 too much for it.

But then what the hell do I know about cash values. I think £140 quite enough.

£8 or £10 for the bronze letter weight ought to satisfy. It would really serve as a letter weight on your desk if it is the thing I think it is. Mrs. W. B. Y.[9] has the alabaster original.

Of course, from Sophie's[10] viewpoint, there is the gallery commission, which she expects you to pay.

I shd. certainly rather have the *Red Dancer* and the *Ballet* than the *Stags*.

And I should prefer my big bust to either lot. I am beginning to grow attached to it. (This is not an oar in on Sophie's sales.) ----

London, 9 October 1920

Dear John Quinn: ---- The first thing I got in England on my return was news of *New Age* reduction of format (grateful for chance to kill B. H. Dias). -/-/

[9]Mrs. William Butler Yeats.
[10]Sophie Brzeska, Gaudier's Polish woman companion, whose name he assumed.

Paris, 21 May 1921

Dear John Quinn: -/-/I congratulate you on getting Brancusi's bust. From what I have seen I think he is by far the best sculptor here. Picabia is alive, but as a thinker, regarding his painting in retrospect. Though I think he has done some good pictures at one time or another.

The honest men here seem to agree with my former impression that cubism is Picasso and that the others are tag ends. Marcoussis is patient and stupid. Pansaers has a little of the élan Matisse HAD (*had*) in 1911–12; Gleizes not the real thing. I hear Braque is good or gooish [*sic*], liked him personally during the only two minutes I have seen him. Lipschitz working in plaster. Looks like Picasso ballet continues.

I am more interested in literature and music than in painting, or rather let us say I am interested in Picasso, whom I have not yet been to see; in Brancusi (as long as he is sculpting, or cooking succulent steaks), in Picabia as a live animal; and I find Cros, Morand, and Cocteau congenial company; also Cendrars probably (if he comes back from Rome); at any rate the air is cleaner here than in London; and there are at least a handful of people who aren't in moribund state of mind. -/-/

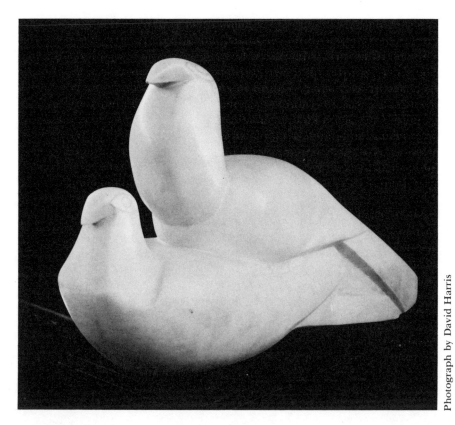

Jacob Epstein, *Doves III* (1913). Marble. The Israel Museum, Jerusalem.

Photograph by David Harris

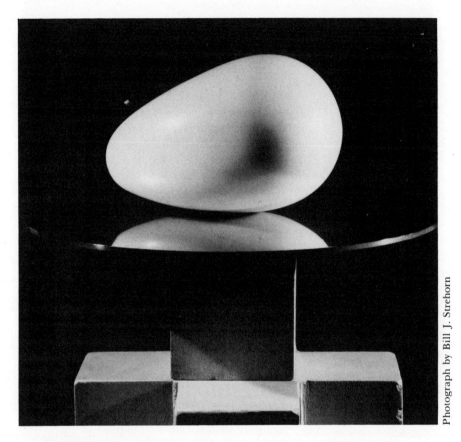

Constantin Brancusi, *Beginning of the World* (*c.* 1920). Marble, polished metal disc, stone pedestal, 11 3/8″. Dallas Museum of Fine Arts, Foundation for the Arts Collection (Gift of Mr. and Mrs. James H. Clark).

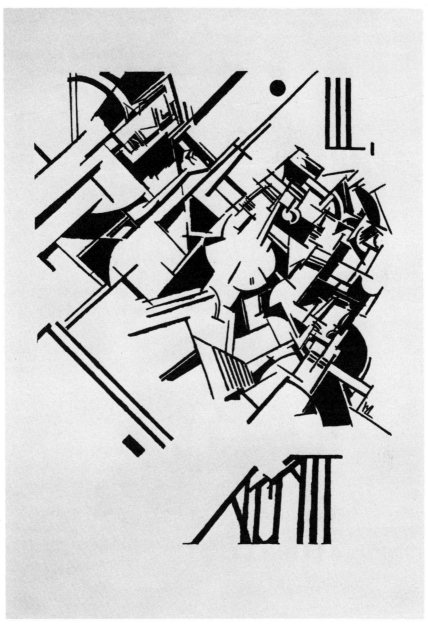

Wyndham Lewis, *Timon of Athens, Composition Act III* (1914). Victoria and Albert Museum, London (© 1980 The Estate of the late Mrs. G. A. Wyndham Lewis).

Henri Gaudier-Brzeska, *Red Stone Dancer* (1913). Mansfield stand-stone. The Tate Gallery, London.

Machine. Reproduced in *The New Review*, Winter 1931/1932. Collection of American Literature, Beinecke Rare Book and Manuscript Library, Yale University.

Edward Wadsworth, *Mytholmroyd* (*c.* 1914). Color woodcut. The
Whitworth Art Gallery, University of Manchester.

5
Selections from Published Books

EXCERPTS FROM *ABC OF READING*[1]

This is nevertheless the RIGHT WAY to study poetry, or literature, or painting. It is in fact the way the more intelligent members of the general public DO study painting. If you want to find out something about painting you go to the National Gallery, or the Salon Carré, or the Brera, or the Prado, and LOOK at the pictures.

For every reader of books on art, 1,000 people go to LOOK at the paintings. Thank heaven![2]

"La sculpture n'est pas pour les jeunes hommes," said Brancusi. Hokusai and Chaucer have borne similar witness.

Pretended treatises giving recipes for metric are as silly as would be a book giving you measurements for producing a masterpiece à la Botticelli.

Proportion, laws of proportion. Piero della Francesca having thought longer, knew more than painters who have not taken the trouble.

"La section d'or"[3] certainly helped master architects. But you learn painting by eye, not by algebra. . . . Give your draughtsman sixty-four stencils of "Botticelli's most usual curves"? And he will make you a masterpiece?[4]

---

[1]*ABC of Reading*, New York and London, 1951.
[2]Ibid., p. 23
[3]Traditions of architectural proportions. (Pound's note)
[4]*ABC of Reading*, pp. 205-6. Pound makes similar statements in his *Treatise on Harmony*, such as the following: "You may reduce the line composition of Botticelli's Nascita to the algebraic equations of analytics, without learning how to paint." (*Ezra Pound and Music*, p. 306.)

EXCERPTS FROM *EZRA POUND AND MUSIC*[5]

As I believe that a certain movement in painting is capable of revitalising the instinct of design and creating a real interest in the art of painting as opposed to a tolerance of inoffensively pretty similarities of quite pretty ladies and "The Tate," the abysmal "Tate" generally, so I believe that a return, an awakening to the possibilities, not necessarily of "Old" music, but of pattern music played upon ancient instruments, is, perhaps, able to make music again a part of life, not merely a part of theatricals.[6]

The cult of little stuffed birds (starting, as *The Athenaeum* obligingly tells us, in Mr. Sickert's studio) may be regarded with some suspicion, as may also the cult or "revival" of Ingres *and* David in France, and the Victorian Renaissance as hinted by prophetic dealers in "Pictures and Works of Art." France wants money, and has on hand a great many more examples of pseudo-classic painting than of, let us say, Clouet; and the British families whose ancestors have provided them with abundance of stuffed birds in glass cases are undoubtedly ready for a change (to machine-made art nouveau or something else than has just been in fashion). . . .[7]

Just as Picasso, and Lewis, and Brancusi have made us increasingly aware of form, of form combination, or the precise limits and demarcations of flat forms and of volumes, so Antheil is making his hearers increasingly aware of time-space, the divisions of time-space.

From Manet to Matisse, the good painters revived and resensitized our colour sense.

Rousseau, Cézanne, Picasso, Lewis, Gaudier revived and revivified our perception of form.

The XIXth century musicians ending with Debussy and Schönberg were occupied among other things with musical colour; in Debussy's case he got it mixed up with visual colour; I mean in his own mind. The arts were in a period when each art tried to lean on some other. Notably painting, sculpture and music leant heavily on bad literature.

All of which means something more than: Picasso was a magnificent draughtsman, Wyndham Lewis is a master of design, George Antheil has a good sense of rhythm. Nobody but a fool will contradict any of these statements; but the point is that Picasso, Lewis, Antheil were or are all doing something rather different in kind from Manet and Debussy; they were or are taking hold of their art by a different extremity.[8]

[5]*Ezra Pound and Music: The Complete Criticism*, ed. with commentary by R. Murray Schafer, New York and London, 1977.
[6]Ibid., p. 39. This paragraph is in somewhat different form in *Literary Essays*, p. 435.
[7]Ibid., p. 50.
[8]Ibid., p. 256.

Let me say here, in my twenty-fifth or twenty-sixth parenthesis, that there are two aesthetic ideals, one the Wagnerian, which is not dissimilar from that of the Foire de Neuilly, i.e. you confuse the spectator by smacking as many of his senses as possible at every possible moment, this prevents his noting anything with unusual lucidity, but you may fluster or excite him to the point of making him receptive; i.e. you may slip over an emotion, or you may sell him rubber doll or a new cake of glass-mender during the hurly-burly.

The other aesthetic has been approved by Brancusi, Lewis, the vorticist manifestos; it aims at focusing the mind on a given definition of form, or rhythm, so intensely that it becomes not only more aware of that given form, but more sensitive to all other forms, rhythms, defined planes, or masses.

It is a scaling of eye-balls, a castigating or purging of aural cortices; a sharpening of verbal apperceptions. It is by no means an emollient.[9]

I wd. readily admit that Vivaldi was in a sense "out of date," meaning out of fashion, out of the received ideas of the general public for a hundred and fifty years, and that he comes *into date* along with the Miro painting, as that painting was in the years immediately following Miro's arrival in Paris.[10]

There is a timeliness in all resurrections in art; whether it be in painting, literature or in music. In Miss Rudge's own rendering of the concerto [of Vivaldi] I have found a close kinship with the line of the surrealist Dali. I don't know whether this comes from the manuscript or from the executant. I have long blamed or at least teased the surrealists for their naive belief that they had invented something which had already been present in Guido Cavalcanti's poetry when Dante was 10 years old. There is plenty of surrealism in medieval poetry. The human spirit has recurring needs of expression.[11]

PREFACE TO THE MEMORIAL EXHIBITION 1918[12]

His death in action at Neuville St. Vaast is, to my mind, the gravest individual loss which the arts have sustained during the war. When I say this I am not forgetting that Rémy de Gourmont, Henry James, and, lastly, Claude Debussy must all be counted among war losses, for in each

[9]Ibid., pp. 256-57.
[10]Ibid., p. 445.
[11]Ibid., pp. 456-57.
[12]*Gaudier-Brzeska: A Memoir*, New York, 1970, pp. 136–39. The Leicester Galleries, London, May–June, 1918.

case their lives were indubitably shortened by war-strain; but they, on the other hand, had nearly fulfilled their labour, each was still vigorously productive, but we could in fair measure gauge the quality of what they were likely to do.

Gaudier was at the beginning of his work. The sculpture here shown is but a few years' chiseling. He was killed at the age of twenty-four; his work stopped a year before that. The technical proficiency in the *Stag* drawings must be obvious to the most hurried observer. The volume and scope of the work is, for so young a man, wholly amazing, no less in variety than in the speed of development.

In brief, his sculptural career may be traced as follows: It begins with "representative" portrait busts in plaster, and with work in more or less the manner of Rodin. Whatever one may think of Rodin, one must grant that he delivered us from the tradition of the *Florentine Boy*, and the back-parlour sculptural school favoured by the Luxembourg. Gaudier was quickly discontented with the vagueness and washiness of the Rodin decadence and the work of Rodin's lesser imitators. We next find him in search of a style, interested in Epstein, but much more restless and in-quisitive. In *The Singer* we have what may seem an influence from archaic Greek, we have the crossed arms motif, used, however, very dif-ferently from the crossed or x'd arms of the splendid *Moscophoros*. (The anti-Hellenist cannot refrain from a slightly malicious chuckle on observ-ing that the Greeks really had a great master (before Phidias), and that they have carefully forgotton his name. *Vide* also the consummate in-anities in the *Encyclopedia Britannica* regarding the *Moscophoros*). In the *Singer* we may observe also an elongation possibly ascribable to a temporary admiration of the Gothic.

In *The Embracers* (plate XXIV) we find a whole pot-pourri of forces: Egypt in the delicate flattening of the woman's right arm, Oceanic influ-ence in the rest of it. Note that all great artists are imitative in their early work; their power lies in the rapidity with which they assimilate, digest, get through with, weld into a style of their own, the forces and qualities of their models. Obvious as one or two acquired qualities are in *The Embracers*, it is perhaps the most complete expression of Gaudier's personality that remains to us. It is also intensely original, the stylization into the bent prismatic shape of the whole does not, I think, occur elsewhere. He has shown the "sense of stone" in the utilisation of this queer-shaped block as Michelangelo showed it in the economy of his *David* (a block, as you remember, which none of his contemporaries could handle, and which was regarded as spoiled, and useless).

Gaudier denied the Chinese influence in *Boy with a Coney*, (plate XXIII), a piece more opulent in its curves than *The Embracers*, though perhaps less striking at first sight, because of its greater placidity.

By the time he got to *The Dancer* (plates XXI, XXII), Gaudier had worked definitely free from influence. This work is his own throughout. I can but call upon the unfamiliar spectator to consider what it means to have worked free of influence, to have established a personal style at the age of twenty-two. There is no minimising such achievement.

The personality is asserted in *The Embracers*, the style is established and freed from derivativeness in *The Dancer*. This last is almost a thesis of his ideas upon the use of pure form. We have the triangle and circle asserted, *labled* almost, upon the face and right breast. Into these so-called "abstractions" life flows, the circle moves and elongates into the oval, it increases and takes volume in the sphere or hemisphere of the breast. The triangle moves toward organism, it becomes a spherical triangle (the central life-form common to both Brzeska and Lewis). These two developed motifs work as themes in a fugue. We have the whole series of spherical triangles, as in the arm over the head, all combining and culminating in the great sweep of the back of the shoulders, as fine as any surface in all sculpture. The "abstract" or mathematical bareness of the triangle and circle are fully incarnate, made flesh, full of vitality and of energy. The whole form-series ends, passes into stasis with the circular base or platform.[13]

I am not saying that every statue should be a complete thesis of principles. I simply point out the amazing fact that Gaudier should so clearly have known his own mind, that he should have been able to make so definite an assertion of his sculptural norm or main urges at the age of but two and twenty.

The quality of his stone animals, his sense of animal life seems too obvious to need note in this preface.

Because our form sense is so atrophied it is necessary to point it out, even to wrangle about it with unbelievers. Again Gaudier's technical power seems too obvious to need explanation, whether it be in cutting of brass, or in the little green charm, or in the splintery alabaster, or in the accomplished ease of the drawings.

If the "more modern pieces" puzzle the spectator there are various avenues of approach. First, by Gaudier's own manifestoes.

"Sculptural feeling is the appreciation of masses in relation.
Sculptural ability is the defining of these masses by planes."

Secondly, by a study of Egyptian, Assyrian, African and Chinese, sculpture, and a realisation that Hellenism, neo-Hellenism, neo-Renaissancism and Albert Memorialism do not contain and circumscribe all that it is possible to know on the subject. Only those shut in the blind alley which culminates in the Victorian period have failed to do justice to Gaudier. My praise of him is no longer regarded as an eccentricity.

[13]Richard Cork considers this passage "one of [Pound's] most closely argued passages of criticism." *Vorticism and Abstract Art in the First Machine Age*, I, London, 1976, p. 175.

He is irreplaceable. The great sculptor must combine two qualities (*a*) the sense of form (of masses in relation); (*b*) tremendous physical activeness. The critic may know fine forms when he sees them embodied, he may even be able to construct fine combinations of form in his imagination. This does not make him a sculptor.

The painter may be able to record or set forth fine form-combinations, to "knock off" a masterpiece in four hours.

The sculptor must add to the power of imagining form-combination the physical energy required to cut this into the unyielding medium. He must have vividness of perception, he must have this untiringness, he must, beyond that, be able to retain his main idea unwaveringly during the time (weeks or months) of the carving. This needs a peculiar equipment. Easily diverted, flittering quickness of mind is small use.

When a man has all these qualities, vividness of insight, poignancy, retentiveness, plus the energy, he has chance of making permanent sculpture. Gaudier had them, even to the superfluous abundance of forging his own chisels.

For the rest, *circumspice!* I can but record the profundity of the cry that came from the Belgian poet, Marcel Wyseur, on first seeing some work of Gaudier-Brzeska's: "Il a eu grand tort de mourir, cet homme! Il a eu grand tort de mourir."

EXCERPTS FROM *GUIDE TO KULCHUR*[14]

I suggest that finer and future critics of art will be able to tell from the quality of a painting the degree of tolerance or intolerance of usury extant in the age and milieu that produced it.[15]

Greek poetry as we know it flows into decadence. Any one with Gaudier-Brzeska's eye will see Greek art as a decadence. The economist will look at their usury. He will find the idea of it mixed up with marine insurance.[16]

STYLE, the attainment of a style consists in so knowing words that one will communicate the various parts of what one says with the various degrees and weights of importance which one wishes.

No man ever knows enough about any art. I have seen young men with most brilliant endowment who have failed to consider the length of the journey. *Anseres*, geese, as Dante has branded them, immune from learning etc.

I have heard Brancusi: la sculpture n'est pas pour les jeunes hommes.

[14]*Guide to Kulchur*, New York, 1952, and London, 1960.
[15]Ibid., p. 27.
[16]Ibid., p. 33.

Brancusi also said that Gaudier was a young chap who had an enormous amount of talent and *might* have done something had he lived.

Brancusi had seen only half-tone reproductions of Gaudier's work. No man except Brancusi had or has a right to such judgement. I mean no one else knows enough about sculpture to have said that in honesty and in modesty.

What we know about the arts we know from practitioners, usually from their work, occasionally from their comments. Our knowledge is sometimes second hand, and becomes more wafty with each remove.

We do NOT know the past in chronological sequence. It may be convenient to lay it out anesthetized on the table with dates pasted on here and there, but what we know we know by ripples and spirals eddying out from us and from our own time.

There is no ownership in most of my statements and I can not interrupt every sentence or paragraph to attribute authorships to each pair of words, especially as there is seldom an a priori claim even to the phrase or the half phrase.

You can write history by tracing ideas, exposing the growth of a concept.

You can also isolate the quality or the direction of a given time's sensibility. That means the history of an art.

For example two centuries of Provençal life devoted a good deal of energy to *motz el son*, to the union of word and music.

You can connect that fine demarcation with demarcations in architecture and re usury, or you can trace it alone, from Arnaut and his crew down to Janequin, where a different susceptibility has replaced it.

But the one thing you shd. not do is to suppose that when something is wrong with the arts, it is wrong with the arts ONLY.

When a given hormone defects, it will defect throughout the whole system.

Hence the yarn that Frobenius looked at two African pots and, observing their shapes and proportions, said: if you will go to a certain place and there digge, you will find traces of a civilization with such and such characteristics.

As was the case. In event proved.[17]

Grosseteste on Light may or may not be scientific but at least his mind gives us a structure. He throws onto our spectrum a beauty comparable to a work by Max Ernst. The mind making forms can verbally transmit them when the mental voltage is high enough. It is not absolutely necessary that the imagination be registered either by sound or on painted canvas.[18]

[17]Ibid., pp. 59-61. On pages 63-68 Pound reproduces Gaudier's Vortex principles as they appeared in *Blast,* June 1914, and as they are reprinted in *Gaudier-Brzeska,* pp. 20–24.
[18]Ibid., p. 77.

A definite philosophical act or series of acts was performed along in 1916 to '21 by, as I see it, Francis Picabia. If he had any help or stimulus it may have come from Marcel Duchamp. Picabia may have been touched up by Erik Satie. I know of no other intelligences implied in the process. There were participants in a "movement" but they were, so far as I know, not sources of movement.

Bayle and Voltaire used a sort of *reductio ad absurdum* for the destruction of hoakum. Picabia got hold of an instrument which cleared out whole racks full of rubbish. . . . That anyone shd. have tried to use Picabia's acid for building stone, shows only the ineradicable desire of second-rate minds to exploit things they have not comprehended.

After Dada there came a totally different constructive movement. Based on the inner need of a couple of painters to paint; in certain permanent facts of human mental existence and sprouting in a field utterly unconscious (as far as one cd. see) of ancestry and tradition.[19]

If I am introducing anybody to Kulchur, let 'em take the two phases, the nineteen teens, Gaudier, Wyndham L. and I as we were in *Blast,* and the next phase, the 1920's.[20]

To establish some table of values as among men I have seen and talked with.

Brancusi in some dimensions a saint.

Picabia a brilliant intellect.

Gaudier had and Cocteau has genius. . . .

By genius I mean an inevitable swiftness and rightness in a given field. The trouvaille. The direct simplicity in seizing the effective means. . . .

A volcanic and disordered mind like Wyndham Lewis's is of great value, especially in a dead, and for the most part rotted, milieu. The curse of England is fugg. A great energy like that of Lewis is beyond price in such a suffocated nation; something might come of disorder created by Lewis "As the giant plow is needed to break intractable soil." (I may err here in agricultural metaphor. Shallow ploughing is useful in proper conditions.)

"Human Greatness" is an unusual energy coupled with straightness, the direct shooting mind, it is incompatible with a man's lying to himself, it does not indulge in petty pretences. [21]

. . . .Of his age, that just before Dante's, we have concurrently a fineness in argument, we have the thought of Grosseteste, and of Albertus. We have a few fragments of enamel, and a great deal of stone work.

[19]Ibid., pp. 87–88.
[20]Ibid., p. 95.
[21]Ibid., pp. 105-6.

A PAIDEUMA carried on, out of Byzantium, or, at least as I see it, the romanesque building ·and the arab building in Sicily, was Byzantine or late Roman *structure*, the difference being merely in expensiveness. With the break down of Constantine's and Justinian's economic system, no one cd. cover church walls with gold mosiac.

Those of us who remember the beginning of the new Westminster Cathedral recall a beauty of stone and brick structure, before the shamrocks (mother of pearl) and the various gibblets of marble had been set there to distract one.

Modena, San Zeno (Verona), St Trophime (when did cloisters become an habit?) the churches in Sicily and the other Veronese structures add nothing that wasn't there in St Apollinaire (Classe, Ravenna).

Mohammed was against usury. There is the like fineness of outline in Cordova (the Mosque) in AlHambra, and AlCazar (Sevilla). Plus the honey-comb plaster.

For European architecture a development occurs in St Hilaire (Poitiers) and the Hall of Justice of Poitiers. Here the architect has invented. The cunning contrivance of lighting and the building of chimneys is, at least for the layman, something there invented, something that has no known fatherhood. In the sense that romanesque forms have a known fatherhood.

This total PAIDEUMA is anti-usura. A tolerance of gombeen men and stealers of harvest by money, by distortion and dirtiness, runs concurrent with a fattening in all art forms.

I have not deflected a hair's breadth from my lists of beautiful objects, made in my own head and held before I ever thought of usura as a murrain and a marasmus.

For 31 years I have carried in my mind as a species of rich diagram, the Prado as I saw it, and heaven knows if my readers will see it ever again. In the long gallery you turned after a time to the left. On your left hand in the great room, *Las Hiladeras*, the spinning girls, with the beamed light, and the duskiness, in the separate smaller room *Las Meniñas*, the young princesses or court ladies, the mirror with glimpse of Velasquez by the far door painting the picture.

On the wall facing the great canvas, alone, his self-portrait. In the great room Don Juan de Austria, the dwarfs, high at the end facing the door, the Virgin enthroned, differing greatly in workmanship, designed shall we say for Church lighting and not for a palace. The *Surrender of Breda* with the spears, new for the American visitor, only years later in Avignon did one see that this composition was not invented ex nihil and ex novo, but had been in fresco.

On the right wall Baldassar Carlos, Philip on foot with his hunting gun, *Philip on Horseback*, the horse's foot having been done first in a different position. Again by the door *Mercury* and *Argos*, and below it the *Drinkers*.

At first go one wondered why Jimmy Whistler had so insisted. A dozen returns and each time a new permanent acquisition, light, green shadows instead of the brown as in Rembrandt, who has steadily declined through 30 years in his power to rouse enthusiasm. I don't mean ceased, I mean that the current in our past three decades has been toward the primitives, WITH a forward current, via Velázquez and, for a surprisingly small number of people if you consider the vast pother and blather about painting that has been used to red-herring thought in our time, a surprisingly small number of people who saw the light, via Manet (as in the *Bar of the Folies Bergères*, or the fragments of the *Execution of Maximillian*). So the background of Don Juan de Austria, the fire, that is there with two strokes or perhaps ONE of the brush.

Où sont . . . ? God knows where this canvas has got to. Russia shall not have Constantinople etcetera.

Our husky young undergraduates may start their quest of Osiris in a search for what was the PRADO. . . .

In 1938 let us say, a bloke with small means wants the best of Europe. Once he cd. have done a great deal on foot. I dare say he still can. In 1911 there was an international currency (20 franc pieces) twenty such in jug-purse and no god-damned passports. (Hell rot Wilson AND the emperor, I think it was Decius.) If a man can't afford to go by automobile, and if he is content with eating and architecture, the world's best (as I have known it) is afoot from Poitiers, from Brives, from Périgord or Limoges. In every town a romanesque church or château. No place to stay for any time, but food every ten miles or fifteen or twenty. When I say food, I mean food. So, at any rate, was it. With fit track to walk on.

I do not say walk in Italy. The sane man will want his Italy by car. Even if it is public omnibus. The roads go over the Appenines, they go over the Bracca. They go over, where trains bore through. It is not a country to walk in because food is a FRENCH possession, when on foot one wants it.

In the territory of the Exarchate there is still some remains of this form of civilization. In twenty and forty and I suppose 400 small towns of France there is the ex-chef of the House of Commons, the ex-chef of the Duke of Bungle, the ex-chef of MiLord of Carogguh, and so forth. And there is food that its concocter respects.

In Italy there are perhaps two dozen restaurants, whereof no man knows more than eight. Inclusive or exclusive of a few stunt places where the boss makes one dish.

Le Voyage Gastronomique is a French paideuma. Outside it, you can get English roast beef in Italy (if you spend 25 years learning how), you can find a filetto of turkey Bolognese. You can get fish in Taormina which (after 30 years absence) may seem as good as American shad. I am writing of civilization. The Chinese have civilization. The Nihon Jin Kwai (London) had a cuisine. Brancusi cd. cook on occasion and Gurdieff made Persian soup, bright yellow in colour, far more delicate—you might say Piero della Francesca in tone, as compared with a borscht (tinted Rembrandt). If he had had more of that sort of thing in his repertoire he cd. had he suspected it, or desired it, have worked on toward at least one further conversion.

The dust on Italian roads, the geographic or geological formation of the peninsula all say go by car. Don't try to walk it. You have enough foot work when you get to the towns. You have a concentration of treasures that will need all your calf muscles, all your ankle resistance. Perugia, the gallery of the Palazzo Pubblico, Bonfigli and co. in a dozen churches. Siena, likewise the gallery, newly set. Cortona, Fra Angelico, in six or eight churches.

Ravenna, mosaics. A less known gallery, and three churches in Pisa. San Giorgio Schiavoni for Carpaccio's, Santa Maria Miracoli, Venice, and a few pictures here and there, a Giovan Bellin' in Rimini, Crivelli in Bergamo, the walls of La Schifanoja (Ferrara), Mantegna's portraits of the Gonsaga (Mantova). Botticelli in Firenze, and the Davanzati if it still be open, Firenze the most damned of Italian cities, wherein is place neither to sit, stand nor walk. The highest aristocracy have or had one very high club, with it wd. seem no windows. The conti and marchesi project from the main portone, the most senile is privileged to the concierge's wooden chair.

Truly this town cast out its greatest writer, and a curse of discomfort has descended, and lasted six hundred years. Don't miss the Bargello. Don't miss the Palazzo Pubblico in Siena.

For fish, try Taormina, for the glory that was Greece try Siracusa, though the Roman marble or white stone is as good as any Hellenic monuments.

So near to a full catalogue, I may as well finish it.

Some good Egyptian sculpture in the British Museum (none in The Louvre though there is a small bit called portrait of Chak Mool or something, with something half like a Chinese inscription). There are, the most hurried tourist has heard it, pictures in the Louvre, the National (and less touted in the National Portrait) Galleries (Paris and London), the early Italians in London, missing their natal light. If any man or young lady will first get this eye-full, this ideogram of what's what in Europe, one will not need greatly to instruct 'em as to why some very great works of art are from it omitted.

Goya, yes Goya. The best one I know is in New York.

How to see works of art? Think what the creator must perforce have felt and known before he got round to creating them. The concentration of his own private paideuma, whereof the shortcomings show, my hercules, in every line of his painting, in every note of his melody (I say melody . . . vide de Schloezer's *Stravinsky* for context). You can cover it up more or less in symphonic or "harmonic" writing, you may even be able to camouflage it a little, a very much lesser little in counterpoint by patience and application of process. But you can't damn well learn even that process without learning a great deal by the way.

A fugue a week for a year wd. teach even a bullhead something.

Loathe the secolo decimonono. What was good from 1830 to 1890 was a protest. It was diagnosis, it was acid, it was invocation of otherness. Chopin carried over precedent virtue.[22]

"Il sait vivre," said Brancusi of Léger.[23]

The Tempio Malatestiano is both an apex and in verbal sense a monumental failure. It is perhaps the apex of what one man has embodied in the last 1000 years of the occident. A cultural "high" is marked.

In a Europe not YET rotted by usury, but outside the then system, and pretty much against the power that was, and in any case without great material resources, Sigismundo cut his notch. He registered a state of mind, of sensibility, of all-roundedness and awareness.

He had a little of the best there in Rimini. He had perhaps Zuan Bellin's best bit of painting. He had all he cd. get of Piero della Francesca. Federigo Urbino was his Amy Lowell, Federigo with more wealth got the seconds. The Tempio was stopped by a fluke? or Sigismundo had the flair when to stop it? You get civilization in the seals. I mean it was carried down and out into details. The little wafer of wax between the sheets of letter paper in Modena is, culturally, level with the Medallions. The Young Salustio is there in the wax as Isotta and Sigismundo in the bronze discs of Pisanello. Intaglio existed. Painting existed. The medal has never been higher. All that a single man could, Malatesta managed *against* the current of power.[24]

. . . the Whistler show in 1910 contained more real wisdom than that of Blake's fanatic designs. Neither monopolizing the truth nor exhausting it.[25]

The worship of the supreme intelligence of the universe is neither an inhuman nor bigoted action. Art is, religiously, an emphasis, a segregation of some component of that intelligence for the sake of making it more perceptible.

[22]Ibid., pp. 108-14.
[23]Ibid., p. 145.
[24]Ibid., p. 159.
[25]Ibid., pp. 180-81.

The work of art (religiously) is a door or a lift permitting a man to enter, or hoisting him mentally into, a zone of activity, and out of fugg and inertia.

L'art religieux est mort? Gourmont's reportage was correct in respect to time and place, Paris 1890. The art of a particular sect dies. Religious art comes to life periodically. M. told me surrealism was not an art movement but a moral discipline.

I am not confirming this view or contradicting it. I register the fact that young M. cd. make such an assertion with considerable fervour.[26]

The London ground rents and entail, lease system etc. have defiled English building. A man will be very hesitant to build permanent beauty if he knows that someone else can bag it at the end of 9 or 99 years. As "B. H. Dias" I spent my odd time for several months observing the decadence of wood-carving, fanlights over London doors.[27]

When the vortices of power and the vortices of culture coincide, you have an era of brilliance. It took the *Manchester Guardian* or froustery six months to discover that *BLAST* was satirical. 24 years have not been enough to teach 'em that vorticism was constructive. In fact, it has passed as a small local movement, and I myself do not care a hoot whether the name remains pasted to it. Kung fu Tseu was a vorticist. Happy is the man who can start where he is, and *do* something.

John Cournos deserves the credit for being the first to see what Gaudier had got into his *VORTEX* (. . . *The whole history of sculpture*). If that phrase be in some senses an exaggeration it exaggerates in the right way. It prods the hearer into getting down into the meaning of a highly delectable document.

The piffling nature of the age can be measured by the time it took a few people to learn the real Gaudier, and the speed with which a faked Gaudier was (two decades later) accepted.[28]

There was in London 1908 to '14 an architect named Ricards (of Lanchester & Ricards), the last pastoral mind, and a man with true sense of form, that is in three dimensions and hollow. His buildings were magnificent until finished. Their structure was the work of genius and their final encrustation the tin-horn ornament of the never sufficiently damned 1900. AND at this same time Gaudier was out of employment and wd. willingly have made architectural odds and ends.[29]

[26]Ibid., pp. 189-90.
[27]Ibid., p. 245.
[28]Ibid., p. 266.
[29]Ibid., p. 346.

SELECTIONS FROM *IMPACT*[30]

I suppose in the long run Jimmy Whistler was not so good a painter as Manet but he had a damn good run for his money. I don't recall any British painter of his time cropping up in a poem by Mallarmé.[31]

One does not discuss painting with a man who is ignorant of Leonardo, Velásquez, Manet, or Piero della Francesca.[32]

KULTURMORPHOLOGIE

To repeat: an expert, looking at a painting (by Memmi, Goya, or any other), should be able to determine the degree of tolerance of usury in the society in which it was painted.

Art is a means of communication. It is subject to the will of the artist, yet goes beyond it.

"The character of the man is revealed in every brushstroke" (and this does not apply only to ideograms).[33]

Let us consider certain facts of literature; let us mark out the categories whenever it may be convenient or possible, but *not* before knowing the facts (i.e., the masterpieces, either of the highest intensity or superior in particular aspects). When we know them we can discuss them—but not painting without a knowledge of Mantegna or Manet, not poetry if we dare not make comparisons.[34]

THE UNEMPLOYMENT PROBLEM[35]

. . . The unemployment problem that I have been faced with, for a quarter of a century, is not or has not been the unemployment of nine million or five million, or whatever I might be supposed to contemplate as a problem for those in authority or those responsible, etc., it has been the problem of the unemployment of Gaudier-Brzeska, T. S. Eliot, Wyndham Lewis the painter, E. P. the present writer, and of twenty or thirty musicians, and fifty or more other makers in stone, in paint, in verbal composition.

If there was (and I admit that there was) a time when I thought this problem could be solved without regard to the common man, humanity

---

[30]*Impact,* ed. with an introduction by Noel Stock, Chicago, 1960.
[31]Ibid., p. 7.
[32]Ibid., p. 56.
[33]Ibid., pp. 61-62.
[34]Ibid., p. 73.
[35]Ibid., pp. 87-90.

in general, the man in the street, the average citizen, etc., I retract, I sing palinode, I apologize.

One intelligent millionaire *might* have done a good deal—several people of moderate means have done "something"; i.e., a poultice or two and bit of plaster hither or yon.

The stupidity of great and much-advertised efforts and donations and endowments is now blatant and visible to anyone who has the patience to look at the facts. The "patron" must be a live and knowledgeable patron, the entrusting of patronage to a group of bone-headed professors ignorant of art and writing, is and has been a most manifest failure. There is no reason to pity anyone. Millions of American dollars have been entrusted to incompetent persons, whose crime may not be incompetence but consists, definitely, in their failure to recognize their incompetence. . . .

This is what American capitalism has offered us, and by its works stands condemned. . . .

For the purpose of, and the duration of, this essay, I am trying to dissociate an objection or a hate based on specific effects of a system *on* a specific and limited area—i.e., I am examining the effects on art, in its social aspect; i.e., the opportunity given the artist to exist and practice his artistry *in* a given social order, as distinct from all questions of general social justice, economic justice, etc.

Autobiography if you like. Slovinsky looked at me in 1912: "Boundt, haff you gno bolidigal basshuntz?" Whatever economic passions I now have, began *ab initio* from having crimes against living art thrust under my perceptions.

It is no answer to say that "my" programme in art and letters has gradually been forced through, has, to some extent, grabbed its place in the sun. For one thing, I don't care about "minority culture." I have never cared a damn about snobbisms or for writing *ultimately* for the few. Perhaps that is an exaggeration. Perhaps I was a worse young man than I think I was.

Serious art is unpopular at its birth. But it ultimately forms the mass culture. Not perhaps at full strength? Perhaps at full strength. Yatter about art does *not* become a part of mass culture. . . .

The Arts[36]

What largely ails the "arts" is unemployment. If painters would paint on walls instead of scraps of paper their work wd. not so easily become prey of speculators, and at fifty an artist wd. not find his most bitter competitors (in the market) the people who had bought his first work.

[36]Ibid., p. 222.

To Senator H. T. Bone[37]

Rapallo, 1936 [?]

. . . In place of St. Hilaire of Poitiers, the GREAT architecture, the great ART wherein DESIGN is the main factor, has been bitched and greased into a luxury trade, where EXPENSIVENESS and the look of costliness has ruined the work of the mind and spirit.

SELECTIONS FROM *LITERARY ESSAYS*[38]

A Retrospect (Excerpt)[39]

I agree with John Yeats on the relation of beauty to certitude. I prefer satire, which is due to emotion, to any sham of emotion.

I have had to write, or at least I have written a good deal about art, sculpture, painting and poetry. I have seen what seemed to me the best of contemporary work reviled and obstructed. . . . I have been battistrada for a sculptor, a painter, a novelist, several poets. I wrote also of certain French writers in *The New Age* in nineteen twelve or eleven.

I would much rather that people would look at Brzeska's sculpture and Lewis's drawings, and that they would read Joyce, Jules Romains, Eliot, than that they should read what I have said of these men, or that I should be asked to republish argumentative essays and reviews.

All that the critic can do for the reader or audience or spectator is to focus his gaze or audition. Rightly or wrongly I think my blasts and essays have done their work, and that more people are now likely to go to the sources than are likely to read this book. . . .

It is difficult at all times to write of the fine arts, it is almost impossible unless one can accompany one's prose with many reproductions. Still I would seize this chance or any chance to reaffirm my belief in Wyndham Lewis's genius, both in his drawings and in his writings. . . .

Cavalcanti (excerpts)[40]

. . . people say that the Quattrocento, or the sculpture of the Quattrocento, discovered "personality." All of which is perhaps rather vague. We might say: The best Egyptian sculpture is magnificent plastic; but its force comes from a non-plastic idea, i.e. the god is inside the statue.

[37]Ibid., p. 274.
[38]*Literary Essays*, New York and London, 1954.
[39]Ibid., pp. 13-14.
[40]Ibid., pp. 152-53.

I am not considering the merits of the matter, much less those merits as seen by a modern aesthetic purist. I am using historic method. The god is inside the stone, *vacuos exercet aera morsus.* The force is arrested, but there is never any question about its latency, about the force being the essential, and the rest "accidental" in the philosophic technical sense. The shape occurs.

There is hardly any debate about the Greek classical sculpture, to them it is the plastic that matters. In the case of the statue of the Etruscan Apollo at Villa Giulia (Rome) the "god is inside," but the psychology is merely that of an Hallowe'en pumpkin. It is a weak derivation of fear motive, strong in Mexican masks, but here reduced to the simple briskness of small boy amused at startling his grandma. This is a long way from Greek statues, in which "the face don't matter."

This sculpture with something inside, revives in the Quattrocento portrait bust. But the antecedents are in verbal manifestation.

Nobody can absorb the *poeti dei primi secoli* and then the paintings of the Uffizi without seeing the relation between them, Daniel, Ventadour, Guido, Sellaio, Botticelli, Ambrogio Praedis, Nic. del Cossa.

All these are clean, all without hell-obsession.

Certain virtues are established, and the neglect of them by later writers and artists is an impoverishment of their art. The stupidity of Rubens, the asinine nature of French court life from Henry IV to the end of it, the insistence on two dimensional treatment of life by certain modernists, do not constitute a progress. A dogma builds on vacuum, and is ultimately killed or modified by, or accommodated to knowledge, but values stay, and ignorant neglect of them answers no purpose.

Loss of values is due usually to lumping and to lack of dissociation. The disproved is thrown out, and the associated, or contemporarily established, goes temporarily with it.

"Durch Rafael is das Madonnenideal Fleisch geworden," says Herr Springer, with perhaps an unintentional rhyme. Certainly the metamorphosis into carnal tissue becomes frequent and general somewhere about 1527. The people are corpus, corpuscular, but not in the strict sense "animate," it is no longer the body of air clothed in the body of fire; it no longer radiates, light no longer moves from the eye, there is a great deal of meat, shock absorbing, perhaps—at any rate absorbent. It has not even Greek marmoreal plastic to restrain it. The dinner scene is more frequently introduced, we have the characters in definite act of absorption; later they will be but stuffing for expensive upholsteries.

Long before that a change had begun in the poetry.[41]

[41]Ibid., p. 153.

263

The Renaissance (excerpt)[42]

Whether from habit, or from profound intuition, or from sheer national conceit, one is always looking to America for signs of a "renaissance." One is open-eyed to defects. I have heard passionate nonentities rave about America's literary and artistic barrenness. I have heard the greatest living American saying, with the measured tones of deliberate curiosity, "Strange how all taint of art or letters seems to shun that continent . . . ah . . . ah, God knows there's little enough here . . . ah . . . ."

And yet we look to the dawn, we count up our symptoms; year in and year out we say we have this and that, we have so much, and so much. Our best asset is a thing of the spirit. I have the ring of it in a letter, now on my desk, from a good but little known poet, complaining of desperate loneliness, envying Synge his material, to-wit, the Arran Islands and people, wishing me well with my exotics, and ending with a sort of defiance. "For me nothing exists, *really exists*, outside America."

That writer is not alone in his feeling, nor is he alone in his belief in tomorrow. That emotion and belief are our motive forces, and as to their application we can perhaps best serve it by taking stock of what we have, and devising practical measures. And we must do this without pride, and without parochialism; we have no one to cheat save ourselves. It is not a question of scaring someone else, but of making ourselves efficient. We must learn what we can from the past, we must learn what other nations have done successfully under similar circumstances, we must think how they did it.

We have, to begin with, architecture, the first of the arts to arrive, the most material, the least dependent on the inner need of the poor—for the arts are noble only as they meet the inner need of the poor. Bach is given to all men, Homer is given to all men: you need only the faculty of music or of patience to read or to hear. Painting and sculpture are given to all men in a particular place, to all who have money for travel.

And architecture comes first, being the finest branch of advertisement, advertisement of some god who has been successful, or of some emperor or of some business man—a material need, plus display. At any rate we have architecture, the only architecture of our time. I do not mean our copies of old buildings, lovely and lovable as they are; I mean our own creations, our office buildings like greater *campanili*, and so on.

And we have, or we are beginning to have, collections. We have had at least one scholar in Ernest Fenollosa, and one patron in Mr. Freer. I mean that these two men at least have worked as the great Italian researchers

[42]Ibid., pp. 218-26. Originally published in *Poetry*, March 1915, pp. 283-87, May 1915, pp. 84-91.

and collectors of the quattrocento worked and collected. But mostly America, from the White House to the gutter, is still dominated by a "puritanical" hatred to what is beyond its understanding.

So it is to the fighting minority that I speak, to a minority that has been until now gradually forced out of the country. We have looked to the wrong powers. We have not sufficiently looked to ourselves. We have not defined the hostility or inertia that is against us. We have not recognized with any Voltairian clearness the nature of this opposition, and we have not realized to what an extent a renaissance is a thing made—a thing made by conscious propaganda.

The scholars of the quattrocento had just as stiff a stupidity and contentment and ignorance to contend with. It is in the biographies of Erasmus and Lorenzo Valla that we must find consolation. They were willing to work at foundations. They did not give the crowd what it wanted. The Middle Ages had been a jumble. There may have been a charming diversity, but there was also the darkness of decentralization. There had been minute vortices at such castles as that of Savairic de Maleon, and later at the universities. But the *rinascimento* began when Valla wrote in the preface of the *Elegantiae:*

Linguam Latinam distribuisse minus erit, optimam frugem, et vere divinam nec corporis, sed animi cibum? Haec enim gentes populosque omnes, omnibus artibus, quae liberales vocantur, instituit: haec optimas leges edocuit: haec viam ad omnem sapientiam munivit, haec denique praestitit, ne barbari amplius dici possent. . . . In qua lingua disciplinae cunctae libero homine dignae continetur. . . . Linguam Romanam vivere plus, quam urbem.

"*Magnum ergo Latini sermonis sacramentum est.*" "*Ibi namque Romanum imperium est, ubicunque Romana lingua dominatur.*"

That is not "the revival of classicism." It is not a worship of corpses. It is an appreciation of the great Roman vortex, an understanding of, and an awakening to, the value of a capital, the value of centralization, in matters of knowledge and art, and of the interaction and stimulus of genius foregathered. *Ubicunque Romana lingua dominatur!*

That sense, that reawakening to the sense of the capital, resulted not in a single great vortex, such as Dante had dreamed of in his propaganda for a great central court, a peace tribunal, and in all his ghibelline speculations; but it did result in the numerous vortices of the Italian cities, striving against each other not only in commerce but in the arts as well.

America has no natural capital. Washington is a political machine, I dare say a good enough one. If we are to have an art capital it also must be made by conscious effort. No city will make such effort on behalf of any other city. The city that plays for this glory will have to plot, deliberately to plot, for the gathering in of great artists, not merely as incidental lecturers but as residents. She will have to plot for the centralization of young artists. She will have to give them living conditions as comfortable as Paris has given since the days of Abelard.

The universities can no longer remain divorced from contemporary intellectual activity. The press cannot longer remain divorced from the vitality and precision of an awakened university scholarship. Art and scholarship need not be wholly at loggerheads.

But above all there must be living conditions for artists; not merely for illustrators and magazine writers, not merely for commercial producers, catering to what they think "the public" or "their readers" desire.

Great art does not depend on the support of riches, but without such aid it will be individual, separate, and spasmodic; it will not group and become a great period. The individual artist will do fine work in corners, to be discovered after his death. Some good enough poet will be spoiled by trying to write stuff as vendible as bath-tubs; or another because, not willing or able to rely on his creative work, he had to make his mind didactic by preparing to be a professor of literature, or abstract by trying to be a professor of philosophy, or had to participate in some other fiasco. But for all that you will not be able to stop the great art, the true art, of the man of genius.

Great art does not depend upon comfort, it does not depend upon the support of riches. But a great age is brought about only with the aid of wealth, because a great age means the deliberate fostering of genius, the gathering-in and grouping and encouragement of artists.

In my final paper of this series, I shall put forth certain plans for improvement.

No, I am not such a fool as to believe that a man writes better for being well fed, or that he writes better for being hungry either. Hunger—some experience of it—is doubtless good for a man; it puts an edge on his style, and so does hard common sense. In the end I believe in hunger, because it is an experience, and no artist can have too many experiences. Prolonged hunger, intermittent hunger and anxiety, will of course break down a man's constitution, render him fussy and over-irritable, and in the end ruin his work or prevent its full development.

That nation is profoundly foolish which does not get the maximum of best work out of its artists. The artist is one of the few producers. He, the farmer and the artisan create wealth; the rest shift and consume it. The net value of good art to its place of residence has been computed in logarithms; I shall not go into the decimals. When there was talk of selling Holbein's *Duchess of Milan* to an American, England bought the picture for three hundred and fifty thousand dollars. They figured that people came to London to see the picture, that the receipts of the community were worth more per annum than the interest on the money. People go where there are good works of art. Pictures and sculpture and architecture pay. Even literature and poetry pay, for where there is enough intelligence to produce and maintain good writing, there society is pleasant and the real estate values increase. Mr. F. M. Hueffer has said that the difference between London and other places is that "No one lives in London merely for the sake of making money enough to live somewhere else."

The real estate values, even in Newark, New Jersey, would go up if Newark were capable of producing art, literature or the drama. In the quattrocento men went from one Italian city to another for reasons that were not solely commercial.

The question is not: Shall we try to keep up the arts?—but: How can we maintain the arts most efficiently? Paris can survive 1870 and 1914 because she is an intellectual and artistic vortex. She is that vortex not because she had a university in the Middle Ages—Cordova and Padua had also medieval universities. France recognizes the cash value of artists. They do not have to pay taxes save when convenient; they have a ministry of fine arts doing its semi-efficient best. Literary but inartistic England moves with a slow paw pushing occasional chunks of meat towards the favoured. England does as well as can be expected, considering that the management of such affairs is entrusted to men whose interests are wholly political and who have no sort of intuition or taste. That is to say, in England, if someone of good social position says that your work is "really literary," and that you are not likely to attack the hereditary interests or criticise the Albert Memorial, you can be reasonably sure of a pension. If your sales have suddenly slumped, you can also have "royal bounty," provided that you respect the senile and decrepit and say a good word for Watts's pictures.

The result is that France gets Rodin's work when he is fifty instead of the day he began doing good work. England gets Rodin's work after it has gone to seed, and rejects the best work of Epstein in his full vigor. England let half her last generation of poets die off, and pensioned such survivors as hadn't gone into something "practical."

But even this is enough to show that bourgeois France and stolid England recognize the cash value of art. I don't imagine that these sordid material considerations will weigh with my compatriots. America is a nation of idealists, as we all know; and they are going to support art for art's sake, because they love it, because they "want the best," even in art. They want beauty; they can't get along without it. They are already tired of spurious literature.

They recognize that all great art, all good art, goes against the grain of contemporary taste. They want men who can stand out against it. They

267

want to back such men and women to the limit. How are they to go about it? Subsidy? Oh, no. They don't want to pauperize artists!

Of course Swinburne was subsidized by his immediate forebears, and Shelley also; and Browning, the robust, the virile, was subsidized by his wife; and even Dante and Villon did not escape the stigma of having received charities. Nevertheless it is undemocratic to believe that a man with money should give—horrible word!—*give* it, even though not all of it, to painters and poets.

They give it to sterile professors; to vacuous preachers of a sterilized form of Christianity; they support magazines whose set and avowed purpose is either to degrade letters or to prevent their natural development. Why in heaven's name shouldn't they back creators, as well as students of Quinet? Why shouldn't they endow men whose studies are independent, put them on an equal footing with men whose scholarship is merely a pasteurized, Bostonized imitation of Leipzig?

How are they to go about it? Committees are notably stupid; they vote for mediocrity, their mind is the least common denominator. Even if there are a few intelligent members, the unintelligent members will be the ones with spare time, and they will get about trying to "run the committee," trying to get in new members who will vote for their kind of inanity. *Et cetera, ad infinitum.*

There is one obvious way, which does not compel individuals to wait for an organization:

Private people can give stipends to individual artists. That is to say, you, Mr. Rockefeller, you, Laird Andy of Skibo, and the rest of you (I am not leaving you out, reader, because you have only one million or half of one); you can endow individuals for life just as you endow chairs in pedagogy and callisthenics. More than that, you can endow them with the right to name their successors. If they don't need the money they can pass it on, before their deaths, to younger artists in whom they believe.

For instance, you may begin by endowing Mr. James Whitcomb Riley, Mr. George Santayana, Mr. Theodore Roosevelt, Mr. Jack London, or anybody else you believe in. And any artist will applaud you. Any artist would rather have a benefice conferred upon him by *one* of these men as an individual than by a committee of the "forty leading luminaries of literature." I take a hard case; I don't suppose for a moment that Mr. Riley or Mr. Roosevelt, Mr. Santayana or Mr. London wants money—in all probability they would one and all refuse it if offered; but none of them would refuse the right of allotting an income, sufficient to cover the bare necessities of life, to some active artist whom they believe in.

If you endow enough men, individuals of vivid and different personality, and make the endowment perpetual, to be handed down from artist to artist, you will have put the arts in a position to defy the subversive

268

pressure of commercial advantage, and of the mediocre spirit which is the bane and hidden terror of democracy.

Democracies have fallen, they have always fallen, because humanity craves the outstanding personality. And hitherto no democracy has provided sufficient place for such an individuality. If you so endow sculptors and writers you will begin for America an age of awakening which will over-shadow the quattrocento; because our opportunity is greater than Leonardo's: we have more aliment, we have not one classic tradition to revivify, we have China and Egypt, and the unknown lands lying upon the roof of the world—Khotan, Kara-shar and Kan-su.

So much for the individual opportunity—now for the civic. Any city which cares for its future can perfectly well start its vortex. It can found something between a graduate seminar and the usual "Arts Club" made up of business men and of a few "rather more than middle-aged artists who can afford to belong."

I have set the individually endowed artist against the endowed professor or editor. I would set the endowment of such grouping of young artists parallel with the endowment, for one year or three, of scholars and fellows by our universities. Some hundreds of budding professors are so endowed, to say nothing of students of divinity.

There is no reason why students of the arts—not merely of painting but of all the arts—should not be so endowed, and so grouped: that is, as artists, not merely as followers of one segregated art. Such endowment would get them over the worst two or three years of their career, the years when their work can't possibly pay.

Scientists are so endowed. It is as futile to expect a poet to get the right words, or any sort of artists to do real work, with one eye on the public, as it would be to expect the experimenter in a chemical laboratory to advance the borders of science, if we have constantly to consider whether his atomic combinations are going to flatter popular belief, or suit the holders of monopolies in some overexpensive compound. The arts and sciences hang together. Any conception which does not see them in their interrelation belittles both. What is good for one is good for the other.

Has any one yet answered the query: why is it that in other times artists went on getting more and more powerful as they grew older, whereas now they decline after the first outburst, or at least after the first successes? Compare this with the steady growth of scientists.

The three main lines of attack, then, which I have proposed in this little series of articles, are as follows:

First, that we should develop a criticism of poetry based on world-poetry, on the work of maximum excellence. (It does not in the least matter whether this standard be that of my own predilections, or crochets

269

or excesses. It matters very much that it be decided by men who have made a first-hand study of world-poetry, and who "have had the tools in their hands.")

Second, that there be definite subsidy of individual artists, writers, etc., such as will enable them to follow their highest ambitions without needing to conciliate the ignorant *en route*. (Even some of our stock-size magazine poets might produce something worth while if they could afford occasionally to keep quiet for six months or a year at a stretch.)

Third, there should be a foundation of such centres as I have described. There should be in America the *"gloire de cénacle."* Tariff laws should favor the creative author rather than the printer, but that matter is too long to be gone into.

In conclusion, the first of these matters must be fought out among the artists themselves. The second matter concerns not only the excessively rich, but the normally and moderately rich, who contribute to all sorts of less useful affairs: redundant universities, parsons, Y.M.C.A.'s, and the general encouragement of drab mediocrity. The third matter concerns millionaires, multimillionaires and municipalities.

When a civilization is vivid it preserves and fosters all sorts of artists— painters, poets, sculptors, musicians, architects. When a civilization is dull and anemic it preserves a rabble of priests, sterile instructors, and repeaters of things second-hand. If literature is to reappear in America it must come through, but in spite of, the present commercial system of publication.

Wyndham Lewis[43]

The signal omission from my critical papers is an adequate book on Wyndham Lewis; my excuses, apart from the limitations of time, must be that Mr. Lewis is alive and quite able to speak for himself, secondly that one may print half-tone reproductions of sculpture, for however unsatisfactory they be, they pretend to be only half-tones, and could not show more than they do; but the reproduction of drawings and painting invites all sorts of expensive process impracticable during the years of war. When the public or the "publishers" are ready for a volume of Lewis, suitably illustrated, I am ready to write in the letterpress, though Mr. Lewis would do it better than I could.

He will rank among the great instigators and great inventors of design; there is mastery in his use of various media (my own interest in his work centres largely in the "drawing" completed with inks, water-colour, chalk, etc.). His name is constantly bracketed with that of Gaudier, Picasso,

[43]*Literary Essays*, pp. 423–24. Originally published in *Instigations*, New York, 1920, pp. 213–14.

Joyce, but these are fortuitous couplings. Lewis' painting is further from the public than were the carvings of Gaudier; Lewis is an older artist, maturer, fuller of greater variety and invention. His work is almost unknown to the public. His name is wholly familiar, BLAST is familiar, the "Timon" portfolio has been seen.

I had known him for seven years, known him as an artist, but I had no idea of his scope until he began making his preparations to go into the army; so careless had he been of any public or private approval. The "work" lay in piles on the floor of an attic; and from it we gathered most of the hundred or hundred and twenty drawings which now form the bases of the Quinn Collection and of the Baker Collection (now in the South Kensington Museum).

As very few people have seen all of these pictures very few people are in any position to contradict me. There are three of his works in this room and I can attest their wearing capacity; as I can attest the duration of my regret for the *Red* drawing now in the Quinn Collection which hung here for some months waiting shipment; as I can attest the energy and vitality that filled this place while forty drawings of the Quinn assortment stood here waiting also; a demonstration of the difference between "cubism," *nature-morte-ism* and the vortex of Lewis: sun, energy, sombre emotion, clean-drawing, disgust, penetrating analysis, from the qualities finding literary expression in *Tarr* to the stasis of the *Red Duet,* from the metallic gleam of the *Timon* portfolio to the velvet-suavity of the later *Timon* of the Baker Collection.

The animality and the animal satire, the dynamic and metallic properties, and social satire, on the one hand, the sunlight, the utter cleanness of the *Red Duet,* all are points in an astounding circumference, which will, until the work is adequately reproduced, have more or less to be taken on trust by the "wider" public. . . .

EXCERPT FROM *POLITE ESSAYS*[44]

. . . There are two kinds of beautiful painting, as one may perhaps illustrate by the works of Burne-Jones and Whistler; one looks at the first kind of painting and is immediately delighted by its beauty; the second kind of painting, when first seen, puzzles one, but on leaving it, and going from the gallery one finds new beauty in natural things—a Thames fog, to use the hackneyed example. Thus, there are works of art which are beautiful objects, and works of art which are keys or passwords admitting one to a deeper knowledge, to a finer perception of beauty. . . .

[44]*Polite Essays*, London, 1937, and Norfolk, Conn., 1940, p. 197.

FROM *RIPOSTES*[45]
THE COMPLETE POETICAL WORKS OF T. E. HULME
(PREFATORY NOTE)[46]

. . . As for the "School of Images," which may or may not have existed, its principles were not so interesting as those of the "inherent dynamists" or *Les Unanimistes,* yet they were probably sounder than those of a certain French school which attempted to dispense with verbs altogether; or of the impressionists who brought forth:

"Pink pigs blossoming upon the hillside";

or of the post-impressionists who beseech their ladies to let down slate-blue hair over their raspberry-coloured flanks. . . .

FROM *SELECTED LETTERS*[47]

To Harriet Monroe[48]

London, [18] August [1912]

Dear Madam: –/–/I send you all that I have on my desk—an over-elaborate post-Browning "Imagiste" affair and a note on the Whistler exhibit. I count him our only great artist, and even this informal salute, drastic as it is, may not be out of place at the threshold of what I hope is an endeavor to carry into our American poetry the same sort of life and intensity which he infused into modern painting.

P.S. Any agonizing that tends to hurry what I believe in the end to be inevitable, our American Risorgimento, is dear to me. That awakening will make the Italian Renaissance look like a tempest in a teapot! The force we have, and the impulse, but the guiding sense, the discrimination in applying the force, we must wait and strive for.

[45]*Ripostes,* London, 1912.
[46]First published at the end of *Ripostes,* p. 59; reprinted in *Personae,* New York, 1949, London, 1952, p. 251. Pound's attack on impressionism comes appropriately in this preface to Hulme's complete poems (five in all), which Noel Stock calls "the first distinctively modern poems in English." (See Stock, *The Life of Ezra Pound,* New York, 1970, p. 65.)
[47]*The Selected Letters of Ezra Pound,* London, 1951, and New York, 1971. For an explanation of deletion symbols, see p. 229.
[48]Ibid., New York, p. 10; London, p. 44.

To Isabel W. Pound[49]

London, November [1913]

Dear Mother: -/-/The Old Spanish Masters show is the best loan exhibit I have yet seen. The post-impressionist show is also interesting.

Epstein is a great sculptor. I wish he would wash, but I believe Michel Angelo *never* did, so I suppose it is part of the tradition. Also it is nearly impossible to appear clean in London; perhaps he does remove some of the grime. -/-/

To William Carlos Williams[50]

Coleman's Hatch, 19 December [1913]

Dear Bull: -/-/Have just bought two statuettes from *the* coming sculptor, Gaudier-Brzeska. I like him very much. He is the only person with whom I can really be "Altaforte."----Yeats is much finer *intime* than seen spasmodically in the midst of the whirl. We are both, I think, very contented in Sussex. He returned $200 of that award with orders that it be sent to me—and it has been. Hence the sculptural outburst and a new typewriter of great delicacy.

----You may get something slogging away by yourself that you would miss in The Vortex—and that we miss. -/-/

To Harriet Monroe[51]

London, 25 May [1914]

Dear H. M.: -/-/You know perfectly well that American painting is recognizable because painters from the very beginning have kept in touch

[49]Ibid., New York, p. 26; London, p. 63.

[50]Ibid., New York, pp. 27–28; London, p. 65. In this letter Pound employs the term "Vortex" for the first time for his circle of artists of the rebel movement soon to be designated "Vorticism." In a later letter to John Quinn (March 10, 1916, *q.v.*), in which he praises Lewis's work, Pound states that he found the word himself.

In a letter to the artist Gladys Hynes, 1956, Pound repeated that he was the namer of the movement. He wrote, "W. L. certainly *made* vorticism. To him alone we owe the existence of *Blast*. It is true that he started by wanting a forum for the several ACTIVE varieties of CONTEMPORARY art/cub/expressionist/post-imp etc. BUT in conversation with E.P. there emerged the idea of defining what WE wanted & having a name for it. Ultimately Gaudier for sculpture, E.P. for poetry, and W.L., the main mover, set down their personal requirements." (See Richard Cork, *Vorticism*, I, p. 236, where this letter is quoted.)

[51]*Selected Letters*, New York, p. 37, London, p. 76.

with Europe and dared to study abroad. Are you going to call people foreigners the minute they care enough about their art to travel in order to perfect it? -/-/

To Harriet Monroe[52]

London, 9 November [1914]

Dear H. M.: -/-/Now about news, I don't quite know what you can use. The stuff I had in mind was material for write-ups of Lewis, Epstein, Brzeska and any other good stuff that might turn up. You said you couldn't criticize stuff you hadn't seen. However I'll get you some photos if you think you can make anything of it.

The general theory of the new art is, I think, made fairly clear in my article "Vorticism" appearing in the September no. *Fortnightly Review*.[52a]

I don't think I can get photos from Epstein unless you really want to use them.

Now about topics of the moment. There is an exhibit of Rodin at the South Kensington Museum, good of its kind but it does look like muck after one has got one's eye in on Epstein's Babylonian austerity. And Brzeska's work, for all that he is only 22, is much more interesting.

Would it be any use to you to have photos of the better Rodins? A couple are fine and some of 'em make me sick. Slime. No form.

Brzeska by the way is at the front, French army. 7 out of his squad of 12 were killed off a few weeks ago, when scouting. He was killed two "boches." The dullness in the trenches for the last weeks has bored him so that he is doing an essay on sculpture for the next number of *BLAST*. Also he has done a figure, working with his jackknife and an entrenching tool.

The exhibition of Modern Spanish Art at the Grafton is a fit exhibit to hang where the show of the Royal Society of Portrait Painters hung recently. MUCK. If it weren't in "aid of the Prince of Wales fund" one would be inclined to sue for one's shilling. On what pretence is it modern! Most of the stuff that has any tendency at all is an archaism of one sort or another. The preface to the catalog which I now look at for the first time is as silly as the show, all anchored about 1875 and amateurish.

Picasso is not mentioned. Even Picabia is a large light in comparison with their twaddle.

The one thing that stands out is the work of Nestor Martin *Fernandez della Torre*. (This is not a fad.) Fernandez has four things, two pictures and two black and white things. The two pictures are very different

[52]Ibid., New York, pp. 45-47; London, pp. 85-87.
[52a]*Q.v.*

superficially. Coburn and I did the show together and these things scattered about were the only things of interest.

He paints hard and clear. As canvases of the masters of Leonardo's time might have looked when *new*. It is as if he had learned from Van Gogh and, in the portrait of the young man "Joselito," been younger and more gentle. In the woman's portrait "La maja del abanico" it is as if he had tried to combine the Van Gogh hardness with the splendour, the ornateness, of Seville or of the Renaissance period.

The two drawings of dances are good, but not sufficiently so to make one remember him apart from the show, had they not been seen with the paintings.

Wadsworth, a young painter, not nearly so important as Lewis, but good, might interest you, as he has a bee for industrial centres and harbours. He is doing woodcuts at the moment. I suppose I could get you a couple, or at least get you impressions of some sort that would give you an idea, if it's any use.

I've mentioned Wadsworth, Epstein, Brzeska and Lewis in hurried scribbles in *The Egoist*. Do you see it? I think it is sent in as an exchange, but am not sure. -/-/

Wyndham Lewis, whose decorations of the Countess of Drogheda's house caused such a stir last autumn (and they weren't very good either) is now decorating the study of that copious novelist and critic, Mr. Ford Madox Hueffer. -/-/

Getting pictures would be fairly simple, in the case of Rodin or Fernandez. I suppose I'd have to buy the prints??-/-/

Tuesday, 10 November

The proof of the College of Arts prospectus has just come and I enclose it.[53] I was going to ask A.C.H.[54] to give it publicity but I guess you can use it as news quite as well. It is, obviously, a scheme to enable things to keep on here in spite of the war-strain and (what will be more dangerous) the war back-wash and post bellum slump. But it embodies two real ideas:

A. That the arts, INCLUDING poetry and literature, should be taught by artists, by practicing artists, *not* by sterile professors.

B. That the arts should be gathered together for the purpose of inter-enlightenment. The "art" school, meaning "paint school," needs literature for backbone, ditto the musical academy, etc.

I was going to ask A.C.H. to boom it, because I think it can be made a valuable model, or starting point for a much bigger scheme for Chicago. This thing here is done by artists *in spite of* the rich, but Chicago should be able to do a really big thing, if, as they seem able to do, they can get

---

[53]See *The Egoist*, November 2, 1914; *The New Age*, May 29, 1913.
[54]A.C.H. refers to Alice Corbin Henderson, assistant editor of *Poetry*.

money and the creative people working together. My third "Renaissance" article will outline something. With three year fellowships, life-endowment, etc.

You see also, that while the vorticists are well-represented, the College does not bind itself to a school. Vide Dolmetsch, Robins and in less degree Dulac and Coburn.

Also the College should be of very real service to American students. I have seen enough of them to know.----

To John Quinn[55]

In *The New Age* of 21 January, Pound had published an article on Jacob Epstein in which he had written that the sculptor had "pawned his 'Sun God' and two other pieces" for sixty pounds. And he continued: "One looks out upon American collectors buying autograph mss. of William Morris, faked Rembrandts and faked Van Dykes." On 25 January, John Quinn wrote to Pound protesting against that sentence as a reflection upon himself. Quinn went on to point out that he had given up collecting manuscripts; that he collected modern art and not faked Rembrandts and Van Dykes and, indeed, had canvases by Matisse, Picasso and Derain; that he was responsible for the new tariff law which broke up the market in faked old masters. He inquired about the possibility of getting some good work by Gaudier-Brzeska and, finally, suggested that Pound might write for *The New Republic*.

London, 8 March [1915]

My dear John Quinn: Thanks, apologies and congratulations. If there were more like you we should get on with our renaissance.

I particularly congratulate you on having shed your collection of mss. and having "got as far as Derain." (Mind you, I think Lewis has much more power in his elbow, but I wouldn't advise a man to buy "a Lewis" simply because it was Lewis. Out of much that I do not care for there are now and again designs or pictures which I greatly admire.) However, there are few such reformed characters as yourself, and I might have as well said, "medals given to John Keats for orthography, first editions of eighteenth century authors," instead of "mss. of Wm. Morris," which allusion would not have dragged you into it and would have left the drive of my sentence about the same. I might have gone on about the way Morgan and a certain old friend of his, whose niece I knew in Paris, used to buy, but Morgan is such a stock phrase (and besides he has done some good in America by bringing in Old Masters). Then there's Ricketts now

[55]*Selected Letters*, New York, pp. 51–54; London, pp. 94–95.

showing Old Masters, collected for Davis I think it is. There are a lot of heads at the fair.

I have still a very clear recollection of Yeats père on an elephant (at Coney Island), smiling like Elijah in the beatific vision, and of you plugging away in the shooting gallery. And a very good day it was. - - - -

As to fake Rembrandts, etc., I carried twenty "Rembrandts," "Van Dykes" and "Velásquez" out of Wanamaker's private gallery at the time of his fire some eight years ago. I know that they aren't the only examples in the U.S., so my sentence was by no means a personal one. My God! What Velasquez! I also know a process for Rembrandts: one man studies the ghetto and does drawings, one the Rembrandtesque method of light and shade and manner and does the painting, and a third does the "tone of time." However, that's a digression. Let me go at your letter as it comes.

I haven't seen much of Epstein of late. He and Lewis have some feud or other which I haven't inquired into, and as Lewis is my more intimate friend I have not seen much of Jacob, though I was by way of playing for a reconciliation. Jacob told me some time ago that the "Sun God" was in hock. He told me, just before the war, it was still in hock. I heard from W.B.Y., after I had written the article and after it was in print, that you had bought "an Epstein" ("an Epstein," not half a dozen.) - - - -

By the way, if you are still getting Jacob's "Birds," for God's sake get the two that are stuck together, not the pair in which one is standing up on its legs. -/-/[56]

About GAUDIER-BRZESKA: I naturally think I've got the two best things myself, though I was supposed by his sister to have bought the first one out of charity because no one else would have it. The second one is half paid for by money I lent him to get to France with. He is now in the trenches before Rheims. However, there is, or was, a charming bas-relief of a cat chewing its hind foot, and there are the "Stags," if you like them. However, money can't be of much use to him now in the trenches. I send him a spare pound when I have it to finish up my payment on the "Boy with a Coney." But when he comes back from the trenches, if he does come, I imagine he will be jolly hard up. In the meantime I will find out exactly what is unsold and let you know about it. Coburn is doing a photo of one of my own things of Brzeska's and I hope it will interest him enough to go on and do a portfolio, in which case you will be able to make your selection from the best possible photographs.

At any rate, I will write to Gaudier at once and see what he has, and where it is, and how much he wants for it, and if there is anything that I think fit to recommend I think Coburn will probably photograph it for me. Then there will be no waste in dealer's commissions.

[56]Pound shows his sharp critical eye here, as Richard Cork notes, for the dove carving Pound refers to, namely, the *Second Marble Doves, c.* 1913, is the finer work. (See Cork, *Vorticism*, I, p. 123.)

Which brings me back to another hobby. Speaking of 30,000 dollars for two pictures, I "consider it immoral" to pay more than 1,000 dollars for any picture (save, perhaps, a huge Sistine ceiling or something of that sort). Your Puvises are big pictures so it don't hit you. But NO artist needs more than 2,000 dollars per year, and any artist can do two pictures at least in a year. 30,000 dollars would feed a whole little art world for five years.

My whole drive is that if a patron buys from an artist who needs money (needs money to buy tools, time and food), the patron then makes himself equal to the artist: he is building art into the world; he creates.

If he buys even of living artists who are already famous or already making £12,000 per year, he ceases to create. He sinks back to the rank of a consumer.

A great age of painting, a renaissance in the arts, comes when there are a few patrons who back their own flair and who buy from unrecognized men. In every artist's life there is, if he be poor, and they mostly are, a period when £10 is a fortune and when £100 means a year's leisure to work or to travel, or when the knowledge that they can make £100 or £200 a year without worry (without spending two-thirds of their time running to dealers, or editors) means a peace of mind that will let them work and not undermine them physically.

Besides, if a man has any sense, the sport and even the commercial advantage is so infinitely greater. If you can hammer this into a few more collectors you will bring on another Cinquecento.

(In sculpture I might let the price run over £200, simply because of the time it takes to cut stone. Drill work is no damn good. Both Gaudier and Epstein cut direct, and there may be months of sheer cutting in a big bit of sculpture, especially if the stone is very hard.) Gaudier does mostly small things, which is sane, for the sculpture of our time, save public sculpture, ought to be such as will go in a modern house. -/-/

. . . If you told Croly of *The New Republic* that I was an art critic he might believe you, but he'd think me very bad for his paper. The fat pastures are still afar from me. And I have a persistent and (editorially) inconvenient belief that America has the chance for a great age if she can be kicked into taking it. ----

To H.L. Mencken[57]

London, 17 March [*1917*]
Dear H. L. Menken: -/-/That is, I think the sum of the London news that I have gathered in the few days I've been up and about, save that we'll

[57]*Selected Letters*, New York, pp. 56–57; London, pp. 100–1.

have out another *BLAST* soon, and that if you touch art, even en passant, Lewis (Wyndham Lewis) and Gaudier-Brzeska are great artists though their stuff is still so far from the public comprehension that I don't expect many people to believe me when I say so. Quinn has, however, written here to know if he can get a good statue by Brzeska; and whatever Picasso has done or is about to do in New York, I think Lewis will be able to go beyond it. I don't know what you intend about covers and posters for the S.S. but if you can get a man with a great future whose work is VISIBLE, mehercule! and at the same rates, probably, as you would pay a nobody, it might in the long run pay, merely as advertising.

I don't know whether you have seen my article on vorticism in *The Fortnightly Review* for last Sept. It is a moderately clear introduction. In any case you might keep in mind the fact that vorticism is not futurism, most emphatically NOT. We like cubism and some expressionism, but the schools are not our school. Even though they are equally distant from Manet or Alma Tadema.

To Felix E. Schelling[58]

London, June [1915]

Dear Dr. Schelling: –/–/Gaudier-Brzeska has been killed at Neuville St. Vaast, and we have lost the best of the young sculptors and the most promising. The arts will incur no worse loss from the war than this is. One is rather obsessed with it. –/–/

To John Quinn[59]

London, 10 March [1916]

Dear Quinn: Lewis has just sent in the first dozen drawings. They are all over the room, and the thing is stupendous. The vitality, the fullness of the man! Nobody knows it. My God, the stuff lies in a pile of dirt on the man's floor. Nobody has seen it. Nobody has *any* conception of the volume and energy and the variety.

Blake, that W.B.Y. is always going on about!!!! Lewis has got Blake scotched to a finish. He's got so much more *in him* than Gaudier. I know he is seven years older. Ma chè Cristo!

I have certainly GOT to do a Lewis book to match the Brzeska. Or perhaps a "Vorticists" (being nine-tenths Lewis, and reprinting my paper on Wadsworth, with a few notes on the others).

[58]Ibid., New York, p. 61, London p. 106.
[59]Ibid., New York, pp. 73–74; London, pp. 121–22.

This is the first day for I don't know how long that I have envied any man his spending money. It seems to me that Picasso alone, certainly alone among the living artists whom I know of, is in anything like the same class. It is not merely knowledge of technique, or skill, it is intelligence and knowledge of life, of the whole of it, beauty, heaven, hell, sarcasm, every kind of whirlwind of force and emotion. Vortex. That is the right word, if I did find it myself. ----[60]

In all this modern froth—that's what it is, froth, 291, Picabia, etc., etc., etc., Derain even, and the French—there isn't, so far as I have had opportunity of knowing, ONE trace of this man's profundity.

Brzeska's "Jojo" sits impassively before me, flanked by a pale mulatto, and something (blue drawing) in spirit like Ulysses in a storm passing the Sirens. If any man says there is no romance and no emotion in this vorticist art, I say he is a liar. Years ago, three I suppose it is, or four, I said to Epstein (not having seen these things of Lewis, or indeed more than a few things he had then exhibited), "The sculpture seems to be so much more interesting. I find it much more interesting than the painting."

Jacob said, "But Lewis' drawing has the qualities of sculpture." (He may have said "all the qualities" or "so many of the qualities." At any rate, that set me off looking at Lewis.)

What the later quarrel with Jacob is, I do not know, save that Jacob is a fool when he hasn't got a chisel in his hand and a rock before him, and Lewis *can* at moments be extremely irritating. (But then, damn it all, he is quite apt to be in the right.)

Oh well, enough of this. You'll soon have the stuff before you.

To John Quinn[61]

London, The Evening of the 24th day January [1917]
Dear John Quinn: -/-/If there is any spending it would be much more fun to spend it on illustrations (even in colour) for the book on Lewis.

I don't believe there's much "oil" of lucre in Pisistratan sculpture, but the blighted Greeks did a few things before Phidias, and it would be amusing to point out Greek art as one continuous decadence. The Moscophoros (alias, "The chap with the calf") is, I think, a good job (possibly better than Yakob).

My wife, trying to find a formula of words, said, "No . . . ah . . . no, Dulac *isn't* an artist."

I: "What?"

[60]Paige's omission of the remainder of this paragraph may be quoted here: "Every kind of geyser from jism bursting up white as ivory, to hate or a storm at sea. Spermatozoon, enough to repopulate the island with active and vigorous animals. Wit, satire, tragedy."

[61] Ibid., New York, pp. 104–5; London, pp. 157–58.

280

She: "No, he's something else, he is different" (that means different from Lewis, me, Gaudier, Eliot, etc.). "He is a . . . dilettante."

Which is probably the answer. He is a nice chap to dine with and probably better at conversation or anything else than at ART.

Don't worry about Lewis not understanding mild delay. Everything turned out all right.

The vortoscope isn't a cinema. It is an attachment to enable a photographer to do sham Picassos. That sarcastic definition probably covers the ground. A chap named Mountsier has seen the stuff and is doing an article on it, also on Lewis and me and Coburn. He is going to N.Y.—on the *Sun*, I think.

The show of Coburn's results comes off here in Feb. He and I are to jaw about abstraction in photography and in art, and old G. B. S. has promised to come out and perhaps chip into the jawing. The vortographs are perhaps as interesting as Wadsworth's woodcuts, perhaps not quite as interesting.

At any rate, it will serve to upset the muckers who are already crowing about the death of vorticism.

It, the vortoscope, will manage any arrangement of purely abstract forms. The present machine happens to be rectilinear, but I can make one that will do any sort of curve, quite easily.

It ought to save a lot of waste experiment on plane compositions, such as Lewis' "Plan of War," or the Wadsworth woodcuts. Certainly it is as good as the bad imitators—Atkinson, and possibly some Picabia—and might serve to finish them off, leaving Lewis and Picasso more clearly defined.

Thanks again for fixing up things with Knopf.

Will say nothing about periodical until I get your next letter, save that it is very good of you to go on being interested after all my varied and divergent propositions.

Am glad the vorticist exhibit is really open. But this letter is already long enough, so I won't expatiate. Regards to Yeats Sr. and remembrances to Brodzky, and thanks again to you.

To Margaret C. Anderson[62]

London, [? June 1917]

Dear editor: -/-/The strength of Picasso is largely in his having chewed through and chewed up a great mass of classicism; which, for example, the lesser cubists, and the flabby cubists have not.

[62]Ibid., New York, p. 113; London, p. 168.

To John Quinn[63]

London, 25 October [1919]

Dear Quinn: –/–/Lewis' portrait of me was on the way of being excellent when I last saw it; have not seen the final form of it yet, but hope to at the Goupil.

Nina Hamnett[64] has greatly improved. Great persistence for a female. –/–/

To Wyndham Lewis[65]

Paris, 27 April [1921]

Dear W. L.: –/–/Am taking up the *Little Review* again, as a quarterly, each number to have about twenty reprods of ONE artist, replacing Soirées de Paris.

Start off with twenty Brancusis to get a new note.

You have had since 1917 to turn in some illustrations for *L.R.*, but perhaps the prospect of a full Lewis number will lure you.

Also, as I have never been able to get a publisher for a book on you, I have the idea of trying one on "Four Modern Artists" *if you* can collect sufficient illustrations. I know there is difficulty re S. Kens. stuff and re Quinn's stuff.

I however give you this chance for a communique to Quinn. Tell him I am contemplating the book. (He has just bought some Brancusi, by the way, and shown good sense in so doing.)

I should take you, Brancusi, Picasso, and, surprising as it will seem to you, Picabia, not exactly as a painter, but as a writer. He commences in *Pensées sans paroles* and lands in his last book. *J. C. Rastaquoère* and there is also more in his design stuff than comes up in reprod.

Also the four chapters wd. give me a chance to make certain contrasts, etc.

Format of *L.R.* will be larger and reprods therein as good as possible. It will also be on sale at strategic points here.

Yr. correspondent Marcoussis is an industrious and serious person who has "done som beeutiful graiynin' in 'is time," not a titanic intellect, but has German market. Very very much concerned with execution. Gleizes isn't. Braque I have only seen for two minutes and am inclined to like. ----

[63]Ibid., New York, p. 151; London, p. 214.

[64]One of the founder members of the Omega Workshops. Quentin Bell, in his review of Frances Spalding's *Roger Fry: Art and Life* (*Times Literary Supplement*, March 21, 1980, p. 308), tells the following anecdote that may be of interet here: "Late in her life Nina Hamnett told me that the difference between Fry and Sickert was this: 'Walter always knew I was a bitch, Roger, bless his heart never guessed.' Nina was in fact wrong; the word with which Roger described her was *putain;* nevertheless the story is illuminating."

[65]Ibid., New York, pp. 166–67; London, pp. 230–31.

To Wyndham Lewis[66]

Rapallo, 3 December [1924]

Wall, ole Koksum Buggle: I have just, ten years an a bit after its appearance and in this far distant locus, taken out a copy of the great MAGENTA
cover'd opusculus [*Blast*]. We were hefty guys in them days; an' of what
has come after us, we seem to have survived without a great mass of
successors. –/–/

I can't and don't believe in Mr. Ingres. In'gress. NOR Seurat, nor Greco,
nor . . . oh damn it all. . . .

I am not very sure about Cézanne. But I like Rousseau's Baboons, and
the warts on Feddy Urbino's nose.

And I think . . . some of the chunks of Manet's execution picture . . . ??? The Timon, on Plate V of *Blast,* still looks O.K. etc. ----

To William Bird[67]

Rapallo, 11 November [1925]

Dear Bill: –/–/However, you can let your fancy play as to the course of
modern art if I had had an income, esp. during the 1912–14 period,
Epstein, Gaudier, Lewis, and also to lesser extent, litterchure, with printing and distrib. facilities. And, later, Brancusi's temple etc. –/–/[68]

---

[66]Ibid., New York, pp. 190–91; London, pp. 261–63.

[67]Ibid., New York, p. 201; London, p. 274.

[68]A note by John Russell in his "Art People" (New York *Times,* February 17,
1978, p. 20) may be of interest:

It was known to Ezra Pound, James Johnson Sweeney and other friends of
Brancusi in the 1930's [*sic*] that the Majarajah has [*sic*] asked Brancusi to
build a temple in India in memory of his wife, who had lately died; but
nothing came of it and no drawings are known to survive.

The temple ranks high, meanwhile, among the works of art that we
should have liked to see. And now, thanks to Radu Varia, a young Rumanian art critic who lives in Paris but is momentarily over here, we have at
least an idea as to how it would have looked. "I recently heard," he said,
"from the Rumanian architect Octav Doicescu, who worked on the project
with Brancusi, that it would have been a meditation temple for one person
only. It was to be almost spherical, with more or less the form of an apple.
The chamber itself would have been where the seeds are, in an apple, and
the daylight would have come from directly overhead, as if the apple had
been neatly cored.

"Access was to be limited to one person at a time. You walked in at garden
level, you went up a few steps, and there you were, alone with the sarcoph-
agus in the small inner chamber. Brancusi never made even a pencil drawing of the project, but he used his spellbinder's conversational power to
make it clear to Diocescu that the temple, with its purity and simplicity of
form, would have the emotional force that we normally find only with the
great anonymous monuments of antiquity."

To John Scheiwiller[69]

Rapallo, 26 November [*1929*]

Dear Scheiwiller: The trouble is that I have never seen any of Modigliani's work. He died in Paris while I was living in London. I know of his position and I know the work by reproduction, and I know how good artists respected him; but my respect for artistic criticism as such prevents me from having or printing opinions on what I don't know.

I don't know what I can say.

"Premature death of Modigliani removed a definite, valuable and emotive force from the contemporary art world."

If that is any use to you?

To E. E. Cummings[70]

Rapallo, 17 February 1930

Dear Cummings: Van Hecke is asking me to help him make up an American number of *Variétés.* -/-/Photos illustrating the number to be mainly machinery, etc. plus the noble and rep. viri murkhani. ---- Van H. has already printed photos of Voronoff operation, the Streets of Marseilles, etc. Bandagistes' windows also a favorite subject.

If you have a photo of a Cigar Store Indian or can get one it wd. be deeply appreciated. Our autochthonous sculpture is comparatively unknown in Yourup though I suspect the c. (or segar) s. i. was possibly of Brit. or colonial origin. Van. H. has got a lot of Berenice [Abbott]'s photos of N.Y. I don't know just what. Still he hasn't mentioned an Indian and B's prob. too young to remember 'em.

To Carlo Izzo[71]

Rapallo, 8 January [*1938*]

---- "With Usura the line grows thick"[72]—means the *line* in painting and design. Quattrocento painters still in morally clean era when usury and buggery were on a par. As the moral sense becomes as incapable of moral

---

[69]*Selected Letters,* New York, p. 225; London, p. 303.
[70]Ibid., New York, p. 227; London, pp. 305–6.
[71]Ibid., New York, p. 303; London, p. 397.
[72]Canto XLV.

distinction as the ....p of ....y or ...t .....n, painting gets bitched. I can tell the bank-rate and component of tolerance for usury in any epoch by the quality of *line* in painting. Baroque, etc., era of usury becoming tolerated. -/-/

To Katue Kitasono[73]

Rapallo, 10 December [1938]

Dear K. K.: -/-/Have just seen W. L. in London. His head on duck; he has done new portrait of me. You can judge the two worlds when you get a photo of it, which I will send when I get one. The Wyndham drawing (done about 1912) that I have brought back is better than the Max Ernst that Laughlin introduced here circuitously. The Max that I had from him (Max) seven years ago is very fine. In fact, it goes away and the other Max approaches revolving. ----

To Wyndham Lewis[74]

Rapallo, 3 August [1939]

Dear Wyndham: -/-/Also I onnerstand Barr (Mod Art Mus) is lookin for *early* W. L. Damn, I told you not to waste them drorinz. I might poifekly well have pinched the lot, and sold 'em for yr. bean-y-fit. Blue gal reposin at my left. Full of characteristics that wd. prob distress you. . . . -/-/

To Katue Kitasono[75]

Rapallo, 29 October [1940]

Dear Kit Kat: -/-/*The Dial* might fool the casual observer; but its policy was *not* to get the best work or best writers. It got some. But Thayer aimed at names, wanted European celebrities and spent vast sums getting their left-overs. You would see the same thing in American picture galleries. *After* a painter is celebrated (and Europeans have his best stuff) dealers can sell it to American "connoisseurs." -/-/

[73]*Selected Letters,* New York, p. 319; London, p. 414.
[74]Ibid., New York, p. 323; London, p. 418.
[75]Ibid., New York, p. 346; London, p. 446.

FROM *TRANSLATIONS*[76]

In painting, the colour is always finite. It may match the colour of the infinite spheres, but it is in a way confined within the frame and its appearance is modified by the colours about it. The line is unbounded, it marks the passage of a force, it continues beyond the frame.

Rodin's belief that energy is beauty holds thus far, namely, that all our ideas of beauty of line are in some way connected with our ideas of swiftness or easy power of motion, and we consider ugly those lines which connote unwieldy slowness in moving.

[76]*Translations* (New York, 1963, and London, 1971), "Introduction: Calvalcanti Poems," p. 23.

6
Selections from Uncollected Manuscripts and Papers

To Isabel W. Pound[1]

London, 7 January 1909

Dear Mother: –/–/There are two kinds of artists: 1) Waterhouse who painted perhaps the most beautiful pictures that have ever been made in England; but you go from them and see no more than you did before. The answer is in the picture. 2) Whistler and Turner, to whom it is theoretically necessary to be "educated up." When you first see their pictures you say "wot't-'ell" but when you leave the pictures you see beauty in mists, shadows, a hundred places where you never dreamed of seeing it before. The answer to their work is in nature. The artist is in the maker of an ornament or a key, as he chooses.

To Harriet Monroe[2]

London, 22 October 1912

Dear Harriet Monroe: –/–/Whistler and Whitman—I abide by their judgment.

–/–/You teach an art student by setting him to make a bad drawing of a fine "antique"—not by telling him his bad work is worthy of public attention.

[1]Paige carbons, Yale University Library.

[2]Special Collections, the University of Chicago Library. The fourth paragraph here and first two sentences of the fifth paragraph are published in *The Selected Letters of Ezra Pound*, ed. D. D. Paige, London, 1951, pp. 46–47; New York, 1971, pp. 12–13.

287

Not by drawing his attention to unsound contemporary work. Unsound work may often have qualities, may often be done meritoriously. But it is not the business of anyone who cares for the arts to put the glamour of popularity in this work in such a way that the student shall forget the more difficult path; the more difficult goal.

–/–/Good art can't possibly be palatable all at once.

–/–/In fact, good art thrives in an atmosphere of parody. Parody is, I suppose, the best criticism—it sifts the durable from the apparent. ---- Yet it is just as ridiculous that one should feel weepy at the *sound* of certain *music* as that one should have a twitching of the lacrimosal glands at the *sight* of certain *colour,* or at a certain mood of the evening when the light has a certain quality.

To Harriet Monroe[3]

London, [6 October 1913]

Dear H. M.: Here is another broad-side. It is not a moment's petulance, but an expression of a very brief and general expression of a conviction against which I have struggled for years. A conviction that it is almost impossible for America to understand WHY Whistler and Henry James and Sargent, and every good artist flee her borders. Why even the minor artists flee when they can, and only return westward in tears. WHY? The patriotic return (even I have returned once) only to find disillusion and to know that they have been made fools of, by their patriotic emotion. –/–/

To Harriet Monroe[4]

London [1914]

Dear H. M.: I am sending you two scraps of Wadsworth's woodcuts, i.e., one is on bad paper (too white) so the colour is wrong, and the other is a proof before the block was finally cleared, so there are slight blurs at the edges. However, you will be able to see the general drift of them. I send also some little photos, of his earlier stuff, so that you can see the development. Quinn bought one of the earlier things. They are of the period when Augustus John designated Wadsworth and Lewis (other way on) as the best of the younger generation of painters. He (Wadsworth)

---

[3]Unpublished letter. Special Collections, the University of Chicago Library.
[4]Unpublished letter. Special Collections, the University of Chicago Library.

is now drilling in the artist's corps. If that gives "topical" or newsy note to the matter.

Brzeska's letters from the front are amusing. I'll send you some extracts as soon as I can get some photos of his stuff from his sister.

I think W. would like the little photos back. These woodcuts make interesting comparison with the Chinese work. There (China) they have their traditional radicals from which each picture develops; i.e., their ideograph for bamboo, or for willow. Here we must find a language.

I think the harbour is admirable. The mast and sails, ideograph. And the splendid organization. Also the Rotterdam (or some Dutch town). The sort of big E, city of canals, bridges and barges, though less obvious.

More anon.

This art should lead us to something occidental which will be as profound an interpretation of life as is the Chinese. It cannot arrive all of a sudden. Nevertheless these woodcuts are good, and pleasant to live with. I have good copies on my wall, which I am not generous enough to send you, but still!

To Homer L. Pound[5]

London, 28 February 1914
Dear Dad: –/–/The papers are full of Wyndham Lewis' cubist room that he has just done for Lady Drogheda. I don't know that I have written of him, but he is more or less one of the gang here at least he is the most "advanced" of the painters and very clever and thoroughly enigmatic.

Brzeska is using up a ton of Pentilicon for my head. Vide *Egoist.* You'll find the mad outline drawing very interesting AFTER you've had it on the wall for a week or two. The tactile values in the that [*sic*] drawing cat's paw, etc. Also the composition.

Epstein is stronger but Epstein is twenty years older. Brzeska is exactly like some artist out of the Italian renaissance. - - - -

To Harriet Monroe[6]

Stone Cottage, 3 August 1914
Dear H. M.: –/–/You must get it into the reader's mind that a capital is the centre of the world, or at least a centre, not an isolated segment.

[5]Paige carbons, Yale University Library.
[6]Unpublished letter. Special Collections, the University of Chicago Library.

All art comes from the or *a* capital. A capital is a vortex. All invention flows into it, and that makes art. It makes the art of awakening and discovery. Paris is not less French for being omnivorous. There is no nation without a capital. America is a colony until she can make a capital. ----

To Harriet Monroe[7]

London, 17 August 1914
Dear H. M.: -/-/VORTICISM being the generic term now used on all branches of the new art, sculpture, painting, poetry. -/-/

To Harriet Monroe[8]

London, 10 April 1915
Dear Harriet: -/-/Please don't call me a futurist in private.
The pictures proposed in the verse are pure vorticism.
As time will show.
The two movements are not synonymous.
Admitted there is a shade of dynamism in the proposition, to treat the pieces as light-potentialities. —Still the concept of arrangement is vorticist.
There maybe a nice book *all* about it soon. Anyhow there's a vorticist show at the Doré Gallery in June—war or no war.

THE BEST IN ENGLISH[9]

---- Here is Matisse, fifteen years late. Five years ago his pictures were selling at 15,000 dollars apiece. If American collectors want contemporary art well represented in their galleries tomorrow they must hear of contemporary art before it becomes too expensive. They still go on buying

[7]Unpublished letter. Special Collections, the University of Chicago Library.
[8]Special Collections, the University of Chicago Library. Unquoted portions of this letter appear in *Selected Letters,* New York, p. 57; London, p. 101.
[9]Part of an unpublished article sent to *Poetry* (?) during May 1915, with the quoted title. Special Collections, the University of Chicago Library.

dealers' back stock, which is not the way to be part of the art force. And the buyer can be very much part of that force if he buys during the years of the artist's stress and gives him leisure and a calm mind to work with. ----

To Harriet Monroe[10]

London, 28 June 1915

Dear H. M.: ---- I went out this A.M. and all that offers is the chance of a ghoul's article on Brzeska. He was killed at Neuville St. Vaast, early this month, but the news is just in.

This is the heaviest loss in personnel the arts have suffered by the war. It is not the case of a beautiful youth who had perhaps done his best work. Brzeska was five years younger than Brooke, but he was a man of full vigorous genius, and there is no one to replace him. Also he had seen months of fighting and had been twice promoted for daring. There is probably no artist fighting with any of the armies who might not have been better spared.

Finis. -/-/

[Addressee unknown][11]   [*Autumn 1915?*]
---- Artists *ought* not to be allowed to fight, but the best one has been killed already, and one can only write elegies and collect reproductions of his sculpture. ----

To Harriet Monroe[12]

London, 15 December 1915

Dear H. M. ---- All that counts is
A. *Knowledge of life.*
B. *Great technical skill.*
A. Knowledge of life, *that is to say,* direct knowledge. -/-/
Ideas got from seeing *life in arrangement,* the designs of life as it exists.
Not the trying to see life according to idea ----.

[10]Special Collections, the University of Chicago Library. For an edited version of this letter, see Harriet Monroe, *A Poet's Life,* New York, 1938, p. 268.
[11]Unpublished letter. Special Collections, the University of Chicago Library.
[12]Unpublished letter. Special Collections, the University of Chicago Library.

Dear Lewis: I am afraid I was rather inconsiderate an hour ago, in asking Miss S. to tell you to come out, if you could, some morning to catalogue the drawings. Also to set prices. As you are bound to be busy.

I think I have now got them in my head. At least I have named 'em so that I can distinguish them. I don't know whether you have named 'em or not.

What is the price of the small blue drawing, like a sea in a storm. White figure, in posture as if hands tied high above head, other figure as if floating in a swish of sea?[14]

I have just writ to Q. to say that I have GOT to do a book on you or on "Vorticists" consisting mostly of you. And that I hope he can get the reproductions made in N.Y.

For this I must have some way of keeping track of the drawings I want used to illustrate it. I dont know whether to scribble my titles on the back of the mounts, or whether you have arranged the numbers you were talking about yesterday. I dont want to "impose" titles, where you've got better ones of your own. It will be easier to talk about particular drawings to Q. if they have names.

I dont know whether you were thinking of a uniform £10. That would certainly be wrong. The dancing "Joyeuse" and "Cholly" have £10 difference between 'em.

Yours
E.P.

Dear Miss Saunders:[15] If you deign to accept £18 of Quinn's money for your three drawings, *Cannon, Dance, Ballance,* I shall be pleased to hand over the said £ as you may direct.

Note, as noted before, Q. has paid £60 freight and insurance, £25 framing the show, there is no commission to be paid to a gallery. On these grounds Mr. Q. has ventured to offer slightly less than the prices set down in our invoice.

With the exception of Ed[ward] Wad[sworth] he has about cleared up the whole show.

Will you write to Miss Dissmorrrrrrrr that Q. offers £12 for her painting *Movements,* and that I will pay it to her as she directs IF she accepts the offer.

Q. has taken practically all the Lewis drawings. It runs to £375, which ought to contradict the premature reports of the death of "le mouvement."

Yours
E Pound

9. 9. 16

[13]Unpublished letter from Pound to Wyndham Lewis. Wyndham Lewis Collection, Cornell University Library.

[14]Pound here makes two pencil sketches of these drawings. Above and below the first he indicates "dark blue."

[15]Unpublished letter. Wyndham Lewis Collection, Cornell University Library.

To Homer L. Pound[16]

London, 22 September 1916

Dear Dad: -/-/Coburn and I have invented *vortography*. I haven't yet seen the results. He will bring them in tomorrow morning. They looked darn well on the ground glass, and he says the results are O.K.

The idea is that one no longer need photograph what is in front of the camera, but that one can use one's element of design; i. e., take the elements of design from what is in front of the camera, shut out what you don't want, twist the "elements" onto the part of plate where you want 'em, and then fire. I think we are in for some lark. AND the possibilities are seemingly unlimited. The apparatus is a bit heavy at present, but I think we can lighten up in time. -/-/

70 bis, rue Notre Dame des Champs[17]
Paris VI.

Dear EdWAD: *Little Review* (27 W. 8th St. New York) seems to be remerging, and getting ready for a special Lewis number. Shd. contain 24 reprods of W L's stuff. Believe he has sent the photos, or part. Shd. send photo of Praxitella.

There shd. be various articles on W. L. as painter and writer. I shd. very much like you to do a few pages "A Painter's view of W.L."

You are the proper person to do it. Know his work better than anyone else etc. Will you send at least a few pages as soon as you can. Make it as long as you like, or as short as you like, but emit something.

Greetings to Fanny.

Yours ever,

Ezra

Cd. Etchells also contribute.

Possibly a brief word on Rebel Art 1912-1922.

Turn on anyone intelligent. Lewis cant ask people himself, and I am not on the spot to do it.

To Jeanne Robert Foster[18]

Paris, 4 August 1924

Dear Jeanne: ---- Both Léger and Marsden Hartley, whom he [John Quinn] never bought, were yesterday talking of the loss to art, or to the upkeep of it. Which shows that there is some disinterestedness still left.

[16]Paige carbons, Yale University Library.

[17]Unpublished letter from Pound to Edward Wadsworth. Wyndham Lewis Collection, Cornell University Library.

[18]Unpublished letter. Houghton Library, Harvard University. Jeanne Robert Foster was a friend of the art patron John Quinn.

Dorothy (is in England) has written to ask whether she ought to write to you. The *Times* last clipping she sent, says a *few* of the pictures go to museums, and the rest are probably to be sold at auction. Is this so, and has the scheme for a memorial gallery fallen through. IF the things are to be sold, I should like the *Red Duet* by Wyndham Lewis. J.Q. paid ten pounds for it. I don't know what it will fetch, but I should like it if it don't run too high. I hope you will get the Gaudier stag drawings. I mean for yourself. I don't know that there was anything else in the collection to which I am personally attached, though there are some admirable Lewis things, especially one *Timon*.

If there is to be a memorial gallery, and they want my mask by Nancy MacCormac they can have it. But if the things are to be auctioned, that mask is a personal souvenir and not an art work, and Nancy had better turn it over to my family. -/-/

To Jeanne Robert Foster[19]

Rapallo, 31 December 1924

Dear Jeanne: ---- Don't see anything to be done re/sale.[20] Bad for artists to have it dumped on market, possibly, but then, half are dead, and I don't care much for the rest save Lewis—and he hadn't had any Lewis for some time. ETC. Barnes the only person who wd. take it in a lump, and keep it whole. As a collection—and possibly that is not the solution J. Q. wd. have wished. Effort can be made toward that end, if you advise—I don't care about being [*sic*] making money on the collection. -/-/

To Henry Allen Moe[21]

Rapallo, 31 March 1925

Dear Mr. Moe: -/-/WYNDHAM LEWIS, I consider without exception the best possible "value" for your endowment, and *the* man most hampered by lack of funds at the moment. Acquaintance with his published work can give you but a very partial idea of why I recommend him.

His work in *design* is, I can not say more important than his *capacity* for writing, but the two capacities very nearly of equal importance. His

[19]Unpublished letter. Houghton Library, Harvard University.
[20]I.e., of the modern art collection from the estate of John Quinn.
[21]Yale University Library. Henry Allen Moe was the secretary to the John Simon Guggenheim Memorial Foundation.

published writings have flaw due to hasty composition between his work as a painter.

His mind is far more fecund and original than let us say James Joyce's; he had at the time of publishing *Tarr* or *The Enemy of the Stars* a less accomplished technique, BUT he had invented more in modern art than any living man save possibly Picasso.

My early critique of him does not appear in my book on Gaudier-Brzeska, although it includes a chapter on Epstein. This was a book on sculpture and not on painting. I hoped at the time to do a book on Lewis as painter, but one was in wartime and the costs of adequate illustration were too great. You understand you can print half-tones of sculpture which, if they don't give a full idea of the work, at least don't give a very wrong one. But the cost of proper colour reprods. etc. etc.

But the fact I did not publish such a book does not in the least indicate that I considered Lewis of less importance than Gaudier. Also Gaudier had been killed and there was an imperative reason to make some sort of record of his work before it was scattered.

Even the gathering of Lewis' work for reprod. presented difficulties. John Quinn had some of it in America, Capt. Baker's collection had gone into the S. Kensington museum, etc.

I don't know what is to become of Quinn's lot. He had, if I remember rightly, about 15 good specimens, and then a lot of things that neither Lewis or I would have recommended him to purchase.

You will find further note on Lewis in my *Instigations*, page 215. This book is out of print, but I have just had a note from my publisher, promising to try to find a copy and send it to Dr. Aydelotte; if it does not arrive, can you consult it in N.Y. Library, or write to my father H.L. Pound, U.S. Mint, Philadelphia and get him to lend you his copy?

I may say that our group in London was getting into swing back in 1914, and then this damn war came down on our heads. Baker who was Lewis' best support, died after six months in hospital, result of having been sent to front when he was in no fit condition to be there. The S. Kensington museum was glad to accept his collection of Lewis "drawings" (this term includes all sorts of work in colour, gouache, etc.).

John Quinn as you know, died last year. From 1915–18 he had worked with me, accepting the idea that the man who keeps the artist in a state of freedom-to-work, participates in the work of the artist.[22]

Quinn was a very sick man during the last years of his life and I could not see eye to eye with his artistic advisors. I don't doubt they advised him to buy a good deal of stuff that has advanced in market value. I have been told that on his death bed or within a few days of his death, he said he

---

[22]An important art-economic principle of Pound.

hadn't lived, and that he wished he had taken my advice, and wanted to come to Italy with me, to "see" etc.

In any case he had done a great deal for the arts and for literature, as much as he could, things being as they were, and he having as much other business to attend to. He had done a great deal more than let us say Mr. Morgan (even though museums and collection have a value).

Lewis was sent to the front, most of his battery killed off; he was taken out to do war memorial painting. This showed considerable breadth of mind on the part of the ex-Austrian in charge of British war memorials; BUT the honoured P.G.K. having got Lewis to work, then proceeded to fuss and to try to get Lewis to "modify" the work etc. etc.

At the present moment Lewis' two chief reliable buyers are dead; England is in a state (intellectually) that I can only treat as I have done, allegorically in my hell cantos. Men like Roberts, whom Lewis has trained and "made" have taken the lower road of compromise. Lewis has I shd. say no market for the part of his work that is of interest to me or to himself.

I can say, from my own 17 years' experience (since 1908) that whenever I have been offered money or had a chance to make it, *even though* the offer or chance came from someone in sympathy with my general aim, that any sum over 75 or 100 dollars has always been offered on conditions that *interrupt* my *main* work and spend my time on stuff of secondary or tertiary importance.

The same is I think true of Lewis. In my case I have existed by a series of accidents, and for a long time I managed by writing articles at 5 dollars a piece in order to write about something that didn't interfere with my work or study. I mean by giving up all thought of placing ANYTHING at 50 to 75 dollars, or even at 25.

IT IS A MISTAKE to think that there is a career in creative or inventive activity; or that things get better as one goes on. I remember in 1909 going to the bank with Yeats, he was going to draw his last 5 pounds, and that was from an advance payment for a play he didn't finish till eight or nine years later. From Nov. 1914 to Nov. 1915, my own takings dropped to 42 pounds 10 shillings for the year. (I give that date because I happen to keep my accounts from my own birthday instead of from new years). Three days after I got to Paris in 1921 my last source of supplies collapsed ab-so-loot'ly.

Yeats didn't begin to get an appreciable income from his work till a year or so after he recd. his government pension, he must have been between 46 and 50, nearer the latter.

Are there any special points I can clear up for you? I don't know what more to say re Lewis' painting; it has a technique that his published writing hasn't. The man has the most fecund and diversely inventive and "volcanic" mind of anyone I know of in Europe or America.

There has been a great hullaballo about Joyce who also has been through a great deal, and who has suffered more than fifteen years of poverty, and latterly any amount of trouble with and operations on his eyes, and who has worked damned hard, even in excess of the international recognition he has received, BUT Joyce has by no means Lewis' originality or mental fertility. Hang it all I know both of these men as well as any one does or can; and I think I have printed the above opinion as far back as 1918.

But if I had to buy the *next* five or ten years' work of either man, with my eyes shut, I should choose Lewis'.

He is I believe writing not painting, at the moment, partly because he has found that he can't do both at once; partly I suspect because he can't afford a studio and it is cheaper to write than to paint.

As for difficulties of temperament ETC. Lewis procrastinates, good artists usually do. And people misunderstand it. The good artist goes on seeing flaws in his work long after the bad artist is glad to have it finished and palm it off onto someone less easy to please.

You can find this in the record of relations between a society woman like Isabella D'Este and Mantegna or Perugino. It is possibly not mere coincidence that Leonardo da Vinci went up to Fiesole when Isabella came to Florence.

What you can get from Lewis' published work is some idea of his general energy; but it is confused, rather with the confusion of an over-abundant source that has not yet got itself sorted out.

I shd. say that a painting like the *Red Duet* in the Quinn collection (an abstract design which has for me rather the charm of a Corot) gives the other pole, i.e. Lewis serene and confined to an area where he GOT things into order; and that possibly from these two points, one cd. plot a curve of potentiality, i.e. what an ultimate work could be, into which he had crammed the fullness, and the originality (as in the alleged play *The Enemy of the Stars*) and attained the order.

I shd. also say that a subsidy to Lewis should be made for not less than a five year period. No earthly use expecting this kind of a man to give results in three months.

NOTE.

There are a number of his things unpublished or scattered in magazines, *English Review* of early dates etc. that ought to be issued in book form.

There are various impediments, one that he has been hampered by need of money and has tried to bargain about prices, so as to get more leisure to go on working. Two: that he had small advance payments from various publishers for work that has not been delivered, and that there are conflicting claims for his books. Three: that as he gets disentangled from his painting and gives fuller attention to writing he is discontented with earlier work and wants to rewrite. I think he has, for example, withdrawn *Tarr* from circulation.

I am trying to obviate some of these difficulties by urging Tauchnitz to do him on the continent, but I don't know that this will suit either party, as Tauchnitz can pay very little for rights of a cheap continental edition; and a cheap continental edtn. might depreciate the value of Eng. publication.

Tauchnitz has, as you know, confined himself in the past, to books that had already had their Eng. or American sales.

The immediate effect of subsidizing W.L. might be to enable him to afford to publish without waiting for advantageous terms.

Also for god's sake DON'T confuse him with D.B. Wyndham Lewis, the jackass writing comic stuff in the *Daily Mail*. Lewis has been put to various straits but he has not come down to that; and the confusion of the two men in the minds of the uninformed has already been sufficient source of annoyance and loss of prestige.

AND nothing can be done about it as the other chap's name IS D.B. Wyndham Lewis, and Lewis' own other name is Percy which can NOT be effectively used in a counter-demonstration.

I don't know what more I can say. He has had a long period of strain. There was certainly a period when, so far as I can see, if he HAD lived in an orderly way and paid his bills, he wd. simply have died of starvation.

He has made spasmodic attempts at advertising when driven to his last trench; balanced by long spells of utter indifference, as for example, as I state in *Instigations*, when he went to the front, I knew him as well as anyone, found the floor of his room covered with piles of coloured drawing which I had never seen, or known of.

Best address at present is: WYNDHAM LEWIS, 5 Holland Place Chambers, London, W. 8.

I don't think you ought to write to him until you are pretty well convinced that you want to subsidize him. You can take up as much of my time as you like, and I can probably further answer any preliminary questions you want to ask.

In writing to him it ought to be made perfectly clear that you don't want to interfere with his work, or grab it, or get him to do something that wd. get immediate recognition from a larger group of people.

He is perfectly reasonable, and orderly and intelligent, when not worried to death and worn into a state of exacerbation.

After a year or two of calm, i.e., financial calm, he ought to have his stuff printed, i.e. what is now ready; at the end of say three years he ought to have a show of painting in New York, these ought not to be condition of his appointment, but as a committee, wanting the goods, and not bound by set regulations, these are collateral utilities; and with a word or two from some member of the committee to the right person or persons, they ought not to present any difficulty. –/–/

To Mrs. Isabel W. Pound[23]

Rapallo, 10 June 1925

Dear Mother: –/–/At present I want photos of machinery and spare parts. Wonder if you know where to get em FREE. I don't intend, and don't want anyone else to spend anything on said photos; also they have got to be good composition AS photos, as well as representing good shapes in machinery. ----

[?][23a] is dead otherwise he might be turned onto U.S. Mint. Spose Jake is too old. Want photos with HARD edge,[24] not muzzy arty.

All credit to photographer and source of machine. Most photos of machines try to give too much, too many parts of machine, or all of it at once. NO use for present purpose. ----

To Mr. and Mrs. Homer L. Pound[25]

Rapallo, 8 August 1925

REEspected Progenitors: The card of Medal Press magnificent. I note it is the Royle [*sic*] Mint. Why can't the Uncle Sam mint do something as good in the way of photos of its internal workings. After all the issue of the mag. ought to regard mainly amurikun machinery. What else is there in the country save howlin lunacy and . . . ???

Get Jake to take the photos. Give him a new lease of life.

Don't think the other photos you mention have yet arrived. The "Medal press" is a post card.

??? What was Baldwin electric supposed to send ???

[23]Yale University Library.
[23a]Name illegible.
[24]Interesting that Pound should use the term "hard edge," a term that became widely current in art circles in the 1960s to refer to the flat color, straight edges, and angular opposing forms of such painters as Kenneth Noland and George Ortman. Pound's use of the term is similar and grows out of vorticist aesthetics, which were not a little influenced by T. E. Hulme. See Hulme's essay "Modern Art and Its Philosophy," in *Speculations*, ed. Herbert Read, New York. 1924.
[25]Yale University Library.

To Homer L. Pound[26]

Rapallo, 11 August 1925

Dear Dad: The Sellers photos are magnificent, and JUST what I want.

Give me particulars. Sellers are?? Makers of machinery?? Who took the photos?? Is there any way of finding out what the individual photos are. I shall tell Walsh[27] to use the whole 15. If can't get separate labels, shall simply catalog them as 1 to 15. Sellers and Co. spare parts. But should like to know wot the bloomin leetle machine is. The photos MUCH better than the Rile [*sic*] Mint post card.

I want this number to be American art.

Does I. W. P.'s question re Baldwin electric mean that they are sending some photos? This fifteen is RIGHT. DEElighted. Can we get anything equally good of some big out door machinery? For contrast.

Not harbour cranes WITH ROMANTIC CLOUDS IN THE . . .[27a] SIDE.

Also let me know the name of the chap who provided you with the photos. Want list of collaborators. Man who finds a lot of photos like this Sellers lot deserves just as big a label as one who rehashes a last month's magazine article under impression he is creating something. In fak a good deal larger one.

Baldwin d. be good ground.

Ships more dangerous. But the engine room of same shd. provide something?? Cramps?

Or cd. Althouse get something from big steamship lines. Are there any American lines? I hate to adv. a company that puts up with the XVIIIth amendment, and makes no fight against visas. But still . . .

Maybe we can stick to the soil. Pumps, drain pipes ???? something Mr. Kipling hasn't enthused about.

Has Jake seen this lot? Can you start HIM doing bits of Mint. A govt. that will elect Wilson, Harding and Coolidge in succession don't deserve recognition, but then the govt. don't know the Mint has any insides so it don't matter.

These Sellers photos are EXACTLY right. It is the clear hard edge, emphasis on the FORM of the machine and parts that one wants.

The NOSE of the big dies, for example, excellent shape. Photos of detail of the coin press, especially at point where the force is concentrated.

---

[26]Yale University Library.

[27]Ernest Walsh, poet, and editor of the magazine *This Quarter* (for which Pound was writing the article and collecting photos). The first issue in the spring of 1925 was dedicated to Pound.

[27a]Illegible.

300

NOT the damn detail of the *coin,* sentimental symbolism. Miss Murphy the belle of the bowery, Liberty before she was lost.

Love to you and mother.

To Homer L. Pound[28]

Rapallo, 23 October 1925

Dear Dad: -/-/Recd. two lots of photos. They are damn good photos, esp. Brown pyrometer. But they don't touch the Sellers lot.

Too much in em that is not forced by necessity.

The good forms are in the parts of the machine where the energy is concentrated. Practically NO machines show high grade formal composition; the minute they hitch different functions, or ?? etc., or have parts NOT included in the concentration of the power, they get ugly, thoughtless. Might just as well be one shape as another. Neither the pyro nor the level is an ENERGY condenser. They are not really machines at all, only measurers.

WOT about the coin presses, are they govt. secret or summat?

What I am gettin at is: MUST distinguish between machinery, motor parts, and mere static structure. The static structure in machines, really part of architecture and employs no extra principle. Governed purely by form and taste.

It's the mobile parts, and the parts REQUIRED to keep them in their orbits or loci that I am interested in.

How about Cramps' machines for making battle ships. NOT the ships.

When machinery not much good, any farm machine being usually two hundred small machines of same sort hitched into one big one with no regard to appearance.

In any case the regard to appearance is merely dillentantism. The beauty comes from the efficiency at one point (vortex). -/-/

What about Whidden—can he nab any photos of *detail* of big printing press??

To Homer L. Pound[29]

Rapallo, 25 November 1925

Dear Dad: Thanks for photo of press. I wasn't grousing about the LEVEL. BUT Sellers' photos are so MUCH better than any of the others. I don't

[28]Yale University Library.
[29]Yale University Library.

301

care a kuss what the press cost. CAN you persuade 'em to PHOTO the DETAILS of it.

A whole show like that in one photo shows the ARCHITECTURE much more than the mechanics. NOT the least interested in the architecture (for the moment), want to distinguish clearly between the machines and architecture. I. E. the very essence of the machine; the parts that *move;* the problems of static stuff are as old as Vitruvius. I mean questions of proportion, balance *for the eye* (as in distinction for balance in *mechanic*).

This aint lack of gratitude to you or inquirer; merely: I know what I want, and the clearer I make it by the photos, the less need for blah; and the more different from other collections of photos of machinery, architecture, etc.

AND, among the DETAILS of machines, I want the PARTS THAT MOVE; also the sockets in which the moving parts move; the points where the energy concentrates. -/-/

TENTATIVE PROPOSITIONS
OR OUTLINE FOR DISCUSSION[30]

1. Beauty of machines in those parts of the machine where the energy is most concentrated.[31] Probably maximum at these points, "points of crisis."

Necessary to redefine the term crisis or to understand it in a particular sense if one is to use it to mean this focus of energy.

2. So far as form is concerned, the static parts of machinery obey, probably, the same laws as any other architecture, and offer little new field for thought.

[30]Yale University Library. Dated *c.* 1927.

[31]Pound's comments in his *Antheil and the Treatise on Harmony* are relevant here. (See *The Criterion*, March 1924, pp. 325–26; *Antheil and the Treatise on Harmony*, Chicago, 1927; *Ezra Pound and Music*, ed. R. Murray Schafer, London and New York, 1977, pp. 260–61.) He writes, in part:

Machines are not really literary or poetic, an attempt to poetise machines is rubbish. There has been a great deal of literary fuss over them. The Kiplonians get as sentimental over machines as a Dickensian does over a starved and homeless orphan on a bleak cold winterrrr's night.

Machines are musical. I doubt if they are even very pictorial or sculptural, they have form, but their distinction is not in form, it is in their movement and energy; reduced to sculptural stasis they lose *raison d'être,* as if their essence [*sic*].

Let me put it another way, they don't confront man like the *faits accomplis* of nature; these latter he has to attack *ab exteriore,* by his observation, he can't construct 'em; he has to examine them. Machines are already an expression of his own desire for power and precision; one man can learn from

3. Interest will therefore lie in the mobile parts, and in those parts which more immediately hold the mobile parts in their orbits.

a. as it is here that the inventor's thought has been most employed.

b. or, better, the thought of the series of inventors.

c. machines are in a "healthy state" because one can still think about the machine without dragging in the private life and personality of the inventor.

4. Farm machinery has been, for the most part, ugly, this ugliness is common to most assemblages of machinery, or to put it another way, farm machinery is usually not a "machine" in the scientist's sense, it is a lot of little machines, of the same sort, or of half a dozen sorts, hitched together.

5. The beauty of individual or "spare" parts of machinery at present much higher than that of the "whole machine."

a. that is to say the machine is now in much better state (even in some cases in a perfect state) than is the accessory architecture of machinery.

The single parts and the foci are made by thought, over thought, layer on layer of attention, and the congeries [are] in many cases, more or less fortuitous, mediocre.

b. . . . . no I shall leave it at that and refrain from comparisons between the Salon, the R. Acad. and a factory full of Bliss Presses, even though some of the latter, at least so far as I can tell from the photographs, seem to offer no room for formal improvement.

My thanks are due to all the firms named in the following list, and in particular to Mr. Coleman Sellers 3rd, Mr. F. S. Bacon, and to my respected progenitor.

E. P.

---

them what some other man has put into them, just as he can learn from other artistic manifestations. A painting of a machine is like a painting of a painting.

The lesson of machines is precision, valuable to the plastic artist, and to literati. . . .

I take it that music is the art most fit to express the fine quality of machines. Machines are now a part of life, it is proper that men should feel something about them; there would be something weak about art if it couldn't deal with this new content. But to return to the vorticist demands:

"Every concept, every emotion presents itself to the vivid consciousness in some primary form, it belongs to the art of that form."

I am inclined to think that machines acting in time-space, and hardly existing save when in action, belong chiefly to an art acting in time-space; at any rate Antheil has used them, effectively. That is a *fait accompli* and the academicians can worry over it if they like.

COLLECTED PROSE[32]

1929—

Fifteen years later I am again able to register the waste of talent in our time, the blatant obtuseness of "art experts" and art buyers. We sit around kicking ourselves for not having "seen" and bought Rousseau in 1910, we probably think Rousseau the best painter of modern times and say that no one has since come up to his level. Perhaps then we saw Rousseau in *Les Indépendants.* In 1911 we did not see his best work. We think no one has since equalled Rimbaud [*sic*].

It appears that no painter can eat of the rich fromage unless he have sacrificed half his work to some dealer who has therefore an interest in booming him. I observe with unspeakable disgust and a matured contempt for continental "criticism" or for the Parisian sense of responsibility that none of their series of brochures on modern painters contains a book on Lewis. The three collections of reprods. of Brancusi's work have all been due to American initiative. Any time from 1914 to '20 I was ready to do a book on Lewis and never found a publisher. My book on Gaudier was due to a series of calamities but its existence does not and did not indicate that I thought Lewis' work of less interest. The obstacles to the satisfactory production of a book on painting are perhaps materially greater, i.e., all photos of sculpture are unsatisfactory, but the more satisfactory reproduction of paintings requires colour, and that makes a proper book on a painter more expensive. One cannot address the art buyer on any terms save the lowest, or appeal to any passion save avarice. On that ground I can say: "Idiot"! to the people who missed the chance of getting Lewis' earlier work for next to nothing. The *Red Duet* and the second *Timon* series are now out of the market. Whatever England's best known art expert says publicly, he has Lewis' work on the walls of the room he lives in. Most of Baker's collection is in the S. Kensington out of the reach of speculators.

Lewis ranks with the best men of the time, not perhaps as a master [?] of paint, but as an inventor of form combinations. In 1914 he showed qualities which Picasso had not. Gaudier in his design of the Horse and Groom antedated a good deal of Chirico's method, though Chirico doesn't know it and is without any indebtedness. Two men then working in England could just as well have worked on the continent. They wd. not have been overshadowed but given greater acclaim.

[32]"Collected Prose," pp. 440–43. Yale University Library.

If I prefer Lewis' most abstract work to any other phase of his, it is possibly because I am not primarily interested in the arts of space. Working in time, by time, by the designing and combination of durations sometimes combined with the conventionalized sound combinations of language there are of necessity periods in which I am comparatively unaware of current developments in the spatial arts. The reader can perhaps the better allow for my personal deflection in preference if I give a paragraph of autobiography. At the age of twelve I found what I thought was a good painting in some Roman or Neapolitan gallery. I liked it because it was a prettier lady than I cd. find in any other frame. (Titian's *La Vanita,* the outlines are fairly clear).

My first bit of written art criticism or rather of description was a freshman theme on Uccello's battle picture in the Louvre. I was occupied with, or largely attracted by, the mediaevalism.

At 21 I entered the Velásquez room of the Prado and wondered what all the fuss was about. Having Whistler as gospel I had the decency to go back if not daily at least with great frequency during the whole of my month or so stay in Madrid, finding each day something worth thinking about. For a long time I cd. have made a map of the room. I haven't seen it for 21 years and I still know that *Los Borrachos* are or were to the right as you enter, same wall as door, that on the left wall are *Las Hilanderas;* and a door by which one goes into the room of *Las Meninas,* faced I think by one portrait; beyond the door are or were Don Juan de Austria and the four dwarfs, the Madonna crowned; at the end, the *Surrender of Breda* (which I thought was a new composition till I saw a fresco in Avignon); on the right wall the child on horseback, Philip with gun, the young prince, etc.

At the same time I still really prefer Carpaccio, and the Bellini in Rimini, and Piero Francesca and in general paintings with clearly defined outlines to any with muzzy edges. I know why these clean edges will not serve for all painting. This however is my personal angle. I prefer Lewis in his clearest and cleanest diagrams; Epstein of the pigeons, as he was when most closely in touch with Hulme and Hulme's ideas, and most like Gaudier and Brancusi. In 1913 I doubt if anyone foresaw Brancusi's preeminence. Purpose firm as a bar of steel.

Perhaps no one outside Guillaume Apollinaire's circle "saw" Rousseau in 1910, or knew enough of the Douanier's work to form a just estimate. Certainly no one now knows Lewis' strength save the few people who, in London in 1912 to '14, saw the wealth of invention registered in the Quinn and the Baker collections. All power of invention which has I suppose continued to manifest itself in secret and probably at rarer intervals. Certain masterpieces of his do exist, and their cash value is indubitably rising with great rapidity, largely outside the "trade."

BRANCUSI AND HUMAN SCULPTURE[33]

If there is ANY locality wherein one hears the SAME idiotic questions, and the SAME idiotic assertions of blatant ignorance with great persistency and flaccidity than in the purlieus of an art movement or in the vicinity of any great artist who does not follow the fashion of the old bozos just dead or about to be buried, I have, thank heaven, never penetrated that cellerage.

It is 13 or 14 years since I heard Madame X, who is the concentration of all the qualities which have made France a nation, clear thinking, straight thinking, and yet detached, impassive in the presence of phenomena for which she is in no way responsible, and to which she tenders no approval, remarking apropos a number of brilliant French artists in the forward reach: Of course, as CHARACTER they are below . . . ANYTHING.

I said: Brancusi?

She said: Brancusi is a Roumanian peasant.

And five years later Brancusi remarked of one of the few men whom I still see when passing through Paris: *Il sait vivre.* That was Brancusi's highest compliment. He didn't discuss the man's talents, and his phrase might be translated as, "He knows how to live with other men, and not stick his own personal vanity into the question." -/-/

The N.Y. courts did override the customs house in the case of Brancusi,[34] but there are a lot of showmen still in the art schools being taught by their great-grandfathers' housemaids. There is even a blighted Briton now governing the London National Gallery who don't know the East [?] from an onion. So one has to go on repeating things.

Brancusi's *L'Ecorché* (the skinned man) is not only in the Art Museum in Bucharest, but it is in the Roumanian academy of medicine, so the medical students can learn where the muscles are.

Brancusi said: Yes, I cut up 300 corpses before I made it. And when I go through doing it, I know that sculpture has NOTHING to do with beefsteaks.

I don't know what Constantin's age is, but the good men of my generation had to perform such demonstrations. It may have been good for their technique. (I used a lot of Provençal rhyme forms once, indeed for some years, as an exercise and as experiment . . . some of the subsequent easy riders might have done better with similar or equivalent exercise.)

---

[33]Yale University Library. Undated.
[34]In this famous case in 1926–28, the United States Customs refused to admit a work of Brancusi's as sculpture, claiming that it was turned metal and thus dutiable.

There's no secret about great art, I mean not in one sense. It is great art because the bloke KNOWS what he is doing. If sculptor he knows MORE about form than does the next bloke.

Sculptural form is ALL THE WAY ROUND, it is not simply a profile on a pivot. It is solid. The great sculptor knows it ALL THE WAY THROUGH. He knows the behind side, while he works on the befront side. You can't tell him by photograph. That is to say a lot of side [?] sculpture can get by on its tintype.

(I dont want to queer anyone's business. You can pick your losers. Will their work stand being seen all the way round.)

Brancusi's goes further. One year when he was thinking about building a temple, he was trying to think if the idea wd. be just as good up on end. In fact he did have a model, that he kept upending, and lying sidewise.

Of course no nation (and by all means certainly the French nation) didn't have sense enough to go on and BUILD it.

There are also the bright-eyed calves who tell me what ISN'T in Brancusi's work. And, naturally, not having known anything about Europe in 1910 they don't know why it happened, or what was done while they were mewling and puking.

When all France (after the war) was teething and tittering, and busy, oh BUSY, there was ONE temple of QUIET. There was one refuge of the eternal calm that is no longer in the Christian religion. There was one place where you cd. take your mind and have it sluiced clean, like you can get in the Gulf of Tigullio on a June day on a bathing raft with the sun on the lantern sails. I mean there was this white wide intellectual sunlight at 5 francs taxi ride from one's door. In the Impasse Ronsin.

The white stillness of marble. The rough eternity of the tree trunks. No mystic shilly shally, no spooks, no god damn Celtic Twilight, no Freud, no Viennese complex, no attempt to cure disease of the age by pasting up pimple. And no god damn aesthetics, as the term is understood in Bloomsbury and similar cloacae. And oh, yes, yes, and very certainly NO CLOACAL OBSESSION.

He (Constantin Brancusi) wanted to get all the forms BACK into the one form, that might be, and what of it; African sculpture HAD certain advantages, it was conceived solid. Had he got the synthesis of African sculpture, or the virtues or merits of African sculpture; nicely canned, potted, condensed, synthesized into. . . .

I damn well think that he has? But what of it. Did he stop there. No! Damn the African sculpture, full of fetishism, black magic, *chichi*. To hell. Was that any use to a man in 1923?

He also had views. And what of it? He can cook; play the fiddle, do stunts with a gramophone, etc. etc. all of which is aside from his sculpture.

The old studio USED to function. I mean I have seen people sick with worry and nerves pretty well cured by a visit.

I heard one visitor murmur: *not like the work of a human being, it's like something created by nature.* That also is part of the truth.

There is a sense of more than PLASTIC proportion, in Brancusi's philosophy or his Anschauung. "Ils sont empoisonnés par la gloire."

We might translate that, "The kids are poisoned by the scrabble to get a reputation."

Or to hell with being today's greatest sculptor; à la Rodin, etc. "You're there. Hang it. There on the POINT OF THE PYRAMID, got no room to MOVE!"

A beefsteak or a melon or Les Folies de la Rue whatsitsname where the old jokes are still so damn funny.

The effect of Brancusi's work is cumulative. He has created a whole universe of FORM. You've got to see it together. A system. An Anschauung. Not simply a pretty thing on the library table.

One of the rewards of a long honest life is that a man can or does build up a universe; that however "dumb" he is, he can by sticking at it do something that a cleverer chap CAN'T do, by just having a half hour's try at it. Or doing it once to show off.

Proof: in Binyon's translation of Dante. Proof in E. Tériade's volume on FERNAND LEGER (Editions Cahiers D'Art. 14 rue du Dragon, Paris vi.)

If one young squib has told me Léger can't do this that or the other; or asked me: "WHATEVER do you see in that man?" thirty have done so.

You might ask it about one or ten pictures but when you get the lot summed up together, you have to get down to Cordell Hull's mental level, not to see that something is working.

What the bright kids don't know is that in 1905 Léger was drawing like Gaudier (meaning he was doing the kind of thing Gaudier did 3 to 6 years later).

"Hell, yes, of course I could do it," meaning "DRAW." Pouvais pas PEINDRE. Couldn't PAINT.

Lot of people still don't know there's a difference. ----

1. Brancusi once said to me: "I wish they would POLISH their sculpture."

What that means is: you can hide any amount of ignorance or uncertainty if you are willing to "leave it rough," if you are willing to "express an idea"; I mean express it more or less, without waiting to find out exactly where it barges into some other idea that just isn't the SAME.

2. The world of forms.

3. Optional. "The more we are together."

4 and 5. Brancusi's only living rivals, Bliss and Company or other realizers of form. The maximum efficiency creating the maximum beauty of FORM. Years ago when Léger and others tried to make "ideal" machines, considering only the form and not the function, they found that the actual WORKING machinery had them flummoxed.

308

4. The Great form, united.
5. Cumulative effect of good forms in conjunction. Compare this with 2 and (3) of Brancusi's accumulation of forms.
6. Optional. Singing light.

ALBERT C. BARNES[35]

One may not agree with all of Mr. Barnes' statements, but one's differences are a marginal matter. If Mr. Barnes is not right, it is on points where there is little question of rightness or wrongness. It is on some 2% question of taste or preference. His personal deflection is of the right kind of deflection for a critic to have, and once noted the reader can allow for; and in so sincere a critic it even adds a certain sort of interest.

That a man so clear sighted as Barnes cares so much about Renoir is perfectly right; Renoir was presumably his first, or at least an early love. The critic has a right to this sort of thing. It makes people whose first love occurred at a later stage of painting see more in Renoir than they otherwise would have. It gives a different perspective. We don't care less for Cézanne. We realize that the kind of jolt we ourselves got from Picasso, or Gaudier or Wyndham Lewis may need just as much explanation to the next generation that is presumably getting its jolt and its sense of liberation from Miro, Arp, and   .[*sic*]

That Barnes' collection should have kept its finger so on the pulse of modernity as to include Chirico as well as Picasso, almost makes one believe in the possibility of a tomorrow in America. (Thirty years ago Mr. Wanamaker's gallery was full of fake Van Dykes, etc. etc. undsoweiter.)

Not only has Monsieur Barnes spent a deal of money on painting by dead and living painters, and spent it with great intelligence, that is to say, I can think of only three living artists of first importance whom up to the crop of 1926 he had overlooked in his selection. But he has put these pictures in a gallery open to serious members of the public, and provided instructors for those who are bewildered by being introduced to so much all at once.

He has also written that very rare thing THE RIGHT KIND of book about painting. By which I mean that he has not criticized art in order to climb on top of the artist, or to fill space in a weekly, or to crab good artists in order to sell second rate work that he has an interest in selling. He has not written in an attempt to prove that his talk about Cézanne is more important than Cézanne; he has not tried to drag down genius to the level of mediocrity, or to tell everybody that it is better for them to do doilies at home than to look at masterwork.

[35]Yale University Library. Undated.

No. He has written a book that aims to make the reader LOOK AT the painting, or even the half tone reproduction of the painting, and SEE what the artist was driving at, and what the artist has attained. He does not, as I see it, try to warp the student into one school rather than another. Barnes' aim is so right that he is almost bound to eliminate the margin of error as he goes on. He wants to augment the visual faculty, or at any rate augment the efficiency of the eye by coupling it with the efficiency of the perceptive intelligence.

With his mind on that and not on the problem of whether the dealers are going to boost the price of some artist, he naturally looks, and looks each year with greater efficiency for the work of men who see MORE, and whose work is likely to develop the visuality of the spectator.

And as his gallery is open as a school, he obviously does not intend it simply as cold storage; any fool can see that he wants painting to exist in America, on a par with, and ultimately above the level of painting in Europe.

Such a man is worth more to the country than 6000 Calvin Coolidges.

Venezia, 10 October [1936][36]

Editor
The Listener

Sir:

May I be permitted to strengthen Marinetti's quotation of me, in yr/issue for 14th inst. Marinetti's force and significance are demonstrated in his keeping hold of the root of the matter for a quarter of a century. The root is: MAKE IT NEW. The branches were the whole opposition made by Wyndham Lewis, Gaudier-Brzeska and myself to overemphasis on the accelerated impressionism practiced by men who called themselves "futurist" painters in 1910. Not that this was bad, but emphasis on structure needed.

There was a basic need of renewal. It functioned in half a dozen "movements" listed by Cremieux. Marinetti has got something done because he did not worry about the differences in detail, and has never lost sight of the basic need: renewal. Ethics of health, if you like. Something fundamental working down under all disagreements as to new modes of expression.

[36]Paige carbons, Yale University Library.

To Mrs. Jeanne Robert Foster[37]

St. Elizabeths, Washington, D.C.,
6 October 1956

Dearest Jeanne: –/–/Phrase "great art collectors." Most of 'em mere
accumulators stuffed-shirts with money. Quinn a reality. ---- Also note
that Wyndham Lewis preface his exhibit now or recently at the Tate two
pages of the best he has writ/----

To Mrs. Jeanne Robert Foster[38]

St. Elizabeths, Washington, D.C.
4 December 1957

Dear Jeanne: Yes these bastardly Foundations will raise monuments but
they will do NOTHING for living artists who aren't working for hire.
    They wdnt give Gaudier 3 cents if he were alive today. They do nothing
to get me out of quod after gornoze how long.
    Gt/Gaudier part in Milano triennale/and one man show now on in
Milano. Stuff placed properly in perspective at Triennale for first time/
hope for photos/etc.

GLOSSARY

ATKINSON, LAWRENCE (1873–1931), English artist. Associated with the Rebel Art
    Centre (q.v.). Signed the vorticists' *Blast Manifesto*. Appeared in the "Invited
    to Show" section of the June 1915 Vorticist Exhibition.
BALLA, GIACOMO (1871–1958), Italian painter. Signed the *Futurist Manifesto* (1910).
BARNARD, GEORGE GREY (1863–1938), American sculptor who studied in Paris
    under Rodin. Exhibited at the Armory Show in New York in 1913.
BARNES, ALBERT COOMBS (1872–1951), American art collector who established the
    Barnes Foundation (Merion, Pennsylvania).
BLAST, publication of the vorticists, in two issues: June 20, 1914, and the "war
    number," July 1915. Its bright puce color, unusual size (12 × 9½), and
    manifestoes, entitled "Blasts and Blesses" accounted, in part, for its notoriety.
    Edited by Wyndham Lewis.

[37]Unpublished letter. Houghton Library, Harvard University.
[38]Unpublished letter. Houghton Library, Harvard University.

BOLDINI, GIOVANNI (1845–1931), a fashionable portrait painter.

BOMBERG, DAVID (1890–1957), English rebel artist associated with the vorticists but who asserted his independence from the movement. Included in the "Invited to Show" section of the June 1915 Vorticist Exhibition.

BRANCUSI, CONSTANTIN (1876–1957), Rumanian sculptor who settled in Paris in 1904. Pound met Brancusi in 1921 and became as enthusiastic over this sculptor in Paris as he had over Gaudier in London. In Pound's studio in Paris, 70 *bis* rue Notre Dame des Champs, the poet had placed about the floor his own Brancusi-like sculpture.

BRODZKY, HORACE (b. 1885), London painter. Gaudier-Brzeska's bust of Horace Brodzky (1913) was exhibited at the Allied Artists Salon in July 1913, at the sculptor's first London exhibition. Pound in a letter to John Quinn said of the painter: "He is an amiable bore with some talent."

CÉZANNE, PAUL (1839–1906), French artist with profound influence on cubists and either through them or through his own work on the London *avant-garde* artists of the early '20s.

COBURN, ALVIN LANGDON (1882–1966), American photographer. (See Vortography.)

COCTEAU, JEAN (1889–1963), French poet, dramatist, and artist, whom Pound had described as "intelligent." Pound had translated his long poem "The Cape of Good Hope" for *The Little Review* and had reviewed his *Poésies 1917–1920* in *The Dial* of January 1921, a review that Noël Stock suggests may have influenced Eliot's *The Waste Land*, with the comment, "In a city the visual impressions succeed each other, overlap, overcross, they are cinematographic." (See Stock, *The Life of Ezra Pound*, New York, 1970, p. 236.)

DAVID, JACQUES-LOUIS (1748–1825), French painter. During the French Revolution and Napoleonic period he received official commissions, including *The Death of Marat* and the *Coronation of Napoleon*.

DAVIES, ARTHUR BOWEN (1862–1928), American painter. Major organizer of the Armory Show of 1913 in New York. Executed cubist and abstract work in later life though he was earlier known for his poetic landscapes.

DISMORR, JESSICA, English artist. She exhibited with the vorticists and signed the *Blast Manifesto*.

DUCHAMP, MARCEL (1887–1968), French painter. His influence on twentieth-century art, particularly on the art of the '60s and '70s, is equal to that of such figures as Picasso and Matisse. His *Nude Descending a Staircase* (1912), *The Bride Stripped Bare by Her Bachelors, Even* (1915–23), and the Readymades are central to the art of our time. It was only after his death that *Etant-donnés* (1946–66), the tableau-assemblage he was working on secretly for twenty years, became known. Pound early recognized Duchamp's dissatisfaction not only with traditional forms but also with the rebel forms of the art of his own time.

DULAC, EDMUND (1882–1953), French artist and illustrator, friend of Pound, whose *Caricature of Ezra Pound* was done c. 1917.

EPSTEIN, SIR JACOB (1880–1959), artist born in New York. He went to Paris in 1902 and lived in England from 1905. He contributed two drawings to *Blast No. 1*. His *Rock Drill* is now on display in the vorticist section of the Tate. He was highly praised by Pound, who encouraged John Quinn's purchases of his works.

312

ETCHELLS, FREDERICK (1886–1973), English artist. He contributed illustrations to *Blast*, Nos. 1 and 2, member-participant of the June 1915 Vorticist Exhibition, included in the January 1917 New York Vorticist Exhibition.

FENOLLOSA, ERNEST (1853–1908), American Far Eastern art and literature specialist, appointed Imperial Commissioner of Art in Tokyo. His widow in 1913–15 entrusted Fenollosa's literary remains with Pound for the poet to edit and publish.

FLENITE. Epstein's descriptive word, of a private and arbitrary meaning, in some of his figure titles, unrelated to the materials used.

FUTURISM. A modern experimental art movement introduced to London by the visiting Italian poet and dramatist F. T. Marinetti in his Lyceum Club lecture in April 1910. At first accepted by English *avant-garde* artists, it was later denounced by Wyndham Lewis and by Pound, who in his attack on the movement called it an "accelerated sort of impressionism." See "Vortex," *Blast No. 1*. The 1910 manifestoes of the futurists, however, influenced *Blast*. Futurist works are characterized by unusual drive, intensity, motion, and "speed."

GAUDIER-BRZESKA, HENRI (1891–1915), French sculptor whom Pound met in London in 1913. Pound's championing of him was the chief cause of his recognition. He wrote the important manifesto "Vortex" on modern sculpture in *Blast No. 1*, reprinted in Pound's *Gaudier-Brzeska*. He was killed in action on June 5, 1915, in World War I. The first one-man show in New York of his work was held in the fall of 1977 at the Gruenebaum Gallery. His *Hieratic Head of Ezra Pound* was carved from a four-foot block of white marble Pound had purchased. The poet always thought extremely highly of Gaudier. As late as January 1939, Pound wrote in the *Musical Times:* "Any ass can draw a face, two eyes, a nose and slit beneath the latter, but we have very few Henry Gaudiers and Pablo Picassos." (See *Ezra Pound and Music*, ed. R. Murray Schafer, London and New York, 1977, p. 444.)

HAMILTON, CUTHBERT (1884–1959), English artist. He contributed illustrations to *Blast No. 1* and signed its manifesto.

HULME, T. E. (1883–1917), English lecturer, essayist, and philosopher. He influenced Pound's aesthetic ideas. Hulme's assertion of the distinction between "geometric" and "vital" art was formulated after his reading the German art historian Wilhelm Worringer's *Abstraction and Empathy* (1908). Hulme advocated a "new geometrical and monumental art making use of mechanical forms." He promoted, therefore, the work of Epstein and the vorticists. Hulme was killed in France during World War I.

INGRES, JEAN AUGUSTE DOMINIQUE (1780–1867), French painter famous for his portraits and nudes, leader of neoclassicism.

JOHN, AUGUSTUS (1878–1961), successful English portrait painter who had studied at the Slade School of Art. Pound along with other advanced critics and artists dismissed John to promote the rebel artists.

KANDINSKY, WASSILY (1866–1944), early abstract painter, born in Moscow. He wrote *Concerning the Spiritual in Art*, translated into English in 1914. Pound considered Kandinsky one of the ancestors of the vorticist movement. See the poet's essay "Vortex" in *Blast No. 1*.

LA TOUR DU PIN, MARQUIS DE (Charles Humbert René, Marquis de la Tour du Pin Chambly de la Charce) (1834-1924), French Catholic sociologist and syndicalist, in whom Pound became interested in the '30s. Author of *Les Phases du mouvement social chrétien* (1907) and of *Vers un ordre social chrétien* (1907).

LÉGER, FERNAND (1881-1955), French painter. By the '20s when Pound was in Paris, Léger's cubism was clearly dependent on dynamic machine shapes. His colors are characteristically strong and unbroken.

LEWIS, PERCY WYNDHAM (1882-1957), English painter, novelist, satirist. He met Pound in 1909 and edited *Blast*. Pound wrote to the artist Gladys Hynes in 1956: "W.L. certainly *made* vorticism. To him alone we owe the existence of *BLAST*. It is true that he started by wanting a forum for the several ACTIVE varieties of CONTEMPORARY art/cub/expressionist/post-imp etc. BUT in conversation with E.P. there emerged the idea of defining what WE wanted & having a name for it. Ultimately Gaudier for sculpture, E.P. for poetry, and W.L., the main mover, set down their personal requirements." See Walter Michel, *Wyndham Lewis: Paintings and Drawings*, p. 67.

MANET, EDOUARD (1832-1883), French painter. His *Déjeuner sur L'Herbe* created a scandal at the Salon des Refusés (1863) as did his *Olympia* in 1865. After the 1870s he tended toward sentimental subjects.

MARINETTI, FILIPPO (1876-1944), Italian poet and dramatist. (See futurism.) A characteristic attack by Pound on the futurist Marinetti follows: "The article on Vorticism in the Fortnightly Review, Aug. 1914 stated that new vorticist music would come from a new computation of the mathematics of harmony not from mimetic representation of dead cats in a fog horn (alias noise tuners). This was part of the general vorticist stand against the accelerated impressionism of our active and meritorious friend Marinetti." (*Ezra Pound and Music*, p. 253.)

MARTINELLI, SHERI, American painter who became a friend of Pound's during his stay at St. Elizabeth's Hospital (1946-58).

MATISSE, HENRI (1869-1954), major twentieth-century French artist. He influenced advanced painters in England especially after Roger Fry organized the Manet and the Post-Impressionists Show at the Grafton Galleries in November 1910.

MERYON, CHARLES (1821-1868), son of an English doctor and a French dancer. He is considered one of the greatest of architectural etchers.

MESTROVIC, IVAN (1883-1962), famous Yugoslav sculptor. He worked in Paris and later settled in America, where he died. He was strongly influenced by Rodin.

MONROE, HARRIET (1860-1936), American publisher and editor of *Poetry*, who sought and obtained Ezra Pound as her "foreign correspondent." The first issue appeared in October 1912 with two poems of Pound, one of which was "To Whistler, American," written following the loan exhibition at the Tate. Pound's indefatigable correspondence with Monroe, some of which is reprinted in this volume, relates more to Pound's activities in poetry than in art.

NEVINSON, CHRISTOPHER (1889-1946), English artist. He participated in the June 1915 Vorticist Exhibition as a futurist and contributed an illustration to *Blast No. 2*.

OMEGA WORKSHOPS, opened by Roger Fry in July 1913 for the sale of items designed and decorated by *avant-garde* artists. Before vorticism, Wyndham

Lewis participated to the extent of decorating (notoriously) the dining room of Countess Kathleen Drogheda's house at 40 Wilton Crescent, in Belgravia. After the publication of *Blast,* such artists as Lewis, Nevinson, Wadsworth, and Etchells dissociated themselves from the Workshops.

PICABIA, FRANCIS (1879–1953), French abstract painter. He influenced such London artists as Wadsworth and Bomberg. Pound valued his wit and intelligence.

PICASSO, PABLO LUIZ Y (1881–1973). Pound acknowledged the dominance of this major twentieth-century artist and considered him one of the ancestors, indeed the "father," of vorticism. See the poet's essay "Vortex" in *Blast No. 1.*

QUINN, JOHN (1870–1924), New York lawyer and pioneer collector of modern art, some of which was suggested for purchase by Pound. Quinn was the patron of such artists and writers as Wyndham Lewis, T. S. Eliot, and Sir Jacob Epstein. He was almost the only buyer of vorticist artists in the New York show at the Penguin Club, 8 East 15 Street, in January 1917.

REBEL ART CENTRE, 38 Great Ormond Street, Queen's Square, London, founded by Kate Lechmere and Wyndham Lewis. The seat of "the Great London Vortex."

RICKETTS, CHARLES (1866–1931), English painter, chiefly known for his work in the development of printing.

ROBERTS, WILLIAM (b. 1895), English artist. He signed the vorticists' *Blast Manifesto.* His work was illustrated in *Blast No. 1,* and he contributed to *Blast No. 2.* A participating member in the June 1915 Vorticist Exhibition, he also showed with the January 1917 New York Vorticist Exhibition.

RODIN, AUGUSTE (1840–1917), a French artist who was highly influential and the most famous sculptor of the nineteenth century. To the vorticist Pound, however, his work was "good of its kind but it does look like muck after one has got one's eye in on Epstein's Babylonian austerity. And Brzeska's work, for all that he is only 22, is much more interesting." (Letter to Harriet Monroe, November 9, 1914.)

ROUSSEAU, HENRI, called "le Douanier" (1844–1910), French painter. Without formal training, he was taken up late in life by the *avant-garde* to the extent of influencing Picasso, Derain, etc.

SAUNDERS, HELEN (1885–1963), English artist. She signed the vorticists' *Blast Manifesto* as "H. Sanders." A member-participant in the June 1915 Vorticist and the January 1917 New York Vorticist Exhibitions, she contributed a poem and illustrations to *Blast No. 2.*

SEVERINI, GINO (1883–1966), Italian painter, a signer of the *Futurist Manifesto* (1910).

SHAKESPEAR, DOROTHY (1886–1973), wife of Ezra Pound, an English painter who wished to remain an amateur artist. Though never seeking exhibitions, she did contribute vorticist work to *Blast No. 2* and did the cover designs for Pound's *Catholic Anthology* and for *Ripostes* (both 1915).

SICKERT, WALTER RICHARD (1860–1942), English painter.

SYNCHROMISM, literally "with color"—a term the American expatriate Morgan Russell chose to designate the kind of abstract art that he and his fellow American Stanton Macdonald-Wright created. The paintings, composed of abstract shapes and colors, were first shown in Munich in June 1913, in Paris the following October, and in New York in March 1914. From January 24 to

315

March 26, 1978, the Whitney Museum of American Art, New York, exhibited some of the Synchromist works in the show "Synchromism and American Color Abstraction."

TANAGRA, name referring to small terracotta statuettes found in tombs of late fourth and third centuries B.C. at Tanagra in Central Greece.

VORTICISM, essentially a movement of English abstraction, An *avant-garde* movement in art and literature, it originated in London around 1914, engineered by the English artist Wyndham Lewis and named by Pound. The rebel movement (including such other artists as David Bomberg, Christopher Nevinson, William Roberts, and Edward Wadsworth) attacked nineteenth-century values, especially those of the '90s aestheticism, and hailed mechanistic energy. In art, it was characterized by experimentation with pure form and geometric abstraction. Pound's definition stresses this emphasis on formalism and his desire for a movement that would encompass all the arts: "Vorticism is the use of, or the belief in the use of, THE PRIMARY PIGMENT, straight through all the arts." (See also Pound's anonymous introduction to the 1917 catalogue of Coburn's vortograph show.) Wyndham Lewis in the introduction to his catalogue for his 1956 show at the Tate Gallery explained the term as follows: "As regards Visual Vorticism, it was dogmatically anti-real. It was my ultimate aim to exclude from painting the everyday visual real altogether. The idea was to build up a visual language as abstract as music. The colour green would not be confined, or related, to what was green in nature—such as grass, leaves, etc.; in the matter of form, a shape represented by fish remained a form independent of the animal, and could be made use of in a universe in which there were no fish." (Reprinted here from Walter Michel, *Wyndham Lewis: Paintings and Drawings*, London, 1971, p. 443.)

VORTOGRAPHY, a form of vorticism, named by Pound and developed by the American photographer Alvin Langdon Coburn in 1916. The method, involving the use of three mirrors fastened together to form a triangle, created abstract photographs. The mirrors, according to Coburn, (*Alvin Langdon Coburn, Photographer: An Autobiography* [London, 1966], p. 102), "acted as a prism splitting the image formed by the lens into fragments." Coburn's earliest experiments utilized Pound's face as the initial image.

VORTOSCOPE "isn't a cinema," Pound wrote to John Quinn on January 24, 1917. "It is an attachment to enable a photographer to do sham Picassos. That sarcastic definition probably covers the ground."

WADSWORTH, EDWARD (1889–1949), English artist. His illustrations and translations from Kandinsky's *Uber das Geistige in der Kunst* are in *Blast No. 1* where he signed its manifesto. A member-participant in the June 1915 Vorticist Exhibition, he showed in the January 1917 New York Vorticist Exhibition and his work was also reproduced in *Blast No. 2*.

WATTS, GEORGE FREDERICK (1817–1904), English painter and sculptor, frequently associated with the revival of mural painting.

WHISTLER, JAMES ABBOTT (1834–1903), American painter. He moved to London in 1859. Pound was interested in Whistler's aesthetic formalism. The following statement from Pound's essay "Vortex" in *Blast No. 1* echoes a famous Whistler statement: "You are interested in a certain painting because it is an arrangement of lines and colours."

316

Index

Abbott, Berenice, 284
Adelphi Gallery, 117, 127, 134
Albert Memorial, 85, 127
Alberti, Leon Battista, 173
Aldington, Richard, 205n
Alma-Tadema, Sir Lawrence, 15, 49, 56, 59, 60, 62, 63, 115, 116, 180, 186, 279
Alpine Club Gallery, 30, 51, 143, 145
American Academy at Rome, 3
Anderson, Margaret C., 281
Angelico, Fra, xii, 70, 257
Antheil, George, 188n, 248, 302n
Apelles, 186
Apple (of Beauty and Discord), xxiiin, 158n
Apollinaire, Guillaume, 166, 199
Arbuthnot, Malcolm, 70
architecture, 37, 46, 47, 73ff, 81ff, 126, 127, 159ff, 173, 174, 222, 247, 259, 264
Aristotle, 36, 39, 179
Arp, Hans (Jean), 164
Atheling, William (pseud.), xxiin
Atkinson, Lawrence, 30, 114, 243, 281, 311

Baker Collection (Capt. Guy Baker), 102, 106, 107, 118, 243, 271, 295, 305
Balla, Giacomo, 53, 102, 191, 228, 238, 311
Barnes, Albert C., 309ff, 311
Barr, Alfred H. Jr., 285
Baxter, Gwen, xxi
Beardsley, Aubrey, 34, 71, 117, 184
Bel Esprit, 146ff
Belgion, Montgomery, 162, 163
Bell, Clive, 128
Bell, Quentin, 282n
Bellini, Giovanni, 257, 258, 305
Berenson, Bernard, 225
Berryman, Jo Brantley, xxiin
Beuys, Joseph, 178n
Bevan, Robert, 30, 70, 88, 90, 94, 103, 114
A Bibliography of Ezra Pound by Donald Gallup, ix, 146n

Bird, William, 283
Blake, William, xiii, 52, 55, 119, 165, 218n, 258, 279
Blast, viii, xiv, xv, xvi, xviii, xxiiin, 19, 108, 128, 150ff, 154, 186n, 205n, 209, 210, 229, 231, 233, 235, 254, 259, 271, 273n, 274, 279, 283, 311
Blasting and Bombardiering by Wyndham Lewis, xxiin
Boccioni, Umberto, 123
Böcklin, Arnold, 65, 97
Boldini, Giovanni, 59, 60, 62, 63, 83, 122, 145, 215, 242, 312
Bomberg, David, xiv, xvi, 94, 136, 312
Bond Street Gallery, 90
Bonnard, Pierre, 141
de Bosschère, Jean, 88
Botticelli, Sandro, 68, 133, 136, 247, 257, 263
Boucher, François, 134
Bougereau, Adolph William, 140
Brancusi, Constantin, xviii, xxi, xxiiin, 101, 161, 163, 164, 167, 171ff, 177, 196, 211ff, 215, 246, 247, 248, 252ff, 254, 256, 258, 282, 283, 306ff, 312
Brangwyn, Sir Frank, 64, 92, 102
Braque, Georges, 169, 246, 282
Breton, André, 165
British Drawings, at the Museum of Modern Art (N.Y.), xv, 20
British Museum, 20, 85, 130, 257
The British Union Quarterly, xix, 161n
Brodsky, Horace, 281, 312
Brzeska, Sophie, 237, 245
Buddhism, 168
Burne-Jones, Sir Edward, 64, 271

Camden Town Group, 184
The Camera Club, 154n
Canadian War Memorial, 91, 94, 108
Canadian War Records Exhibition, 99, 101
Canaletto, (Giovanni) Antonio, 68, 90

317

318

320

Piero della Francesca, 65, 153n, 177, 247, 257, 258, 260
Pisanello, Antonio, 258
Pissarro, Camille, 73, 87, 99, 122, 142
Poetry, xiv, 217, 264, 275n
A Poet's Life by Harriet Monroe, xxiin
pointillism, 38, 52, 73, 118, 129, 223
postimpressionism, xvii, 9, 72, 89, 154, 223, 227, 272, 273, 273n
Pound, Ezra, books referred to: *ABC of Reading*, 247; *A Lume Spento*, xi; *The Cantos*, xx, xxi, 281n, 284n; *Collected Prose*, 150n, 304ff; *Ezra Pound and Music*, vii, 186n, 247n, 248ff; *Gaudier-Brzeska: A Memoir*, xxiiin, 199n, 249ff; *Guide to Kulchur*, xvi, xxiiin, 252ff; *Impact*, 146n, 260ff; *Instigations*, 270n; *Literary Essays of Ezra Pound*, xxiiin, 262ff, 270n; *Patria Mia*, xiii, 1; *Pavannes and Divisions*, 154n; *Personae*, 153n, 272n; *Polite Essays*, 271ff; *Pound/Joyce: The Letters of Ezra Pound to James Joyce*, xxiiin, 150n; *Ripostes*, 272; *Selected Letters of Ezra Pound*, viii, xxiin, 146n, 229n, 272ff, 284n, 285n, 287n, 290n; *Selected Prose*, 1, 218n; *Translations*, 286
Pound, Homer L., 289, 293, 299ff
Pound, Isabel W., 273, 287, 299
Poussin, Nicolas, 186
Prado, xi, 29, 63, 247, 255ff, 305
Praxiteles, 179, 186
pre-Raphaelites, 1, 36, 41, 53, 60, 70, 116, 133, 136
Pryde, James, 96, 103, 145
Puvis de Chavannes, Pierre, 34, 39, 52, 72, 73, 278

Quattrocento, 10, 23, 164, 167, 173, 223, 264, 267, 269, 284
The Quattro Cento by Adrian Stokes, 222ff
Quest Society, 179
Quinn, John, vii, viii, xviii, xxi, xxiin, xxiiin, 106, 147n, 273n, 276ff, 279, 280, 282, 288, 292, 293, 294, 295, 311, 315
John Quinn Memorial Collection, xix, xxiin, xxiiin, 102, 229ff, 271, 305

Rackman, Arthur, 115, 121, 134, 144
Raeburn, Sir Henry, 68
Raemaekers, Louis, 90, 91
Raphael, 24, 26, 169, 242
Ray, Man, 176, 177
Read, Forrest, xxiiin, 150n
Rebel Art Centre, 199n, 293, 315
Reedy's Mirror, 218n
Reid, B. L., viii, xxiin
Reinach, Salomon, 184
Rembrandt, Van Rijn, xi, xii, 6, 46, 51, 73, 102, 133, 256, 257, 276, 277
Renaissance, 23ff, 72, 264

Renoir, Pierre Auguste, xviii, 17, 51, 120, 142, 309
Reynolds, Sir Joshua, 44
Ricketts, Charles, 31, 59, 64, 65, 87, 99, 103, 245, 315
Roberts, William, xiv, xvi, 30, 91, 92, 93, 95, 103, 106, 120, 130, 131, 145, 231, 238, 240, 296
Rodin, Auguste, xiii, xviii, 4, 5, 10, 12, 54, 107, 116; 153, 171, 179, 211, 232, 250, 267, 274, 286, 308, 315
Roger Fry: Art and Life by Frances Spalding, 282n
Rossetti, Dante Gabriel, 64, 116, 177
Rothenstein, Sir William, 38, 49, 55, 61, 73, 93, 98, 131
Rousseau, Henri, 51, 70, 102, 133, 177, 215, 248, 283, 304, 305, 315
Roussel, Ker-Xavier, 142
Rowlandson, Thomas, 106, 119
Royal Academy, 20, 59ff, 85, 91, 93, 94, 103, 113, 129, 158, 187, 189
Royal Institute of Painters in Water Colour, 49, 115, 117
Royal Portrait Painters' Show, 191
Royal Society of Painters in Water Colour, 54, 129, 274
Rubens, Sir Peter Paul, 92, 263
Rudge, Olga, x, 249
Ruskin, John, 54, 55, 76, 85, 122, 187
Russell, John, xvi, 283n
Russell, Morgan, 23
Rutter's Adelphi Academy, 110

Sanders, Abel, xx, 210n
Sargent, John Singer, 33, 63, 97, 104, 122, 123, 130, 145, 187, 191, 288
Sarto, Andrea del, 117, 184
Satie, Erik, 211
Saturday Review, 50
Saunders, Helen, 233, 235, 292, 315
Schafer, R. Murray, 186n
Sea Power Exhibition, 96
Second Post-impressionist Exhibition, xii
Segonzac, André Dunoyer de, 71, 92, 102
Senefelder Club, 99, 141
Serbo-Croatian artists, 34
Seth, Florence, 7
Seurat, Georges, 283
Severini, Gino, xii, xiii, 50, 53, 102, 191, 228, 315
Shakespear, Dorothy, xxi, xxivn, 315
Shannon, Charles, 31, 59, 62, 72, 99, 110, 245
Sickert, Walter Richard, 33, 52, 69, 72, 87, 103, 104, 121, 125, 136, 142, 248, 282n, 315
Signac, Paul, 99, 102
Signorelli, Luca, 101, 210
Smith, William Brooke, xi, xxin
Society of Modern Portrait Painters, 142